Praise for
Human Rights, Perestroika, and the End of the Cold War

"In the summer of 1990, I heard Eduard Shevardnadze publicly credit the U.S. emphasis on human rights in bilateral relations as a major contribution to perestroika. Adamishin and Schifter, their foreign ministries' human rights "tsars" at the time, were less adversaries than they were colleagues in the cause of change in the Soviet Union. Their friendship and imagination regarding the bilateral relationship helped bring the leaderships of the United States and the Soviet Union into a disposition of comity during the Gorbachev years, without which the fall of Communism and the end of the Cold War might not have been nearly as gentle as it was. Their memoir is an important contribution to our understanding of the crucial events of 1987-1991."

—**Kenneth M. Jensen**, editor, *Origins of the Cold War: The Novikov, Kennan, and Roberts 'Long Telegrams' of 1946*

"This unique, joint memoir reveals a behind-the-scenes look at the U.S.-Soviet policymaking process at the end of the 20th Century. The authors provide a fascinating account of their roles in moving the issue of human rights up the foreign policy agenda."

—**Robert Kagan**, Carnegie Endowment for International Peace

"Both authors were effective participants in the process and are, for me, the symbols of where our civilization must head if a civilized world is to be achieved."

—**Max M. Kampelman**, Counselor of the Department of State and Head of the U.S. Delegation to Negotiations on Nuclear and Space Arms with the Soviet Union, 1985-1989.

"In recounting the experience of the senior negotiators on one of the key issues that arose during the Cold War, the authors provide valuable insight into negotiations that have received relatively little attention as compared to those on arms control and geopolitical issues. Their comments are also very useful in combating some widespread misconceptions about the nature and achievements of Gorbachev's perestroika."

—**Jack F. Matlock, Jr.**, U.S. Ambassador to the USSR, 1987–1991

"*Human Rights, Perestroika, and the End of the Cold War* represents a unique effort to combine Russian and American perspectives on the role of human rights in the U.S.-Soviet relationship at the end of the Soviet Union."

—**Dimitri Simes**, The Nixon Center

"Of all the factors that led to the downfall of Soviet Communism and the end of the Cold War, the issue of human rights stands out. Human rights are the very antithesis of Communist ideology and practice, and sapped at their foundation. Adamishin and Shifter offer invaluable insights into how the softest of all elements of soft power triumphed over a regime built on force and fear. More than a study of recent history, this is a much-needed encouragement for all those who aspire to a world with a human face."

—**Dmitri Trenin**, Director of the Carnegie Moscow Center

Human Rights, Perestroika, and the End of the Cold War

HUMAN RIGHTS, PERESTROIKA, AND THE END OF THE COLD WAR

ANATOLY ADAMISHIN AND RICHARD SCHIFTER

UNITED STATES INSTITUTE OF PEACE PRESS
WASHINGTON, D.C.

The views expressed in this book are those of the author alone. They do not necessarily reflect views of the United States Institute of Peace.

UNITED STATES INSTITUTE OF PEACE
1200 17th Street NW, Suite 200
Washington, DC 20036-3011
www.usip.org

© 2009 by the Endowment of the United States Institute of Peace.
All rights reserved.

First published 2009.

To request permission to photocopy or reprint materials for course use, contact the Copyright Clearance Center at www.copyright.com. For print, electronic media, and all other subsidiary rights, e-mail: permissions@usip.org.

Printed in the United States of America

The paper used in this publication meets the minimum requirements of American National Standards for Information Science—Permanence of Paper for Printed Library Materials, ANSI Z39.48-1984.

Library of Congress Cataloging-in-Publication Data

Adamishin, A. L.
  Human rights, perestroika, and the end of the cold war / Anatoly Adamishin and Richard Schifter.
    p. cm.
  Includes index.
  ISBN 978-1-60127-040-5 (pbk. : alk. paper)
  1. United States—Foreign relations—Soviet Union. 2. Soviet Union—Foreign relations—United States. 3. Human rights—Soviet Union. 4. Perestroika. 5. Soviet Union—Politics and government—1985-1991. 6. Adamishin, A. L. 7. Schifter, Richard. 8. Diplomats—Soviet Union—Biography. 9. Diplomats—United States—Biography. I. Schifter, Richard. II. Title.
  JZ1480.A57S653 2009
  323.0947'09048—dc22
                              2008049079

To Svetlana, quite obviously
　　　　　　—Anatoly Adamishin

To the memory of my mother, Balbina Schifter, whom I last saw in 1938, but whose teachings have guided my outlook on world affairs throughout my life
　　　　　　—Richard Schifter

Contents

Foreword
Mikhail Sergeyevich Gorbachev   vii

Foreword
George P. Shultz   xi

Acknowledgments   xvii

Timeline, 1981–1991   xix

Introduction   1

1. The Making of Unwitting Human Rights Officials   7
2. Soviet-U.S. Relations and Human Rights before Perestroika   35
3. Enter Gorbachev   79
4. The Human Rights Agenda   111
5. Vienna   151
6. The End of Perestroika   183
7. Concluding Thoughts   233

Index   277

About the Authors   293

Foreword

Mikhail Sergeyevich Gorbachev

This book by Anatoly Adamishin and Richard Schifter speaks about a time of major changes in the Soviet Union and in the world—a time when, as a result of joint efforts by states and citizens in the still divided world, confrontation between the East and the West came to an end, ridding mankind of the Cold War. The journey to that goal took, historically, very little time and was filled with extraordinary drama.

Of key importance in the interaction between the Soviet Union and the United States at that time were human rights issues. This book's authors were directly involved in that interaction and their account of its evolution, its complexities, and the obstacles that had to be overcome should be of interest and importance to historians and to those who want to learn from the lessons of that period.

I strongly recommend this book to the reader. As I do so, I would also like to share my thoughts about the role of human rights in the context of the problems and challenges that confront mankind in the twenty-first century.

Today, as before, the Universal Declaration of Human Rights, whose sixtieth anniversary we celebrated in 2008, remains our lodestar. Its authors were able to concentrate in one document the key principles of a humane society that would ensure the dignity of every person. However, I think they fully understood that there is a distance between proclaiming the principles of human rights and implementing them in a complex and diverse world.

Movement in that direction is a difficult process with inherent contradictions. The practical realization of human rights was greatly advanced by popular movements that fought for civil rights, against racial discrimination, and against totalitarian and authoritarian regimes. Yet, in a world divided by ideological confrontation, the ideals of human rights were often put aside or distorted. A ruler who suppressed them would receive support from one or other of the world's superpowers if he or she qualified as "our son of a bitch." Human rights problems became weapons in propaganda wars, tools for making political capital, or levers for applying international pressure.

The changes that occurred in our country, in Europe, and in the world as a whole in the second half of the 1980s created a unique opportunity to put an end to the Cold War and to confrontation in various areas, including human rights. The intense effort undertaken in those years by reform-minded political leaders and diplomats is described in detail in this book. Its result was not just the resolution of specific issues but also a new perspective on human rights.

In place of futile disputes about whether political or socioeconomic rights should take precedence, a new consensus began to emerge in the world, a consensus that recognized the interconnectedness of those rights and freedoms. In a way, it harked back to the concept voiced by Franklin D. Roosevelt, who proclaimed as fundamental not only the freedoms of speech and religion but also freedom from want and freedom from fear.

We had an opportunity to move toward those great goals together. This required a real transition from confrontation to cooperation and partnership, the erasing of old dividing lines and the prevention of the emergence of new ones—in short, a transition to a new international politic.

To our regret, this did not happen. The opportunities offered by the end of the Cold War were not seized.

Globalization, which could have brought billions of people closer together and opened the way to a common, humane, and dignified future, took a different course. Politicians proved unable to manage the process of globalization. The consequences of this failure can be seen in the widening gap between the rich and the poor; the global environmental crisis; the growing scale of terrorism; the failures of politics, particularly glaring in the cases of wars in Europe and the Middle East and genocide in Africa; and the real danger of a new arms race.

The current stalemate in world politics will be increasingly aggravated by the global financial crisis, which initially affected the world's economy but which is evolving into a political crisis both in individual countries and in international relations. In all likelihood, this crisis will deal a heavy blow to the rights of hundreds of millions of people, depriving them of any chance of breaking out of poverty and thus of access to the most basic human rights. Things could get even worse if efforts to end the crisis continue to focus on rescuing the pillars of the financial system rather than helping ordinary people—if we are left with a ruthless, cutthroat capitalism for the majority and a "socialist" welfare state for the rich.

We are now in the early stages of building a new financial and economic system. Which principles will form its basis? This is a question of crucial importance that will affect all areas, including the protection of human rights. Success will depend on how democratic this evolving process is, on whether it truly serves the entire international community, and, even more importantly, on whether it contains an ethical, moral core.

In the final analysis, the main challenge that we face is to build the human, moral factor into political, economic, and social architecture that must open the way to a life of dignity for all mankind in the foreseeable future.

This is a challenge not just for nation-states but also for the emerging global civil society and for the academic and media communities. We need a political, intellectual, and moral breakthrough. As in the years when we worked together to end the Cold War, we must again combine our efforts, transcending the stereotypes and barriers of misunderstanding and hostility inherited from the past and persevering on the road to our common future.

Foreword

George P. Shultz

On the afternoon of October 15, 1987, I was asked to be available for a phone call from Jerusalem. At 3:18 p.m., the call came through: "This is Ida Nudel. I'm in Jerusalem. I'm home." My eyes filled with tears, as they still do when I think of that moment. I had met with her in Moscow and worked on her case. She was strong and determined, but I saw no reason to believe that she might get a break. How did this happen and how was it that so many other Soviet Jews were allowed to emigrate? That is one of the key questions addressed in this book of seminal importance.

The authors of this book played a central role in the evolution of these important developments as they worked within the envelope provided them by President Ronald Reagan and General Secretary Mikhail Gorbachev. I was proud to be a part of these efforts with my Soviet counterpart, Foreign Minister Eduard Shevardnadze.

Ronald Reagan was a man of deep convictions that had formed in his mind well before he became president and that resonated with his strong gut instincts. As an Air Force officer, he had seen initial films of the Holocaust camps. He would never forget the images, and he saved the films for his own private collection so he would always be able to demonstrate what happened. There will inevitably be people, he knew, who might later question whether such horrors could be perpetrated by any human being. Reagan also held a long-standing belief that nuclear weapons were immoral and that their numbers should be reduced and, ultimately, eliminated. His convictions about nuclear weapons were another expression of his deep concern for human rights.

I saw his convictions vividly on display when, by the luck of a snowstorm that unexpectedly kept President Reagan and Nancy in Washington, my wife and I were invited to the White House for an informal supper. I could see the president's interest in direct and personal contact with the Soviet leadership and arranged a meeting between him and the Soviet ambassador, Anatoly Dobrynin, the following Tuesday. In almost two hours of talk about a wide range of issues, Ronald Reagan made clear that human rights and Soviet Jewry were at the top of his agenda. He pointed to the Pentecostals being sheltered from religious persecution in our embassy in Moscow as a glaring illustration of the problem. Let them emigrate, he emphasized. You won't hear any crowing from me. Dobrynin and I made this our special project and, in the end, with strong help from Max Kampelman, we succeeded. When sixty Pentecostals were allowed to leave the Soviet Union for Israel, Ronald Reagan didn't crow. So our first deal with the Soviets was a human rights agreement, and the Soviets got the message that President Reagan cared about human rights in a nonpolitical way.

In the meantime, in my periodic meetings with Soviet foreign minister Andrei Gromyko both before and after the Pentecostal event, I would raise human rights as an important issue. Gromyko always diminished it as a "tenth-grade question." He regarded the issue as domestic and none of my business.

On October 22, 1984, the National Assembly of the National Conference on Soviet Jewry gave me an award for our efforts. I was honored but embarrassed. We had achieved very little. The situation of Soviet Jews remained, as I said, "very grim."

On March 10, 1985, General Secretary Chernenko died and I accompanied Vice President Bush to the funeral in Moscow. While there, we met with the new general secretary of the Communist Party, Mikhail Gorbachev. He told Vice President Bush that the Soviets respected "your right to run your country the way you see fit." He insisted that, in the same way, it was up to the Soviet people to make such decisions on behalf of the USSR. Vice President Bush assured Gorbachev that "we have no aspiration of dictating to the Soviets." But he immediately argued against the denial of Jewish emigration, the persecution of Hebrew teachers, and the treatment of dissidents such as Shcharansky, Sakharov, Begun, and Orlov, which he said violated the Helsinki Accords. Gorbachev flushed and offered to think about appointing rapporteurs on human rights to discuss the issue. Bush seized on the idea, and another small step was taken.

A few months later, Gromyko's tenure as foreign minister ended and he was replaced by Shevardnadze. Shevardnadze and I met for the first time in August 1985 in Helsinki. After a lengthy discussion of our broad agenda, with staff members present, we met privately. Once again, I raised the issue of human rights, telling him bluntly, "Until the Soviet Union adopts a different policy on humanitarian issues, no aspect of our dealings will be truly satisfactory, nor will your society be able to progress as it can and should." Shevardnadze's reaction was quite different from Gromyko's. He did not respond in a hostile fashion, but merely smiled and asked whether, on the occasion of our next meeting, he should talk about "U.S. unemployment and blacks."

Then in November 1985 came a big event: the first summit meeting, held in Geneva, between President Reagan and General Secretary Gorbachev. There we not only made significant progress on arms control issues but also, and more importantly, changed the atmosphere of U.S.-Soviet relations.

Foreword

On February 11, 1986, Anatoly Shcharansky crossed the Glienicke Bridge to West Berlin as part of a carefully crafted deal that carried no implication that he was a spy. That deal demonstrated that we could bargain successfully with the new leadership.

We made another deal under tense circumstances in September 1986, after the Soviets arrested Nicholas Daniloff, a reporter they had entrapped to exchange for a Soviet scientific attaché named Zakharov. We secured Daniloff's freedom, the freedom of Yuri Orlov and his wife, and a promise by Shevardnadze that he would work on getting other dissidents and refuseniks released. Zakharov, after pleading nolo contendere to a charge of receiving classified documents, returned to the Soviet Union. Shevardnadze followed through over the next year; all the people on a list I had given him were released or pardoned. Perhaps the biggest bonus from this exercise was the increased trust it created between Shevardnadze and me.

Then came the extraordinary meeting between Ronald Reagan and Mikhail Gorbachev on October 11–12, 1986, in Reykjavik, Iceland. While no full agreement was consummated there, great progress was made on major arms control issues, and the prospect of a world free of nuclear weapons was seriously discussed. Not so well noticed was the agreement by the Soviets, achieved in an all-nighter by Assistant Secretary of State for European and Canadian Affairs Roz Ridgway, to make human rights a recognized and regular part of our agenda.

Under the new Soviet leadership, relations between the United States and the Soviet Union began to improve significantly. Progress was made in our discussions of arms control and there were reports of a loosening of totalitarian controls in the Soviet Union. In December 1986, Andrei Sakharov, who had been exiled from Moscow, received a telephone call from Gorbachev telling him that he could return to Moscow. It seemed that Margaret Thatcher had been right when she said, even before Gorbachev became general secretary, that one could "do business" with him.

It was against the background of these developments that I prepared for my April 1987 trip to Moscow. I wanted to get into deeper discussions with Gorbachev and Shevardnadze about the shape of the future. Our assistant secretary of state for human rights and humanitarian affairs, Dick Schifter, was a member of the delegation that joined me on this trip. At my very first meeting with Shevardnadze following my arrival in Moscow, I asked that he appoint a counterpart for Dick Schifter who would be authorized to discuss human rights issues with him. It was my hope that by moving from generalities to specifics, by getting into a discussion of concrete issues and cases, we might be able to begin to solve the problems of individual victims of repression. Shevardnadze agreed and, as it turned out, he selected a person he trusted, Deputy Foreign Minister

Anatoly Adamishin, to meet with Dick and initiate a goal-oriented human rights dialogue.

On the evening of April 13, 1987, I went to the U.S. ambassador's residence, Spaso House. Everything was ready for the Passover seder. The fancy ballroom had been transformed into a warm and welcoming sanctuary. Dozens of the most famous Jewish refuseniks were there. I put on a yarmulke, met them all, and then said exactly what all of us felt:

> You are on our minds; you are in our hearts. We never give up, we never stop trying, and in the end some good things do happen. But never give up, never give up. And please note that there are people all over the world, not just in the United States, who think about you and wish you well and are on your side.

Their determination amazed me. We held the seder to encourage them, but I realized that they had given me far more strength and resolve than I could possibly have given them.

Then Schifter and Adamishin went to work. This dialogue between diplomats produced concrete results: an end to abuse of psychiatry, the release of political prisoners, the repeal of laws restricting freedom of expression, an end to the repression of religion, and a fundamental shift in the laws and regulations that governed emigration. These changes in Soviet policy significantly helped not only to improve U.S.-Soviet relations, but also to bring greater freedom to the citizens of the Soviet Union.

Understandably, these vitally important details could not be focused upon in meetings of heads of government or in ministerial meetings. That is why it was necessary to set up a working group of experts in the field of human rights to parallel the working groups that focused on arms reduction. What was important was that those entrusted with the task of carrying the human rights dialogue forward knew precisely what was expected of them by their respective superiors and that they were committed to reaching their respective government's policy goals. As Dick notes in this book, his good relationship with me enabled him at a certain point to overcome a bureaucratic obstacle that had been placed in the way of attaining one of my major policy objectives, the adoption of the CSCE Vienna Concluding Document.

Questions have been raised from time to time as to whether personal relationships of U.S. presidents or secretaries of state with governmental counterparts may thwart the attainment of policy goals that are in our national interest. As history has shown, the personal relationships that developed between President Reagan and President Gorbachev, and between me and Foreign Minister Shevardnadze (as distinct from my relationship with Gromyko), set the tone as Cold War tensions gradually eased. But to benefit fully from these momentous events, we had to defeat the devils that are so often in the details. As this book shows, that is what was accomplished as a result of the personal relationship established between Anatoly Adamishin and Richard Schifter in their effort to resolve the key human rights issues that had stood in the way of better relations between the United States and the Soviet Union.

The net result of the close working relationships that had been established at all levels was a feeling of mutual trust. That feeling of trust laid the foundation for increasingly close cooperation on issues of democratic governance and the rule of law. In the years that followed, for example, reciprocal visits played an important role. U.S. judges would travel to the Soviet Union and participate in seminars with Soviet judges. Soviet judges, in turn, came to the United States to visit U.S. courts and observe the proceedings there, including the role played by juries. So better understanding was achieved in both countries, with the benefits spread widely.

This book has much to tell us about the way the Cold War ended, the power of diplomacy, and how diplomatic partnerships help effect profound political changes peacefully. We would not have the opportunity to ponder the important lessons this volume offers were it not for the United States Institute of Peace and its president, Richard Solomon, who granted Ambassador Adamishin a Jennings Randolph Fellowship that allowed him to come to the United States, where he worked with Dick Schifter on the manuscript. Their collaboration was essential to the production of this book.

Acknowledgments

Anatoly Adamishin gratefully acknowledges the invaluable assistance given to him while working on this book by the Gorbachev Foundation, the Historical Documents Department of the Russian Ministry of Foreign Affairs, Stanford University Archives, and the United States Institute of Peace.

Richard Schifter would like to thank Secretary Shultz, who gave him the opportunity to participate in the effort to end totalitarianism in the Soviet Union, and the United States Institute of Peace for its assistance in assembling the needed documentation.

Both authors would like to thank Richard Solomon, president of the United States Institute of Peace, and Virginia Bouvier, a senior program officer in the Institute's Jennings Randolph Fellowship program, for their support and encouragement. The authors are also grateful to the Institute for providing good counsel through the editorial advice of Nigel Quinney.

Timeline, 1981–1991

January 1981: Ronald Reagan is sworn in as president of the United States.

July 1982: George Shultz takes office as secretary of state.

November 1982: Leonid Brezhnev, general secretary of the Central Committee of the Communist Party of the Soviet Union, dies and is succeeded by Yuri Andropov.

July 1983: The Siberian Seven—Pentecostal Christians who had taken refuge in the U.S. embassy in Moscow—are allowed to leave the Soviet Union.

February 1984: General Secretary Andropov dies and is succeeded by Konstantin Chernenko.

March 1985: General Secretary Chernenko dies and is succeeded by Mikhail Gorbachev.

July 1985: Eduard Shevardnadze succeeds Andrei Gromyko as Soviet foreign minister.

November 1985: A summit meeting is held in Geneva between Reagan and Gorbachev.

November 1986: Commission on Security and Cooperation in Europe (CSCE) follow-up meeting convenes in Vienna.

December 1986: Gorbachev calls Andrei Sakharov and tells him that he may return to Moscow from his exile in Gorky.

January 1987: A substantial number of political prisoners are released from the gulag penal labor camps and return home. The first slight increase since 1981 is noted in the number of Soviet exit permits issued.

April 1987: A U.S. delegation, led by Secretary Shultz, visits Moscow. Shultz and Shevardnadze agree on a human rights dialogue. Anatoly Adamishin and Richard Schifter have their first meeting.

September 1987: A ministerial meeting is held in Washington between Shultz and Shevardnadze. Detailed discussions take place between Schifter and Yuri Reshetov, Adamishin's assistant. Significant progress is made on the rules governing the issuance of exit permits; the Soviet representatives assure their American counterparts that the abuse of psychiatry has been ended.

December 1987: A summit meeting is held in Washington; the Intermediate-Range Nuclear Forces (INF) Treaty is signed.

September 1988: Adamishin and Schifter meet in Milan and discuss steps to be taken to conclude the Vienna CSCE meeting, including agreement on a Moscow human rights conference to be held under CSCE auspices.

November 1988: Schifter visits Moscow, carrying personal instructions from Shultz making it clear that Shultz wants the Vienna meeting to be concluded successfully during his term in office, noting that the Soviet Union has made significant progress in dealing with human rights issues, and asking for modest but concrete steps to be taken in the human rights area so as to make possible an agreement on a concluding document.

December 1988: Gorbachev addresses the UN General Assembly, committing his country to democracy and respect for human rights and noting that political prisoners have been released.

January 17, 1989: The CSCE's Vienna concluding document is adopted, calling for a CSCE human rights conference in Moscow and the prompt start of negotiations on a treaty on conventional forces in Europe. In the eyes of many observers, the Cold War comes to an end.

January 20, 1989: George H. W. Bush is sworn in as president of the United States and appoints James Baker secretary of state and Brent Scowcroft as national security adviser. The new administration begins a reappraisal of U.S.-Soviet relations.

March–April 1989: Soviet Union conducts free elections for the Congress of People's Deputies; many officially backed candidates are defeated.

August–December 1989: The Communist dictatorships in the junior members of the Warsaw Pact come to an end.

December 1989: Bush and Gorbachev hold a summit meeting in Malta.

March 1990: Lithuania declares its independence from the Soviet Union.

October 1990: German reunification takes place.

December 1990: Shevardnadze resigns as Soviet foreign minister.

August 1991: Leaders of the Soviet Army, police force, and KGB fail in their effort to take control of the Soviet Union.

September–December 1991: The central government of the Soviet Union gradually disintegrates.

December 1991: Gorbachev resigns and the Soviet Union comes to an end.

Introduction

Richard Schifter and *Anatoly Adamishin*

In 2008, as we write these joint memoirs, there is again tension in the air in the relationship between Russia and the United States. But it is a far cry from where we were twenty-five years ago, when the two nuclear-armed superpowers, the Soviet Union and the United States, confronted each other across the globe in the struggle that had come to be known as the Cold War. In the late 1980s, a tectonic shift took place in our relationship, brought about, in the first instance, by a new Soviet leader, Mikhail Gorbachev, ably assisted by his foreign minister, Eduard Shevardnadze. On the United States end, President Ronald Reagan and Secretary George Shultz recognized the profundity of the change that had taken place in the Soviet Union and responded positively.

As our relationship warmed, the basic decisions were made at the Shultz-Shevardnadze level, albeit within the policy framework approved at the highest level. However, as is often said, the devil is in the details—and there were many details, in many areas of bilateral concern, that had to be resolved. One such area, which acquired increasing importance and played a key role in the warming of the relationship, was human rights. It is in that area that the task of fighting the devil fell to the two of us.

Our roots, strange as it may seem, were in the same corner of the globe, the distance from the original habitat of the Adamishins to that of the Schifters being about two hundred miles. But from the time of our birth to the time we first met, in the Ministry of Foreign Affairs of the Soviet Union, we had traveled significantly different paths, even though they occasionally paralleled each other. Anatoly, a native of Kiev, had left for Moscow, accompanying his mother, as they fled from the invading German army at the outset of World War II. Dick, whose parents had moved to Vienna, Austria, where he was born, fled to the United States after the Nazi takeover in Vienna.

Like all other young people in the Soviet Union, Anatoly received his early political education in the Young Pioneers and Komsomol, the youth arms of the Communist Party. Dick, by contrast, received his political education from his mother, who believed in democratic socialism and vehemently opposed communism. After arriving in the United States he was associated with organizations of the anti-Communist left.

The course of Anatoly's educational preparation led him to the Soviet (and then Russian) diplomatic service, which he entered at the age of twenty-three, and a career of forty years, which included the ambassadorships to Rome and London. Dick had dreamed, as a youngster, of becoming a diplomat, but became a lawyer instead and did not engage in diplomatic work until he had reached the age of fifty-seven. He then spent the next twenty years in diplomatic work as a noncareer appointee.

When we met in April 1987, on the occasion of a ministerial meeting in Moscow between Secretary Shultz and Foreign Minister Shevardnadze, Anatoly was a deputy foreign minister and Dick an assistant secretary of state. Dick had for many years been working in the human rights field, while Anatoly had assumed his new responsibility for that subject at very short notice. We nevertheless very quickly developed a friendly personal relationship and then stayed in touch and worked together to resolve the human rights issues that stood in the way of better relations between our two countries.

While our joint effort was limited to human rights, our work had a significant impact on the field so critically important to the end of the Cold War, the field of arms reduction. The point that Secretary Shultz frequently emphasized was that Soviet progress in the field of human rights would make it that much easier for a feeling of mutual trust to develop, a feeling that would enable us to effect significant cutbacks in our military expenditures.

As these memoirs will show, our close relationship played a particularly important role in the second half of 1988 in helping to bring the Vienna Follow-Up Meeting of the Conference on Security and Cooperation in Europe to a satisfactory conclusion. The work that we had undertaken—and the results that we had attained—allowed the meeting to be brought to a positive conclusion, making it possible for the beginning of negotiations of a Treaty on Conventional Forces in Europe as well as the convening of the conference on human rights in Moscow.

In these memoirs, we trace the years of our close interaction. But before then, to furnish the necessary backdrop, we discuss our respective personal histories that led to our designation as representatives of our countries in this setting, the nature of the relationship between the two superpowers from the mid-1950s onward, and the history of the introduction of the human rights issue into the field of international relations and its impact on relations between the United States and the Soviet Union.

This book has gone through a long gestation period. We first discussed the idea of our joining in this effort as long ago as 1992, even comparing outlines of what we would write about. However, other tasks kept us busy. Anatoly became the Russian ambassador in London. Dick joined the staff of the U.S. National Security Council. But, as we have now demonstrated, the idea of joining in an effort to write a book about our joint endeavor never died.

It was possible to write this book together because while we had represented our respective governments in a highly sensitive and contested area, we had developed a personal friendship. The development of this friendship, in turn, was made possible by the close working relationship that had been established between Foreign Minister Shevardnadze and Secretary of State Shultz. There was no doubt that our task was to remove some of the very important obstacles to better relations between the Soviet Union and the United States.

But did we have a story worth telling that had not theretofore been told? The conclusion that we reached was that the results of our endeavors—the end of abuse, of psychiatry, the change in Soviet policy on emigration, the end of the crime of "anti-Soviet agitation and propaganda,"[1] the positive note on which the Vienna Meeting of the Conference of Security and Cooperation in Europe ended—are indeed either well-known or have been written about by others. What is not well-known and what has not been written about as yet is precisely what the process was by which these results were achieved, results that were important factors in ending the Cold War. And this process was wider than is generally thought, as it included what we called "the new agenda": bilateral humanitarian cooperation, which embraced a number of concrete topics, such as round tables of experts on housing for the elderly or possible U.S. production of prostheses for Soviet soldiers wounded in Afghanistan.

The Soviet-U.S. human rights dialogue of the late 1980s achieved significant results because each of us knew the thinking of our respective bosses, who wanted to remove the obstacle to good relations that disagreement on human rights issues presented. We knew what was expected of us. We, in turn, had come to have confidence in each other. Each of us had concluded that the other was seeking to attain the same objective, namely good relations between our two countries. It was that feeling of trust in each other that enabled us to move forward and attain the results that we sought.

When we first met in April 1987, the system of government that had been installed close to seventy years earlier in the wake of what had become known as the Glorious October Revolution was still in place. But some close observers of the scene, both in the Soviet Union and abroad, had begun to wonder whether change was in the offing. Many Soviet citizens had for years been concerned that their leaders were too old and too ill to function

---

1. Article 70 of the Penal Code of the Russian Soviet Federal Socialist Republic.

effectively. They were pleased when, in March 1985, a vigorous man who had just turned fifty-four became the general secretary of the Central Committee of the Communist Party of the Soviet Union and thus the country's de facto leader.

Less than a year before he moved into the Soviet Union's top leadership position, Mikhail Gorbachev had visited London and met with Prime Minister Margaret Thatcher. She commented after that meeting that she thought one could "do business" with Gorbachev. That did not mean the serious problems that had beset the Soviet-U.S. relationship for the preceding forty years suddenly disappeared with Gorbachev's assumption of the Soviet Union's top leadership position. On the contrary, after decades of hostility and international political competition as well as an arms race, there was skepticism on both sides. To Soviet officials, President Reagan was the man who had dubbed their country an evil empire. To many Americans and their allies in the North Atlantic Treaty Organization, the Soviet Union, irrespective of who might be its leader, was a totalitarian state that had threatened international security.

However, only two days after assuming the Soviet Union's top leadership position, Gorbachev had an encounter with high U.S. officials that left them with the feeling that Margaret Thatcher may have been right after all. Vice President George H. W. Bush and Secretary Shultz had come to Moscow to attend the funeral of the most recently departed Soviet leader, Konstantin Chernenko. That occasion offered an opportunity for the U.S. vice president and the secretary of state to exchange thoughts briefly with the new Soviet leader. In a press briefing following that meeting, Secretary Shultz said: "Gorbachev is different from any Soviet leader I've met. But the U.S.-Soviet relationship is not just about personalities."[2]

Presaging the dialogue of the years to come, the exchange of thoughts between Gorbachev and the Bush-Shultz team on March 13, 1985, covered two topics: international affairs and the arms race, and human rights problems in the Soviet Union. Gorbachev's observations on the first of these two topics were viewed as positive by his American interlocutors. There was a standoff, however, on the issue of human rights. Gorbachev made it clear that he did not consider human rights an appropriate subject for discussion between the Soviet Union and the United States.

It was in keeping with the exchange of thoughts at this first meeting that the U.S.-Soviet dialogue in the early Gorbachev years focused on arms control. More than two years passed until, in April 1987, in the context of

---

2. George P. Shultz, *Turmoil and Triumph: My Years as Secretary of State* (New York: Scribner, 1993), 532–533.

another bilateral meeting on arms reduction, Anatoly and Dick met to initiate a dialogue on human rights.

While we were working on reaching a common goal, our tasks in dealing with our respective bureaucracies differed significantly. To be able to give full recognition to our differing perspectives on the same subjects, we have structured this book to allow each of us to explain how we saw the issues that we had to deal with. Therefore, except for this introductory chapter, each chapter consists of two parts, one written by Dick, the other by Anatoly. For the first five chapters, Anatoly leads off each chapter; in chapters 6 and 7, the order is reversed and Dick's section precedes Anatoly's. Both sections of each chapter (save for the final chapter) cover the same period and focus, broadly speaking, on the same issues. However, the two sections do not, and are not intended to, parallel one another perfectly; to the contrary, just as the Soviet and U.S. perspectives on a given subject varied, with different issues and concerns occupying the foreground, so the perspectives in the paired sections of each chapter vary. In addition, of course, each author's involvement in his country's unfolding political and social history was very different, and those differences are reflected in the chapters, especially chapters 1, 2, and 7.

As our respective bosses and many of our colleagues believe that our roles were significant in the context of the Soviet-U.S. dialogue, we hope we shall not be viewed as exhibiting illusions of grandeur when we begin this book with accounts of our personal backgrounds. There appears to have been a common thread in our vastly different experiences that caused us to be fully dedicated to the desire to help bring our countries closer together and to resolve the differences in the field of human rights.

As noted, at the very first meeting that Gorbachev, as secretary general, had with high-level U.S. officials, he rejected the notion of engaging in discussion of human rights issues. His outlook deserves explanation of the treatment of the human rights issue in the decades that preceded Gorbachev's encounter with Bush and Shultz. We have, therefore, written a general account of the post–World War II evolution of human rights as an issue entitled to receive attention at the international level. We have also reviewed the more specific question of how the human rights issue affected Soviet-U.S. relations in the pre-Gorbachev period. Against that background, we have then provided a chronological account of our interaction in helping bring about an end to Soviet totalitarianism.

As we initiated these discussions, Anatoly found that Dick had framed the expressions of U.S. human rights concerns in a way that improved the chances that the Soviet Union would respond positively. Allowing Jews, Armenians, and Pentecostal Christians to emigrate, for example, was no threat at all to the prevailing system in the Soviet Union. Furthermore the new leadership felt sufficiently confident about its hold on power to agree to end abuse of psychiatry and prison sentences for expressions of dissent. Dick did not ask the Soviet Union to adopt the Swiss model of democracy and move forward to free elections promptly. Also, when Anatoly pointed out that the Soviet Ministry of Justice would not release the documents that Dick requested on criminal cases that were suspected of being politically motivated unless U.S. documents were released on a basis of reciprocity, Dick collected the material on the U.S. cases said to be of concern to the Soviet Union; these involved the conviction of persons for acts of terrorism that happened to be politically motivated.

There was a truly unique feature to our dialogue: While we were focused on issues grouped under the term human rights, our discussions were closely related to those undertaken by different Soviet and U.S. officials in different rooms of the same buildings on the subject of arms reduction. Whether the meeting was in Moscow or in Washington, the initial human-rights discussions took place in the context of so-called ministerial meetings, that is, meetings attended by the foreign minister and the secretary of state, with the largest number of participants focusing on arms reduction and only a small number of officials engaged in human rights discussions.

There is no doubt that arms reduction and human rights issues were closely intertwined, but in a manner that was not quite obvious. As Dick had occasion to say, it was not a matter of trading exit permits for one hundred refuseniks in return for permission to allow ten additional missiles in a particular location. What Shultz had in mind when he frequently emphasized the critical importance of the human rights issue in the context of our bilateral negotiations was that arms reduction was ultimately based on mutual trust and that the U.S. government, particularly Congress, would place greater trust in a government that respected human rights than it would in a government that abused them.

In writing these memoirs, we relied largely on our memories of the events in which we participated, although Dick consulted the memoirs of secretaries of state Shultz and James Baker and was able to retrieve from State Department files the messages that dealt directly with his engagement in the Soviet human rights issue. Anatoly did not have much access to the confidential files of the Ministry of Foreign Relations but was able to draw on his personal papers from the time and to refresh his memory by exchanging recollections with a variety of former colleagues and former superiors, including President Gorbachev and Foreign Minister Shevardnadze.

1

The Making of Unwitting Human Rights Officials

Anatoly Adamishin

This chapter sketches Dick's and my personal histories insofar as they are relevant to the story told in subsequent chapters. In politics and diplomacy, as in so many other areas of life, it always helps to know something about the backgrounds and perspectives, the strengths and weaknesses of the people involved—after all, while vast, impersonal forces may dictate the range of possibilities on the international stage, it is human beings who decide which of those options to take.

When Dick and I began our odyssey in April 1987, I was fifty-three years old and, by the standards of the Soviet Ministry of Foreign Affairs, my career had been brilliant or near to it. I sometimes think that I owe everything to chance. As a matter of fact, only a number of fortuitous circumstances prevented my life from being derailed at its very beginning.

Dawn under the Bombs

On June 22, 1941, the first day of the Great Patriotic War—known in most of the world as World War II—I was awakened by German bombs in Kiev, called the mother of Russian cities, where I had been born seven years earlier. I cried, almost hysterically, to my parents—all three of us lived in one small room—"It is war!" At first, they hushed me; it was early Sunday morning and my young parents were eager to sleep. But they had to get up; the noise we heard differed too much from the usual alarms.

My father, a major in the airborne troops, left very soon for the front and after that I saw him only once, when he was sent to Kiev for a few days and availed himself of this opportunity to organize our departure. My mother held his assessment of the situation in high regard and, contrary to the rest of the family—which decided not to relocate, saying that Kiev would never be surrendered—took my cousin and me to Moscow, where nobody waited for us. (My aunt was a member of the Communist Party, which meant that she was forbidden to leave the Kiev.) Thus, my mother probably saved our lives. Even if I had survived the German occupation, after the war, while filling out bureaucratic forms, I would have to state that I had remained in the occupied territories, a difficult stigma to erase.

My father was lost very quickly, in one of the giant cauldrons that the Germans created during the first months of the war, surrounding large units of the Red Army. We were losing nineteen of our servicemen for one German soldier—and their troops were on the offensive. For a long time, the Soviet official history dedicated just a few words to this shameful period, although our losses were in the millions. Later my mother read to me some of my father's few letters. Even through harsh censorship, we could feel his bitterness about the lack of preparedness for the war, the incompetence of the military leaders, and the complete disorganization of the army. No wonder: Joseph Stalin's repressive actions against the military on the eve of the war were savage. They continued even during hostilities; one of the leaders of perestroika, Aleksandr Yakovlev, writes in his book *Twilight* that firing squads killed 157,000 men, or the equivalent of fifteen army divisions.[1] My father must have known something before the war about the army's deficiencies, but could share his doubts only with his wife. Every incautious word might turn out to be his last.

For almost fifty years, the official information about my father was what we received in August 1941: that he was missing. The organs, as we called state security, periodically summoned my mother, asking whether she knew anything about her husband's fate. The last time was in 1959, on the eve of my departure to the Soviet embassy in Rome as a clerk. The perestroika period, which opened a lot of things, allowed access to the German archives taken as trophies in 1945 and held in a basement for half a century. Strange as it may seem, nobody had ever taken the trouble to examine them.

As our last name begins with A, we quickly found that my father was wounded and taken prisoner in the summer of 1941 and died in captivity in 1943. If it had been known that I was the son of a prisoner of war, I would have been given no chance to receive a higher education. Stalin's infamous

---

1. Aleksandr Yakovlev, *Sumerki* (Moscow: Materik, 2003), 198. Yakovlev was for several decades chairman of the Commission for Rehabilitation of Political Repression's Victims.

order N270, which defined as a traitor anyone captured by the Germans, was not withdrawn until after the dictator's death.

I believe that my father's destiny was that of millions of others who paid a tremendous price in blood for the regime created by the so-called genius of all time.

Growing up in Stalin's Soviet Union

Naturally, I understood all this only much later on. Like so many of my contemporaries, in my early years, I was a member of the Young Pioneers and later of the Komsomol, both of which were Communist youth movements. We were convinced that we were lucky to have been born in the most socially developed and just country in the world.[2] A great revolution and a giant war, in which we had been victorious, were both behind us; a wonderful future lay before us. We believed that, strengthened by the only true doctrine—Marxism-Leninism—we showed the way to a bright future for all mankind. We thought every nation would, sooner or later, follow our lead, and we were extremely proud of this mission. Social or national differences didn't exist for us, and all people were equal—or so we proclaimed and tried to behave accordingly, until cruel reality ended these naiveties. For each of us the path was clear. All we had to do was to prepare ourselves to make a valuable contribution to the common cause. Thus, in due time, I diligently studied all 226 works of the Marxist-Leninist classics officially recommended for higher education students.

"We were coming into this life as if it were a feast entirely for us," I wrote later. How convenient were these idealistic feelings for those who cynically exploited useful idiots. For decades I knew nothing, absolutely nothing, about the terrible deeds that were carried out behind the enthusiastic scenes. Few did. Who could have told me anything about the gulags? There was no man in my family, and my mother was aware of what might happen to those who had, as she put it, a tongue too sharp. Besides, she was busy securing the bare essentials for me. Those first postwar years were truly very hard.

In the early 1950s, the Soviet Union was still a country where the chance for advancement was not a prerogative for the few. There was equal opportunity, based on merit, for many young people, kept alive by the tremendous fear that Stalin's regime had inspired. I gained entry to Moscow University thanks to a

---

2. As Liudmila Alexeyva, our famous dissident, writes about her childhood, "I felt fortunate . . . to be born in my country. The USSR was the best and most progressive in the world." *The Thaw Generation* (London: Little, Brown, 1990), 10.

Gorbachev's wife, Raissa, said once about their youth that they lived in lucky times when a young person could be a Communist and a patriot at the same time. I took her words from an article by Sergio Romano, former Italian ambassador to Moscow, that appeared in *La Stampa*, December 24, 1991.

gold medal awarded by my secondary school, with absolutely no special help to get admitted. The notion that you needed somebody to help you enter a university, "a hair hand," as Russians call it, was alien at that time. There was one troublesome exception: Jews were excluded from this equal opportunity system, and only the most talented among them had a chance to enroll.[3] It would be incorrect to think that we did not say or hear the word right. We did, but never in combination with the word human. We learned by heart: "A person always has the right to study, to work, to take a holiday."

It was in my years at the university that some doubts began to enter my mind, some nagging suspicion that something was rotten in the Soviet state. My new impressions came from contact with fellow students who had already served in the army; they had priority in university admissions and had more experience in life than we young chickens. I became friends with one of them, Volodia Alexeyev, and it was he who, first cautiously and then more and more explicitly, took to enlighten me about Stalin's mass repressions, unjust condemnations, and other appalling actions. Our discussions, at the beginning vague and inconsistent, grew heated enough to pose potentially serious trouble. Volodia hinted at the existence of a secret society and cells of resistance, and there were a lot of KGB informants, as I learned later, in our midst.[4]

Stalin's Death

We were lucky: Stalin died on March 5, 1953, when my classmates and I were only in our second semester. For many of us it meant the end of the world. For hundreds this had a literal meaning: They perished in a terrible stampede that occurred on the night when large crowds tried to push their way through the blockade of military trucks in front of the Columned Hall, where Stalin lay in state. Even now, after more than half a century, I can vividly recall the details of that frosty night: I pushed and ran and used a shortcut, sliding on ice below the closed and locked gates. (As I discovered later, Mikhail Gorbachev, a student of law two years older than I, was part of the crowd that tried to reach Stalin's coffin. He later described Stalin's death as a heavy blow, hard to endure.) At six in the morning, after hours of effort, I reached the hall. What I saw wasn't a giant, but a small man. The coffin had been lowered to allow the crowd to see the body. This seemed sacrilegious to me. Walking back home on a crisp Moscow morning, I wept. So strong was the feeling inculcated in us by long years of Stalin's cult of personality that I thought that

---

3. Many people in these circumstances tried to hide their Jewish origins. The 1989 census data showed a Jewish population of 1,367,910; there were almost three million in 1959.

4. In the first years after the war, small groups of students put forward the slogan "Back to Lenin." All were arrested and jailed.

without him we were dead, that life had lost its meaning.[5] Instead, our life whirled on at higher speed. But politics still did not touch us as students, nor did genuine political activity exist for the general public; to the contrary, it had been excluded once and forever. Yes, the Communist Party continued to exist, as did the Komsomol, but their members were not engaged in meaningful political debate. How could they be? A debate would presume competing ideas, but the comrades were supposed to think in the same way.

A political rivalry was a privilege of the few at the top of the Communist Party pyramid—but such rivalries were conducted out of public view. Most of us weren't concerned about what was happening on high. I realize that such a confession doesn't bring much honor to us, but as a Russian saying has it, you can't throw a word out from the song. Even the most dramatic events, such as Lavrenty Beria's elimination,[6] were not matters of special note. Nor did we pay a great deal of attention to the reshuffling of positions in the party and thus the country's leadership. There was a clear distinction between we, who under all circumstances were expected to behave properly and to perform the duties that were assigned to us, and they, the men in leadership positions who were beyond our reach. The impossibility of influencing the train of events was taken as a given. The people, as our great Aleksandr Pushkin described the state of affairs a century earlier, kept silent.

The Twentieth Congress

What delivered a blow to the whole coordinated system of my generation was Nikita Khrushchev's four-hour secret speech to the Twentieth Party Congress in February 1956 denouncing Stalin's "cult of personality," his violation of "party democracy" [sic], and his unjust imprisonment of great numbers of Communists.[7] With that speech, a tear was produced in our social fabric that still has not healed. It was at that time that the boat of my generation, as in a tsunami, began to be thrown from side to side. Thereafter, it would happen at regular intervals—when Leonid Brezhnev came to push

---

5. The cult was masterfully organized; the entire state machinery supported and propagandized it. Stalin himself played a diabolically shrewd role in order to be held in constant admiration. He wasn't a fool. A brief example: A foreign journalist said to him, following a statement: "You don't even imagine, Marshal Stalin, how right you are." And the reply: "Who knows, maybe I do."

6. Lavrenty Beria was one of the three leaders who delivered an oration at Stalin's funeral. He was arrested four months later, in July, for criminal antiparty and antistate activities and executed in December 1953.

7. It should be noted that those who suffered most were at the top of the party. In 1937 and 1938, the bulk of the Central Committee members and delegates to the Seventeenth Party Congress were executed. Everyone learned from the official historiography that this was the so-called Congress of Winners, but very few knew where the winners ended up.

out Khrushchev, Gorbachev to get rid of the gerontocracy, Boris Yeltsin to preside over the break-up of the Soviet Union, and Vladimir Putin today. Every leader's replacement was supposed to bring remarkable changes in our system of views. These oscillations were not fun.

A lot of people, many in tears, refused to believe Khrushchev. The shift was too great. We had to recognize that for a long period, we had lived in two countries: one in which people marched enthusiastically, singing "broad is my own land," and another in which suffering was just as heavy as it was hidden. There was a strange feeling that many people would have preferred to keep their eyes shut. Even the famous Dolores Ibarrury, the Passionaria, the Spanish revolutionary who fought against Franco, said, after hearing the report, that it would have been better if we had remained unaware of the crimes committed by Stalin. But, again, the truth reached us in drops.[8]

I remember one event in which we students of the economics faculty gathered outdoors. We imbeciles, after a good session of drinking, loudly sang an anthem to our former idol. It was a sort of defiance of those who first made Stalin a god and now were trampling him down, saying at the same time that they couldn't do anything to stop his crimes. How could we trust them if they had lied to us for decades? Some members of the Communist Party had asked the same questions when the closed discussions began. Among young people there were attempts at real resistance to the party's dictatorship. These were not comfortable questions or actions for those in power, so the authorities managed to wind up all that quickly.

Few protested this turn. A poll conducted forty years later among those who lived through the Twentieth Party Congress showed that nearly 40 percent either didn't hear anything about the denunciation of Stalin or were indifferent to it.[9]

In February 2006, I compared my memories with those of Boris Vladimirov, who was at the time of the Congress one of our faculty Komsomol leaders and, unlike me, had been invited to a closed party meeting. Khrushchev's speech had been read to those assembled with a special warning: no discussion. As Boris told me, he too wondered whether these revelations, with their shocking figures of large-scale repression, would harm the country. But, he added, we were miles away from real political life and more concerned with where they

---

8. In those days I had a special source of information: my fellow student Gigi Longo, who was sent by the Italian Communist Party to study at Moscow University. He was thirty then, had passed equal parts of his life in Italy, France, and Russia—mostly as a political émigré—and spoke all three languages perfectly. For this reason he was involved in simultaneous translations when the Soviet Union Communist Party's congresses were held. Sometimes he shared with me what he heard. But when Khrushchev delivered his secret speech, the session was declared closed, and not only Gigi, but even Palmiro Togliatti, the head of the Italian Communists, was asked to leave.

9. See J. Aksiutin's article in *Otechestvennaia Istoria*, no. 26 (1998).

would send us to work and live. Assigned job placement was compulsory for all college graduates, as we studied at the government's expense.

Witnessing Khrushchev's Thaw

What was Khrushchev's thaw, as I remember it? Its main feature was certainly the hundreds of thousands coming back from the gulags. The first trickles began a year after Stalin's death; after the Twentieth Congress, the trickles grew huge.[10] But it was not a triumphant return. I learned much later that nearly ninety special commissions to investigate the circumstances under which people had been imprisoned for political reasons had been created, but at that time, information about their work was practically nonexistent. Some people learned a few details through personal contacts, but they knew the dangers of sharing that information.

After Kiev's occupation by the Germans during World War II, my uncle, Viktor Adamishin, then a young man, had been forced to work as a slave laborer in Germany. Having suffered there and been liberated by the Americans, he was, like many others, turned over to the Soviet authorities—as agreed at the Potsdam Conference—and was then sent to Siberia for two more years. This was a general practice toward such "suspicious elements," who numbered millions. I didn't know about his homecoming right away and learned of it only with a laconic phrase by phone from Kiev: "Vitia's back." People were scared to spread this kind of information. Who knew which turn events might take? The fear spread by thirty years of Stalin's rule had deep roots. Some of them are still here.

Vitia, unfortunately, didn't live long after his return.

I think that Khrushchev, too, when disclosing the truth, was guided in part by fear. Terror came very close to those who surrounded the dictator. Vyacheslav Molotov's wife was put in prison (because she had told Israeli ambassador Golda Meir that she was Jewish) while her husband continued to be second or third in the country's leadership. She was among the very first liberated after Stalin's death in 1953. In 1956, Nikita Sergeyevich wanted to sweep away terror, at least its most insidious forms—such as extrajudicial repression by the Ministry of Internal Affairs—but he did not want to eliminate all fear. Probably, as with Gorbachev later, the door opened more widely than Khrushchev had intended. Attempts to close it began very soon after the Twentieth Congress: Both the Communist Party and its leadership were

---

10. It is estimated that at the time, 5.5 million prisoners were held in the prisons, camps, colonies, and special settlements. See Robert Service, *A History of Modern Russia* (Cambridge, MA: Harvard University Press, 2005), 329. In his turn, Service makes reference to R. W. Davies, "Forced Labor under Stalin: The Archive Revelations," *New Left Review* 1, no. 214 (November–December 1995): 62–80.

absolutely unprepared for serious de-Stalinization. The tug-of-war lasted a long time. Dmitri Ustinov, minister of defense and one of the most authoritative members of the Soviet leadership in the 1980s, used to say that "no enemy brought us such disaster as Khrushchev did with his policy concerning the past of our Party and State and in regard of Stalin."[11]

What was particularly unacceptable for us, the young, was the conclusion reached very soon after Khrushchev's revelations: Yes, there were blunders, misdeeds, and so on, but the most important thing was that the Communist Party was condemning them. So, ultimately, it was claimed, the positive outweighed the negative. How on earth, we used to say in our closed circle—as neither the party nor the Komsomol permitted exchanges of opinions of this kind—could the crimes be defined as errors? And why was no one punished? Something didn't fit. It opened another crucial question: whether the crimes, which were sometimes unimaginable, could be justified by great achievements. The answer to this question divided Soviet society and continues to divide Russian society.[12]

Khrushchev's Pluses and Minuses

It is true that the expectations born with the thaw, with the new literature that emerged[13]—and we were indeed inspired by early Yevgeny Yevtushenko and Andrei Voznesenski and by Vladimir Vysotsky and Bulat Okudzhava—at the end of the day were not fulfilled. Khrushchev's policies were notoriously contradictory and inconsistent.

It was Khrushchev who stopped the infamous investigation that Stalin ordered, just before his death, against physicians, "killers in white gowns," the major part of whom bore Jewish names. But it was also under Khrushchev that a previously little-known dissident, Vladimir Bukovski, was put in a special psychiatric hospital for coercive treatment. Nikita Sergeyevich sincerely considered as enemies those who "stand in the way of the Communist Party," and he strongly believed that Communism would be built in the Soviet Union within twenty years—that is, by 1980 if not sooner. It was Khrushchev who, on the insistence of the famous poet and editor of

---

11. The quotation is taken from the magazine *Big Policy* (March 2006): 102.

12. In polls taken in March 2005, 42 percent of respondents said they would like to have a new Stalin installed in the Kremlin. All of the Soviet Union's achievements, in the minds of such people, are ascribed to him, and the misdeeds have been forgotten.

13. Among them was a novel by Ilia Ehrenburg that gave its name to this period—*The Thaw*. I had a chance to meet Ehrenburg when he came to Rome. The Soviet ambassador Semen Kozyrev—not to be confused with Andrei Kozyrev, the Russian foreign minister, thirty years later—would present me jokingly to the high guests from Moscow as a future ambassador. Usually nobody paid attention, but Ehrenburg did: "You first ask this young man whether he wants to be an ambassador." He guessed my feelings at that time, but in the end it was Kozyrev who got it right: I ultimately did become ambassador to Italy.

New World magazine, Aleksandr Tvardovski, permitted the publication of Aleksandr Solzhenitsyn's first novel, *One Day in the Life of Ivan Denisovich,* a shocking revelation about Stalin's camps. But it was also Khrushchev who shelved the results of the Shvernik Commission, which investigated the infamous trials and purges of the 1930s that took the lives of tens of thousands.[14] And it was also he who made a tumultuous visit to the annual exhibition in Moscow's Manege, during which he vehemently attacked the nonconformist painters;[15] and it was he who compelled Boris Pasternak to refuse the Nobel Prize awarded to him for *Doctor Zhivago,* which was labeled anti-Soviet. I would dare to say that he wanted a more normal life for the Soviet elite, but he was not so eager to offer the same freedoms to the public at large. To the very first signs of Soviet society's political and social awakening, he responded with old methods, though of a much milder version: selective repression and the suppression of information.

All of this is true, but it was a rare case when the aspirations of the leader coincided for a short period with the people's needs, and it had a remarkable effect. Even if independently of his will, what Khrushchev did, and what he provoked by his actions, signified a giant step forward. I would put Khrushchev's attempts to democratize the country in second place among the rulers of the postwar Soviet Union and Russia, behind those of Gorbachev. He was ready to take great risks. Today it is widely accepted that the Twentieth Congress was the first milestone on our way to a more democratic society. A new category of persons started forming in the Soviet Union: "Twentieth Congress's children." I am proud to have been a member of this brotherhood.

Without Khrushchev's thaw, it should be emphasized, Gorbachev's perestroika might well not have occurred.

International Aspects

Khrushchev's performance at the Twentieth Congress had colossal historical implications not only inside the country but beyond its borders, even if he did

---

14. Gorbachev revealed the Commission's results at a closed party meeting in July 1987, during perestroika. He mentioned also that Brezhnev, Andropov, and Chernenko were successively shown the applicable materials as well, but no consequences followed. It was only under Gorbachev that a mighty impetus was given to rehabilitation work. In the summer of 1987, KGB head Viktor Chebrikov reported that 1.6 million people had been rehabilitated. See Gorbachev Foundation, V Politburo CK KPSS [In the Politburo of the CPSU Central Committee] (Moscow: Alpina Busines Books, 2006), 204, 362. Produced by the Gorbachev Foundation, V Politburo CK KPSS brings together notes made by Anatoly Chernyaev, Vadim Medvedev, and Georgi Shakhnazarov, close aides of Gorbachev, at meetings of the Politburo and other closed meetings of the CPSU Central Committee between 1985 and 1991.

15. During Brezhnev's rule, artists had an even harder time. In 1974, the authorities ordered the bulldozing of an illegal exhibition of underground painters. Some of the painters were my personal friends, and their abstract pictures are still in my home.

not foresee them. Just a few months after his speech, in the autumn of 1956, Khrushchev had to cope with a very serious crisis: the Hungarian revolt, which was proceeded by street demonstrations in the Polish city of Poznan. Deprived of prior information, we university students were struck by the harsh repression in Budapest. Khrushchev got away with it. The West limited itself to vocal indignation. The logic of the Cold War was already in action—the zones of dominance were not subject to change unless you were willing to risk war. The West's conduct wasn't very laudable, especially in light of claims that some Western special services had encouraged an armed revolt.[16]

While he was making a show of assertiveness, Khrushchev was also practically liquidating the Soviet navy and drastically reducing the size of the army by more than one-third. For those of us who were students in 1956, these cuts had an unexpected consequence: We enjoyed an unusual softening of our one-month military service in the army camps. Due to Khrushchev's measures, the military was losing its prestige and the military chiefs were not in a position to press us too hard. Khrushchev's perceived antimilitary measures would be recalled to him, among his other sins, when he was ousted in 1964.

As for myself, I was joining the diplomatic service. Back then it was unthinkable to apply for service in the Ministry of Foreign Affairs, as is standard practice today. One had to be invited, after a rather stringent selection process. By chance, the ministry was searching for a person who had some knowledge of Italian, and it found me. In January 1959, I left for Italy as a stageur for our embassy in Rome.

The experience of having overcome two crises—the Suez crisis raged practically at the same time as the Hungarian one—while achieving major advances in space (Yuri Gagarin's flight was in 1961) and in the development of a new weapon, the long-range ballistic missile, seemingly encouraged Khrushchev in a very risky adventure that entered history as the Cuban Missile Crisis. What might I add to its detailed and numerous descriptions? My personal sensations: first, that the crisis could really have ended badly, and, second, of complete helplessness in the face of forces that could decide one's destiny.

Being in the Soviet embassy to Rome in October 1962, I distinctly remember the atmosphere of anxiety and tension that reigned in the Italian capital.

---

16. I was Russian ambassador to London in 1996 when the fortieth anniversary of the Hungarian rebellion occurred. On October 21, the *Times* published an extract from a certain M. Smith's book, where he revealed that American and British agents prepared these events well in advance, delivering weapons, setting up hideouts, and training future insurgents in the Austrian Alps. The topic was hushed up right away; the Foreign Office replied to a journalist's demand that it didn't comment on operational activity, even if it took place four decades ago.

See also Philip Zelikow and Condoleezza Rice, *Germany Unified and Europe Transformed* (Cambridge, MA: Harvard University Press, 1995), 25: "Inflammatory rhetoric contributed to the [Hungarian] uprising which was then bloodily crushed as the Americans stood by, unable to help."

Which would come first, a regular gun salvo from Gianicolo Hill at noon, or an atomic explosion? That was the question on Italian lips. Usually our ambassador shared with me, as his interpreter and assistant, some sensitive information, but this time he kept full silence. Evidently he was not informed about fast and dramatic developments, and for him as well, the only option was awaiting the inevitable. Who cared about the ambassador to Italy when even Andrei Gromyko, the foreign minister, was caught telling a lie: "We have no missiles in Cuba!" Then he had to absolve himself by confessing that he had not dispensed correct information. Thankfully, both Khrushchev and Kennedy managed to keep their heads.

Blame for the Cuban debacle was largely—and correctly—attributed inside Russia's ruling circle to Khrushchev. Some called him a missile-holic. He needed a justification. It was found in the argument that the United States had a twenty-fold superiority in weapons. Thus, if we could not catch up to the United States in food production, even though that was Khrushchev's original pledge, we could switch to arms. And we dashed after the United States. Few understood then that this race would contribute immensely to the demise of the Soviet Union. When, twenty-three years later, on May 6, 1985, the Soviet defense minister, Sergei Sokolov, solemnly confirmed that parity in nuclear arms between the Soviet Union and the United States had been achieved, my country had six years of life left.

The First Moves toward Lessening Tension

Notwithstanding the Cuban crisis, during his reign as Soviet leader, Khrushchev gradually decided to seek better relations with the West, including the Americans. When Khrushchev had ousted one of Stalin's old guard, Georgy Malenkov, in 1955, one of the sins of which he accused Malenkov was of speaking too often about nuclear war as the threat to world civilization;[17] showing firmness was considered to be a more efficient tool. But thereafter the music grew mild. Khrushchev signed the multilateral state treaty with Austria that became the base for Austria's neutrality, and reconciled with Yugoslavian president Josip Broz Tito, who for many years had not been mentioned in the Soviet media as other than a "bloody dog." Our leader met President Dwight Eisenhower on a number of occasions. There followed the famous talks with Richard Nixon in the "typical American kitchen" during the first American exhibition in Moscow in 1959, and finally the June 1961 meeting with the new American president, John F. Kennedy, in Vienna,

---

17. Malenkov used the word détente for the first time, speaking at a session of the Supreme Soviet in August 1953. See R. Pikhoia, Sovietskii Soyuz: istoria vlasti, 1945–1991 (Moscow: RAGS, 1998), 132, 138.

which promised some external thaw, drastically interrupted by the missile crisis. Unexpectedly I came to be privy to one of the first steps toward détente, although not directly.

Rome was an interesting place at that time, due principally to the policies of Pope John XXIII. Within Italy, he tried to reconcile two leading political forces, Catholics and Communists; on the international stage, he sought to promote better bonds between the two superpowers. A practical move in that direction—one that Italians were dreaming about—would have been to convene a meeting in Rome, probably within the Vatican, between the Catholic president of the United States and Khrushchev.

An early stage in this project was establishing diplomatic relations between the Soviet Union and the Holy See. We were actively pushed toward them by leftist Christian Democrats, such as Amintore Fanfani and Giorgio La Pira. Ambassador Semen Kozyrev chose me to make the preliminary contacts with high-ranking Catholic clerics. The relations culminated in Kozyrev's secret rendezvous with Cardinal Agostino Bea, the first such meeting in the history of the Soviet-Vatican relationship. Thanks to the personal intervention of Kozyrev, the Soviet authorities freed Cardinal Slipyi from detention in a gulag as a preliminary condition. The Vatican, however, ratcheted up its requests, and finally my ambassador—who was already conducting a dangerous game, given the resistance of ideologues in the Soviet leadership to contacts with the Vatican—proposed that Moscow give up its attempts to reach an agreement. On that occasion the hawks on both sides won. Even though some improvements were made in the next five years, official relations with the Vatican were delayed for two decades and any hopes of a Roman meeting between the superpowers were dashed. On June 13, 1963, Pope John XXIII died. President Kennedy was assassinated five months later, on November 22, 1963; finally came Khrushchev's political death in October 1964.[18] Still in the Soviet embassy in Italy, I heard the news in a Roman street, as young newsboys shouted, "Look what these Russians have done."

Khrushchev managed to irritate all the strata of high Soviet society. When he left the political scene, as far as I remember, no one mourned.[19] The country was tired of his jostling, improvisations, and mood swings. But he did

---

18. I met Khrushchev at close range only once, when Italian president Giovanni Gronchi paid an official visit to Moscow, the first Western leader to do so. At one of the receptions Nikita Sergeyevich was approached by the Italian minister of foreign affairs, Giuseppe Pella, who asked, "Is it true, Signor Khrushchev, that you pour vodka for your guests while you yourself drink water?" (We suspected that Pella's mission was to watch the Leftist Christian Democrat Gronchi in order to make sure that he did not damage Atlantic solidarity.) Nikita was offended to the depths of his soul. While I translated the scene, trembling, he passed his glass to the Italian, saying, "Drink, Giuseppe."

19. Good evidence of that is presented in his son's memoirs: "Nobody grieved for my father. The news of his resignation was taken with relief." Sergei Khrushchev, *Rojdenie sverkhderjavi* (Moscow: Vremia, 2003), 648.

establish a notable innovation: For the first time in Soviet history, a leader departed office alive rather than in a coffin.[20] His departure allowed the bureaucracy to breathe more easily—he had threatened its dominant position. The motto of the team that succeeded Khrushchev at the helm of the Soviet system was stability. From then on, nobody should fear for his position, whatever his moral or professional qualities. It was a distinct departure from Stalin's characteristically brutal approach to bureaucracy—his firing squads had executed two or three full sets of the senior leadership of the republics and provinces. We now turned to a new page, Brezhnev's. Few suspected how long, and how disastrous for the country, it would be.

Serving under Andrei Gromyko

Andrei Andreyevich Gromyko became minister of foreign affairs in the same year—1957— that I began my diplomatic career in Smolenskaya Square palace (the location of the Soviet Foreign Ministry) in downtown Moscow. When my service in Italy terminated in 1965, I gradually joined his close circle, first as an interpreter, then as a speechwriter and adviser. This situation lasted for two decades. In all this period, he never let me work abroad—except for short missions—rejecting my requests for an embassy posting. For that reason, I spent all of Brezhnev's eighteen-year rule in the central office of our ministry, watching conditions in the country closely.

The first Brezhnev years did give some hope; attempts to reform economic policy, connected with the name of Alexei Kosygin, albeit hesitant and incomplete, brought the most successful five-year plan, 1965–70. Industrial production and productivity increased. Even agriculture saw positive developments; in those years purchases of grain from abroad fell drastically.

But the appetite for reform quickly faded. Our leaders were frightened, especially after the Czechoslovak Spring of 1968, by the prospect of reformist changes that they couldn't keep at bay. So the hopes for reform, like Kosygin himself, died of natural causes.

The end of Khrushchev's thaw, a short and seasonal one, was marked by Brezhnev's assault on intellectuals. Less than a year after Brezhnev came to power, two literary men, Andrei Siniavski and Yuly Daniel, were charged under Article 70 of the Criminal Code with spreading "anti-Soviet propaganda"[21] and were sentenced to seven and five years, respectively, of forced labor—despite Andrei Sakharov's letters in their defense—for having published their

---

20. He plunged into oblivion; through a confidential directive, even his name was prohibited from mention in the mass media. I remember how Julia Khrushcheva, his daughter, rejoiced when this prohibition was removed in 1983, by Andropov almost twenty years later—along, by the way, with Malenkov's name.

21. Article 190, introduced in 1966, was even more generalized and unjust.

literary work abroad. The regime strove to smother all attempts to challenge its monopoly on ideological, political, and even everyday thinking. Few of us knew about the return to punitive psychiatry, which had allegedly been almost suspended under Khrushchev, but we were aware of other methods of punishment, such as sentencing those who disagreed with the regime as if they were common criminals. Particularly convenient for the authorities was the practice of branding suspected dissidents as parasites and then legally condemning persons who had been unemployed for four months to internal exile. This terminology quickly made its way into the language and the practice was applied even to the great Russian poet Iosif Brodsky, subsequently a Nobel Prize winner.

The methods of suppression became more sophisticated. The authorities had to produce a semblance of a legal cause for arrest, an appearance of a fair trial. There was no full-scale repression as in Stalin's time; people didn't vanish into the night. But the feeling that no guarantee existed, that something similar could be repeated, was always present.

"Kitchen" Life

What was our answer? Mainly, our way out was to focus on our private lives, on trying to enjoy those things that were accessible and not extremely expensive. We turned to sport. My friends and I, for example, were fanatics, first of soccer—the playing of which became a real vent for our frustrations and apprehensions—and then, when we grew older, tennis; we also turned to tourism in a huge country with inexpensive train fares and airfares and to Moscow's rich cultural life. As such a subtle expert of our intellectual life as Sir Isaiah Berlin—we used to be good friends while I was the ambassador in London—wrote:

> Despite the difficult and even desperate situation in which persons of independent temperament and education at times find themselves in Russia, they are capable of a degree of gaiety, intellectual as well as social, and of enthusiastic interest in their internal and external affairs, combined with an extravagant and often delicate sense of the ridiculous, which makes life not merely bearable to them but worthwhile; and makes their bearing and their conversation both dignified and delightful to the foreign visitor.[22]

"Kitchen talk," a common term describing pulling inside our own small world, offered escape as well. Birds of a feather flock together, and our circle embraced those who could be called intellectual liberals: film directors like Elem Klimov and Sergei Kolosov; historians like Natan Eidelman; actors

---

22. Isaiah Berlin, *The Soviet Mind* (Washington, DC: Brookings Institution Press, 2004), 26.

like Venyamin Smekhov and his colleagues from the most freedom-loving of the Moscow theaters, Na Taganke, guided by Yuri Lyubimov; the famous bards Jury Visbor and Tatiana and Sergei Nikitin; Khrushchev's daughter Julia; painters; and so forth. What sustained us was hope, the belief that it was impossible that changes would not come. With the means at our own disposal, we tried to speed up their arrival.

Especially gloomy were the years of the full reign of gerontocracy, the late 1970s and early 1980s. Our hopes were being slowly eroded. Almost every day we would hear that someone had left for Israel or the United States. Dick, who knew the general figures better than me, told me in 1987 that during the Brezhnev period, 250,000 Soviet citizens left the country. I am not speaking of forced deportation, as in Solzhenitsyn's case in 1974, or internal exile, as in the case of Sakharov in 1980, but of voluntary emigration. Talented Soviet authors such as Vassily Aksyonov and Georgy Vladimov left the Soviet Union more or less of their own will. Their books had been withdrawn from the libraries and it was forbidden even to mention their names, as well as the names of the great musician Mstislav Rostropovich, his wife Vishnevskaia, and many others. Another thing that narrowed our circle was heavy drinking as a reaction to what was happening. One of our friends was so desperate that he committed suicide.[23]

Coming back to the ministry after a short absence during this period, I asked one of Gromyko's assistants, "How are things going?" He replied with bitterness, "Everything is rotting."[24] My future chief, Shevardnadze, would in 1984 describe to Gorbachev the situation in the country in just the same terms.

Lessening the Damage

Repeatedly I questioned in my mind what I should do in these conditions. My reply was to stick to what I had been doing all my conscious life: trying to improve the system from within—or at least to limit the damage. My background effectively closed the remaining options, such as leaving the Soviet Union or making the passage to open dissent. Harboring doubts about the system was not the same as rejecting it. Whether good or bad, it was my country and, frankly speaking, my establishment. It desperately needed radical reforms to eliminate injustice, demagoguery, the predominance of

---

23. During the reign of Emperor Paul I, one of his dignitaries, Baron Osten-Saken, uttered a sentence: "The only exit for a decent person is a suicide." In later years, though, the Baron preferred to take part in the murder of Paul.

24. My older comrade-in-arms, as we used to say, Soviet diplomat Mikhail Kapitsa, once warned me: "Speak less with foreign ambassadors even if it is part of your job. Everything is monitored, and your own words could be beyond retrieval."

bureaucracy, militarization, and much more. But these could be corrected, and the time for this would come, sooner or later.

In other words, my friends and I tried to pursue a policy of small steps. It was tremendously hard and thankless work. Still, if I may refer to dialectics, changes in quantity, first of all in conscience, were accumulating. Finally they brought a leap of quality, in the policy and the reforms that Gorbachev tried to bring to life.

Meanwhile, I was comforted by the rare occasions that my position in the foreign service helped me make a small but useful contribution. Here is an example. An influential member of the Politburo, Alexey Kosygin, made two rather long visits to Italy, and both times I assisted him as an interpreter. This meant that for many days I had the opportunity to perform "educational" work, showing him the advantages of the Italian capitalist economy, which had been passing through a period of miraculous growth, in order to use something of this experience for our country. Soon thereafter, the Soviet Union decided to develop a big automobile plant, Vaz, and chose the Italian company Fiat to construct it. I like to think that our embassy in Rome made a contribution to that decision.

Another time, I mused to Kosygin, "Do you know, Alexei Nikolaevich, how many holidays the Italians have?" I paused briefly, and then continued, "Nearly twenty, in addition to Saturdays and Sundays. And we?" Kosygin was impressed. Soon thereafter he managed to pass through the Politburo a decree that made Saturday in addition to Sunday a nonworking day. I recall the cartoon that greeted the news: A husband comes home with a bottle of vodka in each hand and cries exultingly, "Masha, we have two holidays!"

As I mentioned, rather than a diplomat I was a ministerial rat. At the end of the day, though, to spend a quarter of a century in the headquarters was not a bad experience. But it was absolutely clear that I couldn't go higher than what we called the working level. To join the high ranks of the ministry you needed the personal benevolence of Gromyko. I never received it and had to wait for perestroika and Gromyko's replacement by Shevardnadze. In line with existing practice, the minister had to ask for Central Committee clearance about my promotion. His request remained unanswered for a long time. One evening, while the case was still pending, Shevardnadze turned to me and asked, "Tell me, please, Anatoly Leonidovich, but frankly: are you a Jew?" I rarely have good answers to unexpected questions, but that time I did: "If I were a Jew, I would be proud of that." "Then why does everybody say that you are a Jew?" he asked. "Maybe because I am so clever," I joked.

Richard Schifter

Anatoly has noted that when he and I met in April 1987, he was fifty-three years old, a professional diplomat who had, by then, had a brilliant career by the standards of the Soviet foreign ministry. After thirty-one years as a career diplomat, he was a deputy foreign minister.

I was sixty-three years old when we met. By contrast to Anatoly, I was fairly new to diplomacy, a field in which I had been engaged full time only for about two-and-a-half years, not as a professional diplomat but as a political appointee. The position that I was then holding was that of U.S. assistant secretary of state for human rights and humanitarian affairs.

The discussion in which we were to engage was to focus on aspects of the governance of Anatoly's country, the place where he was born and had lived most of his life. I, on the other hand, had on the previous day set foot in the Soviet Union for the first time in my life. At first blush, therefore, it would seem that there was a striking difference between us in our respective backgrounds and qualifications to engage in this discussion.

Anatoly's and My Common Roots

It was only as we started to write these memoirs and I reflected on the difference in our background that I fully realized that there were also great similarities in our respective life histories. While I had not visited the Soviet Union prior to April 1987, my roots were in that part of the world. My mother had been born in the Russian Empire, more specifically in Russian Poland, in a village near Warsaw. My father was a native of Galicia, a part of the Austro-Hungarian Empire. His native city, now called Ivano-Frankivsk, was part of the Soviet Union when Anatoly and I met. It is now located in Ukraine. Further, I, too, had been born in Europe, in Vienna, Austria.

Anatoly has explained how as a youngster he had been indoctrinated in school, in the Young Pioneers, and in Komsomol, with a belief in Marxism-Leninism. I, too, had been indoctrinated early in my life, not by any school or organization, but by my mother. My mother had, as a young woman, become greatly interested in world affairs, and by the time she came of political age (probably around 1910) had identified herself with the left-wing democratic movement.

I was very young, not even in elementary school, when my mother began to talk to me about political issues and political developments. In that setting, she could not help sharing her personal outlook with me. Thus, when I was about four or five years old, I recall my mother telling me of a female cousin of hers, who, during the Russo-Polish War of 1920, had become commissar of a Polish town that had been occupied by the Red Army. Shortly after she had been installed as commissar, her brother came to tell her that their father had been imprisoned and to ask her what she would do about that. Her response, as it was relayed to me by my mother, was: "A Bolshevik has neither father nor mother." At the time my mother told me that story, I was also taught that the commandment to honor your father and mother was by far the most important of the ten.

I vividly recall my mother taking me to Vienna's central district, on May 1, 1928, to watch the conclusion of that year's Social Democratic May Day parade. She made it very clear to me that she approved of the people who participated in the parade. They were socialists who believed in and practiced democracy.

My mother had been opposed to Communists even before the rise of Stalin, but once he was in power I heard a great deal about him and was told that he was an evil person. From my reading of newspapers I learned during the 1930s of the increasingly severe repression in the Soviet Union, the execution in 1936 of Marshal Mikhail Tukhachevsky, who had served as chief of staff of the Red Army, followed in the next two years by the trial, conviction, and execution of a group of founding leaders of the Bolshevik movement, persons whom Stalin had come to dislike.

Battling Communists in High School and College

By the time I arrived in the United States in 1938, as a refugee from Nazi-occupied Vienna, I was thus most certainly a thoroughly indoctrinated anti-Communist. Yet I had by then never met anyone who had expressed Communist ideology to me. That was about to change. After my arrival in the United States and my enrollment as a student at DeWitt Clinton High School in the Bronx, New York, I was very quickly exposed to various forms of far-left views. That experience continued when I entered the College of the City of New York in 1940.

In the political setting in which I found myself, we rarely spoke of Communists. We made more precise distinctions. We spoke of Stalinists, Trotskyists, independent Marxists, and various other shades of far-left ideology. After the Soviet attack on Finland, the Trotskyists split further into two movements, the Cannonites and the Shachtmanites. The Cannonites, it was said, believed that the Soviet Union was a workers' state gone wrong, but still a workers' state. The Shachtmanites were said to believe that the Soviet Union was a workers' state gone wrong. Period.

Before I left Vienna, my family and friends had all come to admire President Franklin Delano Roosevelt, so it was not surprising that in the United States I would become a fervent adherent of the New Deal. Not only had

Roosevelt spoken out clearly against Hitler, but he also espoused a domestic economic program of which my mother would have approved.

There were quite a number of Stalinists at City College, both members of the faculty and students. The latter were organized as the Young Communist League (YCL). While we ate lunch in the college's alcoves, we engaged in hot political arguments. The number of Republicans at the school was quite small, and they were rarely heard from. So the political arguments in the alcoves were largely between New Deal Democrats and those to our left. While we New Dealers occasionally argued with supporters of the Socialist Party, whose foreign policy outlook was isolationist, and with Trotskyists, who contended that Roosevelt's only accomplishment was to have saved capitalism, our main argument was with the Stalinists. (Stalinists never debated Trotskyists. Years later, a former leader of the YCL at City College told me that members of that organization were under strict instructions not ever to talk to Trotskyists.)

In 1940 and the first half of 1941, our principal arguments with the Communists were over foreign policy. "The Yanks are not coming," was their slogan.[1] They were opposed to any American assistance to Britain and France and, after France's fall, to Britain. By the early spring of 1941, I had become convinced that Germany was about to attack the Soviet Union and made that point in my arguments with the Stalinists. They did not accept it. What struck me as very strange was how seemingly intelligent persons who had all the information that was available to them in a free society could subordinate their thinking to the Communist party line as formulated by a single individual living in a foreign country. I can readily understand how Anatoly, living in Kiev under Stalin's rule, would accept the party doctrine; I cannot, to this day, understand the thought processes of my Communist classmates in the United States.

Anatoly has described how, as a youngster, he experienced the Nazi attack on the Soviet Union. It came as a surprise to him, but not to me. In letters that I sent to my father, who then lived in Soviet-occupied Poland, not far from the border of the German-occupied area, I urged him to go east. An acquaintance of my father's who was able to get out of the Soviet Union at that time told me that my father had said to him shortly before this acquaintance's departure for the United States, "better Hitler than Stalin."

At City College the adjustment of the Stalinists to the invasion of the Soviet Union by Nazi Germany came fast. The invasion started on June 22, 1941. On Monday, June 23, 1941—literally within hours of the invasion—those of us who came back for summer courses at City College were greeted at the

---

1. A takeoff on the World War I song of the American Expeditionary Force, "The Yanks Are Coming."

entrance doors by YCL members who had faithfully adapted themselves to the new situation and presented us with the new party line. We were handed mimeographed sheets that informed us that the war was now a people's war, in which the United States needed to get engaged. Lenin would surely have been proud of this disciplined party apparatus.

While we pro–New Deal students at City College did not belong to any formally organized movement, the positions we held did reflect a unique aspect of the political life of New York City in the period between the two world wars. The labor movement played an important role in city politics in that period, and developments within the labor movement were followed closely by students at City College—far more than at the city's private colleges.[2]

Within New York City's labor movement, the unions of the needle trades held key positions. The principal needle trades unions were the Amalgamated Clothing Workers, headed by Sidney Hillman, and the International Ladies Garment Workers Union, headed by David Dubinsky. Both Hillman and Dubinsky had been born in the Russian Empire, in Zagare (now Lithuania) and Brest-Litovsk, respectively. Both had become involved in labor union activities in their youth in Russia, both had been arrested, and both had then fled to the United States, where they arrived in 1907 and 1911, respectively.

In the Soviet Union, supporters of democracy were, after 1917, quickly repressed, many of them imprisoned or killed. The Russian social democrats who had emigrated to the United States, however, continued the political struggle in the organizations in which they played an increasingly significant role: the Socialist Party of the United States and the labor movement. In 1919, the followers of Lenin were expelled from the American Socialist Party,[3] but the struggle within the labor movement continued. The Communists would call Hillman, a democratic socialist, a "strikebreaker"[4] and would use similar epithets in their attacks on other labor leaders that opposed the toeing of the Communist line.

The immigrants from the Russian Empire who had identified themselves with the democratic cause and who had risen to leadership positions in the American labor movement came to play an increasingly important role in rallying labor unions beyond the needle trades, such as the steelworkers and autoworkers unions, in opposition to Leninism. In time, a majority of the unions in the American Federation of Labor and the Congress of Indus-

---

2. We also closely observed the local political scene. The congressman representing the district in which City College was located was Vito Marcantonio, who faithfully followed the Communist party line. We anti-Bolsheviks referred to him as Vitorinsk Marcantoniovich.

3. Max M. Kampelman, *The Communist Party vs. the CIO* (New York: Praeger, 1957), 7.

4. Ibid., 9–10.

trial Organizations identified themselves with anti-Communist positions. Some unions, however, did elect Communists to leadership positions, and Communists were very active within the labor movement, both those that they controlled and those in which they were in a minority and in which they fought the union leadership. From 1919 until the collapse of American Communism following the "secret" Khrushchev speech of 1956, the labor movement continued to serve as a platform in which latter-day Leninists and their democratic opponents continued their struggle.[5]

I have discussed this aspect of the history of the American labor movement at length because only as I was writing this memoir did it occur to me that there was a direct connection between this esoteric aspect of the history of the American labor movement and developments in the field of international relations in the late 1980s. For among the members of the labor movement who were drawn into this struggle between Communists and their liberal democratic opponents was a Hollywood actor who had joined the Screen Actors Guild and in due course had become the guild's president. He may not have done a great deal of reading on the subject of Communism, but his experience in the guild in Hollywood taught him a great deal about the behavior of devout followers of the Communist faith. Decades later when, as president of the United States, Ronald Reagan became acquainted with Mikhail Gorbachev, he recognized that this leader of the Soviet Union had broken with the set of beliefs that had inspired the Communist activists whom he had known in Hollywood in the 1930s and 1940s. Thus, the basic shift in the Reagan administration's policy toward the Soviet Union was brought about in significant part because the president had acquired a thorough understanding of the nature of Communism in his dealings with Communist members of the Screen Actors Guild fifty years earlier and was able to apply that understanding to his assessment of Gorbachev. He recognized that under Gorbachev the Soviet Union was moving away from its Leninist moorings.

To return to New York's City College in the early 1940s: The student group of which I was a member, the Student Defenders of Democracy, recognized after June 1941 that, because the Soviet Union was engaged in the war against Hitler, it deserved our full military and economic support. But we remained highly skeptical of Joseph Stalin and the brutal system of repression with which we identified him. Not long after the war started, two leaders of the Bund, the labor organization of Poland's Jews, an organization that had opposed Lenin as long ago as 1903, disappeared. American labor leaders called on the Soviet government to report on their whereabouts, to no avail. Then,

---

5. Ibid.

in 1943, the Soviet ambassador to the United States released a statement announcing that they had been executed.

To us in the Student Defenders of Democracy organization, this was proof of the correctness of our assessment, that while it was good that the Soviet Union was fighting against Hitler, the Soviet Union remained a repressive dictatorship. We were sufficiently exercised over the executions that we organized a rally on our campus protesting Stalin's action. We wondered at the time whether there were anti-Soviet rallies at any other college in the United States, colleges with far more conservative student bodies. We were proud that our school, with its left-leaning student body, would be the site of a protest against repressive action in the Soviet Union.[6]

Joining the Anti-Communist Liberals

Shortly after this event I entered the U.S. Army and once again, for a while, did not encounter anyone who identified himself as a Communist. But when the war was over and I found myself in the U.S. military government in Berlin, I was in a city a portion of which was under Communist control. I could now see firsthand what that meant in terms of repression: the slanted news in the press, no tolerance of dissent, the forced merger of the East German Social Democratic Party with the Communist Party to form the Communist-dominated Socialist Unity Party, the arrest and incarceration of anyone expressing different political views. There was also reason for concern over the rejection by the Soviet Union of efforts by the West to cooperate in what was supposed to be the quadripartite administration of Germany.

In Berlin I joined the local chapter of a new veterans' organization, the American Veterans Committee (AVC). Those of us who identified ourselves as liberal Democrats had decided against joining the old-line veterans' organizations such as the American Legion or the Veterans of Foreign Wars. But soon enough we discovered that among our fellow members of AVC were followers of the Communist party line.

---

6. In 1951, after I completed law school, I worked for a few months on the White House staff in the Truman administration. Early on I was told that there appeared to be a problem with my security clearance. Shortly thereafter I was told that the matter had been resolved and there was no further problem. I remembered this incident years later when the Freedom of Information Act became law, and I asked for my relevant file. I received it in due course; it showed that while I was in college, one of the deans had prepared for the Federal Bureau of Investigation (FBI) a list of students who, he said, were members of Communist organizations. I had been placed on that list. A few years later there was a further entry noting that the organization to which I had belonged and that the dean had labeled communist was, in fact, anti-Communist. Later still, I became acquainted with Louis Freeh when he headed the FBI. I told him of that experience. His response was: "I am not surprised." What can be noted is that false accusations are on occasion made in the United States as they were made in the Soviet Union. Fortunately, the consequences in the United States are not as harsh and we have self-correcting mechanisms in place.

Some of us found it truly amazing that American veterans, who had been involved in the war against Fascist totalitarianism and who were now working for the United States government, would be blind to the events that we could see with our own eyes in East Berlin, the replacement of fascist totalitarianism with Communist totalitarianism. The intramural AVC struggle in which we were engaged was played out at the national level as well.

While still in Berlin, I also joined another newly formed organization, Americans for Democratic Action (ADA). Eleanor Roosevelt was among the organization's founders. Hubert Humphrey was its rising star. We were supportive of the New Deal–Fair Deal program and all that it implied in legislation to help those on the lower rungs of the economic ladder. But we were most emphatic about our belief in democracy. We were, therefore, highly critical of Stalin's police state and the establishment of Communist dictatorships throughout Eastern Europe, under the influence of the Soviet Union's military might. The Bolsheviks did not try to infiltrate the ADA.

When I returned to the United States to enter Yale Law School, I encountered Communists once again among my fellow students. What was principally at issue then was the attitude of the U.S. government toward the international aspirations of the Soviet Union. As I started law school, the 1948 presidential campaign was in full swing. My friends and I supported Harry Truman. But there was a candidate to our left: Henry Wallace. Wallace, who had served as vice president of the United States, secretary of agriculture, and secretary of commerce, had certainly never been a Communist. Yet his behavior in the period immediately after World War II would have qualified him, to use Lenin's terminology, as a "useful idiot." He wanted the United States to ignore the Soviet Union's behavior both on its domestic scene and in its imposition of Communist governments on those East and Central European states that it was able to control. Communists had not directly influenced Henry Wallace to take the positions he took, but once he had made his foreign policy positions clear, they flocked to him and, staying close to him, made sure that he would not deviate from the desired line.

The way the Communists handled Wallace was well illustrated by the following story, told to me by a friend who had served with me in the U.S. military government in Germany. My friend had joined his father, who was an avowed Communist, for what was supposed to be a weekend at the estate of a wealthy supporter of the Communist Party. Henry Wallace was expected to attend for part of the weekend. On the evening before Wallace's scheduled arrival, my friend accompanied his father to a reception for the invited weekend guests. When he was introduced to the other guests as someone who had just returned from occupied Germany, he was immediately asked about the reinstatement of Nazis in positions of authority, a charge made at that time against the U.S. military government. My friend responded by changing the subject to what was going on in the Soviet zone. He mentioned that the concentration camp in Buchenwald was once again operating and that many Social Democrats were imprisoned there. He noticed that the other guests simply stopped talking to him and moved to other parts of the room. Early the next morning, the butler of the establishment came around to tell my friend's father that they had to leave, that their room had been reserved for other guests. As they left, they saw Henry Wallace arriving at the estate. The host later ran into my friend's father and told him that it was simply out of the question to take a chance on the possibility that my friend might talk to Wallace about Soviet concentration camps. Wallace, it turned out, had already expressed some concerns on that subject, and the host was fearful that an encounter with my friend would cause Wallace to make further inquiries.

During my years at Yale Law School, the major intramural struggle with the Communists took place over the creation of a group at the law school that would espouse civil liberties. Pro-Communists wanted to be sure that this new civil liberties group did not associate itself with the American Civil Liberties Union (ACLU), which barred supporters of totalitarianism from its board membership. We, the anti-Communists, wanted to join the ACLU for precisely that reason.

I have described the foregoing experiences in some detail to demonstrate not only how my point of view on Communism was formed, but also to describe the presence of the Communist movement on the campuses of the United States in the 1930s, 1940s, and early 1950s. Communists played a similar role of major significance in organizations that served as transmission belts for the Moscow party line. They also had an impact on Hollywood. Though their total numbers were relatively small, they exercised, through their energy and commitment, a disproportionately significant influence on those segments of American society that Russians would call the intelligentsia.

Let me emphasize that, while those of us who identified ourselves as anti-Communist liberals were ready to oppose American Communists politically, we also believed that their constitutional rights must be protected. In the late 1940s, it was discovered that a high-ranking official of the State Department, Alger Hiss, was a Soviet spy. What was even more troublesome was that a code clerk in the Soviet embassy in Ottawa who defected to the West brought with him the news that a Soviet atomic spy ring had been operating in the United States. Members of that spy ring, led by Julius Rosenberg, were arrested, one by one, in the late 1940s and were tried and convicted.

The reaction of some members of Congress was to enact legislation against Communists. The Truman administration adopted a loyalty-security program that would prevent Communists from serving in government positions. And then came Senator Joseph McCarthy, who, beginning in 1950, made broad accusations against many public figures whom he denounced either as Communists or as stooges for the Communists. Many of the persons denounced by McCarthy had no relations at all with the Communist movement.

The reaction of those with whom I was associated politically was to support measures that were necessary to protect national security, but to oppose measures that would go beyond that, interfering with freedom of speech and association. It was right, we thought, to remove Communists from security-sensitive positions in the U.S. government, but before their employment was terminated, we needed to make certain that they really were Communists. Further, if there were Communists in the movie industry in Hollywood, we said, they should be opposed politically but that should be all.

I graduated from law school in 1951 and began to practice law in Washington, D.C. During my early years as a lawyer, I handled a number of cases of persons who had been unjustly accused of being loyalty-security risks. I am glad to say that I won them all, though the months that passed before a final decision was rendered took a toll on the people who sought to clear their names.

By 1954, the Senate had had enough of McCarthy's unfair accusations and censured him. He died not long thereafter. Thus, in due time, this unfortunate phenomenon in American history, known as the McCarthy era, came to an end.

What I have so far described is my extensive engagement with the American left-of-center opposition to Communism. It was not opposition to the Soviet Union as such, but opposition to its ideology and the gross violations of the human rights of its individual citizens. Most of the events that I have here described took place before Anatoly had begun his higher education at the University of Moscow.

In his account of developments in the Soviet Union, Anatoly has called attention to the profound turning point that came about in the Soviet Union in 1956, while he was a university student: Khrushchev's speech to the Twentieth Communist Party Congress. As Anatoly puts it, "at that time ... the boat of my generation, as in a tsunami, began to be thrown from side to side." The speech had a similar effect on the Communist movement in the United States. Many followers of the party line, who for years had rationalized their political position by telling themselves that reports of Stalin's crimes were bourgeois propaganda, had to consider seriously the revelations by the incumbent general secretary of the Soviet Communist Party.

Journalist Louis Fischer speaks of the suppression of the Kronstadt rebellion as the occasion for the first major incident that caused significant numbers of communist sympathizers worldwide to break with the party.[7]

---

7. In his contribution to *The God That Failed*, ed. Richard Crossman (New York: Harper & Brothers, 1949).

Kronstadt was the location of one of Russia's major naval bases. Its sailors had in 1917 played a key role in bringing Lenin to power. In 1921, appalled by Bolshevik policies, they revolted again, this time against the Bolsheviks. Under the leadership of Leon Trotsky (murdered in 1940, probably on Stalin's orders) and General Tukhachevsky (shot in 1936 as a suspected spy), the revolt was put down. About 2,500 sailors were executed and many more thousands were sent to labor camps, where they soon perished.[8]

Fischer, who had for many years sympathized with the Communist cause, uses the term Kronstadt to describe all those events that have caused Communists to break with the movement. Until one experiences a Kronstadt-like event, he says, "one may waver emotionally or doubt intellectually or reject the cause altogether in one's mind and yet refuse to attack it."[9] But then, he says, an event occurs that causes those who had long put aside their doubts to make the final break. He refers to that break as a person's Kronstadt and explains that his own Kronstadt came with the signing of the Soviet-Nazi Pact of August 1939.[10]

Many American Communists left the party or gave up their sympathies for the party in August 1939, when the so-called Hitler-Stalin Pact was concluded, but many more remained loyal to the cause. It was the Khrushchev speech of February 1956 that was the last straw for them. The secret speech, spelling out Stalin's multiple crimes, was delivered in February, but was leaked and became known worldwide a few months later. As far as I could tell, it ended American Communism as a movement that had to be taken seriously.

The Communist Party of the United States, as such, never played a significant role on the American political scene. At its peak in 1932, its candidate for president attained about one-quarter of 1 percent of the total vote.[11] However, from the early 1920s to the mid-1950s, Communists played a significant, highly contested role in the American labor movement and in the film industry, academia, and among college students.

While American Communism became a movement of senior citizens who could not abandon the beliefs of a lifetime, I and many of my friends took a new look at developments in the Soviet Union. We were encouraged by Khrushchev's speech and by the thaw in the Soviet Union's domestic policy that followed. We were soon disappointed, however, by the way the Soviet Union dealt with Hungary in the autumn of 1956 and the execution of the Hungarian Communist leader Ferenc Nagy, who had broken with Moscow. The Hungarian episode was

---

8. David Shub, *Lenin: A Biography* (Garden City, NY: Doubleday, 1948), 359–361.
9. Crossman, *The God That Failed*, 204.
10. Ibid., 222.
11. Dave Leip, *Atlas of U.S. Presidential Elections,* http://uselectionatlas.org.

followed by other international crises precipitated by Khrushchev, the worst of which was the Cuban Missile Crisis of November 1962.

Focusing on the International Scene

With the battle against Communism in the ranks of the American intelligentsia behind us, my attention was, in light of the Cuban Missile Crisis, drawn increasingly to the issue of Soviet-American relations on the international scene, relations appropriately characterized by the term that had acquired common usage: the Cold War. By that time, Anatoly was in the Soviet foreign service and witnessed developments on the international scene from the inside. I saw these developments from the outside and became involved in organizations that concerned themselves with the Soviet role in world affairs.

In the 1970s, I became one of the founders of the Coalition for a Democratic Majority, a group of Democrats opposed to the party policies associated with 1972 presidential candidate George McGovern (who happened to be a personal friend of mine, but whom I could not in good conscience support in that election; I cast a write-in vote for Hubert Humphrey). We advocated the domestic policies of the Roosevelt and Truman administrations and associated ourselves with Truman's foreign policy outlook. Our opponents, who came to be known as the New Left, called us neoconservatives, a term which today, in 2008, has taken on an entirely different connotation.

In the 1970s, I also met and became friends with Admiral Elmo Zumwalt, the chief of naval operations, who educated me on the military aspects of the Soviet threat. Admiral Zumwalt's wife, Mouza, was of Russian ethnicity. Her family had fled Russia following the Bolshevik Revolution in 1917. Admiral Zumwalt was not only thoroughly informed about Communist totalitarianism, but also followed closely the expansionist policies of the Soviet Union in the 1970s and what he thought was the failure of the United States to maintain adequate military strength to match the Soviet buildup. His basic thesis was that if the United States were to use its economic strength to build up the country's military capability, the Soviet Union would ultimately not be able to keep up with us and would adopt a policy that combined mutual arms reduction with a more cooperative international policy.

When the Committee on the Present Danger—an organization concerned about the Soviet threat and led by Paul Nitze, Eugene Rostow, and Admiral Zumwalt—was formed, I joined it. Although I remained a Democrat and a supporter of the Democratic domestic program, I voted for Reagan in the 1980 presidential election, solely because of his opposition to Communism.

One of the early appointments following Reagan's election was that of Jeane Kirkpatrick as U.S. ambassador to the United Nations in New York. Jeane and her husband had for many years been good friends of my wife's and mine. We had all been active in the Hubert Humphrey wing of the Democratic Party, strongly supportive of a liberal domestic policy and opposed to Communism.

Late in January 1981, my wife and I were having dinner when the phone rang. On the phone was Kirkpatrick. She told me that she was in her car, but was using that new invention; she could telephone me from the car. Then she asked: "Dick, can you be in Geneva next Tuesday?"

What Jeane then spelled out was that she was asking me to participate in the 1981 session of the United Nations Human Rights Commission. I responded affirmatively and thus, at the age of fifty-seven, began a career in diplomacy by entering the Reagan administration as a member of the U.S. delegation to the UN Commission on Human Rights.

As I traveled to Geneva, I was well aware that the United Nations had become a battleground on which the Soviet Union and members of the Soviet bloc clashed in speeches and resolutions with the Western democracies, particularly the United States. I have here reviewed my exposure over a period of decades to the problem that I believed Communism posed to the international community. We did not consider ourselves opposed to Russia and to Russians. What we opposed were the doctrines that had initially been enunciated by one man, Lenin, and that over time had acquired followings throughout the world—including the United States, where I had engaged in verbal battles with Lenin's followers in high school, college, law school, and even in an organization of veterans of World War II. It was truly a struggle based on ideology.

Still, when I answered Jeane Kirkpatrick's question in the affirmative, I was not aware that this would be the beginning of a diplomatic career that would make me a witness and, perhaps, a minor contributor to the end of Leninism, and thus, an end to the Cold War.

2

Soviet-U.S. Relations and Human Rights before Perestroika

Anatoly Adamishin

Whereas the previous chapter sketched some details of Dick's and my personal histories, this chapter centers on a much more important foundation for our work in the humanitarian field in 1986–1990, namely, Soviet-American relations before perestroika. The scope of that subject is huge, of course, and rather than try—and inevitably fail—to cover all its facets, I focus in my section of this chapter on a handful of episodes that seem to me to characterize some particularly striking and salient aspects of the Soviet-American relationship. I hope to help readers realize just how poor that relationship was when the two countries began, spurred by Gorbachev's new thinking, to move toward each other.

Dick's part of this chapter paints a broader historical canvas and offers an American perspective. His section begins by recounting the appearance of human rights on the international agenda after World War II and explains how public opinion and Congress pushed Washington to factor human rights into its policy toward the Soviet Union. Dick also covers the beginnings of the Helsinki Process and U.S. efforts in the 1970s to support Soviet dissidents.

Our Number-One Enemy

After World War II, our leaders always considered the Soviet relationship with the United States to be the most important dimension of foreign policy. And they were right: From both ideological and the geopolitical points of view, the United States was our main rival. In 1952, in one of his rare instructions (effectively, diktats) to the Politburo, Stalin coined the phrase, "Our number one enemy is America."[1] For decades, until Gorbachev rose to power, that assertion was never questioned. In the inner circle, the United States had the label of "eventual adversary"—as, by the way, the Soviet Union did in high places in the U.S. government.

The Soviet attitude toward the United States was largely a reaction to American policy rather than a realization of our own international project.[2] It was a strange mix of hostility and fear, of hidden respect and contempt: respect for American power, and contempt, first, because our leaders thought that armed with Marxism-Leninism they knew the inevitable laws of history and consequently had the ability to foresee the future, and second, because they were sure that their many years of experience—their perennial management of internal and international affairs—gave them an obvious advantage over American presidents, who came to power from who knows where and needed a crash course in foreign policy.[3] Soviet leaders knew the West only in a very approximate way, and faith substituted for real knowledge.

For the thirty-odd years before Gorbachev came to power, our policy was a bizarre combination of peaceful and expansionist, of cooperation with the West—particularly with Western European countries, but with the United States as well, on a bilateral basis—and confrontation, of the rational and the absurd. U.S. policy, it is only fair to note, was also a mosaic of containment and cooperation, shows of strength and concessions.

The Arms Race

In the nuclear age, you ought to live in peace even with your number-one enemy, or at least avoid direct encounters with it. During the late Khrushchev and early Brezhnev periods, a trend toward international détente could be

---

1. See *Kommersant Vlast*, no. 15, April 19, 2004.

2. This certainly did not mean that we lacked our own notion of how to shape our relations with the United States. Dobrynin, who had served as the ambassador to the United States for twenty-five years (evil tongues in the foreign ministry used to say that Gromyko did not want to keep a strong competitor in Moscow), quotes a joint report of the ministry and the KGB (December 1970) with recommendations concerning relations with the United States. I emphasize two items: "1. To continue our offensive against the pillars of capitalism. 2. To fight American Zionism. Masses of Americans should be led to believe that pro-Israeli activities of Zionists are essentially anti-American as they damage the U.S. national interests, especially in regard to maintaining normal relations with the USSR and settling topical problems which cause tension in the world." See Anatoly Dobrynin, *In Confidence* (Seattle, WA: University of Washington Press, 1995); the quotation appears on pages 201–202 of the Russian edition.

3. This is not an exaggeration; I heard statements of this kind several times about Carter and Reagan. After a meeting in Vienna between Khrushchev and Kennedy in 1961, the chief of the Ministry of Foreign Affairs, speaking before the selected members of the ministry, said that it was a meeting between "a giant and a pygmy." Everybody understood who was who.

discerned. In Soviet relations with the United States, the first steps were taken in the field of arms control, with negotiations conducted to limit the arms race, at least in ways that both parties considered convenient.

The Americans were always a step or two ahead of us in that race, and we desperately tried to catch up. Our goal was parity. It was understandable but it was not a wise ambition. Both countries were sucked into an arms-building frenzy, a maelstrom that was especially destructive for the Soviet Union. Many years later I read the following admission by Gromyko:

> In Khrushchev's times, we had 600 nuclear bombs made. He said then: how much further are we going to build up? And under Brezhnev, too, we could have taken a more reasonable position; but we continued to stick to the principle: they are racing—and we'll be racing, like in sports. Science and wise people already made the conclusion that this race was senseless. But both we and they were going on with it. We approached this matter too primitively. And our supreme commanders proceeded from believing that if there was a war, we would win it. And we kept producing more and more weapons. This was a mistaken position, absolutely mistaken. And our political leadership is entirely to blame for it.[4]

My former chief made this confession, speaking at a meeting of the Politburo on June 20, 1988, when perestroika was drastically changing Soviet policy. Sincere or not, these impressive words came too late.

The country was suffocating, but the military-industrial complex was doing quite well, with seemingly no one tallying the amount of money being lavished on defense. The hawks on both sides were giving each other sufficient pretext to keep the arms race moving. It was only much later that news surfaced about how often the Soviet threat and Soviet aggressive capacities had been exaggerated to justify increased American military spending.

The Stubborn Dutch

I experienced firsthand how difficult and professionally dangerous it was to try to slow the momentum of the arms race. This episode concerned SS-20s, Soviet medium-range missiles. When they had been quietly introduced in the late 1970s, we were accused, first, of dangerous irrationality—the Soviet Union already had enough weapons to incinerate Western Europe—and, second, of deploying arms aimed at cities. The Americans responded by persuading NATO to adopt a dual-track decision. Negotiations on the SS-20s would be held, but if they failed to have the missiles removed, hundreds of new American missiles—Pershing-2s and Tomahawk cruise missiles—would be deployed

---

4. Gorbachev Foundation, V Politburo CK KPSS, 377. The same was true on the other side. In his brilliant book, Melvyn Leffler quotes President Reagan, who "was appalled that there were still men in the Pentagon" who claimed a nuclear war was 'winnable.' I thought they were crazy." See Melvyn Leffler, *For the Soul of Mankind* (New York: Hill and Wang, 2007), 359.

in Western Europe. While the SS-20s could hit only European and not American territory, the American missiles could reach the Soviet Union.

We agreed to start the negotiations a year after the American proposal but weren't enthusiastic about them. "What shall we talk about?" Gromyko was said to argue. "We have the missiles, and they don't. Even when the American missiles are ready, the European antiwar movement won't allow them to be deployed." This was yet another miscalculation. The talks, held in Geneva, didn't succeed, and in October 1983 the Americans, as they had pledged, began to deploy their new missiles. We slammed the door in Geneva only to come back to the negotiating table a year later.

Few people in the Ministry of Foreign Affairs were permitted to say a word on vital questions of our security, and there was nothing more vital than talks with the Americans on military matters. An official order forbade anyone not directly involved in the negotiations from dealing with that subject. But when my Dutch colleagues, who were within my area of supervision as the head of the First European Department, shared in 1984 with me an idea that could allow them to avoid having cruise missiles stationed in the Netherlands, I felt inspired to speak up. The Dutch asked us to remove, from our arsenal of hundreds, only forty-eight missiles—exactly the number of American missiles they were required to have on their territory—and they would then try to refuse to accept the Tomahawks. The action wouldn't have made any military sense, but politically, to my naïve mind, it was an excellent idea, offering a chance to break a chain of measures and countermeasures. Needless to say, the idea was rejected by my superiors.

The Dutch didn't give up. They said to me, "If you just declare that your forty-eight missiles are not on duty; that would be enough for us." I resumed work on this issue with greater enthusiasm, banking on the good personal relations I had with First Deputy Minister Georgy Kornienko. We held different points of view, for he usually supported hard positions, but I think we respected each other professionally. Several times I tried to talk Kornienko into seriously considering what the Dutch proposed. He was never moved by my arguments. Finally, on one occasion, when he was no doubt fed up with my insistence, he told me with very rare if not exceptional frankness: "Anatoly Leonidovich, stop it. There are such economic, military, and political interests involved here that you would not be permitted to do anything."

My attempts would probably have seen me dismissed from the ministry had Konstantin Chernenko lived a bit longer or had Gorbachev arrived a bit later. It was Gorbachev who settled this problem in the context of the general efforts to escape the arms race burden.

Entering Afghanistan

In the immediate prelude to perestroika, Afghanistan was one of the most contentious issues on the Soviet-U.S. agenda. It also revealed the infirmities of the Soviet decision-making system, with our top leaders making major miscalculations that many of their subordinates recognized but dared not point out. Some personal recollections should illustrate the point.

On December 22, 1979, the Ministry of Foreign Affairs's collegium—a sort of a ministerial board of directors with practically no responsibilities—held an unplanned meeting. This was a closed one: Only members of the collegium, about thirty people, including me, were present. Minister Gromyko informed us that "a limited contingent" of the Soviet Army had entered Afghanistan in response to an invitation from the local leadership. He then spent thirty minutes explaining why this had to happen. I took notes; this was neither encouraged nor banned. Many years later, in rereading my shabby notebook, I realized how ambiguous my minister had been even when speaking to a very select audience, how many half-truths and how much reticence were contained in his speech. His major rationale was that if the Soviet Union was compelled to deal with such an enemy, first of all the United States, we shouldn't hesitate "to show our teeth."

When the monologue ended, everybody got up and left, trying not to look into each other's eyes.

Days later, on January 1, 1980, I wrote in my diary:

> I will not be writing about the New Year—two days ago we put our troops in Afghanistan. Rarely have we made an unluckier decision. What are they thinking? They're probably just exercising their firmness to each other.
>
> It is said that we're showing our muscles. In reality it is an act of weakness, of despair. Let it burn with a blue flame, Afghanistan. Why on earth are we putting ourselves in a completely losing situation? Why spend the remnants of our moral capital, when no one will believe us?
>
> Since the middle of the last century—the Crimean War—we haven't been in such a mess.
>
> Everybody is our enemy, our allies are weak and insecure.
>
> Timur Gaidar,[5] who came to my dacha, is speechless from bitterness.
>
> If they are such asses that they cannot manage their own country, we are not in a position to teach them anything, with our hollow economy, incapacity to pursue political affairs, to organize, etc. We're much more in the process of being involved in a civil war even if it's fed from abroad.

---

5. Admiral and journalist, the father of the future prime minister.

> Is it possible that the Vietnamese lesson didn't teach us anything? How can we play the mission of the world's savior? It would be better to make up our own minds on what to do in external as well as internal affairs. But our leaders are busy with other things. They care mostly about staying in power; they're interested in internal combinations, in showing ideological purity where, by the way, we are also confused.

But it was to this paper only, beyond confidential talks with a few friends, that I trusted my doubts.

Jumping ahead six years, to 1985: Shevardnadze, who had just replaced Gromyko in the ministry, was getting acquainted with his new staff. Late one evening he had "a friendly talk" with me. Among other topics, he touched upon Afghanistan, seeking my opinion without revealing his. I emotionally explained what a blunder had been made and how urgently we needed to get out of there, mentioning that although I was now being so forthright with him, at that memorable collegium meeting, I had not dared to speak out. "You would have been just destroyed," my new chief replied.

He, too, at that time had had to consider such a fate. In addressing a session of the Communist Party Central Committee in June 1980, half a year after our troops entered Afghanistan, Shevardnadze defined it as "a courageous, solely correct and solely wise step."[6]

Blunders Hard to Correct

In risking the Afghanistan adventure, our three wise men—Andropov, Ustinov, and Gromyko[7]—made three major miscalculations. First, they believed that we were about to lose Afghanistan to the Americans; that Hafizullah Amin, the ruler of the country, was going to "sell" it to the United States, which wanted revenge for the recent loss of Iran and which prized Afghanistan as a bridgehead at our southern borders. What I didn't know in 1979 was that some of our people were artificially fanning these flames, tossing

---

6. *Pravda*, June 26, 1980.

7. At the time, the main foreign policy decisions were made, almost exclusively, by a troika: Dmitri Ustinov, minister of defense since 1976; Yuri Andropov, chief of the KGB since 1967; and Gromyko, foreign minister since 1957. While officially head of the Communist Party and thus the state, Leonid Brezhnev was often excluded due to his health. One of his assistants, Anatoly Blatov, told me that these three gentlemen repeatedly tried to convince Brezhnev to permit them "to bring order in Afghanistan," but Brezhnev hesitated. "Once," says Blatov, when Brezhnev was particularly ill, he conceded—partly because he was told that it would be a short operation of three or four months, "and then we could hold in tranquility the first Olympic games in Moscow." We were stuck in Afghanistan for nine years. I believe that the only silver lining for this black cloud was that, during the crisis in Poland in 1980, the Soviet leadership was almost unanimously against military intervention, limiting its help to General Wojciech Jaruzelski to a substantial amount of economic and other assistance.

out misinformation about U.S. Marines ready to march on Kabul.[8] Our old and suspicious leaders turned out to be easy prey.[9]

Second, they misjudged the reaction of the United States and also of the Muslim world. They thought that the West would content itself with verbal protests, as it had in 1968, when Soviet forces intervened in Czechoslovakia. Why should Jimmy Carter, who was reputed to be weak and content merely to speak about human rights, be tougher than Lyndon Johnson, who had swallowed the Czech repression? In the event, Carter took Afghanistan as a personal challenge.

Third, it was a completely irrational decision to engage militarily in a country with which we had had friendly relations for decades. We succeeded only in making it fiercely hostile to us. Our elderly leaders seem not to have known that Afghanistan had never bowed to a foreign will, be it Alexander the Great or Great Britain. And how could they have believed that it was possible to introduce by force a new social system into a country that was in many respects medieval?

The storming of President Amin's palace under cover of night by our elite detachments was hidden from even the closest circles of the party leadership. A report to the Central Committee, dated December 31, 1979, and signed by the usual troika plus Boris Ponomarev, head of the International Department of the Central Committee, states that "the forces opposed to Amin, on the wave of patriotism embraced by the masses in relation to the entrance of the Soviet Union, set up during the night of December 28th, a military intervention that ended with the toppling of his regime."

When, on December 29, President Carter used the direct line between the White House and the Kremlin to question the Soviet account of events, Brezhnev, with the Politburo's approval, responded that "absolutely unacceptable and non-corresponding to the facts is your assertion that the USSR allegedly did something to overthrow the government of Afghanistan. I have to emphasize with all strength that the changes in the Afghan leadership have been made by the Afghans themselves. Ask the Afghan government about that."[10]

Almost six years later, on November 13, 1986, I attended the Politburo meeting at which Gorbachev, already in power for eighteen months, finally insisted on a decision to quit Afghanistan in two years' time; the decision was revealed to the public only six months later. And it was then that Gromyko, no longer the minister of foreign affairs, confessed aloud that we probably

---

8. See O. Grinevsky, *Tainy Sovetskoi Diplomatii* [Mysteries of Soviet Diplomacy] (Moscow: Vagrius, 2002), 122.

9. In 1980, the median age of a member of the Politburo, the highest ruling body, was sixty-nine years.

10. See A. Liakhovskii, *Tragedia I doblest Afgana* [Afghan's Tragedy and Valor] (Yaroslavl: Nord, 2004), 332, 320.

had not taken into account all the pertinent social and other circumstances when we consented to the Afghan leadership's request for our military assistance.[11] Thus ended his responsibility for the events that created a large and powerful front against the Soviet Union, including the United States, China, and the Muslim countries, and became one of the main reasons for the demise of the Soviet Union.

In December 1990, the democratically elected Second Congress of the People's Deputies of the Soviet Union condemned the decision to send Soviet troops to Afghanistan and pointed out that it had been made in violation of the constitution by a narrow group of persons—Brezhnev, Ustinov, Andropov, and Gromyko. By then all of them had passed away.[12]

Afghanistan, Part Two

I was partially involved in Afghan events at the end of our withdrawal. I remember tough discussions at the March 1988 meeting between Shevardnadze and Shultz, where I had the privilege to chair the Soviet side in the joint working group on Afghanistan. Our general impression was that the Americans, unlike ourselves during the U.S. withdrawal from Vietnam, had not been very helpful; indeed, sometimes we suspected that the United States would be happy to see us stuck in Afghanistan even longer.

I know such thoughts certainly occurred to Shevardnadze. He blamed the Americans for Pakistan continuing to assist the mujahedeen even after the Geneva Accords had been signed (and with the United States and the Soviet Union serving as guarantors) in April 1988. To comply with the accords, we had to pull out all troops no later than February 15, 1989.

Gorbachev preferred that the final formula for Soviet withdrawal would include Washington's obligation not to support militarily the Islamic opposition. Yet, facing the Americans' refusal to accept this clause, he didn't hesitate to go ahead with a de facto unilateral decision. Our people, first and foremost Shevardnadze, retorted that we could not leave Najibullah's regime to its own destiny. "We don't throw away our friends," he used to tell us. "All the world associates this regime with us. We decided to quit and we'll do it, but we can't leave an inimical Afghanistan behind our backs." The Soviet Union did its utmost to help Najibullah economically and left him a lot of armaments from the Fortieth Army, which prolonged his life for three years after our withdrawal. His regime was toppled by the Islamic opposition after the Soviet Union dissolved and after Russian president Boris Yeltsin had changed the policy toward Afghanistan. Still, it is possible that

---

11. Gorbachev Foundation, V. Politburo CK KPSS, 108.

12. See Rossiyskaya, *politicheskaya enziklopedia* (Moscow: Mysl, 1999), 99–100.

if the United States had been more cooperative and had not insisted on our unconditional withdrawal ("let them drink our Vietnamese chalice to the bottom" seems to have been the American attitude), Afghanistan would not have fallen into the Taliban's hands and al Qaeda would not have become powerful enough to launch the attacks of September 11, 2001. But in the Cold War, each superpower was so preoccupied with hurting the other that it often overlooked the danger that its actions might hurt its own interests in the long term. Thus, when the U.S. leaders were happy to see Soviet armies bloodied in Afghanistan, they didn't suspect that U.S. efforts to mobilize and arm the mujahedeen against Soviet troops in Afghanistan would result, two decades later, in the United States having such an enemy as Osama bin Laden.

So-called Human Rights

The vast humanitarian field was practically shut for any dialogue between two superpowers whatsoever: One cannot call mutual reproaches and accusations a dialogue.[13]

From Stalin to Chernenko without interruption, the term human rights was preceded by the word so-called and, when written, surrounded by quotation marks. Human rights were officially presented as a sly, demagogical invention of the capitalist West in its struggle against socialist countries. According to Soviet officialdom, it was hardly surprising that the West's chief target for accusations of human rights abuses should be the Soviet Union, the motherland of socialism. As for real human rights—that is, economic and social ones—the Soviet Union was miles ahead of the West. In that last assertion, at least, there was an element of truth.

The Soviet government blamed reactionary and anti-Soviet forces, first of all in the United States, for disseminating propaganda about alleged violations of human rights in the Soviet Union. According to the official line, Western propaganda sought to divert the attention of the masses in the West from the serious difficulties that infected bourgeois society—especially at this stage of deep economic crisis, of new social and political turmoil—and to weaken the attractiveness of socialist ideas and jeopardize the growing international authority of the Soviet Union. This propaganda campaign, asserted Soviet officialdom, would not damage the stability of socialism but it could negatively influence international détente.

---

13. When I say practically, I mean that there were timid or limited attempts to raise some individual human rights cases in bilateral discussions. In the mid-1970s, there were such discussions in Moscow between Viktor Komplektov, then deputy director of the Ministry of Foreign Affairs's U.S. division, and the American deputy chief of mission in Moscow, Jack Matlock, as both of them later recalled during conversations with me.

Again, our accusations were not entirely wrong. In President Carter's time, there was a firm feeling in Moscow that Carter's public statements on human rights achieved more propagandistic advantage than practical results because his rhetoric was rarely followed by diplomatic action.

As to the substance, we asserted that the Soviet Union, rather than the United States, was the place where real rights and liberties were assured in deeds and not words: freedom from exploitation, the right to have stable work, and the opportunity to enjoy considerable social achievement. The Soviet people, it was pointed out, were not flocking to leave the country—a nuanced claim, given that the Soviet people knew that the doors of the Soviet Union were locked.

A Tiny Flame of Freedom

Despite the stifling ideological conformity within the Soviet Union in the 1970s and the first half of the 1980s, some Soviet citizens dared to assert their disagreement with the official establishment. As Ludmilla Alexeyeva describes in her autobiographical account The Thaw Generation, Soviet dissidents conducted a courageous struggle against the authorities, which began as a fight for individual liberties and became a battle for human rights for all countrymen: "We lit a tiny flame of freedom and kept it burning for the two decades of the Brezhnev period." The dissidents, Alexeyeva writes, were rejected both by the government and by society.[14] Nevertheless, they managed to draw the attention of the West, and particularly of the United States, to the humanitarian situation in the Soviet Union, as Dick describes in his section of this chapter.

I have the greatest respect for people such as Andrei Sakharov and Ludmilla Alexeyeva (whom I have known for many years), who openly challenged power. I would compare them to professional revolutionaries. Still, I agree with Robert Service, who writes: "Yet the dissenters probably had less impact on opinion in society than critics of the regime who stayed on the right side of the KGB."[15] He mentions writers, film directors, composers, and performers. I would add to that list internal dissenters, those who were inside the official compound.[16]

---

14. See Ludmilla Alexeyeva and Paul Goldberg, *The Thaw Generation* (London: Little, Brown, 1990), 5–6.

15. Robert Service, *History of Twentieth Century Russia*, 415. The full name of the KGB translates to the Committee for State Security.

16. Such a great connoisseur of Russia as Richard Pipes remarks with sorrow that in the new democratic Russia, the dissidents did not devote their energies to constructive political work and instead retired from public life to sulk, abandoning politics to the old Soviet nomenklatura. See Richard Pipes, *Vixi: Memoirs of a Non-Belonger* (New Haven, CT: Yale University Press, 2003), 246. They did not join Gorbachev's team either, as Alexeyeva notes. Perhaps a remarkable exception is Sergey Kovalev, who found himself in conflict with other former activists who were completely unprepared for positive change. Later, he too came back to the opposition because of the war in Chechnya (*Moscow Times*, April 1–7, 2005).

Public Pressure or Quiet Diplomacy?

To what extent did U.S. pressure help both the dissidents and those Soviet citizens who wanted to leave the country? In my assessment, the general rule was that quiet, invisible diplomacy involving the leaders or other officials of the two countries was from time to time productive; open pressure, like the famous linkage between trade and emigration, was outright counterproductive.

In this respect, there was a salient difference between Brezhnev's stagnation and mature perestroika. Our old leaders despised Western "human rights tricks" and would make a concession only if they got something concrete in exchange and normally under hush-hush conditions. Gorbachev's team, which was pushing for internal reforms, in particular in the area of emigration policy, used U.S. requests in the humanitarian field as a lever in our internal debates. It is important to note that decisions were not made because "the Americans are asking." And open pressure was never welcomed: Interference from abroad not only offended national pride, but also armed the hard-liners with ammunition for resisting reform.

Hence, linkage itself was negative; public attempts to push those links complicated things even more. Linkage also inspired U.S. groups opposed to any dialogue with the Soviet Union. Measures such as regularly picketing near the Soviet missions in Washington and New York didn't help matters. How could we, recalls Ambassador Anatoly Dobrynin, convince Moscow to ease Jewish emigration when we were daily haunted by the militants of the infamous Rabbi Meir Kahane?[17]

It was in this context that the U.S. government rejected a project to build a Ford automotive plant in the Soviet Union. What was the result? The factory was set up by the Italian Fiat Company. As early as 1968, Congress blocked an attempt by President Lyndon Johnson's administration to concede commercial credits to the Soviet Union. Four years later, President Richard Nixon signed a number of important Soviet-U.S. trade and finance agreements, including some on lend-lease debt. This time the Democratic Congress first delayed ratification and then made ratification altogether impossible by passing the Jackson-Vanik amendment to the Trade Act of 1974. Probably the Congress played an important role, as Dick describes, in the sense of changing some guidelines of American foreign policy, but open and highly publicized requests produced fewer results than working behind the scenes. The Jackson-Vanik amendment, which linked Soviet-U.S.

---

17. Dobrynin, *In Confidence*, 195–96.

trade with internal Soviet rules concerning emigration, very soon acquired an odious significance in Soviet eyes.[18]

In the spring of 1973, President Nixon had encountered fierce resistance in Congress to his request to grant the Soviet Union most favored nation status due to controversy regarding the immigration issue. At that time, he asked for—and received—confidential data from Brezhnev that stated that 95.5 percent of applications for emigration to Israel had been authorized in 1972. Moreover, the Soviet side allowed him to use these data in the administration's discussions with Congress. Many of its members expressed their satisfaction with the news, but not Senator Henry M. Jackson and some others, who continued to escalate their demands.

The statistics showed a continued increase in emigration, but this seemed to concern Senator Jackson less than his political career. He demanded a public commitment by the Soviet leaders to a large and fixed number of émigrés, an act that in their eyes was equal to capitulation. Had it not been for Jackson, concludes Dobrynin, a way out could have been found within the framework of quiet diplomacy.[19]

President Gerald Ford may not have been happy with Congress, which continued to put obstacles in the way of his administration's policy toward the Soviet Union, but he was unable to overcome congressional opposition. It was he who signed into law the amendments that blocked Soviet-U.S. economic relations for many years. The Soviet government immediately answered by rejecting its commitments assumed three years earlier, including the agreement regarding the repayment of the lend-lease debt, which amounted to several hundred million dollars.

When President Carter was attempting to restore normal economic ties with the Soviet Union, he asked the Soviet leadership for a relatively moderate formula to present to Congress and to the Jewish organizations. Moscow refused the request; this refusal reflected a sense of irritation in Moscow with Carter as a person.[20]

According to Dobrynin, Senator Jackson later confessed to him that congressional leaders had got it wrong when they developed the impression that Moscow would eventually concede on emigration if they kept pressing: "The resulting impasse didn't benefit anybody." When I talked with Dobrynin

---

18. Imagine the reaction of the American public to foreign legislatures seeking to influence American internal policy. And the link was selective: In April 1981, at a time when the Reagan administration was delivering some of its harshest anti-Soviet rhetoric, the Soviet grain embargo was lifted by request of American producers.

19. Dobrynin, *In Confidence*, 251, 263.

20. Dobrynin recalls that, Moscow's indignation at Carter was so high that his confidential proposal to swap dissident Natan Sharansky for one of the Soviets arrested by the United States for "illicit activity" was rejected (*In Confidence*, 417). Sharansky had to stay in Soviet prison until Gorbachev's time.

(now in retirement) in March 2006 in Moscow, he told me that Vanik, after he left the Congress, came to Dobrynin with a kind of excuse for his part in this story.

It is worth noting that President Reagan once said to our ambassador that linking Jewish emigration with trade was wrong.[21] In this case, his assessment fully coincided with academician Andrei Sakharov's, who considered the Jackson-Vanik amendment an unfortunate step that did nothing to promote better respect for human rights in the Soviet Union.

In the perestroika years, the Jackson-Vanik amendment weakened Gorbachev's position. After my talks in Washington in 1988, I came home with a firm impression that the amendment would soon be abrogated. Yet nothing happened. In January 1991, Edgar Bronfman, president of the World Jewish Congress, while visiting Moscow and talking with Shevardnadze in my presence, expressed gratitude for the drastically increased outflow of Soviet Jews and said that he was working to abolish the Jackson-Vanik amendment. But in May 1991, the Americans still linked ratification of the U.S.-Soviet trade agreement with the adoption of our new law on emigration. This certainly gave ammunition to those conservative forces in the Soviet Union that opposed the liberal law. As two Americans authors, Strobe Talbott and Michael Beschloss, put the matter: "There was an attempt to sell the horse twice."[22] The horse is still for sale.

---

21. Ibid, 338, 545.
22. Michael Beschloss and Strobe Talbott, *At the Highest Levels* (London: Little, Brown, 1993), 388.

Richard Schifter

The UN Charter and the Entry of Human Rights into the Field of International Relations

As Anatoly has pointed out, in the Soviet Union the term human rights was either placed in quotation marks or was preceded by the word so-called. That did not mean that the term was new to Russia. The ideas of the Enlightenment, including the concept of human rights, had reached the country in the eighteenth century and had a great many Russian adherents in the nineteenth and early twentieth centuries.

By the second half of the nineteenth century, the democratic movement had established itself in the Russian Empire. In the 1860s, serfdom was abolished; local, elected governing councils were established; and the rule of law was introduced. In the following decades, some steps forward on the part of the tsarist government alternated with regression. But the democratic movement persisted.

As a consequence of the serious defeats suffered by the Russian army in World War I, Russia's Romanov dynasty, which had ruled the country for three hundred years, fell in March 1917, and a democratic government that respected civil liberties was established. But in November of that year, the Bolsheviks overthrew the democratic government and established what Lenin euphemistically called the dictatorship of the proletariat.

There was no formal protest from any other government against the forcible overthrow of the democratic government of Russia. For most of the four hundred years in which the democratic idea had spread throughout Europe, a period during which the concept of human rights had evolved, the attainment of respect for human rights had been an issue between the government of a country and its own citizens. Gradually divine-right authoritarian monarchies gave way to constitutional monarchies or to republics, in response to pressure from their own citizenry. Democracy, the rule of law, and respect for civil liberties had not been the subject of dialogue between representatives of sovereign governments; it had been understood in diplomatic circles that what a sovereign did with his subjects was not a matter with which a foreign government should concern itself.

A sharp break with this long-established tradition came with the adoption, in 1945, of the UN Charter. The cause of human rights, including democratic governance, the rule of law, and respect for civil liberties, was now elevated to the international level. Article 1 of the UN Charter makes one of the purposes of the United Nations "to achieve international co-operation … in promoting and encouraging respect for human rights and fundamental freedoms for all without distinction as to race, sex, language, or religion." This commitment is reiterated in Article 55 as follows: "With a view to the creation of conditions of stability and well-being which are necessary for peaceful relations among nations … the United Nations shall promote … universal respect for, and observance of, human rights and fundamental freedoms for all without distinction as to race, sex, language, or religion."

I was a soldier in the U.S. Army in West Germany when the San Francisco Conference convened. As we moved toward the Ruhr area, the German Army Group B was dissolving in front of our eyes. The German soldiers had simply laid down their arms and were trying to get home. We let them pass through our lines and stopped taking prisoners. They were no threat. Processing so many soldiers as prisoners of war was too complicated.

On May 1, we were in Düsseldorf. I recall some of us walking along a major street in that city and two German girls walking in front of us, singing a popular song of the time, but with a change in the lyrics:

> Es geht alles vorueber.
> Es geht alles vorbei.
> Auch Adolf Hitler und seine Partei.
>
> Everything comes to an end.
> Everything passes.
> Including Adolf Hitler and his party.

Six days later, the surrender documents were signed and the war in Europe was over. We of the U.S. Army had by then become used to moving from one badly damaged city to the next. We were in a country whose people had paid dearly for the decisions of its leaders, not only in damaged buildings, but also in loss of life.

But the lives of others had been lost as well. They included my parents. Their last message to me had come from the Polish city of Lublin. Having read about the killings of Jews that later became known as the Holocaust, I suspected that they were no longer alive. Nevertheless, in 1944, while stationed in England and having read that the Red Army had occupied Lublin, I wrote a letter to them. It was returned with the notice "addressee unknown." Although it is hard for me to analyze my own thought processes, I assume that this personal experience has influenced my basic approach to human rights work. I am less interested in broad declarations of human rights principles than I am in how specific decisions affect the lives of individual victims of human rights deprivation.

There is no doubt that in drafting the UN Charter's human rights provisions, its writers were greatly influenced by the horrors committed by Nazi

Germany during World War II. The San Francisco Conference had convened within weeks of the discovery of vivid evidence of Nazi atrocities.

As noted earlier, I stayed in Germany after the end of the war, serving in the postwar military government for the American zone. I had made a point of maintaining my subscription to the *New York Times* throughout the war. Every two weeks or so, our mail clerk would reach my unit and bring a bagful of newspapers for me. I was thus not wholly dependent on the army newspaper, *Stars and Stripes*, in trying to keep up with world events, including the San Francisco Conference of 1945. And I certainly kept up with international developments while personally engaged in them in Germany. Then, in 1948, I returned to the United States to enter law school.

Anatoly has mentioned that he joined the staff of the Soviet foreign ministry in 1956. I, by contrast, did not become a diplomat until twenty-five years later. However, it so happens that I did have an opportunity to get ahead of Anatoly and start a diplomatic career five years earlier than he did.

Washington Rather Than New Delhi

During the summer break in 1950, while attending law school, I worked in the campaign of Chester Bowles for reelection as governor of Connecticut and had gotten to know the governor personally. He lost the election. About half a year later, as I was close to graduating from law school, I had a telephone call from Governor Bowles. "I am going abroad," he said, "and I would like to have you come with me." I asked where he was going. "I can't tell you," was his answer. I then asked whether he was going east or west. "More east than west," he answered. He added that until his appointment was announced and he had been confirmed by the Senate, he would arrange for me to work on the White House staff.

Thus, my family and I came to Washington in 1951, assuming that we would soon be off to a new destination. Before long it turned out that destination was to be New Delhi. Someone suggested that we look at the State Department's New Delhi post report, which described living conditions for embassy personnel in that location. We discovered advice to parents of small children: Do not drink local milk; import powdered milk, then boil the water before the milk is consumed. Our first-born was then less than two years old. My wife and I debated the matter and it was decided that I would write a letter to Ambassador Bowles, explaining why we would not join him in New Delhi.

Decades later I headed the U.S. delegation to a human rights meeting of the Conference on Security and Cooperation in Europe. Every once in a while the heads of the larger Western countries would get together for dinner. I was the only one in that group who was not a career diplomat. The others discovered that many of them had been posted to New Delhi as junior diplomats in the 1950s. I told them that I had been slated to be there, too, and explained why I had not been. At that point my French colleague became very serious and said: "I lost a daughter there."

Because my position in the Truman White House was on the staff of the President's Materials Policy Commission, which was a temporary body, I had to look around for a permanent position. While serving on the commission, I had looked into the question of native rights to Alaska's oil resources. That caused me to contact a law firm that specialized in federal Indian law. Before long I applied for a position at that firm and was hired. For the next thirty-three years my professional career focused principally on the legal representation of Indian tribes. As I look back at the work I did during that period, I believe that the accomplishment that did the most good was my success in persuading the U.S. government to interpret the U.S. Housing Act of 1937 in a way that allowed Indian tribes to establish tribal public housing authorities that could qualify for federal funding. I also succeeded in getting judicial confirmation of the rights of Indian tribes to exercise jurisdiction over law and order on Indian reservations and had the exciting opportunity to argue two cases in the United States Supreme Court. One case established the right of the Metlakatla Indians to use fish traps. The other, a quite different case, established the right of residents of federal reserves, such as the tract that serves as the home of the National Institutes of Health, to vote in the state in which the reserve is located.

While I was gainfully employed as a lawyer, I also engaged in a number of volunteer activities. Thus, I served on the Maryland State Board of Education, where I took the lead in bringing Maryland into full compliance with the Supreme Court decision in Brown *v.* Board of Education. I was also active in the Democratic Party organization of Montgomery County, Maryland, and took charge of the effort, in 1966, to have county newcomers replace the old party organization, which, although not corrupt, was ridden with conflicts of interest.

Human Rights on the United Nations' Agenda

To return to 1945: While I had been well aware of the proceedings of the San Francisco Conference and the ultimate agreement on the UN Charter, I followed the details of developments in the field of international human rights standards for the next thirty-six years only sporadically. It was only after I was named to represent the United States on the UN Commission on Human Rights that I made a point of thoroughly studying the relevant developments over that entire period.

What I found was that the United Nations' efforts to act on human rights standards was taken up in 1946 by a body created under the provisions of

Article 61 of the charter, the Economic and Social Council, which under Article 68 had been entrusted with responsibility to "set up commissions in economic and social fields and for the promotion of human rights." Complying with this mandate, the council created the Commission on Human Rights and under Council Resolution 9 directed it to submit to the council a proposal for an international bill of rights. In the next two years, the commission, led by Eleanor Roosevelt, whom President Truman had selected to head the delegation of the United States, carried out the mandate that had been entrusted to it.

The drafting committee to which the task of preparing an international bill of rights was entrusted in 1947 decided to respond by submitting two proposed texts. One was a declaration for adoption by the General Assembly, which, as a General Assembly resolution, would be hortatory rather than binding. The other text was to be a convention to be signed and ratified by those states that decided to adhere to it and which would be viewed as binding.

The declaration was adopted by the UN General Assembly on December 10, 1948. The Soviet bloc abstained, as did Saudi Arabia and South Africa. All other UN member states voted for this new standard-setting document. Further deliberations followed as to the text of the convention, and it was decided to prepare two documents rather than one: the International Covenant on Civil and Political Rights and the International Covenant on Economic, Social, and Cultural Rights.

The work on the covenants was not completed until 1966, when they were approved by the General Assembly and submitted for signature, ratification, and accession. The Soviet Union acceded to them in 1973.[1] Such accession was not meaningful at the time it occurred, because the Soviet Union considered the document—correctly—as not really enforceable, even though it was a treaty. As is noted later, the accession took on significant meaning fourteen years later.

The drafting of the human rights provisions of the UN Charter, the Universal Declaration of Human Rights, and the human rights covenants had been largely the work of human rights specialists. The task of seeing that these documents were implemented fell, however, to career diplomats. These diplomats had long been trained to consider it a cardinal principle of diplomacy that sovereign governments had the power to deal with their subjects in accordance with their own laws and customs, without interference from foreign entities. Nor did the governmental leadership of UN member states wish to inject human rights considerations into UN deliberations, with one exception: the issue of apartheid in South Africa, which was too reminiscent of the approach to the race issue that was central to the policies of Nazi

---

1. Because of a concern about the covenant's possible interference with states' rights, the United States did not ratify the Covenant on Civil and Political Rights until 1992.

Germany. Yet even on the issue of South Africa, the United States was by no means out in front in criticism of the apartheid regime.

Thus, even though the UN Charter had elevated the human rights concept to the international level, the newly established international human rights standards were rarely applied in the first quarter-century following their adoption. The justification for inaction in the human rights field lay in Article 2, Section 7, of the UN Charter, which provides that the United Nations may not "intervene in matters which are essentially within the domestic jurisdiction of any state." The counterargument was that by committing the United Nations to "promoting and encouraging respect for human rights and fundamental freedoms for all without distinction as to race, sex, language, or religion," the United Nations had internationalized the human rights cause so that it was no longer "within the domestic jurisdiction of any state."[2]

The failure to raise human rights concerns in multilateral fora was paralleled by a similar failure in bilateral relations. As far as the United States was concerned, human rights were for a long time not on the foreign policy agenda with any country, including the Soviet Union. With the Cold War under way, U.S. dealings with the Soviet Union were focused on traditional foreign policy issues, not on what had long been viewed as domestic issues that were inappropriate for consideration at the international level, whether multilateral or bilateral.

U.S.-Soviet Relations: The Cold War

It is interesting to note how developments in history can be viewed quite differently depending on which side of the fence you are. The way it looked to Anatoly, the "Soviet attitude toward the United States was largely a reaction to American policy, rather than a realization of our own international project." It looked quite different from this side of the Atlantic. In the United States, there was increasing concern over what were viewed as Stalin's breaches of the Yalta and Potsdam agreements regarding the status of the states of Eastern Europe.[3] In September 1946, Clark Clifford coauthored a

---

2. As late as 1984, it fell to me, as the U.S. Deputy Representative in the UN Security Council to present this counter-argument against the repeated assertion by South Africa that the United Nations lacked the power to deal with the issue of apartheid.

3. I served in 1946 in Berlin, as an official in the Finance Division of the Office of Military Government, United States ("OMGUS"). In keeping with the agreements reached in Yalta and Potsdam, a quadripartite military government had been set up in Germany, consisting of representatives of France, Great Britain, the Soviet Union and the United States. At the top level of that government was the Allied Control Council, on which each of the four countries was represented by a general. Coodinating committees at lower levels were to effect cooperation on specific issues. We, in OMGUS, had been eager to make this arrangement work, but by the summer of 1946 it became increasingly clear to my colleagues in the Finance Division who were serving on the relevant coordinating committee that the Soviet representatives were not

report to President Truman that contained the following recommendation regarding U.S. policy toward the Soviet Union:

> The primary objective of United States policy is to convince Soviet leaders that it is in the Soviet interest to participate in a system of world cooperation.

> Until Soviet leaders abandon their aggressive policies, the United States must assume that the U.S.S.R. may at any time embark on a course of expansion effected by open warfare and therefore must maintain sufficient military strength to restrain the Soviet Union.

> The United States should seek, by cultural, intellectual, and economic interchange, to demonstrate to the Soviet Union that we have no aggressive intentions and that peaceable coexistence of Capitalism and Communism is possible.[4]

The report also contained an assessment of the Soviet leadership:

> [Soviet policy] is based not upon the interests and aspirations of the Russian people, but upon the prejudices, calculations, and ambitions of a ... group of professional revolutionaries who have survived revolutions, purges, and party feuds for almost thirty years. This small group of able men, headed by Generalissimo Stalin, possesses great practical shrewdness but it is isolated within the Kremlin, is largely ignorant of the outside world, and is blinded by its adherence to Marxist dogma.[5]

This document, which helped lay the foundation for U.S. policy toward the Soviet Union at the beginning of the Cold War, places emphasis only on the danger posed by Soviet expansion through military force. Human rights issues were clearly not on the U.S. agenda at that time. On the contrary, the report emphasizes peaceable coexistence between capitalism and communism.

Located between two oceans, "from sea to shining sea," most Americans do not generally take a great interest in foreign affairs. Wars are, of course, the exception. As it turned out, the period that became known as the Cold War was a period of peace, of the absence of military conflict between the United States and the Soviet Union. But in the early years of the Cold War, many Americans were concerned that the Soviet Union might indeed resort to war.

The general public was, of course, unaware of Clark Clifford's warning that the Soviet Union "may at any time embark on a course of expansion

---

interested in working with their three colleagues. We soon discovered that other Divisions had the same experience. In due course, the system of cooperation broke down. It was clear that Soviet officials were under instructions not to allow that system to work.

4. Clark Clifford, *Counsel to the President* (New York: Random House, 1991), 125.
5. Ibid.

effected by open warfare." However, even without knowledge of the conclusions reached by the counsel to the president, Americans were exposed to sufficient information about Soviet policy to be deeply worried. When our oldest daughter started school in 1955, she and her classmates were given name tags so that if a nuclear alert occurred while the children were there and they had to be evacuated, they could more easily be reconnected with their families.

My own plans at the time were that if the whole family were together during a nuclear alert, we would pack up and drive to the Pine Ridge Indian reservation in South Dakota, far away from any likely target of a nuclear attack, where my friends, the Oglala Sioux, whose lawyer I was, would surely take us in.

As time went on, the concept of mutually assured destruction tended to put our minds at ease, but there was always reason to be concerned about irrationality or miscalculation. The point of greatest danger was reached not during Stalin's time, but when Nikita Khrushchev was in charge. In October 1962, the United States discovered that the Soviet Union had placed missiles directed at the United States in Cuba. The Cuban Missile Crisis ensued, causing many Americans to believe that a nuclear war was in the offing.

I recall being in St. Louis at the time to participate in a meeting on issues of concern to American Indians. When I telephoned my wife to discuss developments, I had the eerie feeling that this was our last conversation. Ultimately, cooler heads prevailed on both sides and the crisis came to an end.

The relationship between the Soviet government and its own citizens was of significantly less concern at that time to members of the general American public. That is not to suggest that those Americans who were interested in international affairs were unaware in the years after the adoption of the UN Charter of the continued forms of repression under Stalin's rule. Shortly after the end of World War II, there was concern that the United States had repatriated Russian slave laborers—such as Anatoly's uncle—from West Germany to the Soviet Union, often against their will. These detainees were upon their return to the Soviet Union either killed or sent to prison camps. Liberated prisoners of war received similar treatment. There was also news of the mass deportation of the Crimean Tatars in 1946 and, in 1949, of the mass execution of the Communist leadership of Leningrad. There was also information about the anti-Semitic measures taken by Stalin from 1947 on, including the killing of Yiddish-speaking authors and actors, done in an effort to stamp out the culture of Yiddish-speaking Jews in the Soviet Union.

After Stalin's death in 1953, note was taken in the United States of the arrest and execution of Lavrenty Beria, a person particularly well-known because of his key role, as minister of the interior, in Stalin's most severe measures of repression. Special attention was paid to Khrushchev's 1956 speech to the Twentieth Congress of the Communist Party of the Soviet Union, in which he exposed Stalin's brutal rule—a rule, to be sure, of which he had been an integral part. In the months that followed the speech, information reached the United States about the greater opportunity accorded in the Soviet Union to intellectuals, particularly writers, to express themselves freely. This period in Soviet history, which became known as the thaw, offered hope for greater freedom in the Soviet Union.

There was indeed a thaw, but it did not melt most of the ice of the Communist system. Loyal Communists or other Soviet citizens were no longer picked up and imprisoned or shot on the basis of malicious denunciations. But persons who tried to exercise their internationally guaranteed rights to freedom of speech or religion were arrested, and though they were no longer likely to be executed, they did face long prison terms.

Nor was there a change in the Cold War atmosphere; as a matter of fact, as noted earlier, it was under Khrushchev that the most dangerous development in Soviet-American relations occurred. That state of affairs, both in the domestic human rights field and in international relations, continued after Khrushchev was deposed in 1964 and replaced by Brezhnev. It was the state of affairs that was in place when, in 1969, Henry Kissinger became national security adviser and initiated a new bilateral dialogue between the United States and the Soviet Union. The priorities in this dialogue, as far as the Nixon administration was concerned, were political and defense related. The term that came into usage to describe the goal of this dialogue was détente.

Neither the human rights provisions of the UN Charter nor the Universal Declaration of Human Rights had been taken seriously by Stalin and his immediate successors. The Soviet Union was and remained a totalitarian dictatorship, in which all civil liberties were severely repressed and the rule of law was a dream but not reality. Yet, despite the significant amount of information regarding repression in the Soviet Union that was available in the West, the issue of Soviet human rights violations was not raised at the United Nations or in bilateral talks between Western democracies and the Soviet Union.

Congress Asserts Itself

There is a significant difference between foreign policy formulation in the United States and foreign policy formulation in other Western democracies. In the other Western democracies, the government in power, controlling both the executive and the legislative branches of government, makes basic foreign policy decisions, often heavily influenced by the diplomatic career service. The separation of powers in the United States leads to a different decision-making process. The executive branch proposes policy, but Congress plays an equally significant foreign policy-making role. When the executive and legislative branches disagree, sharp disputes ensue, which often result in Congress coming out ahead.

The reason for the frequent congressional victories is that members of Congress tend to hear directly from their constituents, acquire a good sense of the prevailing mood at the grassroots level, and transmit strongly held public views to decision makers in the White House. As a result, the president and the White House staff may often modify positions recommended by the State Department; such modifications would not occur if Congress had not been heard from. Public opinion is a major factor in the formulation of U.S. foreign policy.

Thus, while the executive branch of the U.S. government had, for many years, no intention to express concern over human rights issues openly to the government of the Soviet Union, Congress was not similarly inhibited. It increasingly pressured the administration for concrete action on Soviet failure to live up to the norms set forth in the Universal Declaration of Human Rights. Congress was responding to concerns expressed by constituents.

Among the constituent groups from which Congress began to hear in the late 1940s were Jewish groups concerned about the treatment of Jews under Stalin. The Holocaust had caused the American Jewish community to be especially sensitive to developments affecting Soviet Jews. After World War II, many American Jews had concluded that their community had not done enough to persuade the U.S. government to help save Europe's Jews during World War II. They were committed not to stand by idly while the Soviet Union's close to two million Jews were at risk.

As a result of the activities of the American Jewish community, the Soviet Union's treatment of Jews became the very first issue on which the U.S. government departed from the policy of noninterference in the Soviet Union's domestic affairs. The initial step was taken by the Senate, where a resolution on the treatment of Soviet Jews was introduced in 1953, just prior to Stalin's death. The second step was taken ever so quietly in 1963, when the State Department, on express instructions from President Kennedy, set up a meeting of two senators and Justice Arthur Goldberg with the Soviet ambassador in Washington, Anatoly Dobrynin, for the purpose of discussing Soviet discrimination against Jews in education and employment. (Dobrynin vehemently denied these allegations.) The Soviet Jewry issue was dealt with equally informally by Henry Kissinger when he served as national security adviser in the late 1960s. Thereafter, however, it became a formal issue, initially as a result of congressional action, but later fully engaging the executive branch. In the Reagan administration, at the personal insistence of the president and also at the insistence of Secretary Shultz, it was the first issue discussed in our human rights dialogue.

While the issue of the treatment of Jews in Russia appeared in the 1960s to be a new issue in international relations, that was not really the case. The very same issue had been on the Russian-American agenda decades earlier. Following the Kishinev pogrom in 1903, in which the police sat idly by as Jews were killed and crippled while their homes and shops were gutted, Jewish leaders had asked the State Department to raise the issue with the Russian government. They voiced their concerns over this issue in discussions with President Theodore Roosevelt. The State Department contacted the Russian government and reported a short while later to the Jewish leaders "that St. Petersburg had categorically denied any outbreak of violence [and that] the United States could not press further ... without appearing to interfere in Russian internal affairs."[6] It was in light of that response that leaders of the American Jewish community began to focus on Russia's failure to live up to its obligation under the Russian-American Treaty of Commerce and Navigation, which had been in effect since 1832, by refusing visas to American Jews who sought to visit Russia.[7] The treaty was then allowed to expire.[8]

Following the Russian revolutions of 1917, there were years in which Russian Jews experienced equal rights. However, as Stalin consolidated his hold on the country, he increasingly followed in the footsteps of his tsarist predecessors when it came to the treatment of Jews. In 1947, a well-orchestrated anti-Semitic campaign got under way in the Soviet Union. Soviet Jews were denounced in the media, all of which were under government control, as "cosmopolitans." When persons of Jewish ancestry who had Russified their names were mentioned in the press, their original names were added, a practice similar to that of the Nazis. Actors who performed in Yiddish and authors who wrote in Yiddish were arrested, and many were killed. Even the Jewish wife of Foreign Minister Molotov was arrested, charged with treason, and, upon conviction, sent to Siberia.

In 1952, anti-Semitic practices spread to Soviet satellite states. A group of leaders of the Communist Party of Czechoslovakia, almost all of them Jews, were arrested, tried, convicted, sentenced to death, and executed. The most prominent member of this group was Rudolf Slansky, general secretary of the Czechoslovak Communist Party. They were accused of being Trotskyite-Titoist Zionists in the service of American imperialism. As far as anyone knew, they had all been faithful Communists. It was their ethnicity that appeared to be the reason for their arrest and execution. The trial of this group received a great deal of attention in the U.S. media.

---

6. Howard M. Sachar, *A History of the Jews in America* (New York: Alfred A. Knopf, 1992), 224.

7. Ibid., 229.

8. Ibid., 234.

The news of the so-called doctors' plot came in early 1953. Physicians, a majority of them Jewish, who had treated high-ranking Soviet officials were arrested and charged with having tried to kill their patients. Stalin died before the accused had been put on trial, and shortly after his death the defendants were released. Information was later disclosed about his plans to deport all Jews from the European area of the Soviet Union to Siberia.

Just as the general repression of the Soviet citizenry lessened once Stalin was dead, so did the severely repressive measures against Jews. The paranoia that had resulted in the execution of persons who were no threat to Stalin's system, or were in some cases even supporters of the system, was gone. However, institutionalized anti-Semitism persisted and became more pronounced. Because every Soviet citizen was required to possess an identification card that listed, on line 5, the holder's national origin, Jews could easily be identified by the entry on line 5 when they applied for admission to an institution for higher learning or for a job. Many Soviet citizens of Jewish descent came to refer to their experience with discrimination as their "line 5 problem."

The line 5 problem was very much in evidence at the most prestigious institutions of higher learning, such as the University of Moscow. As Anatoly noted, Jews found it increasingly difficult to be admitted to these prestigious institutions, even if they had done extremely well in secondary school. Many job opportunities for which they were well qualified were not open to them. Those who had been able to embark on a career in governmental agencies or in the economic system, which was entirely state run, soon found themselves bumping against a glass ceiling, unable to rise to positions that they would have reached but for their line 5 problem.

The great majority of Soviet Jews was not religiously affiliated. Further, the generation that had come of age after the Bolshevik Revolution had also lost contact with Yiddish culture. Many of its members had no reason to identify themselves as Jews except that the government had classified them as such and they experienced discrimination based on their ethnicity.

These Soviet citizens of Jewish ancestry, who did not identify themselves with the Jewish religion and Yiddish culture and who felt that their Jewish identity was largely a burden that they had to carry, were suddenly, in June 1967, affected by the Six-Day War between Israel and its Arab neighbors. The news that they received through the Soviet media after the outbreak of the war left them with the impression that the Jewish state was about to be wiped out. Even though they did not identify themselves with the Zionist cause, the thought that another mass killing of Jews was taking place troubled them deeply.

When the fact that Israel had been victorious could no longer be withheld, that new development had an electrifying effect on large segments of the Soviet Union's Jewish population. Many Jews took a far greater interest in

Israel than they had earlier. Comparing their experience of discrimination in the Soviet Union—particularly regarding the chances of their children being admitted to institutions of higher education—with the possibility of living in a country in which they would enjoy equal rights with other citizens, they began to give serious consideration to emigration. However, these prospective emigrants soon realized that the Soviet Union was not inclined to give them permission to leave the country.

Before long, members of the American Jewish community became aware of the interest among Soviet Jews in leaving their country and the Soviet government's failure to grant them permission to do so. The American Jewish community appealed for help to members of Congress. Quite a number of members of Congress responded positively to these appeals, but the State Department advised caution. Organizations were formed that came to constitute the Soviet Jewry Movement, whose goal was to persuade the U.S. government to place emigration from the Soviet Union on its agenda in discussions with Soviet officials and to pursue the issue consistently. The Movement called attention to the fact that the Soviet Union was violating international human rights standards.

By the time the Soviet Jewry Movement became an effective operation, Richard Nixon had been elected president, and Henry Kissinger, as his national security adviser, was the person most profoundly engaged in the development of the administration's policy toward the Soviet Union. His goal was to achieve détente. He considered the inclusion of human rights concerns, such as Soviet emigration policy, on the U.S.-Soviet bilateral agenda to be inappropriate.

But the Soviet Jewry Movement kept pressing the point. Members of the American Jewish community who had close relations with the Nixon administration urged that the administration change its policy and include emigration in the U.S.-Soviet political dialogue. Henry Kissinger relented slightly. He continued to resist the idea of placing Jewish emigration on a formal agenda. Instead, he handled the matter informally, in discussions with Dobrynin, the Soviet ambassador to the United States. As he notes in his memoirs:

> Starting in 1969, we had begun to make overtures to Moscow to ease Jewish emigration, emphasizing that such a policy would improve the atmosphere of U.S.-Soviet relations. We did so privately, believing that public confrontation would defeat our ends. We had no great hopes of success. Somewhat to our surprise, Jewish emigration increased from 400 a year to 35,000 in 1973, parallel with the improvement in U.S.-Soviet relations. As the total figures increased, I turned also to hardship cases—individuals denied visas or arrested or harassed for various offenses that the West would consider political. I privately handed [Soviet ambassador Anatoly] Dobrynin from time to time long lists of Soviet Jewish "refuseniks," or prisoners of conscience, given to me by

> American Jewish groups coordinating the public effort. I gave these to him "unofficially"; I never asked for a formal reply.[9]

The focus was thus kept narrowly on emigration. The time had not yet come for discussion of other human rights issues. As Walter Isaacson notes in his biography of Kissinger, "in the world according to Kissinger and Nixon, linkage should not extend to internal matters such as domestic human rights policies. 'What is important is not a nation's internal political philosophy,' Nixon told Mao at their first meeting in 1972. 'What is important is its policy toward the rest of the world and toward us.'"[10] There was dissent, as Isaacson notes:

> Later, the entire goal of détente was assailed on moral grounds by righteous prophets ranging from Daniel Patrick Moynihan to Ronald Reagan to Aleksandr Solzhenitsyn, who criticized it as realpolitik accommodation of Soviet power that gave short shrift to human values and American ideals.[11]

While efforts at improving bilateral relations continued, Kissinger says that in August 1972, both he and the president were "dumbfounded when the Soviets suddenly placed an exit tax on Jewish emigration."[12] The tax was to be graduated to reflect the extent of the prospective emigrant's education. A scientist with an annual salary of 2,000 rubles was to pay a tax of 40,000 rubles. It may very well have been a tax to avoid a brain drain.

The imposition of the tax caused members of the Soviet Jewry Movement to have serious doubts about the administration's effectiveness in pursuing the goal of freedom of emigration. They therefore turned to Congress. As one of the goals of the new dialogue between the Soviet Union and the United States was the improvement of trade relations, the idea that began to take hold was to link emigration to trade. When work commenced on the enactment of a new trade act, consideration started to be given to the idea of conditioning most-favored-nation status on a country's emigration policy. Senator Henry Jackson of Washington was the person most prominently associated with this idea of linkage.[13] He was later joined by Congressman Charles Vanik of Ohio; these two members of Congress became known as the authors of the Jackson-Vanik amendment.

---

9. Henry Kissinger, *White House Years* (London: Little, Brown, 1979), 1271.

10. Walter Isaacson, *Kissinger* (New York: Simon and Schuster, 1992), 610–611.

11. Ibid., 608.

12. Kissinger, *White House Years*, 1271.

13. Relying on Ambassador Dobrynin's assertions, Anatoly suggests that Senator Jackson was seeking to advance his political career when he became the leading spokesman for the cause of Soviet Jewry. My own impression is that Senator Jackson's stand was based on his principles, including his profound distaste for totalitarianism.

The Jackson-Vanik amendment to the Trade Act of 1974, as ultimately enacted, provided that to

> assure the continued dedication of the United Stats to fundamental human rights ... products from any nonmarket economy shall not be eligible to receive nondiscriminatory treatment (most-favored-nation treatment), such country shall not participate in any program of the Government of the United States which extends credit or credit guarantees or investment guarantees ... and the President shall not conclude any commercial agreement with any such country... beginning with the date on which the President determines that such country ... denies its citizens the right or opportunity to emigrate.[14]

Although the language of the text did not specify any country, it was clearly directed at the Soviet Union and, more specifically, at the obstacles that the Soviet Union placed in the way of Jewish emigration. From the time that Senator Jackson initially proposed the amendment in October 1972 until its enactment in December 1974, the amendment was vehemently opposed by the State Department, particularly by Henry Kissinger, who, while the amendment was pending, had become secretary of state.

There also was a significant new development in the attitude of American organizations interested and concerned with U.S. foreign policy. Initially, the Soviet Jewry Movement had been the only citizen organization supportive of the Jackson-Vanik amendment. The amendment did not, at the outset, have the support of those liberal citizen groups active in the political arena that favored the relaxation of tension between the Soviet Union and the United States.

But, as Kissinger noted, by the summer of 1973, there had been further developments in the Soviet Union that changed the outlook of these groups. The historian Andrei Amalrik was sentenced to two years in prison, the physicist Andrei Sakharov was warned about his political activities, the writer Aleksandr Solzhenitsyn was harassed, and other dissidents were put on trial.[15] As a consequence of these developments, organizations whose concerns regarding the Soviet Union reached beyond the issue of Jewish emigration, but focused on civil liberties more broadly, became more sympathetic to the Jackson-Vanik amendment.[16] The fact that the United States was notified in April 1973 that the emigration tax law was to be enforced only selectively did not change the position of key members of Congress on the issue of the Jackson-Vanik amendment.

As a result, Kissinger spent a good deal of time during the next year and a half negotiating with both the Soviet Union and Senator Jackson in search

---

14. Title 19, United States Code, Section 2432.
15. Henry Kissinger, *Years of Upheaval* (London: Little, Brown, 1982), 988.
16. Ibid.

of a formula that would cause the senator not to press for approval of his amendment to the Trade Act. In March 1974, Foreign Minister Gromyko agreed to an emigration figure of up to 45,000 annually, assuming that there were that many applicants for exit permits. The point that Gromyko made at that time was that the Soviet leadership "did not want to put itself in the position where it had to recruit citizens to emigrate to fulfill a moral obligation to the United States."[17]

While the discussions over the Jackson-Vanik amendment were still ongoing, the authority of the Export-Import Bank to extend loans came up in the spring of 1974 for biennial renewal. Given the developments in human rights conditions in the Soviet Union and the increasing concerns expressed by human rights groups, Senator Adlai Stevenson III, who chaired the Senate International Finance Subcommittee, introduced, with support from Senator Jackson, an amendment under which Congress could review every loan from the Export-Import Bank that exceeded $50,000,000. The amendment also placed a ceiling of $300,000,000 on all loans to the Soviet Union.

The administration did not focus immediately on that amendment. Instead, the triangular negotiations among the U.S. administration, the Soviet government, and Congress on the Jackson-Vanik amendment became increasingly intense in the fall of 1974, engaging the intercession of President Ford. Secretary Kissinger emphasized the Soviet commitment to 45,000 exit permits. Senator Jackson demanded a minimum of 60,000. Kissinger wrote to Congress of the assurances that he had received from the Soviet Union on future emigration practices. His letters were made public. But in October, Gromyko handed Kissinger a letter in which he declared that Kissinger's letters to Congress presented "a distorted picture of our position as well as of what we told the American side on this matter."[18] That letter was not released to Congress and the public.

The Senate, unaware of the Gromyko letter, approved on December 13, 1974, a further addition to the proposed Jackson-Vanik amendment. This addition would have allowed the president to grant a waiver of the requirements of the Jackson-Vanik amendment if "he has received assurances that the emigration practices" of the Soviet Union will "lead substantially to the achievement of the objectives" of the Jackson-Vanik amendment. It looked as if the months of hard negotiations had produced a result that could lead to improved U.S.-Soviet trade relations and enhanced emigration. But five days later, on December 18, the Soviet news agency Tass announced that imposing conditions on the reduction of tariffs that would interfere with the Soviet

---

17. Kissinger, *Years of Upheaval*, 994.

18. Isaacson, *Kissinger*, 618.

Union's internal affairs was "unacceptable." It also released the Gromyko letter of the preceding October, which Kissinger had not made public.

The result was that on December 20, two days after the Tass announcement and after two years of debate and discussion of the Jackson-Vanik amendment, Congress passed the Trade Act of 1974, including the amendment. The bill was signed into law on January 3, 1975. No one fully realized at that time that the new law was setting a precedent: Congress was imposing a mandate on the administration to factor human rights concerns into United States foreign policy and was doing so in highly concrete terms. The effort to block the Jackson-Vanik amendment was the last hurrah for the foreign-policy traditionalists who were opposed to an international human rights policy that would intrude into the domestic affairs of foreign countries. Almost thirty years after the adoption of the human rights provisions of the UN Charter, the United States became the first country to implement civil liberties provisions in dealing wih countries other than apartheid South Africa.

Why did the Soviet leadership, on December 18, 1974, decide to torpedo the arrangement that had been worked out by Secretary Kissinger and Senator Jackson, which was about to pass and was expected to improve trade relations between the Soviet Union and the United States? It has been assumed that the reason for this sudden hardening of the Soviet position was the likely adoption of the Stevenson amendment. Looking back at the negotiations on the Jackson-Vanik amendment, Secretary Kissinger suggested that the administration had realized too late that the Stevenson amendment would be another serious obstacle to U.S.-Soviet relations.

As noted earlier, Secretary Kissinger was proud that through his informal negotiations he had been able to increase the number of Soviet exit visas.[19] It was assumed that after enactment of the Jackson-Vanik amendment, that figure would drop precipitously. But that did not happen. Emigration figures dropped temporarily but then continued to rise, reaching 51,333 in 1979.[20] They were reduced sharply thereafter, following the Soviet invasion of Afghanistan and the serious deterioration of U.S.-Soviet relations.[21]

As noted, the Jackson-Vanik amendment was truly precedent setting. It demonstrated how a citizen group, working with Congress, could compel

---

19. According to the tabulation compiled by the Union of Councils for Soviet Jews, the Jewish emigration figures rose from 229 in 1968 to 34,733 in 1973, but then dropped to 20,628 in 1974, the year immediately before the enactment of the Jackson-Vanik amendment.

20. The Jewish emigration figures were 13,221 in 1975, 14,261 in 1976, 16,736 in 1977, and 28,865 in 1978, before reaching the highest level for the decade in 1979.

21. It evidently took a while for Soviet bureaucracy to catch up with changes in policy. The figures were 21,417 for 1980, 9,447 for 1981, 2,658 for 1982, and 1,315 for 1983, reaching a nadir of 876 in 1984.

the executive branch to put aside traditional policies and replace them with what in the Soviet Union was later called new thinking.

It was ironic that the person who more than anyone else represented the old thinking of the executive branch was Kissinger, a Jewish refugee from Europe. As Isaacson notes,

> No one knew better than Henry Kissinger the value of helping people escape repression, and he had worked hard behind the scenes to increase Jewish emigration from the USSR. But it was not, in his view, a suitable subject for formal diplomatic demands.
>
> Nor did he believe that diplomatic pressure should be used to influence the internal affairs of another nation. A peaceful world order depended upon the concept of "legitimacy," which Kissinger wrote about as a graduate student, and upon a respect for national sovereignty. This meant not meddling in another nation's internal matters, such as their emigration rules.[22]

Kissinger's objection to the policy approach advocated by Senator Jackson was not limited to emigration rules. He was opposed to the injection of any human rights concerns into the conduct of foreign policy. Yet it was on his watch as secretary of state that the broad coalition of citizen groups concerned with the issue of human rights succeeded, beginning with the Jackson-Vanik amendment, to persuade Congress to adopt a series of laws that injected the human rights issue into the formulation of U.S. foreign policy.

Here I must note again that historic developments can be seen differently by different observers depending on the angle from which the observation takes place. Anatoly has set forth the assessment of the developments surrounding the Jackson-Vanik amendment from the point of view of the long-term Soviet ambassador in Washington, Anatoly Dobrynin. To Dobrynin, Senator Jackson stood in the way of improved relations between the United States and the Soviet Union because he wanted to advance his political career. To many Americans, Jackson was a stalwart defender of human rights who led a broad-based congressional effort to compel the State Department to factor human rights concerns into the formulation of foreign policy.

While the activities of the American Soviet Jewry Movement and the positive congressional response had forced the issue of the Soviet Union's treatment of Jews onto the U.S.-Soviet agenda, this was not the case, initially, for other human rights issues. The Nixon-Brezhnev summit in Moscow in May 1972 offers an excellent illustration of the nature of the bilateral dialogue of that time. President Nixon, Secretary of State William Rogers, and National Security Adviser Kissinger spent more than a week in Moscow, engaging in extensive discussions with the Soviet leadership on a variety of issues, including arms limitation, the war in Vietnam, Middle East issues, and even

---

22. Isaacson, *Kissinger*, 624.

trade relations. A summary account of these discussions is contained in the first volume of Kissinger's memoirs, *The White House Years*.[23] There is no indication in that account that the parties came even close to discussing issues relating to human rights. Neither the American nor the Soviet side realized when they prepared their concluding communiqué that they were delving into the human rights issue in a way that would resonate for years. As Kissinger later wrote, the

> communiqué contained a favorable reference to a European Security Conference similar to that in declarations Moscow had signed with our European allies; it committed us to no date. Our strategy was to tie the European Security Conference to talks on troop reductions and both of them to an end of the Vietnam War.[24]

The Helsinki Final Act

The proposal for a European security conference had long been on the Soviet foreign policy agenda. The idea had first been suggested in 1954 by Soviet Foreign Minister Molotov. It arose out of the fact that World War II ended without a German government in place and thus without a peace treaty with Germany. As a result, the borders of the Soviet Union, Poland, and Germany that had been put into place at the conclusion of the war had not been formally recognized. Given the state of East-West relations at the time, the idea of a European security conference did not get very far. It was, however, resurrected under Brezhnev and actively pursued by the Soviet Union from 1966 onward. As conceived by the Soviet Union, the conference was to be limited to European countries, excluding the United States and Canada, even though they were NATO allies.

The European members of NATO responded favorably to the concept of a European security conference, but laid down one condition at the very outset of the discussions: All members of NATO (thus including the United States, as well as Canada) had to participate. As East-West relations continued to improve, the discussions became increasingly focused, and preparatory meetings for the European security conference began in Helsinki in September 1972. Agreement was reached on the creation of the Conference on Security and Cooperation in Europe (CSCE), as a permanent institution. It was agreed that the thirty-five participating states—all European states, except Albania but including the United States and Canada—would meet for the purpose of drafting an agreement that would reflect the understandings reached to attain the goals of security and cooperation. The first CSCE meeting began

---

23. Kissinger, *The White House Years*, 1202–1257.
24. Ibid., 1249–1250.

in September 1973 in Geneva and completed its work in July 1975. Its work product, the Final Act, was signed on August 1, 1975.

The text of the Final Act starts with a declaration of principles. The Soviet Union's major concern was addressed in Principle III on the inviolability of frontiers. The text reads:

> The participating States regard as inviolable all one another's frontiers as well as the frontiers of all States in Europe and therefore they will refrain now and in the future from assaulting these frontiers. Accordingly, they will also refrain from any demand for, or act of, seizure and usurpation of part or all of the territory of any of the participating States.[25]

But then we get to Principle VII, on respect for human rights and fundamental freedoms, including the freedom of thought, conscience, religion, or belief. The following text deserves to be highlighted:

> The participating States will respect human rights and fundamental freedoms, including the freedom of thought, conscience, religion or belief, for all without distinction as to race, sex, language or religion.... Within this framework the participating States will recognize and respect the freedom of the individual to profess and practise, alone or in community with others, religion or belief acting in accordance with the dictates of his own conscience.[26]

Principle VII further provides that

> the participating States will act in conformity with the purposes and principles of the Charter of the United Nations and with the Universal Declaration of Human Rights. They will also fulfill their obligations as set forth in the international declarations and agreements in this field, including inter alia the International Covenants on Human Rights, by which they may be bound.[27]

While Principle VII deals unambiguously with basic human rights concepts as mandates that governments have responsibility to fulfill, the portion of the document that became known as the third (humanitarian) basket uses hortatory language. Participating states promise to deal "in a positive and humanitarian spirit with the applications of persons who wish to be reunited with members of their families" in foreign countries, "examine favourably and on the basis of humanitarian considerations requests for exit and entry permits from persons who have decided to marry a citizen from another participating State," and "facilitate wider travel by citizens for personal or professional reasons."[28]

---

25. U.S. House of Representatives, Human Rights Documents, September 1983, 231–232.
26. Ibid., 233.
27. Ibid.
28. Ibid., 262–263.

In the course of the two-year negotiation of the text of the Final Act, the Soviet delegation fought against the human rights provisions but finally acquiesced. Getting the West to agree to Principle III was more important than the insertion of human rights language that the Soviet Union knew it could ignore.

Throughout the process of these negotiations, Secretary of State Kissinger had serious doubts about the value of the conference in general and the human rights provisions of the Final Act in particular. As a result, the West European states took the lead on the NATO side. However, the United States delegation to the conference, though often lacking adequate instructions from Washington, provided behind-the-scenes support.

As one looks back at the Final Act, it needs to be noted that neither the Soviet nor the United States leadership anticipated that the Final Act would, within a very short time, become one of the most significant human rights documents. In international human rights practice, there is no meaningful difference between binding and nonbinding agreements; the nonbinding Helsinki Final Act had a far more profound impact on human rights practice in the Soviet Union than did the binding International Covenant on Civil and Political Rights.

Why should that have been the case? The most important factor appears to have been the publicity given the Helsinki Final Act by the Soviet government. Brezhnev and his colleagues contended that Principle III constituted de jure recognition, accorded by the parties to the Helsinki Final Act, of the borders of the Soviet Union and of Poland and Germany as established at the end of World War II. They pronounced that result an extraordinary diplomatic success and decided to advertise it. So the Helsinki Final Act was reprinted in full in *Izvestia*, the government newspaper. Copies were given wide distribution. Having read the Helsinki Final Act, a number of intellectuals living in Moscow came together to discuss ways in which they might be able to claim the rights that seemed to be accorded to them by that document. Thereafter, Helsinki was the label affixed to the human rights movement in the Soviet Union.

The impact of the human rights provisions in the Helsinki Final Act on Soviet human rights practices was significantly enhanced by the implementation mechanism created under the Final Act and the publicity accorded it. To be sure, such a mechanism was not a novel idea. The International Covenant on Civil and Political Rights also provided for an implementation mechanism, the Human Rights Committee. But that committee never attained the influence and most certainly not the publicity that was accorded to the follow-up meetings provided in the Helsinki Final Act.

An important factor in the newsworthiness of the follow-up meetings was the change in the U.S. position regarding the public discussion of Soviet violations of the human rights provisions of the Final Act. In the post-Kissinger period, there was less resistance from the State Department to such public discussions, particularly in light of the pro–human rights position adopted by the Carter administration, which took office on January 20, 1977. The most important player in the ensuing drama, however, was the person chosen to head the U.S. delegation to the first follow-up conference that began in Belgrade in 1977. This was Arthur Goldberg, former secretary of labor, former justice of the United States Supreme Court, and former U.S. permanent representative at the United Nations. Goldberg and his approach to his task set a powerful precedent for the future functioning of what came to be known as the Helsinki Process. Years later, some West European diplomats still complained that Goldberg had "poisoned the atmosphere" at the first follow-up meeting in Belgrade. What he had done, in fact, was to make the Helsinki Final Act come truly alive.

The Soviet Union's Dissident Movement

While the influence of the West did play a role in the gradual loosening of controls in the Soviet Union, the greatest credit goes to those who, in the post-Stalin period, were prepared to speak up even if it meant taking great risks. It is important to note the distinction between the Stalin era and the era that succeeded it. Expressing dissent in Stalin's era meant committing suicide. In the post-Stalin era, it meant losing one's job or one's freedom but not necessarily one's life. As Yuri Orlov, the leader of the post-Helsinki human rights movement, put it, the human rights advocates "can be compared with people who openly throw themselves on barbed wire, hoping that there will be others who will step on their bodies to cross the wire."[29]

The Soviet Union's most prominent human rights advocate in the period following the death of Stalin was the physicist Andrei Sakharov, who had played a significant role in the development of the Soviet Union's hydrogen bomb. It was largely in light of his role in the development of a weapon of mass destruction that Sakharov became increasingly concerned with the cause of peaceful international relations. In due course, he recognized the close relationship between peaceful international relations and respect for human rights. His advocacy of dissident views led to the termination of his military-related work in 1968. He then proceeded to form the Committee on Human Rights and became a prominent advocate of freedom of speech, freedom of religion, and freedom to emigrate. For these activities he was awarded the Nobel Peace Prize in 1975. Because of the role he had played in the Soviet Union's military effort and because of his worldwide renown,

---

29. William Korey, *The Promises We Keep* (New York: St. Martin's Press, 1993), 48.

Sakharov was never treated as harshly as he might have been. But he did not escape punitive measures entirely. In 1980, he and his wife were banished from Moscow and compelled to live in the city of Gorky.

A much younger dissident was the historian and playwright Andrei Amalrik. In 1968, his essay "Will the Soviet Union Survive until 1984?" was published in the West, causing him to be sentenced to three years in a labor camp. Shortly after his release from the camp, he was sentenced again. In 1976, the authorities pressed him to leave the country, and he agreed. He died in a car crash in 1980 in Spain.

Another opponent of the Soviet system who achieved prominence was Aleksandr Solzhenitsyn. After having served in the Soviet Army, he was arrested in 1945 for making a critical remark about Stalin in a letter. That offense, which did not involve any public statement or any activity, resulted in eight years of imprisonment. Following his release, he started writing novels that remained unpublished for a number of years. After Khrushchev's 1956 speech denouncing Stalin, some of Solzhenitsyn's works were published; before long, particularly with the publication of *The Gulag Archipelago*, he was once again in difficulties with the Soviet authorities, and he was expelled from the Soviet Union in 1974.

What characterizes these three prominent personalities and a few others who expressed dissident views in the pre-Helsinki period is that they acted by and large alone. That was particularly true of Solzhenitsyn, who differed from most other dissidents in that he did not subscribe to the democratic values that stem from the Enlightenment. At any rate, none of these prominent persons thought of forming an organization that would advocate the human rights cause. As Sakharov once explained, working in groups contradicted his psychological make-up. He did not want to attend meetings, engage in debates, or get engaged in details.[30]

Thus, it was a quiet, soft-spoken person who was not at all well-known either in the Soviet Union or abroad who decided to do what no one else had done: organize a group that, claiming the rights of freedom of association and of speech, would challenge the totalitarian system. Yuri Orlov, a professor of physics, had been a member of the Communist Party, but was expelled in 1956 for criticizing Stalin more strongly than was viewed as permissible. In the years that followed, he did not hesitate to express his views clearly. At one point, in 1974, a message from an important official was transmitted to him that he could write and sign letters of protest as long as he did not get involved in forming an organization.

Orlov thus knew the risks he was taking when, after the Helsinki Final Act had been widely publicized, he asked some friends to join with him in forming

---

30. Paul Goldberg, *The Final Act* (New York: William Morrow and Company, 1988), 47.

a group that would seek to advance the cause of human rights in the Soviet Union and would, at the same time, seek to obtain publicity for its activities in the West. He had read the Final Act and had taken due notice of the fact that it was "the first document in which the idea of preserving peace is directly linked to respect for human rights." He noted that the document was "weaker than the Universal Declaration of Human Rights." However, he reasoned, if "the Soviet government said it was important, it was, in fact, important. It was the Soviet government itself that gave us something to work with."[31]

Some of Orlov's friends believed that they should seek to achieve their goal of greater freedom for Soviet citizens by appealing to Western human rights advocates to be more active on behalf of their Soviet counterparts. Orlov, by contrast, decided that "if we wanted compliance with the Helsinki Final Act, it was up to us to monitor it. If we wanted a group started, we were the ones to start it. Nobody would do it for us." By May 1976, a little over eight months following the Helsinki Final Act, Orlov had put together a group that was to call itself the Public Group of Assistance to Implementation of the Helsinki Agreements in the USSR. The group soon became known as the Helsinki Group.

Orlov had hoped that Sakharov would join the group. Sakharov expressed his sympathy with the idea but explained that he was not interested in leading or joining a group, where he would be expected to participate in meetings and debates and focus on details. He was, however, willing to host the first press conference in his apartment, and his wife, Yelena Bonner, was willing to join the group. Orlov had been notified that the KGB wanted to talk to him, which, he thought, meant that he was about to be arrested. Under these circumstances, he asked Sakharov to act speedily, resulting in a press conference being called at Sakharov's apartment at 11 p.m. on May 12, 1976. Only the Reuters representative appeared, but he broke the news of the birth of Helsinki Group. It was quickly picked up by other media. Thus the movement was born that put the issues of freedom of speech and of religion in the Soviet Union on the international agenda.

Although the formation of the new movement had, through Reuters, received some publicity, its sponsors were disappointed by the meagerness of that publicity. They soon received help, however, from the agency that Orlov least expected to assist in his publicity effort: the KGB. Orlov was picked up by KGB agents, taken to a KGB office, and warned to cease his dissident activity. The news of this occurrence was announced by Tass. The result of this encounter with the KGB moved the Helsinki Group story within days from page 8 of the *New York Times* to page 3. From then on, news about the Helsinki Group not only spread abroad, but got back to the Soviet Union

---

31. Korey, *The Promises We Keep*, 48.

and reached various groups that had specific, narrower reasons to consider themselves oppressed.³²

Many of the organizers of the Helsinki Group were of ethnic Russian background; they could have lived a relatively untroubled life in the Soviet Union if it were not for their political beliefs. However, one of the organizers, Anatoly Shcharansky—who has since changed his name to Natan Sharansky—was the victim of both political and ethnic discrimination. It was through him that the Helsinki Group came into contact with another group of persons who agitated for recognition of a right assured them by the Helsinki Final Act: the right to emigrate. They became known as refuseniks, the term used for Jews whose applications for exit permits had been refused on the grounds that, on the basis of their earlier employment, they possessed information that, if disclosed, would have adverse effects on the Soviet Union's security interests.

Foreign radio newscasts about the creation of the Helsinki Group reached many Soviet citizens, including some who were inspired to follow the group's lead. Before long a Ukrainian Helsinki Group had been formed, followed by Lithuanian, Georgian, and Armenian Helsinki Groups.³³ At the same time, Orlov established close contacts with members of the Western press corps in Moscow. The work of the Helsinki Group was now well covered, creating increased attention to political and religious repression in the Soviet Union.

The Soviet Union's criminal code had for years, even in the post-Stalin period, made unauthorized political and religious activities a crime. Under Article 70, a person found guilty of "anti-Soviet agitation and propaganda" would be sentenced to seven years of hard labor, plus five years of internal exile. Persons found guilty of the lesser offense of "defamation of the Soviet system" under Article 190-1 would be sentenced to two years in prison. Religious gatherings, such as prayer sessions, were allowed only if they were held by a denomination registered with and approved by the government. If such meetings were held by a group that had not won approval, the organizers violated Article 142, leading to a sentence of years, and other participants violated Article 227, also leading to a sentence of years.

In cases that were determined by the KGB to be particularly egregious, the dissident was charged with treason and a trumped-up case was presented. In other instances, particularly cases involving members of unauthorized denominations, the punishment was commitment to an institution for the mentally ill.

Throughout the years immediately prior to the organization of the Helsinki Group, hundreds of persons were annually sentenced or committed for

---

32. Goldberg, *The Final Act,* 18–54.
33. Ibid., 91–92.

unauthorized political or religious activities. Yet not a great deal of attention was paid. That state of affairs was profoundly altered by the creation of the Helsinki Group.

The impact of the Helsinki Group was in due course recognized by the KGB, although it took about eight months for that to happen. In January 1977, however, the KGB clamped down hard on Orlov and his associates. After a few more weeks of harassment, Orlov was arrested in February and Sharansky in March. At that point the news got to page 1 of the *New York Times*. A few months later, Orlov was tried for anti-Soviet agitation and propaganda and sentenced to seven years of hard labor followed by five years of internal exile. Sharansky was found guilty of treason as well as anti-Soviet agitation and propaganda and was sentenced to three years in prison followed by ten years of hard labor.[34]

In the short period between May 1976 and January 1977, Orlov, a soft-spoken physicist and former member of the Communist Party, had placed the issue of political repression in the Soviet Union on the international agenda, including the agenda of the U.S. government. It was largely through his efforts and the efforts of the Helsinki Group that the issue of dissidents in the Soviet Union was recognized as a problem that required resolution in order for the Soviet Union to comply with its international obligations.

By sheer coincidence, at the very time that Orlov was exploring the possibility of creating a mechanism in the Soviet Union that would monitor the implementation of the Helsinki Final Act, Millicent Fenwick, a member of the U.S. Congress, was thinking of a way to create such a mechanism in the United States. She had had an opportunity to present her concerns to Brezhnev, who had found her to be "obsessive."[35] Concerned that the State Department would not press the Soviet human rights issue adequately, she proposed legislation to create a congressional commission on security and cooperation in Europe, which would monitor the implementation of the Helsinki Final Act. Although the Soviet Union was not explicitly mentioned, there was little doubt that one of the major purposes of the legislation would be to monitor compliance with the Final Act's human rights provisions.

The State Department, still headed by Secretary Kissinger, reported adversely on the Fenwick proposal because, as the report put it, "[W]e do not believe the proposed Commission would add to the efforts and procedures already established."[36] The proposal passed the U.S. House of Representatives on May 17, five days after the formation of the Helsinki Group in Moscow. The coincidence in timing did not go unnoticed. In the debate

---

34. Goldberg, *The Final Act*, 274–275.
35. Korey, *The Promises We Keep*, 23.
36. U.S. Congress, Senate Report 94-756, 4-5.

on her proposal, just before the vote was cast in the House, Fenwick noted that the Helsinki Group had been created in Moscow. She said: "They and we are hoping that this international accord will not be just another empty piece of paper." The State Department's opposition notwithstanding, the bill establishing the commission was signed into law by President Ford. The commissioners—members of the Senate and House and representatives of the administration—were duly appointed, and the commission started functioning in July 1976.[37] In the years that followed, it spent a significant amount of its time focusing on the Soviet Union's performance in the field of human rights.

The existence of this new monitoring apparatus did not, as noted above, prevent the Soviet authorities from clamping down hard on the dissidents who had dared to form the Helsinki Group in Moscow. But now there was a body within the U.S. government, consisting largely of members of Congress, that did indeed monitor human rights performance in the Soviet Union and publicize violations of the provisions of the Final Act.

There was another body as well, an international body that had the same mandate. The concluding section of the Helsinki Final Act stated that its multilateral process would continue with "a thorough exchange of views both on the implementation of the provisions of the Final Act and of the tasks defined by the Conference." The first such follow-up conference, the Final Act provided, would take place in Belgrade in 1977.

When the Belgrade conference opened in October 1977, Andrei Sakharov sent it a message that noted the "inseparable bond between international security and an open society," including freedom to cross borders, free exchange of information, and freedom of conscience. He then went on to pose the following question: "Is the West prepared to defend these noble and vitally important principles? Or will it, little by little, accept the interpretation of the principles of Helsinki, and of détente as a whole, that the leaders of the Soviet Union and of Eastern Europe are trying to impose?"[38]

The person to whom the task fell to respond to Sakharov's challenge on behalf of the United States was Arthur Goldberg, whom President Carter designated as head of the U.S. delegation to the Belgrade meeting. As a result of his standing and his personality, Goldberg succeeded in establishing the precedent of truly meaningful discussion of human rights problems in international fora.[39]

---

37. Ibid., 23–28.

38. Ibid., 61.

39. Before entering government service, Goldberg had been general counsel to the Congress of Industrial Organization. In *The Communist Part vs. the CIO*, Max Kampelman notes that Arthur Goldberg's "presence was a source of great strength to [Philip] Murray [president of the CIO] in the continued drive against the Communists" (p. 140).

At the outset, as the Belgrade meeting began on October 4, 1977, Ambassador Goldberg followed the established diplomatic protocol of not mentioning any specific countries in the process of reviewing human rights practices in the CSCE region. He emphasized that the discussion of human rights should not interfere with the pursuit of détente. When he sought to express concern over Soviet jamming of Radio Free Europe and Radio Liberty broadcasts, he spoke of continuing interference with foreign broadcasts by an unnamed country with the broadcasts of another unnamed country. Given this tiptoeing around key issues, there was no real dialogue on the issue of human rights.[40]

Ten days after the opening of the Belgrade meeting, on October 14, a letter was delivered to President Carter, signed by 127 members of the House of Representatives and 16 senators, noting the campaign that had been undertaken earlier that year against the Moscow Helsinki Group and urging that these violations of the Final Act be called attention to at the Belgrade meeting and that the U.S. delegation "press this point in as forceful a manner as possible, in closed as well as in open session."

A few days later, Goldberg decided to depart from the protocol of vagueness and indirection. He did so by quoting from the newspaper of the French Communist Party, *l'Humanite*, which was veering toward Eurocommunism and had protested the barring of one of its reporters from the trial in Prague of supporters of Czechoslovakia's Charter 77 movement.

It was this rather innocuous comment that turned the tide. The Czechoslovak delegation protested vehemently, joined by the Soviet Union and other delegations from Warsaw Pact countries. But the genie was out of the bottle. As the Belgrade meeting progressed, Ambassador Goldberg focused specifically on human rights violations in the Soviet Union (as well as Czechoslovakia and East Germany) and broke another taboo by referring to specific cases of violations of Helsinki commitments, such as the incarceration of Orlov and Sharansky.[41] The Belgrade meeting adjourned in March 1978 after agreement had been reached on a number of further follow-up meetings, which would allow the East-West dialogue to continue.

As noted earlier, in December 1979, the Soviet Union invaded Afghanistan, severely rupturing U.S.-Soviet relations. At the session of the UN Human Rights Commission that started the month after the invasion, the U.S. representative to the commission, Jerome Shestack, severely criticized the Soviet Union for a broad range of human rights violations. By the time the Carter administration left office, a U.S. policy of public criticism of Soviet human rights violations was well established.

---

40. Korey, *The Promises We Keep*, 81.
41. Ibid., 82–88.

Yet the fact that U.S. officials would publicly raise questions about the Soviet Union's human rights performance did not bring about any significant change in Soviet policy. On the contrary, the issue posed by the Soviet Union's failure to live up to the obligations it had undertaken under the Helsinki Final Act was brought home most vividly in June 1978, just three months following the conclusion of the Belgrade meeting, when a group of eight Siberian Pentecostal Christians arrived at the U.S. embassy in Moscow. Their intention had been to inquire about the possibility of obtaining entry visas to the United States.[42] The Soviet police at the embassy were able to stop only one of them; the other seven made it onto the embassy grounds. As a result of the altercation with the Soviet police, the seven Pentecostals were fearful of leaving and, under these circumstances, the embassy allowed them to stay. They subsequently became known as the Siberian Seven.

As uninvited guests at the U.S. embassy, the Siberian Seven called attention to a problem that might otherwise have stayed in the background: the treatment of Pentecostal Christians in the Soviet Union. While all religious denominations had suffered persecution from the Soviet state, Pentecostal Christians who were pacifists and whose young men refused to serve in the military were subjected to particularly severe measures. Ethnic Russians were generally disinclined to emigrate from their motherland. Pentecostal Christian pacifists of Russian ethnicity constituted an exception. In the 1980s, they would join Jews, Armenians, and Volga Germans as applicants for exit permits. In the meantime, though, from June 1978 onward, the Siberian Seven's presence in the U.S. embassy compound put the human rights issue high on the agenda of U.S.-Soviet bilateral relations.

---

42. Kent R. Hill, *The Soviet Union on the Brink* (New York: Multnomah, 1991), 25.

3

Enter Gorbachev

Anatoly Adamishin

As we saw in the previous chapter, until the advent of perestroika there was no such notion in the Soviet-U.S. relationship as constructive humanitarian dialogue. Without exaggerating wildly, one could say much the same about the entire two-hundred-year history of Russian-American diplomatic relations. As in myriad other areas, perestroika transformed the situation, creating fundamental changes in Soviet foreign policy and allowing Soviets and Americans to quietly discuss issues that had previously been taboo.

In this chapter, I recount how Gorbachev's new thinking inspired some of us within the Ministry of Foreign Affairs to push for reforms. I pay particular attention to the subject of emigration, a topic of considerable concern to Washington and one that raised issues central to the goals of perestroika. I recount how we battled bureaucratically with conservatives within the Soviet system, especially within the Central Committee, to introduce a more transparent, equitable, and legal process for people wishing to leave the Soviet Union.

Dick's section of this chapter examines the impact on Soviet-U.S. human rights discussions of several new arrivals on the political and diplomatic scene, among them the staunchly anti-Communist President Reagan and Secretary of State Shultz, who brought to his office a deep commitment to human rights issues. Dick, too, was a novitiate of sorts; he began his diplomatic career in the early 1980s as a member of the U.S. delegation to the UN Commission on Human Rights and in 1985 was appointed assistant secretary of state for human rights. Soviet-U.S. discussions of human rights were typically prickly affairs during the first half of the 1980s, and even when Gorbachev, another new arrival, became the Soviet leader, the tenor of Soviet-U.S. relations remained much the same. Gradually, however, American skepticism of Gorbachev's new thinking began to dissolve in the face of the first signs of the dawning of a new era.

Dick's account, it should be noted, chronicles developments between 1980 and late 1986, whereas mine begins with Gorbachev's ascent to power in 1985 and ranges back and forth across the next few years. And whereas Dick's contribution focuses on the often strained relations between the U.S. and Soviet governments, mine centers on struggles between different camps within the Soviet system. It is in the next chapter, chapter 4, that we discuss the beginnings of our joint endeavors in the field of human rights.

A Revolution in Foreign Policy Thinking

Very soon after he came to power, Mikhail Gorbachev publicly declared that the Soviet Union would not interfere in the affairs of fraternal socialist parties and countries, and that their leaders should have full responsibility for their countries' destinies. It meant a clean break with the so-called Brezhnev Doctrine, which practically sanctioned Soviet interference, including military interference, in the internal affairs of the Socialist countries under the pretext of confronting a menace to Socialism. It meant that the methods applied in 1956 in Hungary and in 1968 in Czechoslovakia were no longer acceptable. To proclaim freedom of choice for the East European states allied with the Soviet Union was in itself a revolutionary shift. Subsequent events in Eastern Europe, including the reunification of Germany, proved that Gorbachev kept his word.

Another key decision made by Gorbachev was to deny that the two systems, capitalism and socialism, could not possibly live together on this planet. Such fatalism was symbolized from one side by the famous words of Khrushchev—"We will bury you"—and from the other by President Reagan's claims that America was God's chosen country and that it should not accommodate communism but rather get rid of it. "The West will not contain communism; it will transcend communism," declared Reagan in 1981. "We will not bother to denounce it; we'll dismiss it as a sad, bizarre chapter in human history whose last pages are even now being written."[1] There was no room for compromise with the Soviet Union except on minor issues.[2] De-

---

1. See Ronald Reagan's address at commencement exercises at the University of Notre Dame, May 17, 1981, http://www.reagan.utexas.edu/archives/speeches/1981/51781a.htm.

2. The historian Richard Pipes gave expression to that point of view when he wrote that there is "an impassable line separating the two systems on both historical and ideological grounds. There was no 'convergence' and there could be none; one or another must give way." See Vixi, 130.

ideologizing international policy was one of Gorbachev's great theoretical and practical breakthroughs.

At the Twenty-Seventh Party Congress in February 1986, Gorbachev emphasized that the Soviet Union was ready to do everything it could to change the international situation dramatically. He began with the Soviet-U.S. relationship. At that time, that relationship was the axle around which global stability rotated.

By the arrival in Moscow of Shultz's delegation in April 1987—an event that I consider to mark the beginning of the Soviet-U.S. humanitarian dialogue—two important meetings between Gorbachev and Reagan had already taken place. I had the good fortune to participate in the first, which occurred in Geneva in November 1985.[3] A joint statement issued at the close of that meeting stressed that there could be no winners in a nuclear war and that one should never be fought. At the second meeting, in Reykjavik in October 1986, the U.S. president's advisers had great difficulty pulling him back from concluding an agreement proposed by Gorbachev to eliminate all nuclear weapons in ten years' time. To rein in the arms race and not let it go through another cycle was a major aspiration of Gorbachev's.[4]

A few people noticed, though, that first the Geneva and then the Reykjavik closing statements expressed in writing that human rights were an appropriate topic for bilateral discussion, "in the spirit of cooperation." As Andrei Grachev, the last official spokesman of the Soviet president, told me recently,

> While listening to the very first speech of Gorbachev as the secretary general, I suddenly heard the words "human rights" without the modifying phrase "so-called," like it had always been used before. I thought: Maybe this man doesn't realize what he is talking about and is reading what others have written for him. But if he does, it becomes very interesting because he introduces one of the most explosive topics of his future investiture.[5]

---

3. As a member of the Soviet delegation, I had been introduced to the U.S. president, and I remember the good impression I had of him as a human being. It was difficult to see him as the same person who had declared the Soviet Union to be an "evil empire."

4. Discussing military issues with his closest aides, Gorbachev uttered a phrase that sounded like a directive: "Everything should be done in such a way that the country would no longer be devastated by the build-up of defense" (Gorbachev Foundation, V Politburo CK KPSS, 35).

5. Gorbachev was preparing his new thinking for a long time. In December 1984, before he became number one, when speaking in public he would use such rarely heard terms as stagnation, acceleration, human factor, glasnost, and democratization.
   Speaking at a Politburo meeting on March 11, 1985, immediately following the unanimous vote for his nomination as the next secretary general, Gorbachev mentioned the "dynamism that our democracy needs" but also said, rather ambiguously, "we don't need to change the policy. It is true, correct, genuinely Leninist policy" (National Security Archive, READD Collection, Box 10, Washington, DC).

Thus Gorbachev was the first Soviet leader to give the go-ahead for a full-fledged humanitarian dialogue with the United States and other Western countries. The offer to start talking about human rights topics came from the American side, but Gorbachev had very good reason to accept it. For him—as for my closest colleagues and me—this dialogue was part of the broader agenda of perestroika.

Back to Lenin

In the humanitarian field, as in many others, our motto at the dawn of perestroika was to return to sources. Had not a slogan of defending human rights been written on the Marxism banner from its start? Was not the Declaration for the Rights of Those Who Work and Are Being Exploited one of the first official documents of the Soviet regime in 1917? Yes, we said to ourselves, the luster of these proclamations' appeals had faded in recent decades, but with the assistance of the true Lenin, we would make our ideals shine again. Their long misuse didn't mean that they were wrong. We could echo both Gorbachev and Lenin in declaring all power to the Soviets (not to the party). With Gorbachev de-ideologizing our foreign policy and placing human rights problems high on the global agendas, we could demonstrate to the world that humanitarian issues were not the Achilles' heel of socialism. We could openly talk about the problem with Americans, not to score propaganda points, but to find out something useful for both sides. We were ready to hear criticism and to try to learn something positive from the other side's experience; we were also ready to voice constructive criticism of others. What did we have in mind when speaking about human rights? Did we mean only civil and political liberties or social and economic rights as well? Did we include such issues as unemployment, homelessness, racial discrimination, and social oppression? We certainly didn't want our discussions with Americans to be a one-way street. We wanted to retain our right to be guided by our own ideals. Why, we asked, should Western values rule? Wouldn't it be more appropriate to talk about universal human values? (At their meeting on Malta in December 1989, Gorbachev spoke in this spirit to George H. W. Bush, who agreed.)

I should say that we had certain doubts about the sincerity of Western politicians regarding human rights and personal freedoms inside the Soviet Union. The Carter presidency, as I have mentioned, left a clear impression that the human rights topic had been used primarily as an ideological and propagandistic weapon.[6]

---

6. Those of us who knew history well could refer to the period immediately after World War II, when the issue of building a further relationship with the Soviet Union was not based

On the other hand, I must confess that when, in April 1987, Dick and I began our talks, I knew little about the gray areas of our humanitarian situation. I still harbored some rosy views.[7] Generally I was aware that our laws and particularly their implementation left much to be desired, but I didn't realize how far we were below international standards or how strongly Soviet ideology rejected the notion of civil liberties, which were deemed to be a hollow concept in contrast to substantive economic and social rights. I didn't suspect the extent to which our laws safeguarded the state at the expense of its citizens.

The new minister of foreign affairs had fewer illusions. "A turn of 180 degrees is needed in what concerns humanitarian questions," Shevardnadze told us. "We kicked off this turn, but we are just at the beginning. When, finally, will we be fully convinced that it is a function of socialism to defend human rights? The West, with its mercantilism, its mass consumption, is longing for fresh ideas of justice, of moral purity, of humanism. Instead, often we suffer for these complexes."[8]

Gorbachev was determined to change the situation, but he recognized the scale of the challenge and the fact that we were starting from scratch. "Human rights have never been seriously addressed in our work," he said, "neither in theoretical aspects, nor as a study of practices; we don't even have a database on this issue."[9]

A New Department in the Ministry

It was in this light that the Ministry of Foreign Affairs, for the first time in its seventy-plus years of history, established a special department for

---

on humanitarian matters. As American political scientist Melvyn P. Leffler wrote, "Truman was ready to work with Stalin. U.S. officials were indifferent to the brutality and repression of Stalin's dictatorship at home so long as the Kremlin showed restraint abroad. Truman knew that the regime in Moscow was 'a police government, plain and simple,' but he was willing to ignore its internal nature." See Melvyn P. Leffler, *The Specter of Communism* (New York: Hill and Wang, 1994), 48.

7. This is what we wrote as an official reply to a request from an international organization: "In the Soviet Union cases of arbitrary execution or of execution without trial are completely excluded, since such anti-human practice is in contradiction with the nature and the political system of the Soviet socialist state." Still, in November 1987, we were not free from the notion that socialism not only proclaimed, but almost automatically provided real care of the important needs of the people.

Sometimes our foreign colleagues provided us with figures that we did not possess ourselves. Gorbachev himself exclaimed once, with reference to Hans-Dietrich Genscher's claim that there were 300,000 Germans in the Soviet Union who would like to move to Germany: "In the West, they know about it better than we ourselves know it from our internal information!" (Gorbachev Foundation, V Politburo CK KPSS, 112).

8. I quote these words from the official publication of our ministry, Vestnik MID SSSR, May 1986.

9. Gorbachev Foundation, V Politburo CK KPSS, 111.

humanitarian cooperation.[10] It was a good organizational step to take, but it was certainly not enough by itself. Old conceptions died hard. In the first months of perestroika, Soviet representatives could still be heard taking the old line in the UN Human Rights Commission and in meetings that grew out of the CSCE.

I, as deputy minister, knew very well on which of my colleagues I could rely. Within our small group, we had clear ideas as to what we should do to improve the human rights situation. Usually, two or three persons prepared a draft of such and such document. After some discussion and editing, I would forward the draft to Anatoly Kovalev, first deputy minister, who would masterfully polish our suggestions. He would then send it Shevardnadze, who as a rule didn't soften our initiatives unless he decided, knowing the political climate in the highest reaches of the system, that it was not a good time to "tease the geese." Shevardnadze would sign the document—in our slang, a "memo to instance" or simply a "paper"—either by himself or with other agency chiefs, which was then sent nominally to the Central Committee of the Communist Party of the Soviet Union, but in reality to its departments.

Often, before submitting a memo, the minister would consult with Gorbachev. As far as I remember, Mikhail Sergeyevich did not always readily accept our radical proposals, although he spoke well of the Ministry of Foreign Affairs. He apparently did not wish to traumatize society, particularly the party bureaucracy. He probably remembered Khrushchev's fate. As a rule, Shevardnadze did not protest very strongly, in part because he wanted to avoid doing anything to undermine Gorbachev's authority. In retrospect, it is clear that this tactic was an erroneous one.[11] Many things failed to get done just because the top leadership avoided bold steps and abrupt breaks with the past. This encouraged the conservatives in the Central Commit-

---

10. The search for a person who could head the new department was not easy. Once, Shevardnadze was reading a cable from our embassy in Paris that I had brought to him. It dealt with a human rights topic. He asked, "Okay, the telegram is signed by Ambassador Vorontsov, but, to your knowledge, who prepared it?" "His deputy, Alexei Glukhov," I replied. "Summon him to Moscow; we'll give him a new department." Afterward, we worked in good rapport with Alexei, who joined a tiny group of liberals in the Ministry of Foreign Affairs.

Incidentally, Shevardnadze—in stark contrast to Gromyko—encouraged free discussions and allowed his staff to argue with him and defend their opinions. But we also had to work very hard. The minister himself worked long hours without taking a break even on weekends. One couldn't help recalling the good old times when Gromyko could hardly be found in the ministry by 6:00 in the evening and, consequently, few other people would be there either. Weekends were considered sacred in those days. And there was a special classified resolution of the Politburo to provide its members with two vacations per year.

11. I think that Gorbachev himself recognizes that it was a blunder to try to pull into the new life the enormous train of the Communist Party. Yakovlev and Shevardnadze were not able to persuade him to cause a split in the party, which had 19 million members. Even when Gorbachev was speaking about shortcomings of the one-party system, but he did not have the courage to take practical measures.

tee departments, who, when they had to process our memos, would water down our far-reaching proposals. Ultimately, a draft became a decision that required action by the Secretariat of the Central Committee, or the highest authority, the Politburo. Mostly they approved what they received.

Who Should Have the Right to Emigrate?

The first problem that we discussed in the framework of the Soviet-U.S. humanitarian dialogue was emigration, a subject toward which Russians and Americans have always had very different attitudes.

Historically, emigration had rarely been a feature of Russian civilization. Ours was a huge empire with a prodigious appetite for human resources. From as early as the seventeenth century, Russia required that people be drawn in, not let out. It was a closed country long before 1917. If a subject of Russian ethnicity wanted to go abroad, he had to ask permission from the tsar himself. In the middle of the nineteenth century, Nicholas I required 500 rubles, a substantial sum, for a foreign passport valid for six months. Even our great poet Pushkin was deprived of the chance to travel.

Tsarist Russia followed the pattern of many other governments, using emigration as a tool for regulating social, economic, and political relations. Greater freedom in this field, as in commerce, was advantageous for strong nations. In Great Britain, the cradle of modern democracy, a law that severely limited emigration existed for six centuries. The British finally abolished it in 1827, when they began to feel their worldwide might.

We maintained our prohibition. The emigration of persons of Russian ethnicity—in contrast to the emigration of Jews, Poles, and even Ukrainians—was unknown until the 1920s, after the 1917 Revolution and the subsequent civil war. That window of opportunity was brief, progressively closing until it slammed shut in 1930. Thereafter, the country was almost hermetically sealed for all citizens of the Soviet Union, irrespective of ethnicity. Exits resumed after Stalin's death, but the stream of emigrants was extremely thin and almost exclusively Jewish.

In 1967, after the Six Day War, the Soviet Union severed diplomatic relations with Israel and put an end to this trickle. A small flow was reestablished in 1968 and increased in the 1970s. During that period, every application for an exit permit was carefully examined. In the years immediately preceding perestroika, Jewish emigration dropped substantially.[12] The situation improved only with the dawn of perestroika.

---

12. A yearly quota existed, and it wasn't easy for a Jew to leave the Soviet Union if he or she possessed higher or special education. Among the emigrants were Communist Party members,

How to Fix It?

At the beginning of 1987, before our talks with Dick commenced, we presented to Shevardnadze the following points on the issue of emigration.

1. The interests of the person have become the focus of perestroika. Its primary goal is to ensure the increasing well-being and social protection of the population. The more we achieve this, the less likely it is that people will seek to leave the Soviet Union.
2. Those who want to emigrate from the country should be in a position to do so. It is not only a moral imperative (the state should not keep people within its borders against their will) but also our international obligation (under Article 12 of the International Covenant on Civil and Political Rights).
3. The rules we have after January 1, 1987, regarding the granting of exit permits improve on the past but are still based on the principle of the reunification of families. Some other categories of private contacts for travel abroad are permitted but only based on invitations extended by foreigners. This satisfies the provisions of the Helsinki Final Act but not those of the International Covenant on Civil and Political Rights. Since the covenant was ratified by the USSR in 1976, we have been constantly and rightly accused of not complying with it.
4. The existing administrative rules governing the granting of exit permits are not laid down in the law. At best they are deliberations of the Central Committee, and at worst, the internal instructions of various departments and agencies, closed to the general public.[13]
5. It would not be appropriate to single out Jewish emigration from the general rule. What we ought to do is to create a legal framework for questions of entry and exit from the Soviet Union.

---

too, but few of them. The general figures were as follows:

Year	Number	Year	Number	Year	Number
1968	229	1974	20,628	1980	21,472
1969	2,979	1975	13,221	1981	9,448
1970	1,027	1976	14,261	1982	2,688
1971	13,022	1977	16,736	1983	1,314
1972	31,681	1978	28,865	1984	896
1973	34,733	1979	51,333		

See Albert Szymanski, *Human Rights in the Soviet Union* (London: Zed Books, 1985).

13. Once, we estimated that, in the late Brezhnev period, something like 600,000 normative acts were in place in different fields, substituting for laws and leaving wide possibilities for arbitrary rule.

6. In the present situation, the best practical way to proceed is to prepare a decree of the Presidium of the Supreme Soviet on access and exit. It could include all the necessary provisions and should confine legal limitations on emigration to those provided in the covenant (i.e., limitations necessary for state security, public order, health, or integrity of the population). Furthermore, the decree could be transformed into full-fledged law.
7. At the same time, further steps are required in order to facilitate short-term travel abroad for business, tourism, and professional and personal contacts. Such trips are still restricted at the international level.
8. A positive evolution in this field of human rights will bring not only political and propaganda benefits but eventually material advantages as well; it will help remove such unpleasant phenomena as trade embargoes, denial of most-favored-nation status, and restrictions on technology supplies.
9. What we ought to do immediately is to set up a special commission of the Presidium of the Supreme Soviet to review denials of exit permits. (This was created, and it introduced a legal entity for appeals.)

It wasn't difficult to convince Shevardnadze. The Politburo took longer to persuade, but it too eventually decided to implement our proposals. Here, as usual, Gorbachev played the main role, and he was very eloquent: "Let people travel the way it is done all over the world," he said.[14] Our ministry and other agencies (justice, internal affairs, and security, among the principal ones) were charged with drafting the abovementioned decree and presenting it for final approval.

To Exit or Not to Exit

We in the Ministry of Foreign Affairs who initiated this project were extremely happy. We didn't suspect how long and tormenting the toil would turn out to be. The prospect of new laws, new drafts, and a new order provoked fierce bureaucratic resistance. Our opponents were scattered throughout all the ministries, including the Ministry of Foreign Affairs. Their chief ideological objection centered on preserving state control: Why should a single person and not the government decide a crucial question like leaving the country? It has been this way for decades, and now these "liberals" want to put an end to an order that serves Soviet interests well. There were other, less elevated, motives: A lot of people were busy—and made their living—

---

14. Gorbachev Foundation, V Politburo CK KPSS, 120.

deciding for others, or in fact, forbidding others. For them, the rule of man was much more convenient than the rule of law.

Our opponents were also concerned about "state interests." They argued that unfettered emigration would create a brain drain. They pointed out the dangers of allowing people who knew state secrets to leave the country. And they noted that emigration would saddle the state with a significant financial burden: The ruble was unconvertible, and a person leaving the Soviet Union had to receive from the state the equivalent of his or her rubles in hard currency. In 1988, such currency exchanges totaled 100 million rubles.

Our ally was often the Supreme Soviet or, rather, its commissions. Our main antagonists were some departments of the Central Committee apparatus. I spent many hours in discussions and restricted-access meetings, usually in the comfortable rooms of the Central Committee.[15] I remember well one of the department chiefs, who was a namesake of the great Pushkin by his first name and patronymic; he usually greeted me when I stepped into his office with, "Oh, my sweet one." Then, though, he would denounce the Ministry of Foreign Affairs's proposals while representatives of other agencies would stay silent, even if earlier they had seemed to agree with us. I had to speak out and engage in a one-on-one debate with him.

The situation was aggravated by the fact that different departments of the almighty Central Committee sent their own proposals and memos to the Secretariat or the Politburo. If these were approved, governmental agencies were presented with a fait accompli. The KGB, too, had the right to address the Central Committee on its own. Once I was shocked to learn that our ministry was obliged to take certain steps in the human rights field proposed by the KGB and approved by the Central Committee without our knowledge.

The problem of state secrets was a particularly thorny topic. I used to argue that the problem was real but could and should be addressed by introducing legislation to bring some conformity and predictability to the issue rather than continuing to allow each agency to set its own time frame, which could stretch for decades and were often not made known to employees before they began their jobs. These were precisely the points that we proposed to include in the new rules.

The internal wrestling delayed, conspicuously, the birth of the decree on emigration. In April 1987, the Politburo approved our draft and passed it to the Supreme Soviet. On Gorbachev's insistence, as testified by his closest assistant and supporter, Anatoly Chernyaev, the Politburo held a special hearing to this topic in August 1987. It was stated that of the 250,000 persons

---

15. John Kohan put it this way: "Foreign Ministry staffers, with their boss's encouragement, have lobbied other branches of the bureaucracy to improve the country's human rights image." *Time*, May 15, 1989, 15.

who had emigrated in ten years—remarkably, one in four of them were pensioners—few were in complete discord with the regime. The main reasons for their emigration were, first, ethnic, and second, social. Still, they were viewed as half-traitors. Nationalist writers—and during perestroika they did raise their voices—denounced "those who run" while long-suffering Russian peasants stayed put. Potential emigrants were counted in the hundreds of thousands, but they were of non-Russian nationalities: 400,000 Germans, 400,000 Jews, and 8,000 Armenians, among others. Many people felt that mass emigration was due to shortcomings in our own propaganda and public work. Gorbachev himself had to struggle with that mood, emphasizing that the issue of emigration was rising to the surface thanks to the democratic processes opened by perestroika. The solution, he stressed, also would be found in the context of those processes.[16]

Ups and Downs

Suddenly, in June 1988, there was an open attempt, different from the usual practice, to revise what the Politburo had already decided. Shevardnadze (I remember with how much zest we had prepared the materials for him), in the same open manner, took a very resolute position. We won that fight, but in March 1989, while speaking in Geneva before the forty-fifth session of the UN Commission on Human Rights, I admitted that a decree on exit from and entry into our country had not yet been issued. "But even now," I said, "virtually everyone who wants to leave the Soviet Union may do so. In the previous year 106,000 persons left the USSR to reside permanently abroad. The number of applications turned down was 841, i.e., 0.8 percent of the total." The developments in this area, I concluded, "are clearly gathering momentum."[17]

It was, of course, Gorbachev who had presided over the transformation in our emigration policy, but Gorbachev himself had also undergone a transformation of sorts in his approach to the subject. When in spring 1985 he met George H. W. Bush, then U.S. vice president, who had come to Russia to attend Chernenko's funeral, Gorbachev asked him not to interfere in our internal affairs using the human rights pretext. Four-and-a-half years later, during their presidential rendezvous in Malta, having received from Bush a customary list of about twenty people who wanted to leave the Soviet Union,

---

16. Gorbachev Foundation, V Politburo CK KPSS, 219–220.

17. Years later I found confirmation of these words in a book by the U.S. ambassador to Moscow at the time, Jack Matlock. While describing how the respective law still had not been adopted, he adds, "In practice hardly anybody was barred from leaving the country if he or she desired." Jack Matlock, *Autopsy on an Empire* (New York: Random House, 1995), 524.

Gorbachev said, "Let us know how many immigrants you want, and we'll send them to you."[18]

The law regulating emigration was finally adopted by the Supreme Soviet on May 20, 1991, six months before the Soviet Union ceased to exist. It is some consolation to note that our work turned out to have an enduring impact: The Russian Federation's law on emigration, in place since July 18, 1996, complies with international norms and is very close to the Soviet original. It is easier for Russian citizens these days to leave their country than to obtain even temporary—not to mention permanent—permission to enter the vast majority of Western states. This, at any rate, is the opinion expressed to me by Vladimir Lukin, the human rights commissioner of the Russian Federation, who is, incidentally, a former ambassador to the United States.

It is gratifying to think that our work not only served our country but was appreciated by those Soviet citizens who chose to leave. If I may be permitted a personal reminiscence: In 1994, when I served as the Russian ambassador to the Court of Saint James, I received a letter that enclosed a paid membership to one of the elite clubs that help make London glorious. The dispatch read more or less as follows: "You and I have never met; I am the father of one of the persons who for reasons of secrecy had been denied permission to leave the Soviet Union. I know for certain that it is due personally to you that my son could come to Great Britain. Unfortunately, he died soon after arrival. Nevertheless, I keep a grateful memory of you."[19]

And Other Countries?

As I said above, our approach was not to separate Jewish emigration from the general flow of emigrants. I worked hard on the issue of emigrating Soviet Germans. The West Germans, as they were called in the late 1980s, soon asked us not to encourage this kind of emigration, and even to introduce certain quotas. It was "better if we would help them where they live"—which was mostly in Kazakhstan. As in the case of emigration to the United

---

18. When things turned bad for him in 1990, Gorbachev threatened to stop the emigration to Israel, as he was pressed by both the Arab countries and his colleagues in the leadership who claimed that Soviet Jews had been directed to the Gaza Strip and the West Bank, strengthening Israel's potential. Prime Minister Yitzhak Shamir, in a private letter to Gorbachev, affirmed that only a few people from the Soviet Union settled in the occupied territories. See Beschloss and Talbot, *At the Highest Levels*, 225–226.

19. I would mention also that in Washington in October 2006, I received a similar message from Professor Solomon Alber, to which he attached a copy of my letter to his father dated December 1986, with an invitation to see me at the Ministry of Foreign Affairs. Soon after our talk, he finished his period of being a refusenik—which lasted thirteen years—and he left, with his family, for the United States.

States, we used a dialogue between governments to make the lives of people who had left the Soviet Union easier.

The nation that was particularly active in regard to emigration and human rights issues generally—even if those issues did not affect its own nationals—was The Netherlands. Jokingly, its diplomats would attribute this interest to the "recognized fact" that the Dutch, for various reasons, were the closest to God. Ultimately, I was happy with such assertiveness because it helped us protect ourselves from the reproaches of the defenders of Soviet orthodoxy, who accused us of making concessions exclusively to the Americans. No, we would reply: "Here are the lists of refuseniks brought by the Dutch; we will consider them as well."

I remember one meeting with the Dutch ambassador to Moscow, Peter Kuvalda. I tried to convince him that what we were doing for them we were really doing for our own interests and priorities. "Our answers to you are secondary to our own reforms," I said. "But we are ready for an open and constructive dialogue. So, if you are interested in the situation of some individuals in the Soviet Union, we may put a couple of questions to you, about racial discrimination against foreign workers, for example." The ambassador agreed, saying, "Nobody is perfect."

"Everybody Must Face the Law Like Facing God"

The battle over emigration, and especially the struggle to enshrine rights to and restrictions on emigration in the law, was part and parcel of the wider war for perestroika. With the hindsight of two decades, it is abundantly clear that Gorbachev strove to transform the Soviet Union into a modern and genuinely great power in all respects, to overcome a gap that divided us from the most economically and politically developed nations, to make our country able to enter the twenty-first century with dignity, to make ours a country of laws—to change the very course of Russian history. So ambitious a goal would obviously take a long time to achieve; sadly, time ran out too quickly.

People, Gorbachev stressed throughout the perestroika years, have to learn to respect themselves and their inalienable rights. A cherished and unceasing aspiration of Gorbachev's was to create, for the first time in our history, a state of law: to impose a new character of relations between the state and its citizens, between the party and the citizen, and to protect people with laws. These ideas permeated all his statements, both public and internal, and his talks with aides and supporters. They were also present in instructions given to officials.

In June 1986, as he was instructing his staffers to draft a speech for a trip to Vladivostok, Gorbachev emphasized:

> Now the most important thing is to develop activities based on the law, which is the same for everybody.... There cannot be double standards, that the law is for the masses, whereas the "leaders" would be free from any laws whatsoever.... Everybody must face the law like facing God. ... For we've got the biggest neglect of law in the Party committees, in the obkoms [regional party offices].[20]

It was an immensely challenging task for at least four reasons. First, the country was covered with the birthmarks and scars of the tsarist and the Stalinist regimes, which were hard to eliminate. Second, the larger public was not accustomed to the rule of law and was skeptical that it could prevail in Russia. As a Russian proverb says: "Law is like a harness—where you turn it, there it goes." Third, the bureaucracy, and most important, that of the party, quickly grasped that Gorbachev's project threatened its power. Fourth, almost every sector of the law would have to be rewritten. Add the extreme backwardness of our legal scholarship, the scarcity of defense lawyers—in 1988 there were only 25,000, as many as there had been in Russia before 1917, while the total number of lawyers was merely 200,000—and an archaic court system, and the picture became bleaker still.

Despite the scale of the challenge, a resolute offensive, in perestroika style, was launched. The campaign started with a program of comprehensive judicial reform, along with a revision of the labor and the penal codes. Gorbachev's go-ahead was as follows:

> Here enormous work should be done; all the offices and cadres in this system should be affixed to a solid legal base. A secure mechanism defending the interests of citizens, organizations, and the collective must be created. Nobody has the right to interfere in judicial or prosecutorial activity. For the time being the Party offices are not restricted by any law. It should be done in such a way that all society, all citizens, would know that they may trust the legality provided by the courts. Their role and their authority should be raised.
>
> Nobody is permitted to command the courts, or to interfere with the work of law agencies.[21]

Already by 1988, the chairman of the Supreme Court of the Soviet Union, Vladimir Terebilov, affirmed that we were close to making the courts genuinely independent and that the presumption of innocence, almost forgotten in legal practice, had begun to reemerge.[22]

---

20. Gorbachev Foundation, V Politburo CK KPSS, 71, 83, 318.

21. I found these directives as well as the figures in Anatoly Cherniaev's archive in the Gorbachev Foundation.

22. See his article in Perestroika i prava cheloveka [Perestroika and human rights], a supplement to the magazine *Novoe Vremia* (December 1988).

It was Gorbachev who insisted on ending the Communist Party's interference in court decisions. In many memos sent to the Central Committee by the security agencies before the Gorbachev period, sentences that the courts were supposedly yet to decide were presented as predetermined or already issued. Gorbachev ended this practice. The so-called telephone law, by which a court and a prosecutor could have a person condemned by orders of a party boss, ceased to exist. Unfortunately, however, it reappeared later.

There was a need to uproot the consequences of the legal reforms implemented by Stalin and Andrei Vyshinsky in the 1930s. In the system they fashioned, the prosecutor became the central figure in the judicial process, a situation that permitted arbitrariness and facilitated the repressions of the next twenty years. Pretrial incarceration, for instance, was legally allowed for up to nine months, a very long term in itself; in reality, it sometimes lasted for twelve, twenty-four, or even thirty-six months. In the summer of 1987, the Politburo decided that the 25,000 prosecutors should be completely independent from party offices and that courts should be independent from prosecutors.[23]

Another subject of active discussion was the death penalty. Dissidents such as Andrei Sakharov were definitely against it, but even Sakharov admitted that the public as a whole supported this highest measure of punishment. He appealed to the authorities to take the lead in influencing and educating public opinion. It wasn't easy: The death penalty had been abrogated twice in our country, in 1920 by Lenin and in 1947 by Stalin. Very quickly in both cases, the abrogation of the abrogation followed. Gorbachev requested that we place our provisions regarding the death penalty into compliance with international law and reconsider in this context such terms as "treason of the Motherland."[24]

A New Docket

As early as November 19, 1986, I wrote in my diary: "We have seriously taken on human rights matters, and not only emigration issues. A lot of this docket is being put on my shoulders; sometimes I feel like my head is used by Kovalev and Shevardnadze as a ram to break the walls."

Coming back once from a Politburo meeting, Shevardnadze summoned me and suggested that I get engaged in questions of internal policy, probably because the humanitarian department was closer than the Ministry of Foreign Affairs's other departments to these questions. As a member of the highest ruling body, our minister had to deal with all the problems raised there, and not only international ones. And, he insisted, "don't be afraid of

---

23. Cherniaev's archive in the Gorbachev Foundation.
24. Gorbachev Foundation, V Politburo CK KPSS, 286.

damaging our relations with other players"—the KGB, the Central Committee, and so forth. Three topics were the most important: the arms race, Afghanistan, and human rights.

In April 1987, my duties were expanded in the Soviet-U.S. humanitarian dialogue. A formal structure for it was the so-called working group, a novelty that Shevardnadze introduced as a venue for preparing for various discussions with the U.S. secretary of state. The working group on human rights was set up to fulfill a pledge given by Gorbachev to Reagan in November 1985 in Geneva.

I was not overly enthusiastic about chairing this group from the Soviet side. My main job as deputy foreign minister was settling the armed conflicts in Africa, primarily in Angola, which after Afghanistan was the regional conflict that imposed the heaviest burden on my country. In addition to creating competing demands on my attention, this new job promised to be rather uncongenial. The humanitarian script was already well-known: The Americans usually presented their requests to our ministry, while we, even considering many of them fair, had difficulty obtaining positive answers from our domestic agencies. Those matters were the responsibility of domestic agencies, but the agencies would forward their answers—often unpalatable ones—to us to deliver to foreign representatives. In short, to be involved in human rights issues meant, almost automatically, to be involved in constant disputes with other Soviet government agencies, with little capability to influence them.

Our Americanists, a privileged tribe in the ministry, rarely opened their circle to newcomers. I had seldom dealt with Americans. When some of my colleagues had debated human rights in the past, mostly to counter the Americans at the United Nations or at CSCE meetings, I had not been among them. But if Shevardnadze decided to add a new subject to my portfolio, I obviously couldn't say no.

In the early stages, we approached the dialogue with considerable caution and, most important, uncertainty as to whether dialogue would actually serve our interests. In part because of this attitude, Dick's and my first meeting was, as Dick himself says, not a big deal. I wondered whether the mild manners and quiet voice of my new acquaintance were designed to lull me or if we could find a common language. There was one thing I did notice immediately that gave me hope: The Americans wanted to address troublesome aspects of our system, aspects that I wasn't happy with either, but the American requests did not touch the crucial, fundamental problems of our internal development. So, I thought to myself, it might be possible to push the issues posed to us in the new dialogue through the tight defenses of our conservatives, and to do so in a way that would help the cause of perestroika.

Richard Schifter

Human Rights Advocacy in International Fora

U.S-Soviet relations were an important issue in the American presidential election campaign of 1980. Candidate Reagan expressed the concern that many voters felt about the Soviet Union's aggressive posture in international affairs. Further, there was increasing publicity in the United States about human rights deprivations in the Soviet Union, and there were those who thought there was a close link between the Soviet Union's antagonistic behavior toward the West and the repression of its own people. President Carter had expressed similar concerns, particularly in the second half of his term, but Reagan suggested he would take a harder line, particularly in the buildup of American military strength, which, he said, would cause the Soviet Union to seek an understanding with the United States.

As noted earlier, Reagan brought to his candidacy and ultimately to the presidency a unique experience. As president of the Screen Actors Guild, he had been deeply involved in the struggle within the guild between anti-Communist liberal Democrats and Communist Party members and their followers. He thus was the only president who had ever had a direct confrontation with members of the Communist Party of the United States. It was this understanding of the expressions and tactics of the American Communists whom he had known that caused him to conclude in the summer of 1988 that Gorbachev no longer belonged in that political category.

But when Reagan was sworn in as president of the United States in January 1981, Gorbachev was a little-known junior member of the Politburo of the Soviet Communist Party. The country's leader for more than sixteen years had been Leonid Brezhnev. It was during his incumbency that U.S.-Soviet relations had first improved and then sharply deteriorated; also, repression of dissidents, which had declined under Khrushchev, had once again sharply increased. The new administration was strongly committed to drawing attention to Soviet human rights violations. It was a bipartisan issue, as Congress, with its Helsinki Commission[1] out in front, held to the same view.

The issue of human rights and particularly of Soviet human rights violations was, therefore, very much on the United States agenda when, late in January 1981, I started my diplomatic career as a member of the U.S. delegation to the UN Human Rights Commission. The commission had a full

---

1. The Commission on Security and Cooperation in Europe, established by the U.S. Congress to monitor compliance with the Helsinki Final Act and other OSCE commitments.

agenda, consisting of significant as well as insignificant issues. I soon discovered that almost every issue was affected by the confrontation between the Soviet Union and the United States. My impression was that, as in so many other United Nations fora, the Soviet Union sought to use the commission as another theater in which to conduct the Cold War. It was not that the Soviet Union initiated attacks against U.S. behavior in the field of human rights—although it did just that in response to attacks by the United States against Soviet human rights violations—but that a great variety of issues were placed on the agenda and positions were taken by the Soviet delegation largely to embarrass the United States.

A few months prior to the 1981 session of the UN Human Rights Commission, another international meeting dealing with human rights issues had gotten under way: the Second Follow-Up Meeting under the Helsinki Final Act, which was held in Madrid. By sheer coincidence, the U.S. delegation to that meeting was led by my close friend and law partner, Max Kampelman.

The Madrid meeting, which commenced in November 1980, remained in session for more than two-and-a-half years, while the UN Human Rights Commission met only six weeks of every year in Geneva. While Max and I delivered our speeches on Soviet human rights violations in Madrid and Geneva, not respectively, human rights conditions in the Soviet Union got worse. Yuri Andropov, head of the KGB and, after Brezhnev's death in 1982, general secretary of the Central Committee of the Communist Party and thus the Soviet Union's de facto head of government, had clamped down hard. The number of political arrests, which averaged 89 annually in the period 1975–78, shot up to 238 annually in the period 1980–82. Jewish emigration, which had peaked at 51,320 in 1979, dropped to 1,315 in 1983.[2] There continued to be reports of truly gross abuses of psychiatry.[3]

Anatoly has pointed out that on the Soviet side, the point had been made that we in the West were focused only on political and civil rights, while we failed to respect what in the Soviet Union were deemed the more important rights, namely social and economic rights. It is with regard to these rights that Soviet officials believed that the Soviet Union performed far better than the West, particularly the United States.

As we saw the issue, the concept of human rights as developed in the Enlightenment was built on the precepts that, first, to be able to exercise legitimate authority, a government must have been established by the consent of the governed, and second, individuals have rights of which they may not be deprived, even by a government that has been established with the

---

2. Korey, *The Promises We Keep*, 117

3. Sidney Bloch and Peter Reddaway, *Soviet Psychiatric Abuse* (Boulder, CO: Westview Press, 1984).

consent of the people. In the United States, these rights were enshrined in the Bill of Rights, the first article of which states the essence of the human rights concept: "Congress shall make no law respecting an establishment of religion, or prohibiting the free exercise thereof; or abridging the freedom of speech or of the press; or the right of the people peaceably to assemble, and to petition the Government for a redress of grievances."

The economic, social, and cultural rights to which Anatoly refers are a concept of recent origin. These "rights"—in quotation marks—appear to have evolved in 1947-48 in the context of the negotiation of the text of the Universal Declaration of Human Rights. They include the rights to social security (Article 22); to work; to free choice of employment; to just and favorable conditions of work and protection against unemployment; to equal pay for equal work; to just and favorable remuneration; to form and join trade unions (Article 23); to reasonable limitation of working hours (Article 24); to a standard of living adequate for health and well-being including food, clothing, housing, and medical care and necessary social services (Article 25); to free education, at least in the elementary stages (Article 26); and to participate in the cultural life of the community (Article 27).

There are fundamental differences between the traditional concept of civil and political rights and the recently developed notion of social, economic, and cultural rights. The former are limitations on government, which in democratic countries can be enforced by challenging the constitutionality of a law or of executive action in the courts. The latter are calls upon governments for affirmative action to ensure the enjoyment of these rights, which in democratic countries can be realized by the election to public office of candidates committed to programs that would provide these benefits.

The drafting of the Universal Declaration of Human Rights began after the creation of the UN Commission on Human Rights in 1946. The commission was chaired by the head of the U.S. delegation, Eleanor Roosevelt. It is my understanding that the Soviet delegation insisted on the inclusion of economic rights in the declaration. Mrs. Roosevelt and her American advisers, many of them veterans of the New Deal administration, saw no particular problem in including principles of government policy that had been essential elements of legislation espoused by the Roosevelt and Truman administrations. The wording of the economic rights articles of the declaration closely resembles wording used in the statements of political principles of the New Deal.

The fact that in spelling out rights, there is a need to distinguish between limitations on government and what some would view as the affirmative obligations of government seems to have been overlooked by the drafters of the Universal Declaration, with the result that both types of rights are now set forth in that text. Anatoly is right in noting that the Soviet Union adopted policies that avoided unemployment and that provided health care for all. But when we argued the issue in the UN Commission on Human Rights in the early 1980s, we pointed to the fact that the Soviet Union had violated many of the economic rights, such as the right to form trade unions (which was a government monopoly) or the right to free choice of employment. At one point I took the floor of the commission to make the point that the collective farm system deprived Soviet citizens of the right to adequate food supplies. I told the story, well-known in the Soviet Union, of collective farmers working in the fields of collective farms at a leisurely pace all day, returning home in the early evening, and then rushing to their small private plots to work hard for the next few hours to maximize their own crops.

These digressions were minor episodes in the work of the U.S. delegation to the commission. Our principal activity was to engage in the effort initiated by Justice Goldberg in Belgrade, that of using international fora to expose Soviet human rights abuse. We had no indication that what we were saying would bring about change in the Soviet Union in the near future. We hoped it would register above all with West Europeans and, although their influence was limited, with East European diplomats at our meetings. Most important, we thought that our messages would, through radio news reports, provide hope for the courageous dissidents in the Soviet Union so that they would know that they had not been forgotten.

Evidence of our influence on East European diplomats came to me in 1990, after the collapse of Leninism. On a visit to Sofia, which had just shaken off its Stalinist dictatorship, I was told by a Bulgarian diplomat: "In Madrid we were listening to what your people were saying and we recognized that you were right. We also saw that the speech texts that were sent to us from Sofia to deliver in Madrid were full of lies." Later that year a Soviet diplomat with whom I had sparred in Geneva asked me: "You knew all along that I did not believe a word I was saying. Didn't you?"

The answer to that question was that we were not sure. What we most certainly did not anticipate, but what appears to have happened, is that our statements at international meetings registered with the men who took over the leadership of the Soviet Union in 1985.

Shultz's Commitment to the Human Rights Cause

But before then, a highly important personnel change had taken place in the United States. In July 1982, George Shultz became secretary of state. His tenure in the secretary's office was characterized by an active interest in the field of human rights. In September he had his first meeting with Soviet

Foreign Minister Andrei Gromyko. In his memoirs, he offers the following deeply moving account of his personal outlook:

> As an important part of my preparation for the Gromyko meetings, I focused on human rights practices in the Soviet Union. I assembled lists of people who had been denied permission to emigrate, reviewed the special problems of Soviet Jewry, and expanded my knowledge of the full range of our human rights concerns. I met with Avital Shcharansky, the intense and compelling wife of the famous dissident. Afterward, I was wrung out. The woeful treatment of her husband, his courage, and my inability to provide any real assurance about his release made for immense frustration. Avital's pleas dramatized the human side of the tension in U.S.-Soviet relations. "The president and I will never give up on pressing the cause of human rights and the case for your husband's release," I told her.[4]

In his meeting with Gromyko, Shultz indeed paid "particular attention to the human rights area: problems faced by Jews, dissidents, and families divided by Soviet refusal to allow emigration, as well as the persecution of people monitoring Soviet compliance with their obligations under the Helsinki Final Act. Gromyko's answer was: 'Is it so important that Mr. or Mrs. or Miss So-and-So can or cannot leave such and such a country? . . . I would call it a tenth-rate question.'"[5] A few months later, when Shultz was in Moscow following the death of Brezhnev, he had his first meeting with the new general secretary, Yuri Andropov. In a brief exchange of views, "Andropov made clear that no one should tell the Soviets how to run their internal affairs."[6]

But that did not prevent the U.S. president from pursuing the human rights agenda. Secretary Shultz writes about a very informal meeting between President Reagan and the Soviet ambassador to the United States, Anatoly Dobrynin, in February 1983. After discussing arms control, Afghanistan, and Poland, Shultz says, Reagan "spoke with genuine feeling and eloquence on the subject of human rights, divided families, Soviet Jewry, and refuseniks. He also talked with sincere intensity about the Pentecostals, a small group of Christians who had taken refuge in our embassy in Moscow almost five years earlier." Shultz then quotes Reagan's statement to Dobrynin: "If you can do something about the Pentecostals or another human rights issue, we will simply be delighted and will not embarrass you by undue publicity, by claims of credit for ourselves, or by 'crowing.'"[7]

---

4. George P. Shultz, *Turmoil and Triumph* (New York: Charles Scribner's Sons, 1993), 121.
5. Ibid., 122.
6. Ibid., 126.
7. Ibid., 165.

It was this concluding statement that produced amazing results. After intensive negotiations that involved discussions by the head of the U.S. delegation to the Madrid CSCE meeting, Max Kampelman, with a member of the Soviet delegation to that meeting who was a high-ranking KGB officer, the Siberian Seven were allowed to leave the Soviet Union. In that process, a precedent was set for allowing Pentecostal Christians, most of whom were ethnic Russians, to leave the Soviet Union: They would get Israeli visas and ostensibly travel to Israel. Because there were no direct flights from Moscow to Israel, they would fly initially to Italy. Once they arrived there, they did not proceed to Israel, but to the United States. As President Reagan had promised, the United States did not crow over this concession.

The Pentecostal case was the first Soviet human rights case to be resolved during the Reagan administration, and it was done through the president's personal intervention. If the Soviet leadership wanted to send a signal that it wished to have better relations with the United States, it had succeeded. As Secretary Shultz put it, "This success, unnoticed because of its terms, encouraged President Reagan and me to continue to pursue our efforts to turn the superpower relationship into something far more positive."[8]

This did not turn out to be a very easy task. In January 1984, Shultz met with Gromyko in Stockholm. The major topic was once again arms reduction, but as he had done before, Shultz started with a discussion of human rights. Gromyko's response was once again very sharp. Shultz's position, he said, was "entirely pervaded by falsehood." He went on to say that "nowhere else are human rights violated as in some of the places in the Western Hemisphere that are so dear to U.S. hearts, not to mention in the United States itself."[9]

As it was, it took quite a while and a number of additional changes in the Soviet leadership before it was possible to move forward with further constructive discussions between the United States and the Soviet Union, whether in the human rights field or in the area of arms limitation, the latter being the most profound subject on the bilateral agenda.

Representing the United States at the UN Human Rights Commission, I joined my colleagues year after year in 1983, 1984, and 1985 to rise in memory of the most recently deceased general secretary of the Central Committee of the Communist Party of the Soviet Union—respectively, Brezhnev, Andropov, and Chernenko. And year after year I would deliver, on behalf of the United States, the same complaints about Soviet violations of human rights. In 1985, I made a point of spelling out our reason for this annual speechmaking ritual:

---

8. Ibid., 171.
9. Ibid., 469.

> Those who hear our presentations or might read reports thereof might ask themselves what these exchanges of words seek to accomplish, what good they will really do. It is a good question. Let me seek to answer it from our point of view.
>
> Our purpose . . . is to advance the cause of human rights throughout the world. In the case of the United Nations Human Rights Commission and the procedures which have evolved over the years, we are dealing, speaking from a historical perspective, with a relatively young institution, with a relatively recent history. The notion that governments may comment on the manner in which governments of other countries deal with their own citizens is fairly new. What we hope is that through such comments, through such discussions, governments can be made aware of the fact that the rest of the world takes notice of the human rights violations they are committing and disapproves of them. But for the entire process to work, to be taken seriously, there is need for a high standard of intellectual honesty to be applied, a sense of fairness, of objectivity, and a commitment by those who make presentations to the notion that the facts should speak for themselves, with a minimum of hyperbole and emendations.

These remarks were delivered on March 11, 1985. On that very day the Politburo of the Communist Party of the Soviet Union had elected Mikhail Sergeyevich Gorbachev as the party's general secretary.[10] Vice President Bush and Secretary of State Shultz went to Moscow to attend Chernenko's funeral but stayed on for an extended meeting with the new leader.

U.S. Officials' Initial Impressions of Gorbachev

Secretary Shultz writes in his memoirs about his impressions of Gorbachev at this first meeting. He noted that Gorbachev emphasized "that there will be continuity in both the domestic and foreign policy of the USSR," and concluded that while Gorbachev "displayed a breadth of view and vigor . . . his basic positions were ones we had heard before." On the issue of human rights, Gorbachev had this to say: "The Soviets respect your right to run your country the way you see fit. In the same way, it is up to the Soviet people to make such decisions on behalf of the USSR, and the USSR will never permit anyone to teach it how to govern itself."

When it was Vice President Bush's turn, he responded to these remarks: "We have no aspirations of dictating how to administer the Soviet Union. This is the farthest thing from our thoughts." Having made the point that the United States had no intention of changing the basic nature of the Soviet

---

10. A few days after Gorbachev's accession, with the UN Human Rights Commission still in session, I attended a reception at which I asked one of my Soviet colleagues what he knew about the new general secretary. His answer was: "He is a nice guy." He then grinned and added: "I read it in the *Herald Tribune*."

system, the vice president went on to say that issues such as denial of Jewish emigration and the treatment of dissidents were issues that the United States wanted to discuss, consistent with the spirit of the Helsinki Accords. At that point, Gorbachev became quite agitated and accused the United States of "brutally" repressing human rights. He called for the appointment of rapporteurs to investigate human rights violations in the United States. In spite of this sharp exchange on the subject of human rights, Secretary Shultz came away from the meeting "genuinely impressed with the quality of thought, the intensity, and the intellectual energy of this new man on the scene."[11]

A few months later I represented the United States at the CSCE Human Rights Experts Meeting in Ottawa. The head of the Hungarian delegation took me aside to assure me that a new day was dawning. There was a new spirit in the hall, he told me: the spirit of Gorbachev. I failed to notice that new spirit in the behavior of the Soviet delegation. Not at all anticipating the changes that were in the offing in the Soviet Union in the years immediately ahead, I went out of my way to explain, as the vice president had done in Moscow, that the U.S. position was not to effect fundamental changes in the Soviet system of governance, but to persuade the Soviet Union to end oppressive measures that directly affected the lives of individual citizens:

> The U.S. delegation, in selecting issues for discussion at this conference, decided deliberately to limit itself to problems which, though of great concern to the American public, would not require systemic changes in the Soviet Union to effect correction. Every one of the problems we have raised so far about conditions in countries which describe themselves as Marxist-Leninist could be eliminated while staying within the system.
>
> It so happens, therefore, that the Soviet human rights problems of greatest concern to the American public are the problems which could be most easily solved by the Soviet Union. They concern, as we have pointed out, the incarceration of persons guilty only of giving expression to their thoughts, the persecution of religious believers, the commitment of sane persons to institutions for the mentally ill, cultural repression, and discrimination against certain people on the grounds of ancestry. The Soviet State could, as I have said, correct these problems without effecting fundamental structural change.

Later that year, in November, Reagan had his first meeting with Gorbachev. It took place in Geneva. In the course of the meeting, Gorbachev invited Reagan for a private session of the two of them and their interpreters. As Secretary Shultz reports in his memoirs, President Reagan "had decided to use the opportunity to take up human rights issues again." Shultz then describes the outcome of that discussion:

---

11. Shultz, *Turmoil and Triumph*, 529–532.

> When the two leaders emerged, they were not smiling. The atmosphere had been highly charged. The president told me that after he made his points, Gorbachev attacked human rights practices in the United States, citing discrimination against blacks and women and unemployment figures, which he contrasted with full employment in the Soviet Union. The president had argued back. The exchange had been intense.[12]

Gorbachev appears to confirm this account in his memoirs:

> Reagan began by saying that if the Soviet Union intended to improve its relations with the United States, it would do well to change its reputation with respect to individual freedom. He argued that the American public was very sensitive about this issue and that therefore no American politician could ignore it. I said that I did not think the United States had a right to impose their standards and way of life upon other countries.[13]

Before the Geneva meeting concluded, an effort was undertaken to formulate a statement that would outline the points on which agreement had been reached. Such a statement was produced after some difficult negotiations, in which the U.S. delegation was led by Assistant Secretary of State Roz Ridgway, who headed the Bureau of European Affairs (EUR). In addition to arms control, air services, people-to-people contacts, and other similar matters, the statement included the following sentence. "They [Reagan and Gorbachev] agreed on the importance of resolving humanitarian cases in the spirit of cooperation."[14] That sentence, it was believed by some at the time, constituted a major breakthrough. I was skeptical.

With the president, vice president, and secretary of state fully engaged in the issue of human rights performance in the Soviet Union—albeit performance limited to the issues of immigration and the treatment of dissidents—there was no doubt any longer as to where the executive branch of the U.S. government stood. The administration and Congress were now of one mind on this subject, calling for specific action by the Soviet Union.

Taking Charge of the State Department's Bureau of Human Rights

Having been engaged in the Soviet human rights issue in the context of multilateral diplomacy, delivering speeches that criticized Soviet actions in broad terms, my appointment as assistant secretary of state for human rights in the autumn of 1985 caused me to face new challenges. I did not see my job as merely

---

12. Ibid., 602–603.
13. Mikhail Gorbachev, *Memoirs* (New York: Doubleday, 1996), 408.
14. Shultz, *Turmoil and Triumph*, 606.

issuing statements criticizing the Soviet Union. As I saw it, my task was to determine precisely what my office could do to attain concrete results in specific cases and then take the steps necessary to attain these results in terms of people released from unjust confinements or denied exit permits in violation of the principles set forth in the Universal Declaration of Human Rights.

In his memoirs, Secretary Shultz spells out the broad challenge that he felt we faced at that time: "Gorbachev was proving to be a skillful and adroit tactician in the politics of the Politburo and was now solidly entrenched.... What would cause him to alter course, I felt, would be a combination of U.S. determination and strength combined with persuasive arguments that the Soviet Union would benefit from a different approach to its own people and to foreign affairs."[15]

Although Secretary Shultz had never taken me aside to spell out this point in the words he used in his memoirs, I certainly understood that to be the U.S. policy relevant to the work of my bureau and was prepared to act in conformity with it. Before long, however, I ran into a serious but unexpected problem—not with the Soviet Union, but within the State Department bureaucracy. Specifically, I encountered difficulties with EUR and its Soviet desk. After all, the officers in EUR thought, it was their assistant secretary who had negotiated the sentence in the Geneva agreed statement that referred to the resolution of humanitarian cases and it was their bureau that should be engaged in detailed work on Soviet human rights issues.

In retrospect, I find EUR's position perfectly understandable. Like every other regional bureau of the State Department, EUR viewed itself as responsible for the management of bilateral relations between the United States and the countries within the area of its jurisdiction. It did not want any bureaucratic interlopers.

On the other hand, while I recognized the role of the regional bureaus generally, I saw a difference regarding the Soviet Union that my colleagues in EUR were not prepared to recognize: I believed that the issue of the relationship between the United States and the Soviet Union was the most important foreign policy issue on the United States agenda and that in our relations with the Soviet Union, the human rights issue ranked very high. As distinct from our human rights concerns regarding military dictatorships, the Soviet human rights issue was central to the international conflict between communist totalitarianism and democracy. This was an area in which I believed the Human Rights Bureau (HA) could make a contribution not only to the formulation but also to the execution of bilateral policy. I emphasized that if EUR were to handle the human rights negotiations with the Soviet Union, neither the EUR assistant secretary nor a deputy assistant secretary—nor an

---

15. Ibid., 702.

office director—would be able to give the matter concentrated attention. The task would fall to a junior officer, with the result that the Soviet Union would assign a junior officer to serve as a counterpart, quite a number of bureaucratic steps removed from the foreign minister. If, on the other hand, an assistant secretary took responsibility for the human rights negotiations with the Soviet Union, I argued, the Soviet side would choose a counterpart of much higher rank and thus much closer to the foreign minister. At the time I made this argument, I did not realize that I was, in effect, seeking to draw Anatoly into human rights work, but that is what I ultimately, unknowingly, did.[16]

The fact that EUR and HA were debating their respective roles in dealing with Soviet human rights issues did not prevent the U.S. government from pursuing these issues in the context of the Geneva agreed statement. In February 1986, Anatoly Shcharansky was released from prison and was allowed to leave the country, but only in the context of an exchange in which the United States released a number of Soviet citizens who had been convicted of spying.

Aside from the Soviet willingness to exchange an imprisoned human rights advocate for Soviet spies, we failed to note any change in Soviet human rights performance. In the summer of 1986, I received a visit from a Soviet foreign ministry official, Yuri Kashlev, who told me that a new emigration law was about to be promulgated, but that was all.

During 1986, much of the time and effort that both sides devoted to the U.S.-Soviet relationship focused on arms reduction. Another summit meeting devoted entirely to that issue took place in Reykjavik in October, bringing both sides somewhat closer, but not close enough to reach agreement. Earlier, in August, another flare-up had received a great deal of attention in the United States: the arrest by the Soviets of Nicholas Daniloff, the Moscow correspondent of *U.S. News & World Report*, on a charge of spying, a case that was resolved through difficult negotiations.

In the autumn of 1986, as plans for the next follow-up meeting under the Helsinki Final Act, which was to be held in Vienna, were under way, I participated in a session at the National Security Council at which we sought to reach agreement on U.S. policy at the forthcoming Vienna meeting. In light of the months that had passed since the Geneva summit without any indication of change in Soviet policy on human rights, I held out at that meeting for our taking a hard line with the Soviets in Vienna. EUR differed. I was later told that, following that meeting, the EUR deputy assistant secretary

---

16. The controversy between the EUR and HA ended in the middle of 1986 when an EUR foreign service officer who specialized in Soviet affairs notified me that EUR had agreed to work cooperatively with HA.

responsible for Soviet affairs had said: "The problem with Schifter is that he is a Menshevik ideologue and he hates the Bolsheviks."

The difference in outlook between EUR and HA caused me to send a memorandum to Secretary Shultz on November 6, 1986, which stated in its summary:[17]

> We have been clear and unequivocal in expressing our dismay at the manner in which the Soviet government deals with its own people. We tell the Soviets that their behavior with regard to human rights will prevent us from developing satisfactory relations with them. Your recent speech in Los Angeles made that point most forcefully.
>
> But I am concerned that we do not follow through as effectively as we can. I have the greatest admiration for you and the President's sincerity and deep commitment to the cause of human rights. I have also no doubt that all other U.S. Government officials involved in dealings with the Soviet Union on human rights matters are committed to that cause. My concern relates to our tactics. With your recent speech we have clearly ended our period of quiet diplomacy at the Secretarial level, but we have not decided what adverse consequences continued unacceptable behavior by the Soviet Union might have. In fact, we have conveyed the impression to the Soviets that there would not be any adverse consequences as far as the Executive Branch is concerned.

Later that month, I reported to Secretary Shultz on the new Soviet emigration law, the one heralded by Yuri Kashlev during his visit to me the preceding summer. It allowed some emigration, but also codified some severe restrictions on the right to leave the country. As I wrote in my memorandum to the secretary, "it would . . . appear that for the time being this is the definitive answer to our appeals for freer emigration from the Soviet Union. It's 'nyet' on the basic question with a 'da' for a relatively small subgroup."[18] It was estimated that the da would benefit between 30,000 and 40,000 prospective emigrants.

Regarding Gorbachev's announced policy of glasnost, I wrote to the secretary on November 26:

> The developments under Gorbachev which have left some observers with the impression that there is a new "openness" consisting of the following: (a) freedom of expression for the purpose of exposing corruption and inefficiency; (b) adherence by government officials to rules and regulations instead of the exercise of bureaucratic arbitrariness; (c) the exercise of repression only if it serves the purposes of the state; (d) the use of public relations tricks of greater openness where none exists.

---

17. Memorandum from Schifter to secretary, "Our Soviet Human Rights Policy," November 6, 1986, 1. Like other State Department memoranda cited in this volume, this document was obtained by the author under the Freedom of Information Act.

18. Memorandum from Schifter to secretary, "The USSR's Answer on the Emigration Question," November 14, 1986, 2.

I concluded:

> The foregoing is to emphasize that no meaningful improvements in the Soviet Union's human rights performance are now in evidence. That does not mean that meaningful improvements could not occur if we keep pressing for them. But it does suggest that no such improvements will take place if we are prepared to characterize these make-believe or token steps as the real thing.[19]

On December 19, I circulated a memorandum among colleagues for submission to Secretary Shultz in which I wrote:

> At the Geneva Summit we assumed that the Soviets were prepared to improve their human-rights performance significantly and that, hand-in-hand with these improvements, we would warm our commercial and exchange relations with them. . . . [T]heir human-rights performance has not improved; but driven by our post-Geneva momentum, we have moved vigorously ahead with efforts to increase substantially our commercial contacts and exchange programs. We have also tended to go out of our way to commend the Soviets for what we deem positive developments in the human rights field. . . .
>
> The Soviet Union's failure to perform in line with our hopes and expectations has created a significant imbalance in our bilateral relations. Continued failure on our part to relate our human-rights concerns to concrete measures, combined with continued expressions of appreciation for the few acts of Soviet "kindness," will cause the Soviets to conclude that our statements of concern are largely for public consumption. They will further conclude that these statements are either not sincerely meant or, if they are, that we are satisfied with the small steps they have taken.

I concluded with a checklist against which Soviet performance should be measured:

> (a) the release from mental institutions of persons committed for their political or religious beliefs and an end to this abuse of psychiatry;
> (b) the release from imprisonment or internal exile of the Helsinki monitors and a clear indication that Helsinki monitors shall be allowed to function;
> (c) the release from prison or internal exile of persons punished for unapproved religious activity and change in the laws and practices to permit freedom of religion;
> (d) the release from imprisonment or internal exile of persons punished for the mere expression of dissenting views and, at a minimum, less severe enforcement of the provisions of the criminal code dealing with anti-Soviet activities and defamation of the Soviet Union;
> (e) release from imprisonment or internal exile of persons punished for the teaching of Hebrew and an end to interference with any private teaching of languages;

---

19. Schifter memorandum to the secretary, "Human Rights and Gorbachev's 'Openness,'" November 26, 1986, 2–3.

(f) an end to jamming of foreign broadcasts;
(g) emigration levels of at least 1,000 per month.[20]

On the very same day on which I circulated this memorandum, an event occurred that, in retrospect, heralded a new era. Two workmen had appeared at an apartment in the city of Gorki to install a telephone. Not long after they had completed the task, the telephone rang. As Andrei Sakharov picked up the phone, he heard, at the other end, the voice of the general secretary of the Communist Party of the Soviet Union. He invited Sakharov to return to Moscow. In his memoirs, Gorbachev reveals his train of thought that led to this highly significant decision, a train of thought that reflected his gradual emergence from the totalitarian system that had brought him to the highest office in the land:

> I had, of course, heard about that disgraced scientist, who had been a great patriot in his youth, and then had "slid" into dissidence and anti-Soviet activity. Along with everyone else, I was outraged that he had, as the newspapers reported, advised the Americans not to agree to our proposal to commit themselves to the nonuse of nuclear weapons. Our propaganda machine had described many other such "treacherous" actions to Sakharov by twisting various statements that he had made.
>
> The newspapers were silent on the attempt to take away his title of Academician and his colleagues' opposition to this. People expressed their surprise at the patience shown by the leadership, which tolerated this rebellious academician's "infamous" statements and had exiled him "only" to Gorky (Nizhny Novgorod), instead of forcing him to emigrate. . . .
>
> When I became General Secretary, I considered it an important task to rescue Academician Sakharov from exile. . . .
>
> After Sakharov's return to the capital, the president of the Academy of Sciences, A. Aleksandrov, tried, with my encouragement, not only to create conditions for Sakharov to continue his normal scientific activity, but also to provide him with position in the scientific world that corresponded to his status.[21]

I must confess that I did not recognize at the time the significance of this event. I was convinced that Gorbachev was committed to carrying on the Leninist tradition and that we were treated to a few theatrical performances that appeared to hide this unpleasant truth. In an interview that I gave to Radio Free Europe/Radio Liberty (RFE/RL) shortly after Sakharov's return to Moscow, I offered the following comment:

---

20. Schifter draft memorandum to the secretary, "Recommendations Concerning Our Soviet Human Rights Policy," December 19, 1986, 2, 4.
21. Gorbachev, *Memoirs*, 295–297.

> We have not seen any turn in Soviet policy as yet, any significant turn. If we are going to suggest to the Soviet Union that the relatively minor steps that they have taken so far deserve a great deal of praise, then it may very well be that there is not going to be any further move. . . .
>
> We are now looking for major steps. An excellent touchstone would be the abandonment of the use of psychiatry for political purposes and the release of imprisoned psychiatrist Anatoly Koryagin. It would be symbolically significant for them simply to say that from here on in, we are not going to continue this barbaric practice of committing to mental institutions persons who are perfectly sane.

As I saw it, abuse of psychiatry was the worst feature of Soviet totalitarianism. I used to tell my colleagues that if we kept highlighting it, there might come a day when the members of the Politburo would turn to the head of the KGB and say to him: "Comrade, we know all these reports about abuse of psychiatry are false, capitalist propaganda. But whatever you are doing, please stop it."

Only a few months following my statement to RFE/RL, Dr. Anatoly Koryagin[22] was released from prison and allowed to emigrate. As far as we could tell, from the spring of 1987 onward there were no new commitments to psychiatric institutions as punishment for political dissidence. When I made my pessimistic comments about Soviet human rights conditions at the end of 1986, I certainly did not expect that a new day would dawn within just a few months.

---

22. Koryagin, a psychiatrist who had publicized the Soviet policy that had come to be known as "abuse of psychiatry" had been convicted in 1981 of "anti-Soviet agitation and propaganda" and had been sentenced to twelve years in prison and enforced internal exile.

4

The Human Rights Agenda

Anatoly Adamishin

The Soviet-U.S. humanitarian dialogue initially embraced an agenda which reflected that the United States had proposed the dialogue. Several months after the dialogue began, a new and broader agenda emerged, one that included more spheres of cooperation and was the result of joint Soviet-U.S. efforts. In my part of this chapter, I discuss both the old and the new agendas, but my focus is on the former and more particularly on four of its five major issues: the use of psychiatric confinement to punish political dissidents, political prisoners, prisoners of conscience, and freedom of expression. (The fifth issue was emigration, which I discussed in chapter 3.)

Although the agenda was drawn up mostly by the Americans, I, like other reform-minded officials in the Soviet government, also considered these issues to be matters of serious concern. Convinced that Gorbachev's quiet revolution would transform Soviet society into a modern and democratic one, we regarded international cooperation as a means of furthering our internal reforms by helping to reveal our shortcomings, allowing us to learn from the experiences of other countries. In theory, such possibilities were always present in our minds, but it was only Gorbachev's perestroika that permitted us to realize them in practice. In this way, we were giving our leaders additional ammunition with which to combat the conservative resistance.

Dick's section of this chapter presents the perspective from the other side of the negotiating table. The two of us first sat down to discuss humanitarian issues in April 1987, and over the course of the next twelve months, as Dick describes, our conversation broadened and deepened. More than that, it produced concrete results. While the leaders and foreign ministers of the two countries developed close and productive relationships, Dick and I did much the same, albeit at a much less elevated level, wrestling with the concrete aspects of the topics in discussions that included individual human rights cases.

Insane Psychiatry

The use of psychiatry to silence political dissenters was undoubtedly one of the most pernicious sides of the Soviet regime. As a political tool, psychiatric incarceration was subtle: Nothing was made public, everything was kept murky. One could deny charges of abuse because hardly anybody was permitted to see the patients and hospitals. When Dick, in his mild but convincing manner, put this issue on the agenda for our talks, I had absolutely no objections, as we had already begun our work on this topic. At the start I suspected that something sinister was behind our psychiatrists' resignations in 1983 from the international organization of psychiatrists. The reality, however, turned out to be much worse than I had expected. Some features were shocking.

Punitive psychiatry had been in use since the earliest days of Soviet power, when Maria Spiridonova, a leader of the Socialist-Revolutionary Party, which opposed the Bolsheviks, was placed in a psychiatric sanatorium. The first Penal Code of the Russian Federation, introduced in 1926, provided "means of social defense" that included not only penitentiaries but also forced medical treatment. Prison-type psychiatric hospitals were inaugurated by the NKVD chief Beria in 1939; their numbers increased over time.[1]

After Stalin's death, Sergei Pisarev, a prisoner in such a hospital, wrote a letter to the party's Central Committee demanding an investigation into the use of psychiatry for punitive purposes. A special commission was set up. It found that abuses had indeed taken place. The harsh conditions, humiliation, and severe beatings to which prisoners were subjected were denounced. Sane and insane persons were deliberately held together in the same cell. Things changed—but only for a while. Pisarev's friend Pyotr Grigorenko, a decorated Soviet Army general and World War II veteran, was committed to a mental institution; when his file was opened, in perestroika's time, in 1991, an authoritative commission determined that he had never suffered from any psychological ailment.

In 1978, a special party commission studied the psychiatric state of Soviet society. It found that 4.5 million people had a record of mental illness, including 75,000 persons who were potentially dangerous to society and who were secluded in psychiatric hospitals; about 15,000 of these were political prison-

---

1. The full name of the NKVD translates to the People's Commissariat of Internal Affairs; it existed from 1934 to 1946 and was the precursor to the KGB.

ers.[2] Nikolay Shvernik, the president of the party control committee under whose name the commission had worked, shelved its findings, and the practice of incarcerating political prisoners in psychiatric hospitals continued.

Persons who were considered dissidents were sent to medical experts; almost half of them were determined to be mentally ill and sent to special psychiatric hospitals.[3] Formally, such incarceration could be authorized only by court decision and was not considered a repressive measure because the court would not impose penal punishment on the accused, instead deciding that he or she was an ill person requiring hospitalization. The reality was that such a hospital was often a prison and its patients were detained for an indeterminate period ("How can you know when a patient will get well?" was the authorities' cynical argument). A special unpublished instruction issued in 1960 legitimized increased commitment without trial of "mentally ill persons who are dangerous to the public." The common definition of the illness in these specific cases was "sluggish schizophrenia," which could be diagnosed in anyone. The rationale was simple: Only a schizophrenic would criticize Soviet power.

When I said that we'd already been working on the issue, I meant that it was the Ministry of Foreign Affairs that first drew attention to the situation in psychiatry. In the second half of the 1980s, on the wave of perestroika, we forwarded several memos to the Central Committee insisting that measures be taken to curb the insidious practice of psychiatric punishment. Over a period of one to two years, we achieved some success. First, new rules for delivering psychiatric help were promulgated in 1988. They drastically reduced the grounds for coercive treatment of the mentally ill and their hospitalization for social (more appropriately, antisocial) reasons. Mental patients were granted access to legal counsel. Second, political dissidents charged with anti-Soviet activity were released from psychiatric clinics. Third, maximum security institutions were dissolved or transferred from the Ministry of the Interior to the Ministry of Health. Fourth, several hundred thousand people who had been diagnosed with marginal mental disorders were dropped from the psychiatric registers.

So already by the fall of 1987, Dick could report to Secretary Shultz that "the practices which we have labeled 'abuse of psychiatry' have been ended."

---

2. See A. S. Prokopenko, "Bezumnaia psikhiatria" [Insane psychiatry], *Trud*, April 17, 1997, 6. Prokopenko was a consultant on the Commission for Rehabilitating Victims of Political Repressions who explored this issue.

3. *Nezavisimaia Gazeta*, July 3, 1992.

A Remarkable Visit

In March 1989, we extended an invitation to a representative team of twenty-seven American psychiatrists. They didn't just talk with their Soviet colleagues; they visited psychiatric hospitals, read patients' files, and examined the patients. Specific patients' names had been provided to them not by the Soviet authorities, but by various human rights organizations.

This breakthrough cost us—a small group of enthusiasts in the Ministry of Foreign Affairs—a lot of blood. Our psychiatrists, many of them linked to the KGB, built a wall of denial and found help among some influential conservatives inside the leadership of the Communist Party. The senior psychiatrist of the Ministry of Health publicly said, "It is with full responsibility that I can declare: I have not encountered any cases when a mentally sane person would be deliberately certified by doctors as mentally ill, not to mention that this would be in accordance with state policy, as some people in the West try to present it."[4]

If this was indeed true, we countered, then why not prove it to the American colleagues? Shevardnadze not only welcomed our idea, but pushed it with vigor and publicly supported it. There was quite a bit of tension when the Central Committee's resolution on Soviet-American contacts in the field of psychiatry was debated. The results were astonishing. The U.S. delegation's investigation, wrote Richard J. Bonnie, provided unequivocal proof that persons who were not mentally ill had been hospitalized for expressing political dissent or engaging in unauthorized religious activities. Patients typically were arrested and locked up without ever seeing an attorney or appearing in court. Sometimes they were deprived even of the right to correspondence.[5]

The Americans' visit helped us pursue the fight. The goal was to replace a sheaf of unpublished administrative guidelines, which had regulated this sensitive field, with a coherent law on providing psychiatric help. One of our arguments was based on the Soviet Union's international obligations, in particular those that had been assumed at the Vienna meeting of the CSCE countries. This approach—first, to achieve the desired results at the international level, then, to introduce them into our internal procedures—had

---

4. See his article in Perestroika i prava cheloveka [Perestroika and human rights], supplement to the magazine *Novoe Vremia*, December 1988, 11. It may be that the author of this article didn't know that a certain Vladimir Bukovski—this name became very well-known when he was swapped for one of the Soviet intelligence men—had been arrested in June 1963 for distributing the book *New Class* by M. Djilas. Bukovski was found criminally not liable on grounds of insanity and placed for coercive treatment.

5. R. J. Bonnie, "Political Abuse of Psychiatry in the Soviet Union and China: Complexities and Controversies," *Journal of the American Academy of Psychiatry and Law* 30, no. 1 (2002): 137.

worked before, and it worked this time, too.[6] The Ministry of Health (thanks to academician Evgeny Chasov) and the Academy of Sciences sided with the Ministry of Foreign Affairs. The new law protected the rights and legitimate interests of persons suffering from mental diseases. As Bonnie writes, "The end of political hospitalization in the Soviet Union was attributable to changes in Soviet politics, not to changes in Soviet psychiatry."[7]

Soviet-American cooperation in this field bore reciprocal advantages. Bonnie recognizes that the controversy surrounding the Soviet political abuse of psychiatry had an impact on the evolution of mental health legislation in the United States. In turn, our psychiatry could take advantage of the American experience: Russia's mental health law, enacted in 1992, codified some freedom-protecting norms and the core ethical principles embedded in the American law. What we began during perestroika continued after the Soviet Union ceased to exist.

Political Prisoners

The subject of political prisoners, or as Dick put it, those imprisoned for the expression of dissenting political views, was discussed from the very beginning of our bilateral talks in April 1987. Once again, the American side took the initiative, although in this case too perestroika's team moved to correct the situation before we were pushed to do so from outside.

The Soviet totalitarian system did not provide space for civil activity. The system had only one response to individuals who chose to act independently or who harbored thoughts that were considered harmful: repression. As Stalin's hangman, Lavrenty Beria, liked to repeat: "A people's enemy is not only who damages but who has doubts about the party's line." In one form or another, repressive measures were present throughout Soviet history.

By the early 1950s, fifty-two million politically motivated court sentences had been meted out in the Soviet Union, six million people had been banished without sentence, and one million people had been executed.[8] Four hundred and thirty labor camp administrations were formed from 1930 through 1953, the year of Stalin's death. There were more than 150 prison

---

6. The Vienna document contained a special provision (23.6) that obliged the participant states "to defend persons from any psychiatric or other medical practice, which violates human rights and main liberty of people, as well as to undertake effective measures in order to prevent such a practice and punish it."

7. Bonnie, "Political Abuse of Psychiatry," 139.

8. "History of Stalin's Gulag" (presented at the Aleksandr Solzhenitsyn Russian Public Foundation, October 30, 2005).

camps and settlements in the Perm region alone; every third resident of the Perm region lived behind bars.[9]

Political repression influenced the entire nation. The country's leadership deemed the stability of the Soviet system to be more important than the rights of Soviet citizens.

What is less well-known is that resistance to the regime, including insurgencies in the gulags, was as perennial as repression, even if it was sporadic and uncoordinated and rarely involved many people.

Stalin's mass purges caused many people, including the elite, to conclude that such practices should never be repeated.[10] But even though he denounced the despot's cult, Khrushchev did not entirely eliminate the repressive system that Stalin created. True, the so-called extrajudicial practice, under which thousands of people were arbitrarily sent to death, was abolished under Khrushchev. But at the same time, the infamous Article 70, which provided for very harsh punishment of "anti-Soviet agitation and propaganda," was introduced. The new article was immediately employed: In its first two years, more than three thousand people were imprisoned under its provisions.

During Brezhnev's years, use was also made of Article 190-1, introduced into the penal code in 1966 and formulated in even more vague terms than Article 70. It punished those who "slandered" the Soviet establishment, and thus allowed for the imprisonment of anyone who voiced an opinion that dissented from the official point of view. Sixty percent of prison sentences that were handed down were pronounced for verbal expressions of dissent.[11]

Perestroika Begins to Make Itself Felt

As early as October 1986, Gorbachev said to KGB chief Viktor Chebrikov during a Politburo meeting: "It is necessary to free political prisoners from jails. They are there for saying the words that I, as the Secretary General, am saying today."[12] And so it was done. The famous telephone call from Gorbachev to Sakharov, liberating academicians from exile, took place in December 1986; political amnesty, as it was labeled, soon followed.

---

9. As reported by Agency ITAR-TASS, October 30, 2005.

10. Even as late as 2006, a new mass grave containing the remains of 144 victims of Stalinist purges was uncovered near the provincial town of Voronezh. See Interfax (Russian press agency), October 30, 2006.

11. In the period 1956–60, 4,676 persons were condemned under Article 70; in 1961–65, 1,072; in 1966–70, 295; in 1971–75, 276; in 1976–80, 62; and in 1981–85, 150. The numbers condemned under Article 190 were 384 in 1966–70; 527 in 1971–75; 285 in 1976–80; and 390 in 1981–85. See *Istochnik* [Source], no. 6 (1995): 153, quoting the Russian president's archive.

12. Gorbachev Foundation, V Politburo CK KPSS, 83.

A year and a half later, I was in a position to assert at the Geneva meeting of the UN Commission for Human Rights that "there are no persons convicted for their political or religious beliefs now in prison." I had informed Dick about this development a little earlier.

Gorbachev not only made the release of political prisoners possible. The shameful articles of the Penal Code were first suspended and then, in 1989, abrogated by the Supreme Soviet. Another positive step was undertaken by the Politburo, at Gorbachev's demand, when it decided to legally abrogate the sentences passed in the 1930s by the dvoika, troika, and other extrajudicial organs, completing the job left half-finished by Khrushchev. The reports on repressions, including that produced by Shvernik's commission and ignored by Khrushchev, Brezhnev, Andropov, and Chernenko, were finally acted on by Mikhail Sergeyevich.

In trying to make the dialogue with Americans a two-way track, I occasionally touched on the issue of political prisoners in the United States. Dick was ready to discuss this issue, though we couldn't prove that those for whom we appealed were political and not common criminals. Frankly, it mattered to me less than our own misfortunes.

Prisoners of Conscience and Freedom of Religion

The newly formed Humanitarian Department in the Ministry of Foreign Affairs was charged with watching the reaction abroad to what happened in the Soviet Union in the humanitarian area. Among other tasks, it polled Soviet embassies on our weak points.

Our colleagues in London informed us that we had been criticized most for problems associated with the reunification of families and for the treatment of religious dissidents.[13] Reading this report, I said to myself: "So, Dick Schifter is right when he presents cases of people committed for holding religious meetings that were not properly authorized." This provided an additional reason to bring Shevardnadze's attention to the so-called prisoners of conscience—who had been released relatively quickly within the wider framework of the liberation of political prisoners.

Dick urged me to press for greater freedom of religion, which should include the freedom to practice one's religion without the need for governmental authorization. We ourselves felt that a comprehensive law on religion was necessary. Preparing it, however, turned out to be a difficult and lengthy job.

---

13. This information was prepared by Andrei Kostin, second secretary of the embassy at the time. He is now president of one of Russia's largest banks. I mean that sometimes dealing with human rights pays off.

Gorbachev kicked things off in his meeting in 1988 with Patriarch Pimen and the members of the Synod of the Russian Orthodox Church. The press release issued after this meeting was sensational for those times:

> Worshipers fully have the right to express their convictions with dignity. Perestroika, democratization and glasnost apply to them as well, and without any limitations. This especially concerns the sphere of morality where universally human norms and customs can facilitate our common cause.... We have many points of contact for an interested and hopefully fruitful dialogue. We have a common history, one fatherland, and one future.[14]

Gorbachev informed religious leaders about the Politburo decision to start drafting a law on freedom of conscience, but two years of struggle followed before such a law appeared. The progressive wing's opponents did everything to maintain the Communist Party's control over this domain, battling to preserve official uniformity of thought and to stifle the development of real religious pluralism. The autumn of 1990 finally brought the law of the Russian Federation on the freedom of faith, which declared the right of each citizen to freely choose, to have, and to disseminate religious and other convictions; to practice any religion or none; and to act in accordance with his or her convictions as long as the laws of the state were observed. Under the law, parishes as well as centralized religious associations could register as legal entities. The Russian Orthodox Church registered its bylaws on March 27, 1991, and obtained the first registration number. The next important step was embodied in the constitution of the Russian Federation, which was approved in a referendum in December 1993. According to Article 13 of the constitution, the "Russian Federation recognizes ideological diversity" and "no ideology may be established as state-forming or compulsory." Article 28 echoed the provisions of the law on the freedom of faith.

Here, again, reform was made possible by Gorbachev's perestroika, even though the results became visible only after he left the political scene.

Freedom of Expression

As Gorbachev gradually loosened the state's grip on public expression of opinion, a bustling, independent mass media quickly sprang up. Without waiting for the law to formalize the growing freedom, newspapers and journals began to assert their right to publish and broadcast what they wanted. In the mid-nineteenth century, Alexander Herzen, one of Russia's greatest intellects, famously published a plea for freedom of speech in his magazine *Kolokol* (The Bell); that plea and that magazine, however, had had to be

---

14. *Pravda*, April 30, 1988.

printed in London, beyond Russia's borders. Not until the February Revolution in 1917 did Russia enjoy such freedom, and then only briefly. On the third day after they seized power in October 1917, the Bolsheviks established strict control over the press. The decree introducing the administrative restrictions pledged that control of the press would end "when the new order gets strength." That didn't happen for seventy-three years.[15]

Gorbachev originally believed that the country, given its Russian and Soviet traditions, could live with just one political party. Political rivalry would be excluded, but it could be substituted for by glasnost—openness and transparency in the affairs of government. An adequate law regarding mass media was urgently needed, because the old regulatory tools based on strict control of the media by the party and the government were ceasing to exist.

The right wing of the party, headed by Yegor Ligachev and Anatoly Lukianov, couldn't even think about releasing the mass media from party control. Many officials were sincerely convinced that without the party's guidance, everything would swiftly degenerate and fall apart. How could we live without the party determining who ran the country's newspapers and magazines and what stories they could publish? The left wing didn't deny that such control was necessary, but insisted that it be exercised only over the media belonging to the party; media not controlled by the party had to be allowed.

Another sensitive issue was secrecy, as the media were bringing much previously secret information to the surface. Glasnost, in the eyes of many party conservatives, was a step too far, giving birth to permissiveness and score settling.

A big problem was to regulate the relations among the different sides participating in the work of the media: journalists, founders of media outlets, state organs responsible for media registration, state and public organizations that provided the media with information, and, of course, citizens, readers, and viewers. The existing system practically had to be turned upside down. No wonder it took years to elaborate provisions that could accommodate the different strata of society.

The Politburo discussed a media law more than once. Gorbachev pressed for the broadest version of glasnost together with fidelity to socialist choice and to the people's interests. He emphasized the media's responsible behavior. Characteristic of the perestroika period, an alternative approach was suggested by three young lawyers, Yuri Baturin, Mikhail Fedotov, and Vladimir Entin. Their proposal eventually formed the basis for the first progressive

---

15. M. Fedotov, *Birth and Development of the Media Law of the Russian Federation* (Moscow: International Relations, 2002), 137.

law on the status of mass media in Russian history, approved by the Supreme Soviet on June 12, 1990.

Democratization

While the Soviet-U.S. dialogue on human rights focused on a handful of particular issues—psychiatric abuse, political prisoners—that dialogue took place against the backdrop of sweeping democratic change in almost all areas of Soviet life. Gorbachev's relaxation of government control precipitated the appearance of thousands of civic associations, clubs, and movements. For the first time in their lives, people could join together to form informal voluntary organizations. Conservative circles in the Communist Party of the Soviet Union (CPSU) demanded compulsory registration of public organizations as well as legal norms regulating foreign aid to voluntary societies. The issue was brought to a divided Politburo. Gorbachev was on top of the situation and he instructed the Ministry of Justice to elaborate a basic law. Voluntary organizations must not be closed down, he said, and they could work without bylaws. In his mind, the public associations would become the foundation of the new social-political system.

Although the broader canvas of change was not part of the agenda that guided Dick's and my official endeavors, a couple of brief sketches of my personal involvement in the tide of democratic change may help to convey a fuller picture of the environment within which Dick and I worked.

Culture Wars

Every step forward on the road of democratization required a tough struggle. I witnessed many examples of that struggle in the cultural arena.

Representing the Ministry of Foreign Affairs, I attended several CPSU Secretariat meetings called to decide on various aspects of the nation's intellectual life. I heard conservative bosses saying that they would never abolish the party's control over culture, be it foreign travel for cultural envoys—a matter that still remained tightly regulated—transformation of giant state-owned publishing houses into smaller public or cooperative ventures, or the rehabilitation of writers previously forced to emigrate and unlawfully deprived of their Soviet citizenship, such as Solzhenitsyn, Vassily Aksyonov, and Georgy Vladimov.

One episode struck me particularly. In the Ministry of Foreign Affairs, we prepared proposals designed to make it easier for representatives of creative and scientific intelligentsia, as they were officially called, to travel abroad. At the time, any artist invited to tour abroad first had to get approval from his collective or party gathering as well as tacit approval from the local KGB; he then had to hope his or her application would survive scrutiny by innumerable organs in the party pyramid before being considered by the relevant department in the Central Committee. Many of my friends among cultural envoys, including the very popular Georgian movie director Otar Ioseliani, had said to me, "Tolia, try to do something, it is a shameful practice to depend on 'my collective' or on a department of the Central Committee." We called the Department for Exits the Department of Nonexits. The situation improved only with perestroika. By then the department was chaired by Ambassador Stepan Chervonenko, a convinced supporter of new thinking. Apart from everything else, the workload was enormous: As the heads of various departments reported to the Central Committee on March 17, 1987, in the preceding five years foreign trips were made by 105,000 artists, writers, soloists, and performers. Each trip required considerable paperwork.

After traveling a tortuous and bitterly contested bureaucratic route, our proposals reached the Secretariat under the chairmanship of Yegor Ligachev and were approved—or so we thought. Two or three days later, I received the Secretariat's resolution in writing and discovered that it was very different, and much more restrictive, than what had been approved. I called the woman in charge of official records of the Secretariat and told her that I had recorded all the remarks and corrections made at the Secretariat's meeting; thus, I said, I had the text approved by the Secretariat. How on earth had it been revised? The woman calmly explained that the person who chaired a meeting had the right to introduce his remarks into the "preliminary adopted" document, giving it its final format: "The decision is as you see it now." I went to see Shevardnadze, to be consoled by this: "Egor is known for that trick. The decision as a whole is a good step ahead. You did a good job, we'll do the rest later."

The Glasnost Wave Grows Bigger

Despite the fierce opposition of the right wing of the CPSU, the conditions of intellectual life improved. Publishing houses were given the right to decide for themselves which books and articles to publish. Progressive-minded magazines, such as *Ogonek*, edited by Vitaly Korotich, and *Moscovskie Novosti*, edited by the late Egor Yakovlev—both my good friends—urged greater democratization than even Gorbachev envisaged.[16] Previously restricted masterpieces of literature, as well, unfortunately, as poorer-quality literature, flooded bookstores. When, in the late 1970s, the so-called gray cardinal of the Politburo, Mikhail Suslov, read extracts from Vassily Grossman's book

---

16. As I registered in 1988 in my diary, I received a severe reproach from Ligachev for providing the ministry's facilities for a press conference by editor V. Korotich and writer M. Shatrov, both "perestroika men."

Life and Destiny, Suslov allegedly said that the book wouldn't be published in the Soviet Union in the next three hundred years.[17] It was published in 1989.

The adage that a poet in Russia is more than a poet is confirmed by the odyssey of Yuri Lyubimov, director of the theater Na Taganke, a center of artistic dissent during Brezhnev's times that was just barely tolerated by the authorities. His specialty was the use of Aesopian language. In 1984, half a year before Gorbachev came to power, Lyubimov lost a long and exhausting struggle and was deprived of Soviet citizenship.

Several years later, another extended political wrestling match took place, this time to get the artist back. In May 1988, Shevardnadze and Yakovlev signed a memo, drafted by me and directed it to the Central Committee, proposing that Lyubimov be granted a Soviet visa. Yuri Petrovich had an Israeli passport at the time. Intervention from Gorbachev was needed to settle this "highly ideologically charged issue."[18] On May 15, I showed up at the apartment of Nikolai Gubenko, then the comrade-in-arms of Lyubimov, to say to the famous director, "Welcome back to the USSR." Mine was the first official greeting.

Is UNESCO a Romanian Countess?

At the time of my appointment as chairman of the Soviet commission for the UN Educational, Scientific, and Cultural Organization (UNESCO), I found UNESCO to be a tool of propaganda and ideological combat between the two superpowers' blocs. We managed to get the go-ahead from the Politburo for changes that would make UNESCO an instrument of cooperation that could bring concrete results to the Soviet Union.

I remember the heavy silence of the Politburo members when I finished my report on UNESCO proposing such changes. Few members knew much about the organization. Gromyko, who by then was no longer the minister of foreign affairs, relaxed the tension with an anecdote: "At first, we thought that UNESCO was the name of a Romanian countess." The discussion that followed went smoothly.

Our major endeavor was as follows. In October 1987, on vacation with my wife at a Bulgarian beach, I heard the news that UNESCO was to hold an

---

17. Service, *History of Twentieth Century Russia*, 416.

18. Browsing through the Hoover Institution archives in Stanford, I found further confirmation of the close attention that the Soviet government always paid to artistic life. I discovered there a curious document: Klement Voroshilov, people's commissar for military and navy affairs, writes on January 29, 1929, to the Politburo and to Comrade Stalin, recommending that Mikhail Bulgakov's play *Run* be "listed as non-opportune politically . . . [for] performance in a theater." The next day the Politburo accepted Voroshilov's recommendation.

Today, I console myself with the thought that Voroshilov's name is practically forgotten, but a lot of people, not only in Russia, read Bulgakov, a great writer.

assembly in Paris at which it would elect a new director general. I immediately interrupted our vacation and, upon arriving in Moscow, learned that the Politburo had already approved instructions to vote for the incumbent director, Senegal's Amadou-Mahtar M'Bow.

For me, such a vote would be disaster. The United States and Great Britain had already quit UNESCO; other countries, including Japan, the biggest donor, were ready to do so as the result of M'Bow's bad management. The candidate presented by the socialist countries, Professor Todorov from Bulgaria, had no chance. Only Spain's Frederic Major remained. "We ought to vote for him," I told my direct supervisor, First Deputy Minister Anatoly Kovalev, who, a proven liberal, was persuaded in no time. We both went to Shevardnadze. At first, he was unshakable: New thinking was good, but to prefer a politician from a NATO country to a third-world candidate was unacceptable. But by arguing that M'Bow's continued tenure would be a death knell for UNESCO, we broke through Shevardnadze's remaining orthodoxy. The Politburo changed its decision, and I flew to Paris to organize the voting process, which was not simple either. Under the guidance of Major, who lasted two terms in office, UNESCO was returned to a constructive path.

We united our new elite around the Soviet commission for UNESCO. My deputies were Academician Alexander Sheindlin and writer Alesia Adamovich; other members of the commission included the poet Andrei Voznesenski, the painter Tair Salachov, the rector of Leningrad University, Stanislav Mercuriev, and Dmitri Lichachev, who later was named "the conscience of the nation." The first time he left the Soviet Union was to attend a UNESCO assembly at my invitation. The same might be said about Metropolitan Uvenaly. We did our utmost to involve UNESCO in the celebration of Russia's Christian millennium.

A New Agenda

Gradually, the Soviet-U.S. dialogue on human rights widened its parameters. The time had come to form a more coherent approach. I suggested calling it humanitarian cooperation and Dick, very good at dealing with philological nuances that have clear political significance, agreed.

Remarkable from this point of view was the visit to Moscow in November 1987 of the second-highest official in the State Department, John Whitehead, accompanied by Dick. When talking with me, Whitehead welcomed the fact that many more Jews had received permission to leave the Soviet Union in 1987 than during the immediately preceding years, but lamented that something like six thousand otkasniks (refuseniks) still lacked permission to emigrate. I had done my homework before the meeting and replied that in the ten months of the current year, 6,466 persons had left the country and 420 applications were under consideration. I stressed that, unlike in the past, we had neither quotas for permission to leave the country nor plans to introduce them.

I insisted on the extradition of two criminals, father and son Brasinzkas, who had killed a Soviet airline hostess during an attempt to hijack an Aeroflot plane. Unfortunately, they were never extradited. Dick later explained that the U.S. rationale for refusing to extradite the Brasinzkas was that the two had already been tried in a Turkish court and been punished (to my mind, very mildly). We were more fortunate regarding some Nazis who had found shelter in the United States; one of them, Karl Linnas, was extradited to the Soviet Union in May 1987.

Considering that a Gorbachev-Reagan summit was in the making, I put forward to Whitehead a program of further humanitarian cooperation:

1. Regular specialized contacts between Soviet and American parliamentary members.
2. The exchange of information concerning changes in the laws of the two countries, including those of the republics in the Soviet Union and the states in the United States. (The Americans were worried about some articles already abolished in the penal code of the Russian Federation but still existing in the codes of the republics.)
3. Direct contacts between Soviet and U.S. ministries and agencies that dealt with human rights issues.
4. Common action against terrorism; we had already affirmed the need to act in this field within the strict limits of international law.
5. Consultations on psychiatric problems.
6. Annual bilateral meetings of writers and journalists.
7. Regular discussions between lawyers and specialists in international humanitarian law.
8. Joint efforts to combat drug trafficking, in regard to which Shevardnadze and Shultz soon signed a special agreement.

The new agenda was born. Dick confirmed it by stressing that the U.S. side had considered Soviet criticism of the American use of the death penalty for teenagers. A Soviet representative attended the session of the U.S. Supreme Court at which that question was litigated. As a final compliment, Whitehead said that the United States had begun to believe in perestroika. Yet he remained deaf to my request to support Shevardnadze's proposal to make Moscow the place to convene an international conference on the "human dimension."[19]

Let the Experts Talk

One of the new features that Shevardnadze brought into the life of the Ministry of Foreign Affairs was asking political science experts to participate in ministry discussions. He invited several dozen Soviet officials and political scientists to hold a two-day discussion on foreign policy and diplomacy. Such an event had not occurred for many years. I remember how hard I worked with my colleagues on Shevardnadze's report of the discussions.

In part because of Shevardnadze's great respect for science, Dick and I decided to set up direct contacts between Soviet and American scientists. Our efforts culminated in an extraordinary event: expert participation, in Washington in March 1988, in the framework of the official working group on humanitarian problems. The experts had a separate roundtable as well, again under the aegis of Dick and me. Among the Soviet experts were several who saw the United States and talked with their American colleagues for the first time, such as Veniamin Yakovlev, director of the Scientific Center for Soviet Law, Gennadiy Melekhin from the Serbsky Institute of Psychiatry, and Vassily Vlasikhin from the U.S. and Canada Institute of the Russian Academy of Science. Many more specialized meetings followed.

Replicating the Model

Using the Soviet-U.S. dialogue as a model, we established relations with a few Western and non-Western countries, among them Great Britain. I remember with pleasure my talks with David Ratford, assistant to the permanent undersecretary of state, who chaired our working group for the British side. I was the first Soviet official to hold contacts with Amnesty International in its London headquarters. Before perestroika, Amnesty International had a bad reputation in Soviet eyes. We broke the ice; Amnesty International opened an office in Moscow and still keeps it.

---

19. This topic was, at the time, our "must" in contacts with foreign representatives. Sometimes in private conversations we faced such objections: "To have a conference on human rights in Moscow is the same as to suggest discussing pork in a Semitic country." Yet finally it did, as we'll see, take place.

Richard Schifter

A Goal-Oriented Human Rights Dialogue Begins

Within weeks of Andrei Sakharov's return to Moscow, another major development occurred: Substantial numbers of political prisoners were released. At a senior staff meeting at the State Department, Secretary Shultz asked for my opinion on this development. I said: "It is significant." The secretary then said: "If even Dick Schifter thinks it is significant, it must be significant." There was laughter in the room.

Later that day, I sent a memorandum to Shultz elaborating on my statement:

> It is important to try to assess the prisoner releases correctly. They are obviously important on humanitarian grounds for the people directly affected, their families and their friends. What we need to ask ourselves is what they mean politically.
>
> The fact that this is the largest political prisoner release since 1953/54 does not tell us much. For 24 years, from 1953 to 1977, the number of persons newly imprisoned for political reasons was minimal. Only since 1977 has there been a substantial rise in the number of Soviet political prisoners. Gorbachev has released a greater number because during the last ten years, including the Gorbachev years, a far greater number of persons was incarcerated on political grounds and for longer terms than had been the case in the period immediately preceding.
>
> In my discussions with Soviet representatives in recent years, I have put the question: "Isn't the Soviet state strong enough to let people such as the Helsinki monitors go free without really taking any risks?" It is clear that someone has now answered this question in the affirmative. . . .
>
> There is no doubt that we are now seeing some payoff on our repeated appeals, including most importantly your repeated appeals, for improvement in the Soviet human rights record. If we are to expect further movement, particularly a truly significant political opening, we need to be sure that we neither understate nor overstate the significance of the recent release of prisoners and that we keep pressing for further progress.[1]

It was around this time that Secretary Shultz came to the conclusion that, given relatively positive messages from the Soviets in fields other than human rights, the time had come to move forward with bilateral negotiations on arms control. The latter was the major purpose of the trip that Secretary Shultz planned for April 1987. As he put it:

---

1. Schifter memorandum to the secretary, "Soviet Prisoner Releases," February 10, 1987, 1, 2.

> I was set to arrive in Moscow on April 13, 1987. I thought of this as a real opportunity, extending beyond the traditional issues on our agenda. I wanted to engage in deeper discussions with Gorbachev and Shevardnadze about the shape of the future: the shape of the world five to ten years ahead. Arguments about specific problems tended to consume all the time and therefore set the tone of the relationship. I wanted to look at a different range of problems and opportunities that did not set us against each other but would affect us both in powerful ways. Gorbachev seemed highly alert to a new set of realities. The information age was changing the basis for material and intellectual advance: That is what I wanted to get across to the new Soviet leaders.[2]

Gorbachev's memoirs confirm that Shultz attained the result that he tried to achieve:

> On April 14, 1987, I welcomed George Shultz in Moscow. Today I view this meeting as a milestone. The American Secretary of State focused the conversation on intermediate-range nuclear forces and the continuation of strategic arms negotiations. But the issues we discussed went far beyond our prepared briefs. It was the first time that we touched on the philosophical aspects of the new policy, on the roles and responsibilities of our countries....
>
> I think that both sides basically pursued the same object. Rhetorical exchanges of "compliments"—including the traditional accusations of spying—were one thing. But the talks had shown that underlying considerations and intentions were far more important. As we could see from his subsequent actions, the Secretary of State genuinely wanted to sustain the dialogue. His position seemed to influence the American administration in general, President Reagan in particular.
>
> I realized, maybe for the first time, that I was dealing with a serious man of sound political judgment. Subsequently he developed his potential even more—as a statesman, an intellectual, a creative and at the same time a far-seeing person.[3]

The feeling of mutual respect and confidence that had developed between Gorbachev and Shultz extended also to the Soviet foreign minister:

> Despite all the tension and cliff-hanging about the future of superpower contacts, I was well aware and appreciative of how much easier it was to deal with Shevardnadze than with Gromyko. The difference was absolutely dramatic. We could have a real conversation, argue, and actually make headway in resolving contentious issues. Shevardnadze was comfortable and candid with the press when he wanted to be, whereas Gromyko repeated the ideological line and compulsively denounced every aspect of American policies and actions.[4]

---

2. Shultz, *Turmoil and Triumph*, 879.
3. Gorbachev, *Memoirs*, 774–775.
4. Shultz, *Turmoil and Triumph*, 744–745.

In the human rights field, the task was indeed made easier when Foreign Minister Shevardnadze agreed that, in addition to the high-level dialogue between him or Gorbachev and Shultz, there would also be a working-level dialogue, in which specific issues and cases could be discussed systematically; the parties to the dialogue would then seek to resolve these cases. That is what brought Anatoly and me together in April 1987.

Although, as just noted, the principal purpose of the April 1987 Shultz visit to Moscow was to deal with a truly far-reaching set of issues, the secretary's decision to take me along with a group of experts in the field of arms control sent the message that there was some linkage between arms control and human rights. This is not to suggest that a carefully thought-out strategy had been developed to provide for such a linkage. It just so happened that the two issues, which had been in the forefront of both the president's and the secretary's thoughts about the Soviet Union, happened to be joined through the make-up of our delegation. I used to say that linkage did not mean that we would trade the release of a hundred political prisoners for permission for the Soviet Union to keep one additional intercontinental ballistic missile. Instead, Congress would provide the linkage: If it was satisfied with progress in the human rights field, it was more likely to approve arms reduction agreements.

But we were not there yet. Shortly before our departure for Moscow, on March 25, I sought to recapitulate where matters stood regarding the absence of civil liberties in the Soviet Union:

> In the years immediately following Stalin's death in 1953, the Soviet Union gradually emerged from the state of fear engendered by his despotic rule. With the Secret Police less powerful and less oppressive, the Soviet people discovered that they could speak more freely and intellectuals began to assert their independence. This state of affairs, known as "the thaw," continued through the Khrushchev years (ending in 1964) into the early part of the Brezhnev era. Thereafter, however, the Soviet government began to resist the efforts of intellectuals to broaden their freedom of expression. The intellectuals responded by forming human rights groups, which engaged the government in a continuing struggle. This struggle, which began in 1965, ended in 1977 with a sharp clampdown by the Soviet government on what had come to be known as the dissident movement. Arrests, long-term imprisonment or commitments to a mental institution became the price paid for dissidence. With the return of the Secret Police to the center of governmental authority, the period 1977–86 became a period of severe repression.[5]

A few days later, I followed up with a memorandum that assessed developments in the less than two years since the ascension of Gorbachev:

---

5. Schifter memorandum to the secretary, "Human Rights in the Soviet Union during the Period 1953–1986," March 25, 1987.

> Driven largely by domestic concerns, namely his desire to reinvigorate the Soviet Union and improve the operations of the economy, Gorbachev has initiated major programs to open up to public scrutiny and debate governmental operations at the local level. For the same reason he has loosened somewhat the rigid controls recently in effect with regard to cultural activities. Change with regard to other aspects of freedom of expression has been far more limited and driven more by efforts to improve the Soviet Union's public relations image. . . . There is no indication as yet of any change in the Soviet Union's basic structure as a totalitarian dictatorship.[6]

U.S. Human Rights Goals

It was with the foregoing thoughts and the basic notion that in order to achieve progress, I should present only issues of a purely humanitarian nature—issues that could be resolved without fundamental change in the Soviet system—that I sat down with Deputy Foreign Minister Anatoly Adamishin at our first meeting on April 14, 1987. The issues that I planned to raise in our dialogue included abuse of psychiatry, restrictions of freedom of expression and religion, and emigration.

Abuse of Psychiatry

I considered abuse of psychiatry to be the most serious of the human rights violations that was practiced in the Soviet Union. It was never clear to me why it was necessary to commit to mental institutions persons who could easily have been convicted for anti-Soviet agitation and propaganda or for practicing a religious faith that had not been properly licensed. To be sure, to get a commitment, the KGB needed only the signatures of two psychiatrists. But it was equally simple to go through a criminal procedure that would result in a conviction. After all, no Soviet judge would find a person innocent whom the KGB had already pronounced guilty. It occurred to me at that time that a commitment, which would place a perfectly sane person in an institution for the mentally ill and subject him to treatment with painful drugs, would be a greater deterrent to those contemplating expression of political dissidence than mere imprisonment.

Legal Restrictions on Freedom of Expression and Freedom of Religion and Incarceration of Persons Convicted under These Laws

Many non-governmental organizations had provided us with long lists of persons who had been convicted under provisions of the Soviet criminal code that made it a felony to say anything—or to write or distribute written

---

6. Schifter memorandum to the secretary, "Human Rights in Gorbachev's Second Year: 'Openness' and 'Restructuring,'" March 28, 1987, 1.

material—that the government deemed objectionable or to organize or practice religious activities of a denomination that had not been authorized by the government to function. Our goal was to persuade the Soviet government, first, to release all those who had been convicted under these laws, and, second, to repeal the laws that were clearly in conflict with the legal obligations that the Soviet government had undertaken.

Restrictions on the Right to Emigrate

The great majority of those who sought to emigrate from the Soviet Union were Jews. They had given up on attaining equality in education and employment in the Soviet Union.[7] Their interest was focused on getting exit permits. Four main obstacles stood in the way: the contention that some of them had done classified work that must not be revealed to foreigners; the need to be sponsored by a relative of the first degree, that is, a child, parent, or sibling who lived abroad; the need for a formal statement of permission to emigrate from relatives in the first degree and of divorced spouses who lived in the Soviet Union; and an overall quota on the number of permits that would be issued each month. The existence of the quota system was never admitted. The monthly statistics made it clear, however, that it was in place.

While most applicants for exit permits were Jews, there were also Volga Germans, Armenians, and Pentecostals among those who wished to emigrate from the Soviet Union and whose right to leave the country was not recognized.

Of the four categories of issues, it seemed to me that, except for the security-sensitive emigration cases, the first and third issues were the easiest for the Soviet government to handle. As for emigration, getting persons whom it viewed as troublemakers out of the country could only benefit the system. It was a way of accommodating the United States at no real cost. As it was, I had wondered why the emigration restrictions were in place and had assumed that it was for demographic reasons, the fear that many ethnic Russians would leave the country. Anatoly later told me that he did not think that Russians were likely to leave the country in large numbers, and developments since the lifting of emigration restrictions have proved him right. Thus, the only imaginable reason for the emigration restrictions was that the state viewed emigration as an embarrassment, suggesting that some people did not like life in the vaunted motherland of socialism.

---

7. There was a joke during the Gorbachev era about a scientist who had applied at a scientific institute to fill a job opening. The persons in charge of personnel looked at the applicant's biographical sketch and told him that on the basis of his professional background he was highly qualified. The personnel director then said, however: "This is the time of glasnost [openness]. I need to tell you that we don't hire any Jews." The applicant responded: "But you have told me that I am well qualified. This is the time of perestroika, the time to place the best-qualified people in the right jobs." The answer of the personnel director was: "If you believe that, you are very dumb and we certainly don't hire any dumb Jews."

As for the abuse of psychiatry, the problem could be handled by resorting to criminal proceedings against those who had offended the laws on political speech or unauthorized religious activities.

Allowing emigration and abandoning abuse of psychiatry could be handled by the Soviet government without a basic change in the system. Releasing prisoners of conscience, on the other hand, would mean that the laws repressing dissenters would no longer be enforced. That would be a significant move toward a more open society. Yet while the Soviet Union considered our requests regarding prisoners of conscience as calling for fundamental political change, we viewed this as an issue that we had to tackle from a purely humanitarian point of view. That is why we stressed, initially, the mistreatment of prisoners in the gulags. What was not on our human rights agenda was a call for free, democratic elections or a change in the country's economic system.

These were the policy considerations that were in my mind as we arrived in Moscow on April 13, 1987. That evening I attended a seder at Spaso House, the U.S. ambassador's residence. Dozens of refuseniks, applicants for emigration permits who had been turned down, were present. The high point of the evening was when Secretary Shultz arrived, put on a yarmulke, and went around the room shaking hands with the refuseniks. He then delivered a brief speech. His conclusion rings in my mind to this day, as it will in the minds of the others in attendance: "Never give up. Never give up. For we won't give up."

Our First Meeting

The next morning, I paid my first visit to the Soviet foreign ministry for a meeting with Deputy Foreign Minister Anatoly Adamishin. It was the beginning of a truly unique dialogue that established a continuing working relationship between the Soviet Union and the United States in the field of human rights. It is important to underline how this dialogue was brought about. First, the U.S. president and secretary of state had made it clear in their conversations with their counterparts in the Soviet government that human rights issues were of major concern to the United States. Second, these Soviet counterparts were interested in good relations with the United States, reflected, in particular, in mutually agreed arms reduction, as arms were placing a heavy burden on the Soviet economy. Third, these Soviet leaders had come to share our concerns about their country's totalitarian system and favored liberalization for the sake of their own people and not just to accommodate the United States. Thus, when Secretary Shultz, at the very outset of the April 1987 ministerial meeting, told Foreign Minister Shevardnadze that he hoped that a working group on human rights would be created and that

Shevardnadze would designate appropriate ministry personnel to meet with the U.S. human rights team, Shevardnadze agreed.

As Anatoly notes elsewhere in this book, he was notified quite late that he would lead the Soviet delegation in our dialogue. He had no previous exposure to the Soviet-U.S. discussions of human rights and was most certainly not familiar with the issues that I would raise. As a matter of fact, the designation of Deputy Foreign Minister Adamishin to head the Soviet delegation to the human rights working group came as a surprise to the U.S. embassy, which had assumed that the head of the Soviet delegation to the Vienna CSCE conference would be called back to Moscow for this purpose. Adamishin, I was told, was a specialist in African affairs. I was further told that he was tough but civilized. In retrospect it would appear that he was chosen because Shevardnadze had full confidence in him.

Once we sat down to talk, it was soon clear that the Soviet Union had operated on a need-to-know system and that Adamishin had, as of April 1987, not been deemed to be in need to know about the Soviet Union's human rights violations that were of greatest concern to the United States. This reality became most obvious when I initiated a discussion of Perm 36. Perm is a city about 850 miles east of Moscow, located in the Ural Mountains. There were a series of prison camps in the vicinity of Perm, of which Perm 36 was the most notorious. Perm 36 was well-known to those of us who monitored human rights abuses in the Soviet Union as a camp in which prisoners lived under particularly rigorous conditions. When I started the conversation about Perm 36, Anatoly responded that he did not know what I was talking about. Our conversation regarding Perm 36 took place prior to our lunch break. After the lunch break, he told me that he had checked on the matter and found out that Perm 36 was just one of the Soviet Union's many penal institutions. He had evidently not been told that it was a prison in which especially harsh measures were applied to inmates.

On a positive note, Anatoly told me that the cases of political prisoners would continue to be reviewed, as would the provisions of the criminal code relating to political crimes. Our expression of concern with regard to Perm 36 was noted. The matter would be looked into. I used the opportunity to present a list of political prisoners and an appeal prepared by the American Association for the Advancement of Science calling attention to the high standing of the association in the United States and its apolitical character.

We also discussed emigration at the first session, and I was informed that a very small number of pending refusenik cases, perhaps three, had been resolved. By the time we met, we had seen the first small uptick since 1981 in exit permits issued to Jewish applicants, from less than one hundred per month to about three hundred per month in early 1987. However, Anatoly made a point of reading to me Section 20 of the new emigration decree concerning nondiscrimination among ethnic groups in the issuance of exit permits.

Anatoly told me of progress on the list of refuseniks that had been presented to Soviet representatives theretofore, persons whose applications for exit permits had been refused on the grounds that the applicant possessed security-sensitive information. I made the point that some of these determinations may have been wrong in the first instance or, in other cases, the information at issue was no longer sensitive. Anatoly told me that in recent weeks, a process had been set up under which requests to review such determinations could be filed with the presidium of the Supreme Soviet. He told me further that the presidium was required to decide simple cases within thirty days and complex cases within six months.

It seemed to me at the time that both the political prisoners and the refuseniks were at long last among the beneficiaries of Gorbachev's bureaucratic reforms, at least regarding procedure. A few years earlier, when I had tried to present a list of names to a Soviet official whom I had gotten to know at the UN Human Rights Commission in Geneva, his response was: "Richard, Gromyko does not accept any of these lists. How can I?" The question that I asked myself now was: "Will these lists really be reviewed or is all of this a charade?"

When we adjourned, it was clear to both of us that we had not accomplished much of substantive significance, but it seemed to me that the very fact that we met, that a working-level dialogue had started, was of some significance. So were the changes in procedures to qualify for exit permits and the assurances that the matters that we had identified as of concern would be examined. As we said goodbye to each other, Anatoly noted that we could expect to meet again.

During this visit to Moscow, I also met with the chairman of the Religious Affairs Commission. Here, too, I noted minor progress within a highly confined space. I was told that recognized denominations would be allowed to open more places of worship, import bibles and prayer books, and maintain contacts with coreligionists abroad. The existing scheme of governmental regulation of religion would, however, be maintained; the sphere of authorized activity would remain limited to ritual functions; and religious education outside the home would remain prohibited. The Ukrainian Catholic Church, about which I had made specific inquiries, would remain outlawed.

The issue of human rights came up on the same day in a conversation between Shultz and Gorbachev. Gorbachev said that the Soviet side was prepared to consider any proposal that emerged in the humanitarian area. But then he brought up Shultz's attendance the previous night at the seder for refuseniks held at the U.S. embassy. As Shultz describes the exchange in his memoirs, Gorbachev "launched into a bitter attack on me." He complained that Shultz dealt "only with a certain group of Jews, people who do not like it here and have complaints." He accused Shultz of showing "no interest in the millions of other Soviet Jews, who are out of your field of vision" and added that Shultz's activities were "stimulating" discontent.[8]

Despite these harsh words, we kept in mind that there had been progress. As Shultz puts it in his memoirs: "Gorbachev did not understand the United States, but he was willing to discuss human rights in the Soviet Union as long as the transcript showed that he had hit back."[9]

How to Measure Progress?

Given both the progress that had been made and the clear limits to that progress, the question arose as to how the State Department should respond in public to Soviet developments in the human rights field. My assessment was that we had seen only limited progress regarding grants of permission to leave the country:

> We do also need to keep in mind that Jackson-Vanik is not limited to emigration of a particular ethnic group. While we were in Moscow, I met with Ludmilla Yevsukov, a most intelligent young woman, who is a member of an ethnically Russian Refusenik family. They, too, have become outcasts, but what makes matters worse, is that her father, a former Aeroflot navigator, has twice been committed to an institution for the mentally ill and has suffered the excruciating pain of being administered neuraleptic drugs (which, I am told, are not painful when administered to schizophrenics but very painful when administered to sane persons). He has been warned that if he does not stop demonstrating for emigration, he will be committed again. The daughter told me: "We hate the totalitarians. We want to live in a democracy." It was so sad to think that unless there is a real outcry over the fate of the Yevsukov family, her chances of being allowed to leave are close to nil.[10]

At the Vienna CSCE meeting, the Soviet Union had floated the idea of holding a conference on humanitarian cooperation in Moscow. A year and a half later, I became one of the strong advocates of such a conference, but in May 1987, I was strongly opposed:

> I believe the Soviets are eager to involve us in a "Humanitarian Cooperation" spectacular in Moscow in which they are going to pull out all the stops in portraying the problems of the West as to unemployment, homelessness, racism, etc. I don't think we should walk into that trap. Also, I do not believe that we are going to get any significant, long-

---

8. Shultz, *Turmoil and Triumph,* 894.

9. Ibid., 895.

10. Schifter memorandum to the secretary, "Post-Moscow Human Rights Strategy, HA Views," May 15, 1987, 1.

lasting human-rights concessions from the Soviets for agreeing to a Conference. It does not stand to reason.[11]

In another memorandum, on May 27, I outlined the progress that had been made in the Soviet Union and the continuing limits of that progress:

(a) Some political prisoners are released, a few harmless demonstrations are allowed, but it is made clear through the continued imprisonment of many political figures and the continued dreaded abuse of psychiatry that organized dissent will not be tolerated.

(b) Some accommodations are made to allow greater opportunities for religious observers to engage in religious ceremonies, but all of that within the limits of the state-controlled system of management of religion. Believers are also subjected to discrimination in education and employment.

(c) Some hitherto forbidden books, plays and films are allowed to be shown, but none that would challenge the system.

(d) History is once again being rewritten, this time to show Lenin's friends and associates, including those killed by Stalin, in a more favorable light, but not to tell the unvarnished truth, particularly as to Lenin's opponents.

(e) Foreign broadcasts which the powerful Soviet propaganda apparatus believes it can handle are no longer jammed, but broadcasts which it believes it can't handle continue to be jammed.

(f) Pre-1967 applications for exit visas are processed but a policy to discourage new applications is clearly in evidence. At the same time Jews continue to be discriminated against on grounds of ethnic origin.[12]

I noted that three different approaches had been suggested for U.S. policy to encourage further progress in the field of human rights in the Soviet Union and made it clear which I believed would be the right course:

(1) We can view the Soviet Union as receptive and responsive to praise and resentful and rejecting of reproach. . . .

(2) We can conclude that the Soviet Union is led by persons so deeply committed to maintaining themselves in power, so cynical in their view of human nature, so distrustful of us that no significant change can be expected of the present leadership.

(3) As is so often the case in analyses of this kind, there is also a golden middle way. It starts with the assumption, as in (2), that the Soviet leaders want to maintain themselves in power, are cynical, distrustful, and also deceitful, but it takes into account that the present leadership group seems to have realized that the Soviet economy and Soviet society are beset with problems and seems to be

---

11. Schifter, "Post-Moscow Human Rights Strategy," 2.

12. Schifter memorandum to the secretary, "Operational Suggestions for Our Soviet Human Rights Policy," May 27, 1987, 2.

committed to remedying the situation. To remedy the situation they seem to be more interested in reaching out to the West than their predecessors were. This fact offers us opportunities to effect Soviet behavior change not by obscuring their human-rights violations but by exposing them, thoughtfully and deliberately, so as to cause the Soviet leaders to move further on human rights because improving their standing in the West would be to their material advantage.[13]

I soon had an opportunity to test that approach. While human rights had been an item on the agenda of the Gorbachev-Shultz meeting in April 1987, the major issue, as it had been for some time, was arms reduction. Both sides were deeply interested in further progress in that field. To carry negotiations on arms control forward, Shevardnadze was to arrive in Washington for further negotiations in September 1987. But while arms reduction was to be the major theme, there was no doubt that Shultz would again raise human rights issues with the Soviet foreign minister. Given that fact, I thought I should travel to Moscow for discussions of human rights issues to see whether it might be possible to lay the groundwork for positive developments at the September meeting.

Progress on the Emigration Issue

As already noted, we had not seen any significant movement on the civil liberties front in the summer of 1987, and I did not expect the Soviets to move soon on any issue that might be viewed as a challenge to the basic precepts of the police state. On the other hand, the number of exit permits issued each month kept climbing. That development fit into my assessment of the attitude of the Soviet leadership. It seemed to me that the powers that be had concluded that getting rid of potential troublemakers was a boon to the system rather than a detriment. If the leadership had decided as much, it was now advisable to try to remove the obstacles that the bureaucracy had set up to prevent progress in this field and to place the emigration issue high on the agenda of the working-level bilateral talks in which we were engaged. Therefore, after having arranged my visit to Moscow in August 1987, I sent word ahead that I planned to focus on the emigration issue and expressed the hope that appropriate interlocutors would be selected for me.

I have heretofore mentioned that there were four groups of potential emigrants from the Soviet Union, namely, Armenians, Volga Germans, Pentecostals, and Jews. It soon became clear to me that Armenians in Armenia did not want to see their country depopulated. It also appeared to me that many members of the Armenian-American community felt the same way,

---

13. Schifter memorandum, "Operational Suggestions," 2–3.

so that there was not a great deal of pressure for substantially enhanced Armenian emigration.

The German government appeared interested in accepting Volga Germans, clearly for purely humanitarian reasons and not as a result of Volga German activity or political pressure from the German public.

For some reason that I am not familiar with, there did not appear to be a great deal of interest in the United States in fostering Pentecostal emigration. As it turned out, however, beginning in 1988, the KGB wanted to get rid of Pentecostals. But how could that be done without setting precedents for the emigration of other Soviet citizens of Russian ethnicity? The KGB found an answer to that problem, namely, to follow the precedent of the release of the Siberian Seven. The Pentecostal Christians were for emigration purposes to be treated as if they were Jews who were emigrating to Israel. To smooth the way for them, the KGB would give them a telephone number in Rome that they needed to call to get a vyzov, an invitation from a presumed Israeli relative. The Russian-speaking person who answered the phone in Rome would take the necessary information and, in due course, produce the vyzov that would invite the recipient to Israel.

But before an exit permit could be granted, there was still one other complication that had to be overcome: the issuance of an Israeli visa. Because the Soviet Union had broken diplomatic relations with Israel years earlier, there was no Israeli embassy or consulate in Moscow. Israel's interests in the Soviet Union were represented at that time by the Netherlands. The Dutch consular officials decided to issue the Israeli visas, well aware of the role they were playing in a game of deception, albeit one with a humanitarian objective. Thus, like many emigrating Jews, the Pentecostals traveled to Italy and there qualified for refugee status that allowed them to enter the United States.

As I planned my trip to Moscow in the summer of 1987, the resort to the ruse that ultimately allowed a great many Pentecostal Christians to leave the Soviet Union was still off in the future. As it turned out, their chance of emigrating depended on how the Soviet authorities would handle the issue of Jewish emigration.

Nearly thirty years of activity by the American Soviet-Jewry movement had placed Jewish emigration high on the U.S. government's agenda. Jewish emigration had been adopted as a major issue by President Reagan and Secretary Shultz, who put it at the very top of their list when engaged in conversations of human rights with the Soviet leadership.

As noted earlier, in addition to the problem posed by the restrictions on the total number of exit permits, there was the problem of the refuseniks, quite a number of whom had become well-known in the West and in Israel. In the hope that we could make progress regarding the refusenik cases at the September Shultz-Shevardnadze meeting in Washington, I picked that theme as the central one for a meeting that I had arranged in Moscow in August. The Shultz-Shevardnadze meeting was again to focus on arms reduction, but the human rights working group was scheduled to meet as well, and I thought it would be appropriate to lay the groundwork for such a meeting through preliminary discussions in Moscow.

Something unusual happened when I arrived at the Moscow airport. I was greeted not only by an officer of the U.S. embassy but also by an official of the foreign ministry. What was striking about this official was that he spoke excellent American English. When I asked him how much time he had spent in the United States, he told me that he had not spent any time in the United States. When I then asked him about his American accent, he explained to me that he had learned English from a couple who had emigrated from Brooklyn to Moscow in the 1930s.

As I later reflected on this conversation, I concluded first that anyone emigrating from Brooklyn to Stalin's Soviet Union in the 1930s must have been a thoroughly believing Communist. Second, when I wondered how this couple would have been recruited to teach American English to potential foreign service officers, it appeared most likely that this had been arranged by the KGB, or its predecessor, the NKVD. Be that as it may, my newfound Russian friend escorted me to all the meetings I attended in Moscow and also joined me at the airport as I departed Moscow.

The first person in the Soviet government whose office I visited was Anatoly. He welcomed me, told me that he was fully aware of the principal objective of my visit, and explained that the matter that I wanted to discuss was in the province of the Office of Visas and Registration (OVIR). A meeting had, therefore, been set up for me with the appropriate OVIR officials.

At the OVIR meeting, I started out with a list of cases of refuseniks who had close relatives in the United States. I received responses to my inquiries—not necessarily satisfactory responses, but coherent nevertheless—that enabled me to figure out what our next steps needed to be. (As our work developed over the following year, the next step was often an appeal to Shevardnadze.) But when I got to the names of refuseniks who had invitations to go to Israel, my interlocutors at the OVIR refused to respond. They told me that if I wanted to get information about people who wanted to emigrate to the United States they were prepared to respond. But as for Soviet citizens who wanted to emigrate to a third country, that was none of the business of the United States. I argued about our basic concern regarding Soviet adherence to its international human rights obligations, but that did not get me anywhere.

In due course, I returned to Anatoly's office. When he asked me how things had gone at the OVIR, I told him that my experience was quite disappointing. I told him further that my disappointment would most certainly be shared by Secretary Shultz when he got this unpleasant information. I said that this would cast a shadow over the September meeting. I received no concrete answer, but it soon became clear that my message had been understood.

I was scheduled to leave for Warsaw the next morning. As I arrived at the airport, my Soviet escort for this visit, the one who had been tutored by the couple from Brooklyn, greeted me there. He led me into the VIP lounge, asked whether I wanted a cup of tea, brought the tea, and sat down next to me. He then turned to me and said: "That list of names that the OVIR refused to discuss: Give it to me." I was, of course, greatly surprised but happy to give the list to him. He said: "We shall review it."

When I got on the plane, I drafted a cable reporting on my visit for Secretary Shultz's personal assistant, Charlie Hill. I reported, in particular, on the last minutes at the airport and concluded with the famous words of Secretary Rusk as the Cuban Missile Crisis wound down: "I think the other side has just blinked."

As planned, Shevardnadze and his delegation arrived in Washington in September. One member of that delegation, Yuri Reshetov, came for the specific reason of meeting with me. Reshetov—who, unlike Adamishin, was not a very friendly type—nevertheless had good news. I had the impression that the message of my August meeting in Moscow that the human rights issue might cast a shadow over the September meeting in Washington had reached the right place. Reshetov made it clear that the policy position taken by the OVIR at my meeting the previous month had been reversed. Following my meeting with Reshetov, I was able to report to Secretary Shultz several important developments.

First, the Soviet foreign ministry was prepared to discuss all emigration cases with us. Second, it was prepared to intercede with other Soviet authorities on emigration cases at our request. Third, changes in emigration regulations were likely. Fourth, the commission created in the presidium of the Supreme Soviet to review denials of exit permits could be expected to overrule some denials by local offices. Fifth, what we called abuse of psychiatry had been ended. Finally, the criminal code provisions dealing with violations of the religious-control laws and with defamation of the Soviet Union were likely to be repealed and persons heretofore convicted under these laws were likely to be released from prison, but anti-Soviet agitation and propaganda would remain a crime.

As noted earlier, one of the aspects of Soviet emigration law that had been of concern to us was the requirement that the vyzov, the invitation from abroad on the basis of which emigration could be allowed, needed to come from a first-degree relative, defined to include parents, children, and siblings. It was clearly a severe limitation on the right to emigrate. By early September, we had received word from Jewish organizations concerned with Soviet Jews that quite a number of the most recent emigrants had been permitted to leave even if their invitations did not come from first-degree relatives. I was able to report to the secretary that when I asked Reshetov about the continuation of the first-degree requirement, he told me that it "would not be applied rigidly."

Early in October 1987, quite a number of the refuseniks who had been on the list that I handed to the Soviet official at the Moscow Airport the preceding August were notified that they could leave. They included Ida Nudel, whose case had been of particular concern to Secretary Shultz.

Turning to the Prisoners of Conscience Issue

Later in September, I was back again in Moscow for further human rights discussions with Soviet officials as part of another secretarial visit devoted primarily to arms reduction and designed to lay a foundation for a summit meeting in Washington before the end of the year. Illustrating the intensity of our dialogue was that I was in Moscow again in early November, accompanying Deputy Secretary Whitehead. It was during that meeting that I participated in a conversation with Foreign Minister Shevardnadze that did not seem extraordinary to me at that time, but appears to have had significant results in the long run.

The one human rights issue on which we had made no progress at all was the issue posed by the criminalization of what Soviet law called "anti-Soviet agitation and propaganda," for which a person could be sentenced to seven years of hard labor and five years of internal exile. I suggested to the deputy secretary that the first human rights item that he should raise at our meeting with Shevardnadze was the issue posed by the continuing imprisonment of political dissidents. He did just that, handing Shevardnadze a list of the names of persons who were serving long prison sentences for the expression of political dissent.

Shevardnadze responded in a truly thoughtful manner. "I understand your point," he said. "But please recognize that these people were convicted by the courts of the Soviet Union under the laws of the Soviet Union. They are in prisons that are under the jurisdiction of the Ministry of the Interior. I am the foreign minister. What can I do about this?"

At that point an idea popped into my head. "Mr. Minister," I said, "the provisions of the criminal code that lead to the sentencing and imprisonment of persons for political or religious activity, Sections 70, 190-1, 142, and 227, are in conflict with the International Covenant on Civil and Political Rights. That covenant was negotiated by the foreign ministry, and its ratification was arranged by the foreign ministry. It would seem reasonable to assume that it is the task of the foreign ministry to bring the Soviet Union into compliance with the international obligations which the foreign ministry had negotiated and which the appropriate Soviet authorities had then ratified. That would mean repeal of the code provisions that I mentioned and the release of anyone convicted under these provisions."

My words were interpreted to Shevardnadze. He did not respond. But I thought I saw a sign of recognition in his eyes.

In the course of the same visit, Whitehead and I stopped off to see Anatoly Adamishin for a discussion of human rights. After we had said goodbye and were out in the corridor of the foreign ministry, I suddenly decided to turn around and walk back into Anatoly's office. I then said: "I think there is a struggle going on here. I hope the good guys will win." Anatoly did not say a word. He grabbed my hand, pressed it, and smiled. There was an expression of friendship in his eyes. That was the first time that I realized that Anatoly was most definitely on the side of reform.

My remark to Anatoly was based on what had become obvious by then: the struggle to which Gorbachev refers in his memoirs as "the battle between the reformist and the orthodox-conservative currents in the Party."[14] As the news of that struggle filtered out to the West, it became clear to many of us that it must have been the reason for the mixed signals we had received from Moscow during 1987: some forward movement, but movement that was severely limited in scope. It may also have been the reason for the troublesome comments by Gorbachev about human rights in discussions with Shultz. Could these comments have been made largely for the benefit of the notetakers, to send the message to members of the Politburo that the general secretary was acting within the Politburo's consensus?

Our Human Rights Dialogue Takes Hold

In early December 1987, another step forward in the improvement of relations between the Soviet Union and the United States took place with Gorbachev's visit to Washington for a summit meeting. The main event was the signing of the Intermediate-Range Nuclear Forces Treaty and arms control issues were thus high on the agenda. However, a few days before Gorbachev's arrival, a massive rally, for which 250,000 people turned out, took place on the Mall to support the cause of emigration for Soviet Jews. That fact came up in an interesting fashion during the summit.

What I was told by the person who served as President Reagan's interpreter for his initial meeting with General Secretary Gorbachev was that, after the starting formalities had been completed and the two leaders had

---

14. Gorbachev, *Memoirs*, 361.

sat down, Reagan turned to Gorbachev and said: "Have you heard about that rally on the Mall last Sunday?" Gorbachev responded that he had heard about it and wanted to get on with the business of the meeting, which was principally arms control. But Reagan did not let him. He started to talk about the size of the turnout, how much the Soviet emigration issue meant to many Americans, and how important it was that the Soviet Union responded positively. As Reagan talked, Gorbachev grew increasingly impatient, but Reagan insisted on completing his observations. What he made crystal clear was that emigration continued to be an important issue in the relationship between the United States and the Soviet Union.

While the talks got underway at the presidential level, I met with Alexei Glukhov, a Soviet foreign ministry official subordinate to Anatoly, to discuss details. On the issue of emigration, we reviewed both policy and specific cases. As the first-degree relative requirement had been viewed, quite rightly, to constitute a sharp limitation on emigration, I pressed Glukhov on the question of flexibility. Could we assure the interested groups that this requirement was no longer enforced with regard to certain nationalities? (I assumed that for demographic reasons it would not be waived for ethnic Russians.) He told me that that was so. I asked whether we could assure the interested groups that the policy would remain in effect from then on. He said we could. This change in the rules was critical in that it expanded the population that was in principle eligible for emigration from a mere fraction of Soviet Jews (and Armenians and ethnic Germans) to all members of those groups.

I then discussed what seemed to me to be a quota policy in the issuance of exit permits. By the time of our conversation, the number of Jews allowed to leave monthly was slightly more than one thousand, ten times the number it had been one year earlier, but still a clear limitation on the freedom to leave. There seemed to be similar quotas for Armenians and ethnic Germans.

Glukhov started out by denying, for the record, the existence of quotas. Later, during a break in our talks, I showed him the month-by-month figures for each of the groups. They followed a pattern. Over the immediately preceding months, the number of monthly departures had been constant for each of the groups. Glukhov admitted that it seemed as if a quota system was in place. (I was prepared to assume that Glukhov was truly unaware of it. It appeared that he was not one of the persons who needed to know facts about emigration policy.) I urged that the foreign ministry intercede to end the quota system and make an effort to speed up the processing of applications for exit permits.

Given the spirit of the Gorbachev visit and my discussion with Glukhov, we were quite optimistic by the time Gorbachev departed Washington that the human rights situation in the Soviet Union, including its emigration policy, would improve significantly.

In January 1988, I was once again back in Moscow and had lunch with Anatoly. Referring to my conversation of the preceding November with Foreign Minister Shevardnadze, I asked him about political prisoners. He responded: "We have decided to bring ourselves into compliance with our international obligations."[15]

It seemed to us that a new day was dawning. In September, we had been told by Reshetov that what we called abuse of psychiatry had ended; we had not received any reports of inappropriate commitments since then. Regarding political prisoners, I now received assurances from Anatoly that the Soviet Union would comply with the commitments it had made under the International Covenant on Civil and Political Rights and the Helsinki Final Act.

The year 1988 indeed turned out to be the most intensive year in the bilateral human rights dialogue between the Soviet Union and the United States. It was also a year of profound progress as the Soviet Union, under Gorbachev, emerged from totalitarianism and began its gradual transition to democracy.

As the year began, there was no doubt that the word from the very top of the Soviet governmental pyramid was to open up. The impression of those of us who were looking at developments from the outside was that the key policy decisions of greatest concern to the United States were taken by a triumvirate consisting of Gorbachev, Shevardnadze, and Politburo member Aleksandr Yakovlev.

As already noted, Shevardnadze struck Secretary Shultz from the very outset as a thoughtful and considerate person. Over time it became clear that his personal outlook was in harmony with democratic thought. Yakovlev had lived for ten years in a democracy, as Soviet ambassador to Canada. Gorbachev, although he had climbed up the bureaucratic ladder to the top of a totalitarian structure, appeared to be open to the ideas and suggestions that may have originated with his colleagues.[16]

---

15. It is worth noting in this context that human rights theorists tend to distinguish between nonbinding human rights documents, such as the Universal Declaration of Human Rights and the Helsinki Final Act, and binding documents, such as the International Covenant on Civil and Political Rights. In reality, that distinction does not have a great deal of meaning. Even when we are dealing with a binding document, the absence of an enforcement mechanism makes it de facto nonbinding. It is, above all, the publicity that is given to breaches of human rights standards, whether binding or nonbinding, that makes the critical difference. It was the publicity surrounding the Final Act—publicity, strangely enough, provided in the Soviet Union by the Brezhnev government—that caused it to have a major impact on developments in the field of human rights in the Soviet Union and its satellites.

The binding covenant, by contrast, though ratified by the Soviet Union in 1973, had not played a role in the discussion of human rights in the Soviet Union until I raised it fourteen years later in a meeting with Foreign Minister Shevardnadze. From what he told us, Shevardnadze clearly wanted to see political prisoners released from prison. My calling attention to the covenant provided the foreign minister with a bureaucratic hook that would allow his intercession on the issue presented by prisoners of conscience.

16. When I read Gorbachev's memoirs, I came across, on page 24, an item that I thought might explain what it was in the background of this successful apparatchik that caused him to bring

A vitally important additional factor in the democratic evolution of the Soviet Union was the U.S. position on arms reduction. The Soviet leadership had been increasingly concerned about the pressure that an arms race would impose on the country's economy. From their dialogue with the U.S. president and secretary of state, the Soviet leadership had concluded, first, that it would be possible to reach fair agreements on arms reduction, and second, that in light of the emphasis that both Reagan and Shultz placed on human rights, the chances of arms reduction would be greatly enhanced if the Soviet Union would accommodate U.S. concerns in that field.

Combating the Naysayers

While it was indeed increasingly clear that a decision had been made at the very top to move away from totalitarianism, the devil was in the details. And the task of working on the details had been left to Anatoly and me.

Neutralizing the work of the devils was indeed the challenge before us. We, at the U.S. end of the dialogue, had, over the years, been used to the existence of a monolithic Soviet system. We did not think it possible that one agency—namely, the foreign ministry—would adopt one line while another agency adopted another line.

But that is precisely what happened. In early January 1988, we received word that applicants for exit permits were once again turned back if they could not furnish a vyzov, an invitation from a first-degree relative living abroad. They were told that the waiver of the first-degree relative requirement applied only for 1987. That waiver, they were further told, had expired and as of January 1, 1988, an invitation from first-degree relatives living abroad was once again required. It appeared that what we had considered a major breakthrough on the emigration front had not been a breakthrough after all.

But that was no reason to give up. Early in February 1988, I attended an international human rights conference in Venice at which I encountered Glukhov. I immediately pulled him aside and reminded him that I had, on his recent visit to Washington, asked him expressly whether the waiver of the first-degree relative requirement would stay in place and that he had assured me that it would. Glukhov confirmed that conversation. I then told

---

about fundamental change in the Soviet state. When he was six years old—in 1937, one of the years of Stalin's major purges, he tells the reader—his maternal grandfather was arrested on suspicion of being a Trotskyist. Gorbachev's grandmother then moved to his parents' house. Gorbachev describes the events that followed in the following words: "Our neighbors began shunning our house as if it were plague-stricken. Only at night would some close relative venture to stop by. Even the boys from the neighborhood avoided me. Now I understand that one cannot blame them: anyone who maintained contact or simply associated with the family of an 'enemy of the people' was also subject to arrest. All of this was a great shock to me and has engraved in my memory ever since."

him that I was truly shocked to hear that the first-degree relative requirement was once again being enforced. I added that the assurances we had received had been passed on to interested groups. The Soviet Union's backsliding was, therefore, not only substantively wrong but also was a significant embarrassment to the U.S. government, which had evidently allowed itself to be misled. Glukhov seemed genuinely surprised. He promised to look into the matter immediately. He pointed out that I was due in Moscow later that month and promised to have an answer for me by then.

Later in the month, I was indeed in Moscow. On the Soviet side, the meeting was again chaired by Anatoly. He began the meeting with an apology. The waiver about which I had talked to Glukhov had indeed been a waiver for 1987 only. It was sheer bureaucratic oversight that it had not been renewed by the end of the year. It had just been renewed, he said. I asked whether it was a waiver for 1988 only or a permanent waiver. Though the response was unclear, I was left with the impression that the waiver would remain in place for good. It did.[17]

There were other challenges as well. Although Anatoly had informed me of the Soviet government's decision on the release of political prisoners in principle, there was the further problem of making sure that the prisoners who were to benefit from that decision—those who had violated the political provisions of the criminal code or its provisions regulating the practice of religion—were properly identified and then released. This required the cooperation of the Ministry of the Interior, which had responsibility for prisons.

Then we discovered another, truly complex problem: Some persons who had been placed on our list of political prisoners had been convicted under trumped-up charges, including treason. In those cases, I asked for the official record of the case. Anatoly did not reject my request outright, but told me that the relevant offices of the Soviet government would not release the files. He suggested that we try to solve the problem by arranging for reciprocity. I responded by noting that the United States did not have political prisoners. He suggested that he would give me some names and hoped that I would supply the records.

In due course, I did get the names. They turned out to be Puerto Rican nationalists who had been convicted of acts of terrorism. I went about the business of writing to U.S. attorneys across the country, asking for the relevant documents. I had no problem collecting all the records and duly delivered them to Anatoly. The problem of getting Soviet records of the cases we had asked about turned out to be quite difficult. We were told that documents could not be released for cases in which the evidence was secret. I suppose it was understandable

---

17. During our lunch break, Anatoly invited me to go on a walk with him. As we walked through the snow-covered streets, he made some further remarks to me that confirmed once again that he was on the side of the reformers.

that prosecutors who had manufactured a case at the behest of the KGB were not prepared to release files that revealed what they had done.

Then, in the spring of 1988, I received information that an Armenian nationalist leader had been arrested, tried, and sentenced to a prison term for "defamation of the Soviet system." On another of my visits to the Soviet Union, I mentioned the case to Anatoly, pointing out that I had been expressly told by his ministry that laws such as the one that criminalized defamation of the Soviet system, Article 190-1, would no longer be enforced and would ultimately be repealed. Anatoly wrote down the name of the Armenian leader and said he would look into it.

A few weeks later, I received a visit in Washington from the same Armenian leader. He told me that he had suddenly, without any formal proceedings, been released from prison and taken to the Moscow airport, from where he was flown to Addis Ababa. Once the plane landed there, he was driven into the center of the city. At a certain point the car stopped and he was asked to get out. His guide then pointed to a nearby building and told him: "That's the American embassy." He was soon processed for entry into the United States as a refugee, thus bringing his saga to an end.

Another case that demonstrated the limits of the foreign ministry's authority, and yet its ability to solve problems that we raised with it, involved a person on our refusenik list named Irina Varshavskaya. As the Soviet contention was that the persons whose applications for exit permits had been turned down were persons who possessed classified information, I had decided to order our refusenik list by the year in which a refusenik had stopped working on classified information. Thus, the list was headed by the person who quit security-sensitive work earlier than any of the others. That person was Irina Varshavskaya, who had last been engaged in security-sensitive work more than forty years earlier, in 1947. She wanted to join her son, who had been allowed to emigrate to Denmark.

I do not recall ever meeting Varshavskaya, but I did inquire of my friends in the refusenik community what kind of work she had done that still needed to be kept secret after almost half a century. The interesting answer that I received was that she had worked for the secret police, the NKVD—the predecessor of the KGB. I was also told that she had had a nervous breakdown that caused her to quit. At one of my sessions with Alexei Glukhov, as I started to read my list, beginning with the name of Irina Varshavskaya, I asked: "What's the problem with her after forty years? Did she work for Beria?"[18]

About a month later, I met with Glukhov again and, reviewing our refusenik list, started again with Varshavskaya. When I again asked why she was not being allowed to leave, Glukhov's response was that he had heard

---

18. Lavrenty Beria was the dreaded chief of the secret police, executed in 1953 after Stalin's death.

that she had worked for Beria. I then reminded him of the fact that what he had remembered was a joke of mine at the earlier meeting. Following our formal session, I had a private talk with Glukhov, in which he told me that the foreign ministry was prepared to be of general help regarding human rights matters of concern to us, but that cases involving the KGB were quite difficult to handle.

A few months later, I saw an article in the *New York Times* reporting the appointment of a new head of the KGB, Vladimir Kryuchkov. The *Times* also printed a picture of the new KGB chief. I recalled that I had met a Soviet official by the name of Sergey Kryuchkov in Paris about five years earlier. What's more, Sergey Kryuchkov, though much younger, did resemble the picture of Vladimir Kryuchkov. I had met Sergey while representing the United States on the human rights committee of UNESCO. He was with the Soviet delegation to UNESCO's human rights committee and seemed to hover around the Soviet representative, Samuil Zivs, a Lithuanian Jew well known for his leadership of the Soviet Union's Anti-Zionist Committee. I had come to the conclusion at that time that Sergey was Zivs's KGB overseer.

On the next ministerial trip to Moscow, the U.S. and Soviet delegations once again assembled in the foreign ministry's elegant guesthouse, the Osobnyak. I used the opportunity to ask whether Sergey Kryuchkov was related to Vladimir Kryuchkov. As I had suspected, I was told that Sergey was Vladimir's son. I then asked where I could find Sergey, as I wanted to discuss a case with him. I was told that he was with the Soviet delegation in the very building in which we were gathered, and my interlocutors offered to look for him. Before long they brought us together. After discussing our days in Paris, I said to Sergey: "There is a matter that I would like to ask you to discuss with your father." I then told him about the Varshavskaya case. He shrank back and said: "I have nothing to do with that organization." My response was: "I am not saying that you do. I am just asking you to mention this case to your father. I am sure he would listen to you. I would certainly listen to my son if he talked to me about a matter in which I am officially involved." Sergey did not agree. He reiterated that he would not get involved. As he left, I thought I had struck out.

A few minutes later, however, Sergey reappeared with one of the higher-ranking officials of the foreign ministry and said to me: "Tell him about the case." I did just that. A few weeks later Varshavskaya was on her way to Denmark to join her son. I assume that if Sergey did not talk to his father, he talked to some other high-ranking person in the KGB, someone beyond the reach of the foreign ministry who had the power to allow Varshavskaya to go.

The New U.S.-Soviet Friendship

During the first half of 1988, we saw our Soviet friends—they had indeed become our friends—about every six weeks, alternating between Moscow and Washington. From one visit to Moscow to the next, I saw the fog of the dictatorship lifting. People seemed to be less afraid. The media opened up. Political prisoners were released. There was greater religious freedom; the number of emigration permits increased sharply. It was an exhilarating time for those of us who had hoped for decades that the Soviet totalitarian system would come to an end.

The change in the relationship between our two countries was demonstrated most vividly in May 1988, when President Reagan visited Moscow for another summit meeting. On that occasion, the president and the general secretary took a stroll together through Red Square. Shultz saw it as "a powerful visual symbol of the immense change well under way. There the two men were, easy in their relationship, greeting Soviet citizens. Gorbachev held a baby. Reagan's winning smile came through. Body language and imagery told the story: A dangerous cold war was ending."[19]

The feeling of warmth and cooperation reflected in the interaction of the two heads of government also characterized the interaction of those of us at the working level. We had not as yet resolved all the outstanding problems in the human rights field, but it had become increasingly clear that even though the Soviet foreign ministry did not always have the full cooperation of other agencies of the Soviet government, it was ultimately able to deliver because it was carrying out the policy endorsed by the country's top leadership. Under these circumstances, I began to see our role as one in which we dealt with the Soviet foreign ministry as a partner in the effort to bring respect for human rights to the Soviet Union.

During the spring of 1988, my conversations with Anatoly broadened. As the Vienna CSCE follow-up conference began to focus on the drafting of a concluding document, Anatoly told me that the Soviet Union would be greatly interested in including in that document a provision that would arrange for a human rights meeting in Moscow as one of the CSCE meetings to be held between the Vienna follow-up conference and the next CSCE follow-up conference. He also raised the question of the possibility of repealing the Stevenson amendment, which severely restricted loans by the U.S. Export-Import Bank to the Soviet Union.

Ambassador Warren Zimmermann, who headed the U.S. delegation to the Vienna Conference, shared my view that the proposed Moscow meeting should be agreed to, as did my good friend Ambassador Max Kampelman,

---

19. Shultz, *Turmoil and Triumph*, 1103.

who then served as counselor to the State Department. Max also shared my thoughts regarding the Stevenson amendment. Both of us had for decades been hard-liners regarding the Soviet Union and Communism. We had generally found the State Department's European Bureau to follow an approach that was significantly softer than ours. Now, I discovered, the European Bureau was much more hard-line than the policy that I was advocating. Two years earlier, as noted above, a European Bureau official had said: "The problem with Schifter is that he is a Menshevik ideologue. He hates the Bolsheviks." That same official was now quoted to me as having said: "The problem with Schifter is that he is a Menshevik ideologue. He thinks the Mensheviki have taken over in Moscow."[20]

It was against that background—one of recognizing the changes that were occurring in the Soviet Union—that I thought we could be of help to the foreign ministry in its struggle within the Soviet government, if we were to respond to a letter from Anatoly that had emphasized the Soviet label under which our dialogue had been started, that label being humanitarian cooperation. Thus we started exchange programs that dealt with the problems of the handicapped, to which we later added the elderly and, later still, the mentally ill.

---

20. He may very well have been close to being right on both occasions.

5

Vienna

Anatoly Adamishin

The positive changes brought into the international arena by Gorbachev's perestroika, the feeling among Eastern and Western politicians that the end of the Cold War was around the corner, and the dramatic improvement in Soviet-U.S. relations has been labeled as a new détente. Although unprecedented in many of its features, the new détente actually had much in common with the old détente of the 1970s, which brought a lessening of international tension for the first time. The bridge between the new and old détentes was the so-called Helsinki Process or, more officially, the Conference for Security and Cooperation in Europe. The Final Act of the CSCE was signed in the Finnish capital on August 1, 1975. The signatures of the leaders of thirty-three European countries, plus the United States and Canada, placed them on record as supporting sovereign equality, territorial integrity, nonintervention in internal affairs, and respect for human rights. The Final Act also called for periodic follow-up meetings of all the signatories to review how the Helsinki Process was progressing. Such meetings took place in Belgrade, Madrid, and Vienna; Dick and I happened to be involved in crucial decisions regarding the third of these.

This chapter focuses on the Helsinki Process leading up to the Vienna meeting and the course of that meeting, which began in November 1986 and concluded in January 1989. My part of the chapter begins in the mid-1960s with Soviet initiatives in the CSCE's creation and development, which set us on the path to Helsinki, and wraps up in the late 1980s with Soviet efforts to implement the agreement reached at Vienna. I was personally involved over the course of these years at different stages and at various levels, from interpreter to deputy minister. Dick's part of the chapter starts in September

1988 and discusses how our humanitarian dialogue helped facilitate the agreement reached several months later. Both of our contributions tell a tale of bureaucratic infighting within our respective governments as well as tough negotiations between them, but a tale, too, of remarkable progress on a number of human rights fronts and of a successful conclusion to a meeting that brought about a transformation of the international landscape.

In this chapter, as in previous ones, Dick and I seek to show that a breakthrough in Soviet-U.S. cooperation on humanitarian issues, as well as on some other issues, was due almost exclusively to the changes provoked by Gorbachev's new thinking. The link was evident and direct; our part was to help set up a delicate and sometimes controversial process of rapprochement between the positions of the two teams of political leaders, headed by Gorbachev and Reagan, that were initially separated by opposite ideologies and different political cultures but that came to work together in a spirit of confidence and mutual trust.

Europeans at One Negotiating Table

In suggesting a convocation of European countries, the Soviet Union in the mid-1960s sought to perpetuate, on a multilateral basis, the political and territorial outcomes of World War II and the postwar period, that is, the division of Europe into two opposing blocs. The implementation of this concept would fix the boundaries of Europe without the need to discuss the delicate issue of a peace treaty with Germany. In any event, the slogan "Europeans should sit down at one negotiating table" was an inviting one.

Minister Gromyko was the first to test the West's reaction to the idea of an international conference in April 1966, during negotiations with Italian leaders in which I served as interpreter. At that time, Italy had special relations with Russia: The two countries had just signed an agreement for the construction of a huge Italian automobile-manufacturing plant in the Soviet Union. The Italians immediately supported the Soviet minister's proposal. However, they suggested that the Soviets' name for the conference—the Conference on Security in Europe—also include the word "cooperation." This innovation allowed human rights topics to be included on the agenda.

The road to Helsinki lasted almost ten years. It survived the Soviet intervention in Czechoslovakia in the summer of 1968 and was given added momentum by the Ostpolitik (Eastern policy) of West German chancellor Willy Brandt and the treaties that Bonn concluded with Poland and the Soviet Union in 1970.

The Soviet Union gave its consent to U.S. participation in the conference, although originally Washington had been excluded from the list of the participants. The United States had been a signatory to the postwar Yalta and

Potsdam agreements and was one of the guarantors of the quadripartite agreement on West Berlin.

The Soviet Union resorted to an arsenal of diplomatic techniques to convince the West to participate. At a certain stage, it became clear that the West would display goodwill with regard to accepting the territorial and political realities in Europe. But the West wanted to exact a price: broadening Soviet practical adherence to a number of specified human rights. President Richard Nixon and Secretary of State Henry Kissinger did not hide their negative attitude toward the European plan; the United States agreed to participate only after Nixon's visit to Moscow in May 1972, which resulted in the signing of the Strategic Arms Reduction Treaty.

In November 1972, multilateral consultations at the ambassadorial level commenced in Helsinki, continuing for almost nine months. In July 1973, the foreign ministers of thirty-five countries gathered in the Finnish capital. Europe had not seen such a representative assembly since the Congress of Vienna in 1815. The first stage of the conference was a success, as the ministers agreed on how they believed Europe should henceforth exist and gave instructions to experts to prepare a conclusive document.

Concession or Advantage?

Sometimes it was more difficult to reach agreement among ourselves than with our Western partners. Andrei Gromyko liked to repeat that internal diplomacy is much more important than the external kind. Our leadership's objective was to make the deal as advantageous as possible by reducing the price the West demanded under the pretext of noninterference in internal affairs. As Gromyko publicly stated, internal laws are a boundary at the gate of each state, at which others must stop.

But there were other points of view as well within the Soviet establishment: Some people believed that moving forward in the field of human rights was not a concession to the West but an indispensable prerequisite for the country's development, which needed long-overdue democratic reforms. If foreign policy could help promote such reforms, the policy should only be welcomed. Thus, the human rights issue was not a price but an advantage—and if we could get the West to accept post–World War II territorial and political realities through the CSCE, the gain would be double.

The individuals who held such views never came together as a formal group—even among ourselves we rarely discussed the issues openly—but some were influential, particularly the assistants to Leonid Brezhnev. People such as Anatoly Blatov, Andrei Aleksandrov, Aleksandr Bovin, and Georgi Shachnazarov; those in the Ministry of Foreign Affairs, such as Anatoly Kovalev; and academicians such as Georgi Arbatov managed to convince

Brezhnev that without a counterbalance—the human rights issue—the West wouldn't sign the Final Act and we wouldn't have closure to World War II. Brezhnev, a war veteran, understood. Because he gave his consent, no one inside the Politburo objected.

Putting into writing the ideas proposed at the ministerial conference proved to be an enormously difficult task that took almost two years. One dissenting voice was enough to make all participants revisit wording. The concluding document—the Final Act—had thirty-five authors, including the Vatican; it was the first time the Holy See had participated in a major international forum since 1824. Never before had the principle of consensus, the highest manifestation of democracy, been implemented on such a scale. The Final Act comprised every possible aspect of international agreement, from the principle of the inviolability of frontiers and various military aspects of security to specific matters of economic and humanitarian cooperation. The call for periodic follow-up meetings provided for further development of the Helsinki Process.

In the end, we realized a double gain: the Final Act contains sections on both the inviolability of frontiers and human rights, including a wide range of practical improvements in this area. For the first time, the Soviet Union took steps to permit people to emigrate for the purpose of family reunification.

What about Implementation?

The ten years following the Helsinki meetings were gloomy times for moderates in Soviet foreign policy. Despite early hopes, very little changed in Russia's domestic affairs. Because the Final Act was not binding, our geriatric leaders decided on a course of nonaction: We would simply not implement the provisions we didn't like.[1] Two years after the Final Act was signed, Gromyko told President Carter: "We don't believe that in the world there could be one person or even a group of persons who can claim an exclusive right to gauge human rights. We will never permit others to interfere in our internal affairs. Each state must settle these questions independently. That is how it is done in reality." Gromyko was in line with our legal system, which declared that "human rights, as such, lie beyond the limits of international law. It is an internal affair of a state to dispose of these rights regarding the population and individual citizens."[2]

---

1. Recently I spoke about this practice with an ex-colleague, who tried to defend it with the motivation of political expediency. "Look," he said to me, "they [the West] made the same argument, ignoring the principle of inviolability of borders when Yugoslavia was breaking down."

2. From a collection of articles published by the Diplomatic Academy, *Oktiabrskaia revoluzia i sovremennoe Mejdunuarodoe Pravo* [The October Revolution and Modern International Law] (Moscow: Diplomatic Academy, MID SSSR, 1978), 137.

The CSCE follow-up meetings were constantly on the verge of being ruined. One reason was the Soviet leadership's position on implementation. Yet the other side was at fault as well, trying to present the multifaceted Final Act as dedicated exclusively to human rights. The Soviets, those who promoted détente, tried to keep the Helsinki Process alive, and countered efforts to transform the follow-up meetings into propagandistic wrestling, facing a long and difficult battle.

One example from 1983, probably the worst year for détente, illustrates the struggle we waged. The Madrid Conference, which reunited the thirty-five countries to examine the progress of implementing the Final Act, was in danger of becoming a debacle. For reasons still unclear to me, Minister Gromyko was ready to allow the conference to end in failure. By deciding not to share with the Politburo the cables containing alarming information that the ministry was receiving from Madrid, Gromyko could present a debacle as a fait accompli. When I saw that all my attempts to influence Andrei Andreevich were futile, I called up Anatoly Blatov, assistant to the secretary general, Yuri Andropov. This worked as it had worked eight years earlier with Brezhnev: Gromyko's behavior changed at once.[3] I prayed that Gromyko would never discover my exploit.

Madrid ended with a compromise, including a decision to convene a conference on military détente and disarmament in Europe. The human rights issue, although it didn't come to the forefront, was at any rate not discarded.

Historical Defect

The habit of signing international agreements in the humanitarian sphere without any intention of fulfilling them dates back to Stalin and the Universal Declaration of Human Rights,[4] which was consigned to oblivion for forty years until perestroika gave it new life.[5]

---

3. The head of the Soviet Union at that time was less sensitive than Gromyko to accusations that he was conducting a weak foreign policy. Gromyko, as foreign minister, might be assumed to be a dove rather than a hawk, but he tried to dispel that idea. Andropov sometimes had more subtle views than his colleagues in the Politburo. On December 14, 1982, I marked in my diary the words he told to us, his speechwriters: "Even if we cannot make concessions now in the human rights field, it wouldn't be appropriate to pull down 'the friends' [allies in the Warsaw Pact] from their positions"—which were slightly more liberal than ours.

4. It is remarkable that the Soviet delegation headed by Vyshinsky, having failed to put off the vote on the Universal Declaration, abstained in December 1948 at the UN General Assembly—even though it voted for the great majority of the articles. Vyshinsky, by the way, tried to exclude the passage about citizen's obligations toward their state. The reason, albeit not declared, was that we could not support the obligations toward the bourgeois state.

5. In 1988, the third year of perestroika, the fortieth anniversary of the Universal Declaration of Human Rights was solemnly noted at the All-Union level. We in the Ministry of Foreign

The International Covenant on Civil and Political Rights, ratified by the Soviet Union, went into force in 1976. As a treaty, it is considered binding and has compelling authority; thus, once it was signed and ratified, it should have been implemented. But that was never going to happen. We simply did not replicate the provisions of the covenant in our internal laws even though the document contained specific obligations to do so. Why did we feel we could flaunt such obligations? Because our legislation had priority over international norms; as we saw it, Soviet law was the best in the world and our social system was the most perfect and humane. In addition, the Soviet constitution guaranteed social and civil liberties. Finally, we could point out that the United States hadn't signed or ratified the bulk of international agreements that concerned human rights either.

The Vienna Meeting

The first two CSCE follow-up meetings, in Belgrade (1977–78) and Madrid (1980–83), were discordant. From the beginning, we hoped that the Vienna encounter would be different, thanks to the leadership of Gorbachev. Yet it did not become an immediate venue for constructive diplomacy. Although there were new ways of thinking within the Soviet Union, these innovations didn't reach the members of the CSCE for some time. Once they did, the Western countries needed time to adjust to the revised Soviet approach. Our Western colleagues did not immediately realize that the new Soviet leadership's declared intention to make advances in all four of the main Helsinki topics, or "baskets"—political, military, economic, and humanitarian—was not just an opportunity to show off. Overcoming our historically confrontational reputation in the humanitarian-legal arena turned out to be a difficult job.

The meeting began on November 4, 1986. For almost the entire first year, NATO countries did not react to our political-military proposals. They preferred to concentrate, as in the past, solely on human rights matters. Presenting the CSCE meetings as dedicated exclusively to humanitarian problems and to the respective shortcomings of the socialist countries was a Western propagandist modus operandi.

Affairs prepared a plan of events that was subsequently approved by the CPSU's Central Committee, including the publication of the Universal Declaration of Human Rights in leading Soviet newspapers, as well as a full collection of international human rights documents. We defined the international standards of the Universal Declaration as "universal human values"—a term proposed by Gorbachev. For the first time, a specialized UN seminar on human rights would be held on Soviet soil, which led to the issuing of a commemorative postal stamp and other events. The most remarkable event was a special meeting of the Supreme Soviet.

The situation began to shift as the substantial changes in the Soviet Union became evident. There was a newfound responsiveness to the concerns and suggestions of other nations. Yuri Kashlev, the head of the Soviet delegation in Vienna (and a good friend of mine), recalled that Shevardnadze's proposal in Vienna to convene a pan-European conference on humanitarian cooperation in Moscow was initially viewed as surreal. Some Western delegates even made bets with Kashlev that such an event had no chance of being held during their lifetime.[6]

It's Time to Act

During 1988, Dick and I met frequently to discuss bilateral human rights matters. But in due course our conversation turned to the multilateral CSCE forum and to Soviet-U.S. cooperation at the Vienna meeting, which was still going on. The compromise being reached in Vienna included three main concepts. First, human rights had universal applicability, existing for both the East and the West. Second, the humanitarian complex embraced the entire gamut of freedoms—political, social, civil, economic, and cultural.

Third, participating countries could establish their own respective legislation, but it had to comply with international commitments, in particular those voluntarily adopted by the states under the Helsinki Process.

When Dick came to Moscow in May 1988, Yuri Kashlev participated in one of our talks. The previous year, Yuri had frankly described our weak points in a Politburo meeting: psychiatric abuse, as 183 confined people had diagnoses that were at best dubious, and refuseniks, some of whom couldn't leave the country even though many years had passed since they had had access to state secrets. "How could this happen," exclaimed Yuri, "when the general secretary himself had declared publicly that the terms of security restrictions could not exceed five to ten years."[7] During these Politburo discussions, Mikhail Gorbachev, appropriately prepared by our proposals, instructed Evgeny Chasov (Ministry of Health), Albert Vlasov (Central Committee), Fillip Bobkov (KGB), and Vladimir Terebilov (Prosecutor General) to transfer the management of special psychiatric hospitals from the Ministry

---

6. For a while, the United States used its power to consent to or oppose such a conference as a diplomatic tool. In a conversation with me on February 28, 1989, the U.S. ambassador to Moscow, Jack Matlock, while complaining of a decline in the number of exit permits for the Soviet refuseniks (in particular, he mentioned a person called Samoilovich, who had not been connected with secret matters for sixteen years), wondered if George Shultz hurried too much in giving the consent for the conference in Moscow.

7. When we, from below, raised the issue of secrecy before our chiefs, we used to say that the political leadership was interested in creating some order, if for no other reason than to have more knowledge about what was occurring behind the closed gates of the military-industrial complex.

of Internal Affairs to the Ministry of Health. Not long after this, Kashlev was able to announce at the Vienna meeting that this transfer had been accomplished. He added that the jamming of foreign radios had been brought to a close. We were confident that the U.S. side—namely, President Reagan and Secretary of State Shultz—would recognize these concessions, and as a consequence, a breakthrough was more likely.

Trouble Is Not Over Yet

That's why we were surprised when, in the middle of November 1988, the U.S. embassy in Moscow delivered a message stating that it was not ready to sign a comprehensive document. As had been the case in Belgrade more than a decade earlier, the United States preferred to issue a brief, formal paper. We suspected that something was happening inside the U.S. administration and guessed that certain people in Washington worried about the military aspects of the conference. It seemed likely that the prospect of future negotiations on reducing conventional forces in Europe scared those preoccupied with the status of U.S. troops in Western Europe.

A few days later, we received word from our embassy in Washington that the U.S. assistant secretary of state for human rights, Richard Schifter, would come to Moscow for further discussion of the outstanding problems and that he was acting on instructions from Secretary Shultz.

The job of arranging the visit fell to me. I scheduled a meeting between Dick and the first deputy minister, Anatoly Kovalev, who held the second-highest position in our ministry. The discussions focused on two main issues in the humanitarian field: political prisoners and emigration. After Shevardnadze had been briefed, he instructed us to find solutions to the issues raised by Dick. The task of preparing the agreement between the United States and the Soviet Union was assigned to me.

Regarding remaining issues of emigration, the problem was that our Ministry of Defense and the KGB objected to granting exit permits to certain refuseniks. Dick told us that we needed to resolve 120 of those cases by the end of 1988 in order for the United States to sign a statement in Vienna while Secretary Shultz was still in office.

The problem of political prisoners proved to be more complicated. The Soviet leadership had decided to release from prison persons who had been convicted for either political offenses or holding religious meetings of denominations not recognized under Soviet law. The United States raised the issue of prisoners convicted of treason on what it claimed were false charges. Dick and I met in December 1988 in New York to discuss that issue. I made a commitment that we would review the cases that the United States had raised with our Justice Ministry and that anyone improperly convicted would be released.

It was in light of these understandings that agreement was reached in Vienna and a final statement adopted on January 17, 1989—during Secretary Shultz's final days in office. Dick eloquently describes this episode from the American angle.

This time the gain for the Soviet Union was more than double: The Vienna concluding agreement had, as an integral part, mandates for negotiation on conventional armed forces in Europe. These negotiations began promptly after the close of the Vienna meeting. In addition, a three-phased conference on human rights and humanitarian issues was convened in Paris (1989), Copenhagen (1990), and Moscow (1991). The American concessions—and Secretary Shultz was criticized in the United States for conceding too much, exactly in the same way that some Soviet hard-liners condemned our concessions—turned out to be advantageous for consolidating détente in Europe.

To Implement

Mindful of how the old (in both senses) Soviet leadership had dealt with international humanitarian agreements, we ensured that their strategy would not be repeated. The Politburo gave the go-ahead for the process of implementation immediately after signing the Vienna statement.

In March 1989, a meeting of more than two dozen agencies, departments, scientific institutes, and the like was held at the Ministry of Foreign Affairs. Yuri Kashlev, Yuri Deriabin, and I were responsible for the CSCE in the ministry. We reviewed the work accomplished thus far in implementing the Vienna agreements, urged its acceleration, and stressed that an important series of laws was in preparation in areas such as mass media, religion, emigration, and voluntary societies.[8] These new laws had to correspond to international standards and Vienna obligations, and we insisted, correcting our earlier practice, that the Ministry of Foreign Affairs's experts were needed to participate in implementation. Our arguments prevailed, and a special working group on fulfilling CSCE human-rights requirements was created, with our ministry at its head.

Half a year later I was invited to the Supreme Soviet's Committee on International Affairs to report on the follow-up to Vienna. I informed the parliamentary members that we had kept our pledge to clean up the backlog of exit applications in six months. Three years before, there had been 11,000 refuseniks; in January 1989, there were 2,000; six months later, those who could not leave the Soviet Union for security reasons numbered 299. I listed

---

8. Vestnik MID SSSR, April 1989, 20–21.

some of our other accomplishments, focusing on what was yet to be done, primarily in the field of legislation. I was well received by the legislators, who were usually rather critical of executive government officials.[9]

In the aftermath of Vienna, there were few skeptics regarding our association with the Council of Europe. We started joining the council's numerous conventions to aid our law-building activity.

In September 1991, two months before the Soviet Union fell apart, there was an event that, in different times, might have been a culmination of our human rights efforts: the Moscow stage of the humanitarian conference, which had been envisaged three years before at the Vienna meeting. Gorbachev put forward five concepts. First, if human rights were being suppressed—if violence was present not only in international relationships, but inside a country—this repression should be the subject of general attention and common reaction. Second, our main objective was freedom—economic, political, national, and spiritual; a system based on violence and trampling upon freedoms would be rejected. Third, a monopoly on power was as perishable as one on property. Fourth, exposing our weak humanitarian points met our own internal needs and could not be considered politically harmful for the Soviet Union. Fifth, when the Soviet Union voluntarily joined international pacts, it made international law a part of its internal policy. Thus, *pacta sunt servanda*.

Using the Moscow conference as a lever, those who participated in the human rights struggle succeeded in introducing many changes in legislation and in everyday life. It was a kind of triumph—though behind this triumph was the deteriorating national situation. As for me, I watched the Moscow conference from Rome, where I had arrived in May 1990 as Soviet ambassador, not suspecting that I would be the last Soviet envoy to this country—and the first one from the Russian Federation.

---

9. *Pravda,* September 28, 1989, 1, 5.

Richard Schifter

Putting the Vienna CSCE Meeting on Our Bilateral Agenda

During the second half of 1988, the U.S.-Soviet human rights dialogue, while continuing to deal with specific cases and categories of cases, came to focus increasingly on the CSCE's Vienna follow-up meeting and to the drafting of a final document for that meeting. In August, the Soviet delegation reminded the meeting participants that the Soviet suggestion of a CSCE human rights meeting in Moscow was still on the table.

The UN Human Rights Center had arranged for a conference in Milan in early September that was to be devoted to the subject of international human rights standards. Both Anatoly and I had been invited. Before leaving for Milan I received a message from Anatoly to the effect that he wanted to be sure to see me there.

We encountered each other in a lecture hall at the University of Milan. Anatoly, who is fluent in Italian, delivered a ringing endorsement of the human rights cause in that language. He had written it out in longhand. It was indeed a sign of the times that a Soviet diplomat had the courage to deliver a speech at a public event that he had personally written and that, it would seem, had not even been cleared. I spoke after Anatoly and made the point that human rights were by no means a purely Western cause.

As soon as the proceedings were over, Anatoly pulled me aside and urged that we go for a walk. We stepped outside, and as we walked around the quadrangle of the University of Milan, our conversation turned once again to the issue of the proposed Moscow human rights meeting, which was the key to agreement on the concluding document of the Vienna CSCE meeting.

Anatoly was quite direct in his approach. "Let's not haggle as if we were in an Oriental bazaar," he started out. "What will it take to reach agreement?" I responded that I did not deem the situation hopeless and had no doubt that George Shultz was genuinely interested in reaching an agreement, but that, while there had been progress in the human rights area, it was not sufficient. I warned in particular that the staff of the National Security Council was still quite skeptical and needed clear evidence that the Soviet Union had turned a corner on the issue of human rights.

For the rest of the day, as we walked through the streets of Milan, we went through the details of our human rights dialogue: the problems of persons still imprisoned for mere speech or for religious practice and restrictions on emigration that were still in place. Anatoly made an important point to me regarding the significance of the Moscow meeting. Gorbachev, he explained, planned to convene a Party Congress in the autumn of 1991, at which the cause of perestroika was to receive very special attention. It would be helpful to hold the Party Congress immediately following a CSCE human rights meeting in Moscow. I told Anatoly that immediately upon my return to Washington, I would deliver a report on the observations that he had shared with me and that we would be in touch with each other.

From then on, our dialogue played a special role in the broad outlines of the relationship between the United States and the Soviet Union. That was so for two reasons. First, it became increasingly important to close the Vienna meeting while the Reagan administration was still in office, as the concluding document was expected to provide for the early start of negotiations on a treaty regarding conventional forces in Europe. Second, agreement to hold a human rights meeting in Moscow had become a matter of special domestic importance to the Gorbachev leadership.

I came to support the Soviet proposal quite strongly because of the progress that I had noted on the human rights front in the Soviet Union prior to our Milan meeting and the further progress that I noted in the period immediately following the meeting. We had started the year with a list of more than seven hundred prisoners of conscience and had seen that list decline sharply. There had been no further reports of abuse of psychiatry, namely, the commitment to a mental institution of persons who were clearly perfectly sane but had engaged in political or religious activity of which the authorities disapproved. The issue remained on our agenda because the private organizations that kept the lists of detainees contended that some persons who had been wrongfully committed were still in mental hospitals. There had also been significant progress in the field of emigration. Although many refusenik cases were still on our list, their number had declined. The number of emigrants that were not on the refusenik list had increased substantially, as Armenians, Jews, Pentecostals (under the pretense of being Jewish), and Volga Germans were now allowed to leave the country.

Significant Soviet Progress on Key Human Rights Issues

Not long after our Milan meeting, a question as to the status of patients committed without justification to Soviet mental hospitals was raised with Foreign Minister Shevardnadze at a public meeting in Washington. His response was that if anyone was concerned about this subject, the Soviet Union would let American psychiatrists visit the hospitals and talk to the patients whose mental illness was in doubt. Of the three lists of persons that were the subject of our human rights dialogue with the Soviet

Union—prisoners of conscience, persons improperly committed to mental hospitals, and refuseniks—the second category was by far the smallest. Yet most observers of human rights conditions in the Soviet Union considered it to be the most heinous violation. We therefore responded promptly to the foreign minister's invitation.

I first contacted the American Psychiatric Association, which had taken a deep interest in the psychiatric abuse issue. The association, in turn, put me in touch with Dr. Loren Roth of the University of Pittsburgh, who expressed an interest in working on the issue. The U.S. embassy in Moscow initiated the needed contacts with the foreign ministry.

On my next visit to Moscow, I raised the issue with my usual interlocutors in the foreign ministry. I was told that we had a problem. When I asked about the nature of the problem, I was told that it lay with the health ministry, and more specifically with the minister himself, who was a holdover from the Brezhnev era. When I asked why he had not been replaced, the response was: "Don't you know?" When I responded that I did not know, I was enlightened on that subject. The health minister, Dr. Chasov, was being kept in his position and was able to exercise significant influence because he was the cardiologist for a number of members of the Politburo. As we discussed the question of how we could overcome the problem, it was suggested that I discuss the issue with the staff of the Central Committee of the Communist Party. Alexei Glukhov agreed to set up an appointment for me.

The appointment was set and off I went to the headquarters of the Communist Party of the Soviet Union. When I arrived there I thought of what my mother might have said about my visit to the headquarters of the Bolsheviki. The officials with whom I met, I gathered, were the Central Committee liaison officers to the health ministry. They were very polite and clearly had instructions to be cooperative. I explained that we were interested in following up on Shevardnadze's invitation; I hoped we could arrange for a delegation of U.S. psychiatrists to visit Moscow for the purpose of developing the necessary ground rules for a later visit, during which they would interview persons who might have been improperly committed to mental hospitals. My interlocutors promised to take the necessary steps to make the initial visit possible and kept that promise. In the months that followed, Dr. Roth engaged in extensive negotiations with the appropriate Soviet officials; an unprecedented visit by U.S. psychiatrists to the Soviet Union took place in early 1989.

As for the right to leave the Soviet Union, it turned out that increased Jewish emigration raised an issue that was the subject of discussion between the U.S. and Israeli governments. Jews were being granted permission to emigrate to Israel. They first traveled to Italy. Once there, however, most of them changed course and traveled to the United States, where they were admitted as refugees. Israel's prime minister, Yitzhak Shamir, had expressed his concern to Secretary Shultz over this change in the routing, urging that Jewish emigrants not be allowed to enter the United States when another country, Israel, was ready to receive them. In his response, the secretary had observed that Jews who were leaving the Soviet Union might not go unless they could come to the United States. We could not, he said, exclude the possibility that, if Gorbachev were deposed, conditions might turn very bad and there would once again be mass killings. In that case, the secretary concluded, "I would not forgive myself and you would not forgive yourself either."

That discussion took place as the number of Jewish emigrants was gradually increasing above one thousand per month. When I visited Moscow in the summer of 1988, it became increasingly evident to me that the restrictions on Jewish emigration were being relaxed to the point that it would be difficult for the United States to accept the ever larger number of refugees if another country was ready to receive them. The problem for the U.S. administration was that, under the Refugee Act of 1980, an amount of money had to be set aside for each arriving refugee to reimburse state and local governments for the expected cost of supporting the newly arrived immigrant.

In September 1988, I traveled from Moscow to Jerusalem and arranged to meet with Prime Minister Shamir. At the very outset of our conversation I said: "Mr. Prime Minister, I sense that in the months ahead there will be a very large number of Jews who will receive permission to leave the Soviet Union, too large a number for the United States to accept under the provisions of the Refugee Act. You can, therefore, expect a sharp increase in emigration to Israel. You better get ready to provide housing and jobs." Shamir nodded and then went on to talk about other matters. At a certain point, I returned to the topic of prospective immigration to Israel and the need for housing and jobs. Eli Rubenstein, then secretary to the cabinet, broke into the conversation to say: "Keep in mind that the name of our economics minister is Nissim." (Nissim is the Hebrew word for miracles.) Everyone laughed and we left it at that.

The U.S. Intramural Conflict over the Vienna Meeting

By autumn of 1988, I had concluded that the changes that we had witnessed in the Soviet Union would make it possible for us to come sufficiently close to a series of understandings on the issues on the human rights agenda, including a Moscow CSCE human rights meeting, to enable us to conclude the Vienna meeting before the end of the Reagan administration. As it turned out, the question of whether to agree to a Moscow human rights meeting was not the most serious issue in the intramural controversy in the State Department. Before long, the broader question arose regarding whether it was wise to complete the Vienna meeting while the Reagan administration, and thus Secretary Shultz, were still in office.

Although the secretary had made it clear that he wanted the work of the Vienna meeting to be concluded on his watch, there were officials in the U.S. government who seriously questioned the wisdom of moving forward quickly. What came increasingly into focus was a difference in outlook between the idealist and the realist camps. Most interestingly, the former included the president and secretary of state, who believed that there had been a profound change in the ideology that motivated the leadership of the Soviet Union, a change that needed to be considered in formulating the U.S. position on geopolitical and trade issues.

The realists, by contrast, were likely to hold key positions in what was expected to be the incoming administration of George H. W. Bush. They were heavily influenced by the thinking of Henry Kissinger, who considered it highly inappropriate to inject ideological considerations into the issue of the political relationship between the United States and the Soviet Union. Fifteen years earlier, he had led the camp that opposed letting human rights issues prevent the United States from moving forward with a policy of détente with the Soviet Union. The realist camp was consistent: In 1988, it opposed allowing human rights consideration to warm our relationship with the Soviet Union. What I heard from this camp was that Reagan had gone soft on Communism in his old age and that Shultz simply did not understand world affairs.

What I did not know at the time was that George Shultz was well aware of these divisions of opinion in the foreign policy community. It was only years later that I found the following passage on the last page of his memoirs:

> As I worked in early January to persuade President Reagan that we should agree to a prospective human rights conference in Moscow, I argued Andrei Sakharov's point of view that such a gathering of human rights activists could spur on human rights progress in the Soviet Union.
>
> But I worried. George Bush and Jim Baker seemed concerned and wary that Ronald Reagan and I had become too impressed with Soviet personalities—Gorbachev, Shevardnadze—too ready to believe that genuine change was occurring in the Soviet Union. Brent Scowcroft had been named early on as NSC adviser, and I knew he would be influential. He had opposed the INF Treaty, had raised severe doubts about the prospective START Treaty, and was highly skeptical about the reality of change in the Soviet Union and Eastern Europe. I was apprehensive that the "new team" did not understand or accept that the cold war was over. I heard that a "top-to-bottom policy review" would be undertaken. Fair enough. But President Reagan and I were handing over real momentum. I hoped it would not be squandered.[1]

---

1. Shultz, *Turmoil and Triumph*, 1138.

Although I was not fully aware of the secretary's strong feelings, as expressed in his memoirs, it soon became clear to me that the sharp division of opinion between the idealists and the realists would have a significant impact on my work as we sought to conclude the Vienna meeting. I was aware, though, that those who wanted to delay final action in Vienna were not concerned with human rights—which even the realist camp articulated as major issues—but by the fact that the draft Vienna concluding document provided, as noted earlier, that immediately following the conclusion of the CSCE meeting, negotiations were to start on a treaty for the reduction of conventional forces in Europe (CFE). There were those who worried that NATO might be placed at a disadvantage by a CFE agreement.

It did not take long for me to get directly engaged in this division over U.S. policy. On November 8, 1988—Election Day—I voted in the morning and then had a series of meetings outside the State Department; I got back to my office in the late afternoon. As I started to read the material that had accumulated on my desk while I had been out, I found the draft of a message that was to be sent to the U.S. embassy in Moscow for delivery to the Soviet foreign ministry regarding the Vienna CSCE meeting. It was on my desk for my clearance. As I read the text, I concluded that the intent of this message was to tell the Soviet government that the United States was not prepared to reach prompt agreement on the outstanding CSCE issues and thus bring the Vienna meeting to a conclusion in the very near future.

As soon as I had completed reading the draft message, I telephoned the State Department's executive secretary, Mel Levitsky, who was responsible for reviewing messages that were sent out over the signature of the secretary. I told him that I was not clearing the message to the Moscow embassy because it did not reflect the secretary's views. Mel's response was that it was too late, the secretary had signed off on the message. My response was: "It does not reflect his policy. He probably did not have the time to read it carefully. Please arrange a meeting for me with him as soon as possible." Mel arranged for me to meet with Secretary Shultz two days later, on November 10.

On that day, I met the secretary in his small, personal office. I started out by asking him to restate his policy regarding the Vienna CSCE meeting so that I could be sure that I understood it correctly. The secretary then repeated what I had heard him say frequently, that he hoped that we could all try hard to resolve outstanding issues so as to allow the Vienna concluding document to be approved before January 20 and thus on his watch. I told the secretary that he had confirmed my understanding of his position. I then pulled out the message that had been sent to the Moscow embassy for presentation to the Soviet foreign ministry. I had underlined the sentences and phrases that I believed would be understood by the foreign ministry as indicating that the United States was not prepared to move speedily to resolve outstanding controversial issues so as to allow the prompt completion of the Vienna meeting. As I handed the paper to the secretary, I made the point that, when reading this message, the officials of the Soviet foreign ministry would reach a conclusion regarding U.S. intentions that was the opposite of the policy that the secretary of state had just articulated.

The secretary read the document that I handed him. He then sat there utterly silent. I had been told that when George Shultz is very angry, that anger expresses itself through his silence. After what may have been a minute of silence, I said: "Mr. Secretary, I am scheduled to be in Moscow next week with the Congressional CSCE Commission. If you want to give me oral instructions as to a message that I should carry that would make your policy clear, that would be an opportunity to get that message to Moscow quickly." The secretary indicated immediately that he was in favor of that suggestion and called in an assistant to make a record of our discussion. He and I then reviewed the specific issues on our human rights agenda, and the secretary spelled out his position on each of the relevant points.

Once we had completed our meeting and I was bidding the secretary goodbye, George Shultz got out of his chair and escorted me through his outer office to the entrance of his office suite. When we were out of earshot of the notetaker, he turned to me and said: "And you can tell them that I have problems with my bureaucracy, too."

As I walked back to my office, quite pleased about the progress that we had made in advancing toward a satisfactory conclusion to the Vienna meeting, I suddenly had a disturbing thought. It was Thursday. The message to the Soviets that I had been concerned about had probably been delivered to the foreign ministry the day before, on Wednesday. I would not be able to deliver the new oral message until the following Monday or Tuesday. I thought there was a danger that, once the message that both the secretary and I had found troublesome was read and analyzed at the foreign ministry, it would be understood as a rejection of an early conclusion of the Vienna meeting and attitudes on the Soviet side would freeze. The question with which I then struggled was what I could do to avoid that result.

The bureaucratically appropriate course of action would have been to get in touch with the European Bureau, tell the appropriate official of the oral instructions that I had received from the secretary, and suggest that the Moscow embassy be instructed to tell the Soviet foreign ministry that I would arrive with new instructions regarding the completion of the Vienna meeting in the near future. It did not take long for me to conclude that this option would nullify the progress that had just been made in my talk with Secretary Shultz. My colleagues would make every effort to persuade the secretary to reverse his decision. I was confident that he would remain firm, but in the meantime valuable time would have been lost, in which Soviet attitudes could indeed freeze.[2]

The next option was for me to call the U.S. ambassador in Moscow, Jack Matlock. I ruled that out for the same reason: It would lead to an effort to change the secretary's mind.[3] As it was, one of George Shultz's favorite comments about Washington was that no decision was ever final—that when a decision had been made, the struggle to get it changed started the next day.

I then took a highly unbureaucratic step that I would probably not have taken if I had been a career government official. My task, as I saw it, was to carry out the policy of Secretary Shultz. If, after Shultz had left office, the new leadership did not want me around any more, I could always go back to my law firm. So I asked my assistant to call the Soviet embassy and ask for the deputy chief of mission, Sergey Chetverikov, whom I had come to know quite well. When he got on the phone, I said to him: "Sergey, there was a message from the State Department that was delivered to your ministry yesterday. Please tell your people that it has been superseded by oral instructions from the secretary that I shall convey when I am in Moscow early next week." Sergey promised to convey the message.

A Critically Important Mission to Moscow

I arrived in Moscow on Sunday, November 13. On the following day, I had another meeting with Alexei Glukhov at the foreign ministry. Anatoly was not present at the outset of that session, but he appeared soon and asked me to step outside. When we were in the corridor, he said: "We have received your message. A meeting has been set up for you for this afternoon with Anatoly Kovalev, the senior first deputy minister."

For much of the day I conferred with officials of the ministry's Department on Humanitarian Cooperation and Human Rights. That office had theretofore been known as the Department of Humanitarian Cooperation; human rights had not been recognized as a matter to be dealt with by the foreign ministry. It was clear that the renaming of the department reflected a fundamental change in the Soviet leadership's outlook on the subject of human rights.

---

2. I may have been wrong in my assessment. When I recently recounted this chain of events to Roz Ridgway, who had headed the European Bureau at that time, she told me that she had not been aware of this development. She thought the team managing the transition to the new administration might have been responsible for the troublesome wording of the secretary's message.

3. Only when I read Jack Matlock's memoirs did I discover that his outlook was the same as mine; that he, too, believed that Gorbachev's "blanket endorsement of common human values as the basis of foreign policy implicitly abandoned the class struggle concept." Matlock, *Autopsy on an Empire*, 154.

Our goal at this point, as I had put it to Secretary Shultz, was to stop the practice of pulling teeth one by one and instead see whether they could all be replaced by new dentures. That was the goal that I had in mind when I met with Kovalev, who held the number-two position in the Soviet Foreign Ministry. The meeting began at 4 p.m. on November 14 and lasted for three hours. The time required by the meeting was, of course, extended by the fact that our conversation had to be translated.

Kovalev began by saying to me: "I understand you have a message from Secretary Shultz. When did you receive that message?" I told him: "Last Thursday." He then said something in Russian to one of his staff members, and that member responded. The U.S. deputy chief of mission, who accompanied me on this visit, whispered to me that Kovalev had asked when the U.S. embassy had delivered its last message and had been told that it was last Wednesday. It was thus clear that the message that I was conveying trumped the earlier one.

I quickly came to the basic theme of my message: Secretary Shultz was greatly interested in concluding the Vienna meeting before January 20, 1989, and believed that we should work very hard to find solutions to all outstanding issues so as to allow the adoption of a Vienna follow-up meeting concluding document. As our conversation proceeded, I spoke largely in terms of the bilateral human rights dialogue. Then it occurred to me that the head of the U.S. delegation to the Vienna meeting, Warren Zimmermann, might be offended by my failure to mention the CSCE process, and I therefore suggested we work on the issues in Vienna as well.

Kovalev responded quite sternly to this point. There were certain issues, he told me, that the Soviet Union was prepared to discuss and resolve in a dialogue with the United States. But he emphasized that the Soviet Union had no intention of making these issues the subject of discussion with thirty-three other countries (at that time, the CSCE process had thirty-five participating states). Kovalev was so emphatic that I recognized that there was no point in arguing the point further. I suggested that the matter of engaging the CSCE process could be handled by having the Soviet Union make a public statement as to its plans to move forward in the human rights field in 1989 and hoped that my colleague in Vienna, Ambassador Zimmerman, would forgive me for this departure from the CSCE process.

I then reviewed the understandings that we sought to reach with regard to the issue of prisoners of conscience, namely, repealing the provisions of the criminal code that made political dissent and unauthorized religious observance an offense and releasing all persons who remained incarcerated under these provisions of the code. As to persons convicted under other provisions of the criminal code for what we called trumped-up charges, it was understood that the foreign ministry would request that the procurator general allow the release of the relevant court documents, allowing us to discuss these cases further.

I noted that agreement had been reached that U.S. psychiatrists would be allowed to visit Soviet mental hospitals for the purpose of examining persons alleged to have been committed even though they were not mentally ill. It was understood that the details of that visit would be worked out in the very near future.

As to emigration, I laid out our continuing concerns regarding parental vetoes of the emigration applications of adults, the numerical limits on the exit permits issued each month, and our list of persons denied exit permits on the grounds that they possessed security-sensitive information. I noted that, while we had made progress regarding refusenik cases, we were still in a process of going through the cases one by one, which was quite tedious and prolonged the period of uncertainty for these prospective emigrants.

At that time, about five hundred names remained on our list of unresolved refusenik cases. Including spouses and children, the total number of persons who were denied the opportunity to emigrate was about two thousand. Earlier in the day, a Soviet official had indicated to me that perhaps six to ten cases could be resolved in short order. I had made it clear that that would not be enough, that the number of cases to be resolved in the near future would have to be substantial.

That was the word I now used in my discussion with Kovalev. I suggested that in order to allow for the wholesale release of refuseniks, a clear message would have to be sent from the leadership to all the relevant offices that it was the leadership's intent to resolve the issue. I added that it would be helpful if, as the United States proceeded to its decision on the Vienna meeting, a substantial number of refuseniks were allowed to emigrate within the weeks immediately ahead.

At that point, Kovalev interrupted to ask: "What do you mean by substantial?" I thought for a moment and made the following calculations in my head: It should be possible to get the relevant Soviet authorities to handle four cases a day, two in the morning and two in the afternoon. With five working days in the week, therefore, it should be possible to complete twenty cases per week. I further calculated that we would have to decide on the Vienna final document by the end of the year, which meant that we had six weeks left. Six weeks at twenty cases per week multiplied to 120—which was my response to the question of what I meant by "substantial." As our meeting adjourned at 7 p.m., Kovalev said that he had found it constructive and would report his conclusions to the minister, whom he was to see immediately after our meeting had ended.

I had no idea as to how and when the Soviet side would come back to us. In the Glukhov meeting earlier that day, we had once again gone through the details of our human rights dialogue, dealing with individual cases one by one. We had spent a significant amount of our time trying to resolve the issue of prisoners of conscience. Our side now raised a few related questions. To start, we made it clear that we did not deem cases that involved acts of violence to be political even if the motivation for committing the act was political. On the other hand, we called attention to the case of a person convicted and imprisoned under Article 227—participation in an unauthorized religious gathering—who had sought to flee and was then given a new prison sentence for attempted escape, a violation of Article 188. If he was improperly imprisoned in the first instance, we contended, his attempted escape should no longer be punished.

We also raised the issue of persons convicted on charges that we considered trumped up. We did not hesitate to use the term "trumped up," and the Soviet side did not object to it. The foreign ministry officials agreed to ask the procurator for documentation on the cases for which we claimed that the defendants had been convicted on trumped-up criminal charges, when the real intent was to punish them for political activities.

Once both my meeting at the working level and my meeting at the policy level were behind me, I assumed that part of my visit to Moscow was over and that I would return to Washington and await the Soviet response, presumably a message delivered to the U.S. embassy in Moscow.

Because the initial reason for my trip to Moscow was to participate in meetings arranged by the Congressional CSCE Commission, I planned to be active, for the rest of the visit, with the members of Congress who were in Moscow in the capacity of commission members. I was able to join the group on Tuesday morning, November 15, and sat in on a meeting that the commission staff had arranged. Not long after our meeting started, I was told that there was an urgent telephone call for me from the U.S. embassy. When I got on the phone I was told that a foreign ministry official had called and asked that I get to the ministry as soon as possible. I was also told that the embassy would send a car to take me there. The car arrived soon thereafter, and off I went for another meeting at the ministry. Once I arrived, I was promptly taken to the office at which I had evidently been awaited. Alexei Glukhov was once again ready to talk to me.

After I had taken my seat, Glukhov smiled and said: "All right, give me the 120 names." This was the Soviet response that I had hoped for, but what was truly amazing was that it came in less than a day. The mission on which I had embarked with specific instructions from Secretary Shultz had been successful.

To be sure, the specific request for 120 names caught me unprepared. After all, in my conversation with Kovalev, I had simply made a calculation as to what would be a reasonable number. I had not come prepared to present a list. Glukhov and I agreed that I would submit the list promptly following my return to Washington.

The difference in the spirit of the Monday meeting and the Tuesday meeting was striking. I concluded that, following my meeting with Kovalev and his meeting with Shevardnadze, the word had come down for an active Soviet engagement in resolving our outstanding areas of concern.

One of the problems that had arisen in our dialogue was our insistence that the Soviet Union make a public statement that it would enact legislation that would bring it into full compliance with the provisions of the Helsinki Final Act. Glukhov took me aside to explain that the Soviet Union was prepared to make the kind of statement that we were looking for, but that it had to be in a setting that preserved the country's dignity. It could not be made in the multilateral context of the CSCE meeting in Vienna, nor could it be made in the context of our bilateral human rights dialogue. It had to be done in a unilateral setting. He assured me that the statement would be made, that it would deal with the issues of concern to us, and that it would be made before the end of the Reagan administration. I had come to know Glukhov and trusted his word, particularly because it was so clear that he was speaking under instructions.

We once again reviewed other outstanding problems, particularly the issue of persons convicted on trumped-up charges. On all these matters, Glukhov made it clear that the Soviet Union was changing course, not merely because we asked for it but because a fundamental change in governance was taking place in the Soviet Union.

We made progress and reached understandings across the board. It was now clear to both sides that, first, both of us wanted to reach agreement on the Vienna concluding document within weeks, and second, to accomplish that result, we needed to clear all obstacles out of the way. These obstacles were now exclusively in the human rights area. We had to come up with formulas that would allow Secretary Shultz to convince the president that reaching an agreement in Vienna promptly was the right thing to do, irrespective of what the president might hear from other sources. The reformers in Moscow, in turn, had to look for formulations that, while meeting our concerns, would be swallowed by the hard-liners in the Soviet system.

Success

Moving the process forward, Secretary Shultz addressed the following letter[4] to Foreign Minister Shevardnadze on November 25:

> Dear Eduard:
>
> It was with considerable pleasure that I received Ambassador Schifter's report on the results of his recent talks in Moscow and the steps he learned you are planning to take in the area of human rights. I believe that this painstaking approach is producing significant and positive results. Final resolution of the outstanding cases he raised can provide a great impetus to our relationship, as well as facilitate settlement of the final issues at the Vienna Conference. This would also enable the United States and, we would hope, other Western governments to say "yes" to your proposal to host one of three human rights meetings.
>
> As I wrote you on November 9, my Government will be able to say "yes" to your proposal if the steps I described in that letter are taken prior to the end of the Vienna Meeting and we receive public assurances of the further measures you intend to take in 1989. While we, of course, welcome advance assurances in private, it may be most appropriate for the Soviet Union to announce these steps publicly along the lines of recent announcements of legislative changes you plan to make. We will understand it if such public statements were made without reference to the Vienna Meeting or the views of other countries, inasmuch as they are, in any case, a manifestation of the ongoing process of reform inside the USSR. . . .
>
> Sincerely yours,
>
> George

On November 30, we sent our list of 120 names to Moscow.

On December 7, the Soviet Union delivered on its promise of a clear statement of policy in keeping with the provisions of the Helsinki Final Act. It took a form that we had not expected: a speech by Gorbachev, now president of the Soviet Union, to the UN General Assembly. In the context of a speech that dealt broadly with international affairs, the role of the United Nations, and developments in the Soviet Union, we found the language that we had been looking for:

> We have gone substantially and deeply into the business of constructing a socialist state based on the rule of law. A whole series of new laws has been prepared or is at a completion stage. Many of them come into force as early as 1989, and we trust that they will correspond to the highest standards from the point of view of ensuring the rights of the individual. Soviet democracy is to acquire a firm, normative base. This

---

4. State Department message, "Moscow Conference—Letter to Shevardnadze, Points for Kashlev," November 25, 1988.

means such acts as the Law on Freedom of Conscience, on glasnost, on public associations and organizations, and on much else. There are now no people in places of imprisonment in the country who have been sentenced for their political or religious convictions. It is proposed to include in the drafts of the new laws additional guarantees ruling out any form or persecution on these bases. Of course, this does not apply to those who have committed real criminal or state offenses: espionage, sabotage, terrorism, and so on, whatever political or philosophical views they may hold.

The draft amendments to the criminal code are ready and waiting their turn. In particular, those articles relating to the use of the supreme measure of punishment are being reviewed. The problem of exit and entry is also being resolved in a humane spirit, including the case of leaving the country in order to be reunited with relatives. As you know, one of the reasons for refusal of visas is citizens' possession of secrets. Strictly substantiated terms for the length of time for possessing secrets are being introduced in advance. On starting work at a relevant institution or enterprise, everyone will be made aware of this regulation. Disputes that arise can be appealed under the law. Thus the problem of the so-called "refuseniks" is being removed.

We intend to expand the Soviet Union's participation in the monitoring mechanism on human rights in the United Nations and within the framework of the pan-European process. We consider that the jurisdiction of the International Court in The Hague with respect to interpreting and applying agreements in the field of human rights should be obligatory for all states.

Within the Helsinki process, we are also examining an end to the jamming of all the foreign radio broadcasts to the Soviet Union. On the whole, our credo is as follows: Political problems should be solved only by political means, and human problems only in a humane way.[5]

I was deeply moved by this speech. Yes, Gorbachev had invoked the name of Lenin. But when he spoke of a socialist state, he spoke of a socialist state based on the rule of law. From my own understanding of what he said, the speech did not reflect the spirit of Leninism; quite the contrary. As the U.S. official group took the ferry to Governor's Island, where the two presidents were to have a brief meeting, I encountered Secretary Shultz and said to him excitedly: "He has just repudiated Leninism!" Shultz smiled. He thought in practical terms, not in terms of the history of the ideologies that had contended for power in Russia seventy years earlier. But to me it meant that the Mensheviki had indeed returned, to use Trotsky's famous phrase, from the ash heap of history.

---

5. The text of the speech can be retrieved at CNN, *Cold War—Historical Documents: Gorbachev's Speech to the United Nations*, http://www.cnn.com/SPECIALS/cold.war/episodes/23/documents/gorbachev.

With only a few weeks left for the Reagan administration and Secretary Shultz's term in office, the State Department became fully engaged in the effort to remove all obstacles that stood in the way of concluding the Vienna meeting before January 20, 1989. Secretary Shultz wanted to be sure that the Soviet side understood that he was serious about concluding the Vienna meeting, but needed resolution of some of the outstanding issues in the human rights area. On December 15, the secretary sent a message to Ambassador Matlock in which he instructed him as follows:

> I would ask that you underscore for the Soviets that the time for this Administration to make a final decision on the Moscow Conference proposal and to end the Vienna Meeting is running extremely short. (All the more so if Shevardnadze genuinely wants to wrap things up by January 6.) And we will not be in a position to take the positive decision unless the conditions the Secretary outlined to Shevardnadze are satisfied. For our part, we would like to finish Vienna as soon as possible as long as the substance is right. But the calendar will not push us into an unsatisfactory conclusion.[6]

As I recently reviewed the final version of this December 15, 1988, message, I noted a handwritten note from my principal deputy to me at the end of this document, which read: "This is what finally went out as toughened by NSC." Some of the terminology of that message would not have come from State Department officials aware of the secretary's attitude. Still, the specific talking points to be transmitted to Shevardnadze had a highly positive ring to them:

- The Secretary was especially encouraged by Minister Shevardnadze's comment in their New York meeting that the positive evolution of the Soviet Union's approach to human rights and humanitarian questions is a result of the unfolding process of perestroyka in Soviet society, and not primarily a response to the views of Western countries.

- As President Reagan told Chairman Gorbachev, the United States supports the process of change in the Soviet Union and believes that its continued vitality represents an important factor in building greater trust and stability in our bilateral relationship and in the world at large.

- The progress we have seen in the past several months has been most heartening and goes a substantial way toward satisfying our concerns.

- For example, your Government's decision to end jamming of all Western radio stations was a major step forward. . . .

- There has also been tremendous progress on emigration . . . though we would like to see more explicit recognition of emigration as a right in accordance with the Universal Declaration of Human Rights.

---

6. State Department message, "Demarche on Moscow Human Rights Conference," December 15, 1988.

- The release over the past two years of more than 600 individuals whom we in the West have considered to be prisoners of conscience is also viewed by my government as of great significance.

- We particularly welcome the steps Chairman Gorbachev announced in his UNGA address regarding legal reform, exit-and-entry procedure, secrecy restrictions, and the USSR's participation in UN and CSCE human rights monitoring arrangements. . . .

- At the same time, we need to learn more about the details of the planned changes. For example: the abolition or amendment of key criminal code articles, the contents of future legislation on religious freedom, the time limits for refusals on security grounds, the nature of the appeal process and the like.

Ambassador Matlock responded the next day, informing Secretary Shultz that he had delivered the message that was to be transmitted to Foreign Minister Shevardnadze and had been told that

> the USSR shared the U.S. goal of wrapping up the issues raised in the demarche by January 6. Much had been accomplished in the Reagan Administration. He continued drawing a comparison between the current situation and that of three years ago. He attributed these changes to both internal developments and improved Soviet-American relations, and said he was encouraged by the good forms of discussion that had been established with the aim of resolving problems.[7]

The ambassador was also told that, first, progress was being made in legal reform, but that final action would have to await the convening of the Supreme Soviet in April 1989; second, a new decree on emigration was virtually complete; third, new criminal legislation was "ready in its essence"; and fourth, a new law on conscience, in the planning stage, would permit religious organizations to register officially and to allow religious education.

A follow-up message from the U.S. embassy in Moscow on December 22 suggested that no progress had been made as yet on developing a mechanism for the exchange of information on criminal convictions for ostensibly nonpolitical crimes when the basic cause of the conviction was political.[8] Anatoly and I had discussed that topic at some length, but our colleagues had not been able to progress on this issue.

That very evening, Anatoly—who happened to be in New York City at the time—and I had dinner in a restaurant and discussed the outstanding issues, particularly the proposed Moscow human rights meeting, at

---

7. State Department message, "Demarche on Moscow Human Rights Conference," December 16, 1988.

8. State Department message, "Moscow Human Rights Conference: December 22, Demarche to MFA," December 22, 1988.

length. The following day, I prepared a memorandum of conversation on our talk.⁹ Here are highlights:

> On the evening of December 22 I met with Soviet Deputy Foreign Minister Anatoly Adamishin for a discussion of the conditions under which we would be prepared to support a Moscow human rights conference.
>
> Adamishin emphasized that in his view both sides need to get away from the notion that what is good for the Soviets is necessarily bad for us and vice versa. He reminded me of what he had told me in Milan: that anyone could see the Moscow human rights meeting could no longer be viewed as a public relations coup for the Soviets, that it is of value principally to the reform element in the Soviet Union in its internal struggle.
>
> He said that the remaining items on our agenda were relatively minor matters, but the fact that we keep coming back to them for more has left the Soviets uncertain as to (1) whether we intend ever to agree to the Moscow Conference, or (2) if we do, whether we intend to close the Vienna CSCE meeting during the Reagan Administration.
>
> To underline the Soviets' seriousness in responding to us he pointed out that the Foreign Ministry had drafted the human rights section of Gorbachev's December 7 UNGA speech to cover all the points of basic principle which we had raised. He emphasized that the resolution of cases presented by us would be pursued as part of the Soviet Union's efforts to change its ways even after the Vienna meeting closes.
>
> My answer . . . was that the Secretary is a person who means what he says and that he had made it clear to Shevardnadze that he was prepared to agree to a Moscow human rights meeting under the circumstances which we had spelled out. What seemed . . . as our coming back time and again with minor items was to us a matter of tying up loose ends on the package previously proposed, that the Secretary, who would take responsibility for the final decision, wanted to be sure that all the points we have raised have been fully covered.
>
> We then got down to specifics. I explained that we needed movement on three items: (1) A mechanism dealing with the list of prisoners convicted of ordinary crimes. (2) Resolution of the remaining bilateral cases. (3) Resolution of the remaining old Refusenik cases.
>
> The first of these turned out to be the most difficult problem. . . . Adamishin said that the Soviets might be prepared to give us material on some of the cases but not on all. What became evident was that he had a problem with an agreement which would promise us access to secret files in treason cases [when we deemed the treason charge to have been trumped up]. He was surprised when I told him that in the United States even persons convicted of treason and espionage can be convicted only on evidence placed in the public record. . . .

---

9. State Department message, "A/S Schifter Conversation with [redacted] re 'Proposed Moscow Human Rights Conference,'" December 24, 1988.

> We concluded with a discussion about the future. Deputy Foreign Minister Adamishin said that so many problems in the world could be solved more easily if we got together. To my question whether the present trend in the Soviet Union will last, he answered: "There is not an evening at which intellectuals gather when that question doesn't come up. We all wonder. The presently prevailing opinion is that while we may slip back temporarily or here or there, we have passed the point of no return. We just can't go back to the way it was."

I had concluded that Anatoly's observations should be taken seriously, that they fairly reflected developments in the Soviet Union. I continued to be of the view that there was sufficient movement on the Soviet side to allow us to agree to the Moscow human rights meeting and the ending of the Vienna meeting with the adoption of a concluding document that would make provision for further arms reduction negotiations. On December 28, I sent a further memorandum to the secretary on our human rights dialogue with the Soviet Union in which I summarized my view of the state of affairs as follows: "On my last visit to Moscow I told the Soviets that we hoped that we could discuss an entire new set of dentures rather than pulling one tooth at a time. During the last thirty days we have, in fact, seen rapid progress on quite a number of our lists. On one list we have gotten down to zero."[10]

A week later, on January 4, 1989, Secretary Shultz wrote Foreign Minister Shevardnadze:

> Dear Eduard:
>
> We have talked and corresponded over the last few months regarding the Soviet proposal to host a CSCE human rights conference in Moscow. I have expressed to you often and in the clearest terms possible the concerns my government has had about the Moscow Conference with regard to the need for significant positive changes in Soviet human rights practices as well as the need for specific commitments on access and openness for anyone who is interested in attending a human rights conference in Moscow.
>
> I have been encouraged by the progress you have been making on all fronts. Significant positive action has been taken on a number of issues of particular importance to the U.S., including resolution of all the cases of persons convicted under Articles 70, 190-1, 142, and 227 of the Soviet criminal code, a significant reduction in the number of bilateral and Refusenik cases, and the end to jamming foreign radio broadcast. We noted particularly what General Secretary Gorbachev said in his UN speech regarding the rights of individuals and freedom of conscience and association, as well as changes to be made in the penal code, in the regulations regarding access to secrets as a bar to emigration and with regard to entry/exit procedures generally.

---

10. State Department memorandum from Schifter to secretary, "Our Soviet Human Rights Dialogue—Lists and Statistics," December 28, 1988, 1.

Against the background of steps already taken and with the firm expectation that the progress to date is a part of a longer term process that will continue in the Soviet Union, the United States agrees that the meetings to be agreed upon at the Vienna Conference *include the Moscow human rights conference* [emphasis added]. . . .

Much has been accomplished since the beginning of the Vienna CSCE meeting in November 1986. Through our discussions and the actions which have resulted from them we have helped to move the CSCE Process forward on the path to reduced tension in Europe. Perhaps most gratifying to me, we have taken steps which have a direct and beneficial effect on a great number of individuals and families. I am confident that the U.S. and the USSR will find it in the mutual interest of their peoples to continue the dialogue that we have established.

Sincerely yours,

George[11]

On January 17, 1989, a U.S. delegation led by Secretary Shultz traveled to Vienna to witness the adoption at the Vienna meeting. The Concluding Document contained the following text:

The participating States decide further to convene a Conference on the Human Dimension of the CSCE in order to achieve further progress concerning respect for all human rights and fundamental freedoms, human contacts and other issues of a related humanitarian character. The Conference will hold three meetings before the next CSCE Follow-up Meeting.

The Conference will:

- review developments in the human dimension of the CSCE including the implementation of the relevant CSCE commitments;
- evaluate the functioning of the procedures described in paragraphs 1 to 4 and discuss the information provided according to paragraph 4;
- consider practical proposals for new measures aimed at improving the implementation of the commitments relating to the human dimension of the CSCE and enhancing the effectiveness of the procedures described in paragraphs 1 to 4.

On the basis of these proposals, the Conference will consider adopting new measures.

The first Meeting of the Conference will be held in Paris from 30 May to 23 June 1989.

The second Meeting of the Conference will be held in Copenhagen from 5 to 29 June 1990.

---

11. State Department message, "Letter from the Secretary to Shevardnadze Regarding the Moscow Human Rights Conference," January 4, 1989.

> The third Meeting of the Conference will be held in Moscow from
> 10 September to 4 October 1991.[12]

In 1987, the Soviet Union had celebrated the seventieth anniversary of the Glorious October Revolution. Within two years of that anniversary, the entire edifice erected by Lenin, modified by Stalin, and maintained by their successors had crumbled. There were a number of reasons for the end of Bolshevism. First, it had been rotting from within. As one of the directors at a training school for Communist Party cadre told me in 1990, "in this place we lost our faith about twenty years ago." Second, the system had become increasingly inefficient, inept, and corrupt, deeply disappointing the general public. Third, and very important, in what continued to be a police state, the system had produced a group of leaders who shared this lack of faith and the deep disappointment with the system's multiple failures and wanted to loosen the reins. Fourth, and only fourth, U.S. engagement in a human rights dialogue encouraged the leadership to effect the changes that they themselves thought were needed. The informal linkage between human rights issues and arms control also caused the leadership of the military, concerned about the Soviet Union's failure to keep up with the United States in the arms race, not to oppose the Gorbachev policies.

The successful conclusion of the Vienna CSCE Meeting began the resolution of a highly important issue that may very well have been troublesome to those officials in the U.S. government who preferred to postpone the Vienna agreement: namely, negotiations on conventional armed forces in Europe. The member-states of the Warsaw Pact and NATO committed themselves to meet within seven weeks of the closure of the Vienna CSCE meeting to negotiate

> a stable and secure balance of conventional armed forces, which includes conventional armaments and equipment, at lower levels; the elimination of disparities prejudicial to stability and security; and the elimination, as a matter of priority, of the capability for launching surprise attacks and for initiating large-scale offensive action.... These objectives shall be achieved by the application of militarily significant measures such as reductions, limitations, redeployment provisions, equal ceilings, and related measures, among others.[13]

The Soviet-U.S. human rights dialogue, in which Anatoly and I had been engaged by then for a year and three-quarters, had by January 1989 produced significant results in the field of civil liberties for Soviet citizens, including

---

12. The Vienna CSCE concluding document can be retrieved at the Organization for Security and Cooperation in Europe Web site, http://www.osce.org/item/15808.html.

13. Mandate for Negotiation on Conventional Armed Forces in Europe, January 10, 1989.

the right to leave the country, an end to psychiatric abuse, and the release of prisoners of conscience. But beyond that, the agreement on the Vienna Concluding Document and the resulting start on the work to conclude a treaty on conventional forces in Europe had a truly profound impact on international relations. Gorbachev notes that fact in his memoirs:

> The heads of delegations and foreign ministers [of the CSCE member states] convened at the Elysee Palace on the eve of the opening of the European summit [November 18, 1990] for the signing ceremony of the conventional force reduction in Europe treaty (which had been negotiated in Vienna). The signatory powers pledged that henceforth they were no longer enemies and would build new relations based on partnership and friendship. This was indeed a historic event. An era marked by two world wars and nearly fifty years of "nuclear antagonism" between the two military-political blocs and political systems was about to become a thing of the past.[14]

---

14. Gorbachev, *Memoirs*, 548.

6

The End of Perestroika

Richard Schifter

Unprecedented U.S-Soviet cooperation that resulted in the successful CSCE meeting in Vienna was the high point of the U.S.-Soviet human rights dialogue. Soon thereafter, all the major problems on our agenda having been resolved, Anatoly's and my close working relationship came to an end. In the three years following Vienna, bilateral work in the human rights field was productive but less spectacular. Thanks to the groundwork that Anatoly laid as perestroika had advanced, I was able to deal directly with Soviet agencies that foreign diplomats would normally have dealt with only through the foreign ministry. Anatoly helped when needed, but he was increasingly given other responsibilities, and in May 1990, he left for Rome.

In this chapter (and the next), we reverse the order of the previous chapters. I lead off by recounting the work I did in direct contact with officials of the newly democratic Soviet Union—what we accomplished and what I saw, as an outsider, of political developments in the Soviet Union. I also discuss the hesitation of the George H. W. Bush administration in following up on the policies pursued at the end of the Reagan administration and the U.S. failure to provide the support that Gorbachev, who had brought democracy to the Soviet Union, needed to stay in office.

Anatoly then describes how developments in 1989–1991 looked to a Soviet insider. It was a period in which hope for a brighter future began to erode under mounting domestic economic problems that undermined Gorbachev's popularity, continuing political resistance from conservative forces, a split in the democratic movement precipitated by Boris Yeltsin, and a reduction—or at least a suspension—of U.S. support for Gorbachev.

As I have heretofore noted, during 1988, as I visited Moscow every few months, I saw how the totalitarian fog was gradually lifting. For those of us who had hoped for this change for years, it was truly an exhilarating time. But it was exhilarating not only for visitors to the Soviet Union. More important, it was exhilarating for many Soviet citizens.

Many members of what was called the intelligentsia—that is, persons who had received a higher education—had lost their faith in Leninism some years earlier, but had been afraid to speak out. As Anatoly once said to me: "Each of us was in a hole, with a lid on top of us. Then, along came Gorbachev and lifted that lid and we came out of our holes." With so many members of the intelligentsia finally out of their holes, the Soviet Union, under Gorbachev, moved toward a free society and a genuine democracy. In the summer of 1988, Gorbachev reportedly said to the Politburo: "We have given power to the people. Let us hope they use it wisely."

A Change of Administrations

The fundamental change in conditions in the Soviet Union had been fully recognized and understood by President Reagan and Secretary Shultz. But on January 20, 1989, a new administration took office.

The first task of any new administration is to select and then bring in its new team. At the State Department, James Baker succeeded George Shultz as secretary. There were substantial other personnel changes, but I was asked to stay on as assistant secretary of state for human rights and humanitarian affairs.

Although, as mentioned heretofore, I had heard expressions of concern, attributed to persons connected with the incoming administration, that Reagan had gone soft on communism and that Shultz could not be trusted, it was not entirely clear to me what the new administration's policy approach to the Soviet Union might be. What was announced was that U.S. policy toward the Soviet Union would be reviewed.

In his memoirs, James Baker states that the "top-to-bottom policy review" undertaken by the new administration produced mush.[1] When he delved into the matter personally, he discovered a sharp split among the experts whom he consulted. On one side were hawkish analysts who thought that "perestroika was just a breathing space, designed by the Soviets to overcome the stagnation and technological backwardness of the Brezhnev era, and to revive the Soviet economy for further competition with democracy and capitalism into the next century."[2] The dovish analysts, by contrast, believed that "perestroika was a fundamental shift in Soviet policy. To them, Gorbachev

---

1. James Baker, *The Politics of Diplomacy* (New York: G. P. Putnam's Sons, 1995), 68.
2. Ibid., 69.

was the Soviet Union's Dubcek, a man who would usher in a new era of 'socialism with a human face.'"[3]

The split between hawks and doves regarding Soviet policy was not a new phenomenon; it had been inherited from the previous administration. After Gorbachev had persuaded some leading figures in the Reagan administration, particularly the secretary of state, of his sincerity in moving the Soviet Union in a different direction, the Reagan administration had been divided. In his memoirs, Shultz describes a session that he had with representatives of the intelligence community, including the Central Intelligence Agency's (CIA) deputy director, Robert Gates, in November 1987:

> Bob Gates described Gorbachev as a Leninist: "He's tried to jump back over Stalin to a time when Leninism was not encased in Stalinism." . . . Gates said there was consensus in the Politburo for "a breathing space with the West." The Kremlin was seeking "a period of dampened tensions with the West" while they revived themselves internally and gathered strength for another era of conflict with us. "Gorbachev hasn't cut military research and development and has poured in more weapons to regional conflicts," Gates said.
>
> I disagreed with Gates's assessment, I told them . . . I felt that a profound, historic shift was under way: the Soviet Union was, willingly or unwillingly, consciously or not, turning a corner; they were not just resting for round two of the cold war. . . . We should, I thought, work with Gorbachev in order to pull him in the right direction—and as fast as possible.[4]

In the Reagan administration, the president relied fully on Shultz's recommendations regarding Soviet policy, and there was no high-level dissent. The national security adviser during the critical years of 1987–1989 was Colin Powell. As the Reagan administration was about to leave office, Powell used the opportunity of a dinner in honor of Shultz to note that "the NSC adviser and the Secretary of State had not gotten on so well since the days when Henry Kissinger held both jobs simultaneously."[5]

But there was a significant difference between the Reagan and Bush administrations. Gates, as deputy CIA director, was not in the policymaking loop in the Reagan administration, but he was in the White House in the Bush administration as deputy to the national security adviser, Brent Scowcroft, and he had not changed his outlook. Both Scowcroft and Gates weighed in heavily on the hawkish side, or, as they would have viewed it, on the realist side.

---

3. Ibid.

4. Shultz, *Turmoil and Triumph*, 1003. As noted earlier, in 1986 I held the same views as Robert Gates, but had changed my assessment of Gorbachev in the course of 1987.

5. Ibid., 1138.

Baker started out as a skeptic regarding U.S. policy toward the Soviet Union, but Baker was impressed by Shevardnadze's sincerity just as Shultz had been. Following their first meeting in Vienna in March 1989, Baker reported to the president that "Shevardnadze . . . very much wanted to establish a personal relationship and ensure continuity in U.S.-Soviet relations. [Gorbachev and Shevardnadze] felt a real urgency to see perestroika succeed quickly. They're leaders in a great hurry, possessing a sense of urgency but lacking a plan."[6]

While Secretary Baker had thus been persuaded of Gorbachev's and Shevardnadze's good intentions—but not of their ability to carry them out—his outlook was not shared by Scowcroft and Gates. With his principal foreign policy advisers in disagreement on the question of U.S. relations with the Soviet Union, the president did not commit himself to a clear policy approach for quite some time. As Baker relates in his memoirs, in July 1989, President Bush finally agreed that he should meet Gorbachev "sooner rather than later." When Scowcroft argued that such a meeting would confuse U.S. "support for the principles of perestroika with the personality of Gorbachev," the president rejected that line of reasoning by saying: "Look, this guy is perestroika."[7]

A face-to-face meeting between Bush and Gorbachev was finally arranged and took place in Malta in early December 1989. As Baker puts it, "Malta did for George Bush's relationship with Gorbachev what Jackson Hole[8] had done for my relationship with Shevardnadze: enabled it to break through to establish a personal bond. Before the meeting, the President's understanding of Gorbachev naturally had been theoretical. . . . But with Malta, the relationship became human and personal."[9]

Human Rights Work Continues

Unaware of the policy conflict at the highest level, and without specific instructions as to a change in U.S. policy, I continued the Human Rights Bureau's work with the Soviet Union in 1989 along the lines that had been laid down in 1988. For one major project pending in the human rights field, the

---

6. Baker, *Politics of Diplomacy*, 67.

7. Ibid., 168.

8. The May 1989 ministerial meeting in Moscow had been followed by a September meeting. Secretary Baker had chosen Jackson Hole, Wyoming, as the venue for that meeting, so as to allow for greater informality and to develop his personal relationship with Foreign Minister Shevardnadze. Secretary Baker's interpreter later told me that, on the flight from Washington to Jackson Hole, the two principals had extensive conversations that helped them bond. I was told that Shevardnadze discussed in great detail the increasing difficulties faced by the Gorbachev leadership.

9. Baker, *Politics of Diplomacy*, 169–170.

planning had sufficiently far advanced to give it the momentum to keep going without further clearances from the top. This was the project that resulted from U.S. acceptance of Foreign Minister Shevardnadze's invitation for U.S. psychiatrists to visit Soviet mental hospitals and check for themselves whether there was anyone left who had been committed for political reasons.

Following my initial contacts with the Central Committee liaison officers for the health ministry, which had paved the way for full cooperation, Dr. Loren Roth, the director of the Law and Psychiatry Program at the University of Pittsburgh, had undertaken the task of negotiating the ground rules for the visit to the Soviet Union by a team of U.S. psychiatrists. The objective of the visit was to interview persons whose names had been given to the U.S. government as persons who had been committed to mental institutions without medical justification and who had still not been released.

The agreement that Dr. Roth reached with the Soviet authorities was, in retrospect, truly amazing in terms of the intrusiveness of the scheduled visit. Soviet officials had agreed that, first, Russian-speaking psychiatrists who had emigrated from the Soviet Union would be included in the American team; second, no Soviet personnel were to be present at the interviews with the patients (to avoid possible intimidation); third, to guard against the patients being drugged, urine specimens were to be taken from them before each interview; and fourth, to guard against tampering with the urine tests, the U.S. delegation was to bring dry ice along so as to take the samples back to the United States for analysis in U.S. laboratories.

That key Soviet officials would agree to such intrusive terms suggested that they, too, had found the abuse of psychiatry both inherently appalling and also damaging to the new image that the incumbent Soviet leadership wanted to achieve for the Soviet Union. These key officials wanted a clean-up, just as we did.

That there was something to clean up was vividly stated by Professor Richard Bonnie, the director of the Institute of Law, Psychiatry, and Public Policy at the University of Virginia, who participated in the visit. He subsequently reported:

> The investigation by the U.S. delegation provided unequivocal proof that the tools of coercive psychiatry had been used, even in the late 1980s, to hospitalize persons who were not mentally ill and whose only transgression had been the expression of political or religious dissent. Most of the patients interviewed by the delegation had been charged with political crimes such as "anti-Soviet agitation and propaganda" or "defaming the Soviet state." Their offenses involved behavior such as writing and distributing anti-Soviet literature, political organizing, defending the rights of disabled groups, and furthering religious ideas.[10]

---

10. Bonnie, "Political Abuse of Psychiatry," 137.

May in Moscow

My first visit to Moscow under the new administration took place in May 1989, in anticipation of Secretary Baker's initial ministerial meeting with Foreign Minister Shevardnadze. Once again, I had a series of working-level meetings, but they were vastly different in content from what they had been in earlier times. The subject matters that we discussed reflected that the Soviet Union had turned over a new leaf and was getting ready to build a democratic system.

To be sure, some matters still had not been fully resolved and required attention. That is what we came to call the old agenda. In addition, however, we started to discuss programs to assist the Soviet government in its efforts to advance the democratic cause in the Soviet Union. These programs were called the new agenda, a term that Anatoly had coined. It was not a matter of the United States pressing new agenda issues; it was a matter of our responding positively to interests expressed by our Soviet colleagues for advice and technical assistance in democratizing the country.

Thus, in the course of my May 1989 visit to Moscow, I had an extended meeting with representatives of the Ministry of Justice. The principal topic of our dialogue was the establishment of the rule of law. I was told that the country was moving in that direction, though my interlocutors conceded that the process would be gradual. Lawyers were playing an increasingly important role in Soviet society. But the country's 28,000 judges, I was also told, were far from enough. Further, there had been controversy over the issue of constitutional review of legislative actions. There were those who advocated giving that authority to the Supreme Court. Others favored placing that responsibility in the hands of "more political people." The matter had been resolved by creating a Constitutional Review Commission, whose members would be divided equally "between lawyers and others."

There had been debate, I was told, as to whether to introduce a jury system; a decision had been made not to do so. There was also division of opinion over access by criminal suspects to lawyers. There were those who believed that suspects should have access to lawyers immediately after their arrest. Others argued that this would hinder investigations and, therefore, hamper the fight against crime.

Finally, I was assured that the role of the prosecutor's office had changed drastically. The office was now independent. To underline the fact that a new era had arrived, I was told that the prosecutors now devoted time to fighting "antiperestroika" activities of bureaucrats and enforcing antipollution laws.

Following this truly encouraging discussion with officials of the Ministry of Justice, I met with members of the staff of the Human Rights Section of the

Central Committee of the Communist Party. The mere fact that I would be going to Communist Party headquarters for a meaningful and comprehensive discussion of human rights was, against the historic background, a true sign that we had entered a new era. The candor with which my interlocutors discussed developments at the Central Committee was striking. They made it quite clear that they had played a critically important behind-the-scenes role in resolving human rights issues that had been of concern to us.

It was explained to me that the Human Rights Section had been part of the Ideology Department. That department, in turn, was a conglomerate of three previous departments, namely, the departments for propaganda, culture, and scientific and educational institutions. The new, consolidated department employed one-half the number of people that had staffed the three earlier departments. The new Human Rights Section had three functions: first, to inform the leadership on human rights issues; second, to analyze developments with the help of experts; and third, to foster international cooperation on human rights. However, I was told, the Human Rights Section was gradually being phased out. Its responsibilities were to be assumed by ministries and other governmental agencies. This was clearly in line with the perestroika goal of reducing the power of the Communist Party apparatus, which had dominated the ministries since Lenin's time.

My Soviet interlocutors did, however, express regret over the fact that Soviet reforms had not had a great impact on public opinion in the West. It would have been helpful, I was told, if the media had cheered the release of prisoners and the grant of exit permits to refuseniks. The coverage of the unprecedented recent visit of a U.S. group of psychiatrists was a perfect example of the failure of the Western media to give the Soviet Union full recognition for the progress that had been made. That was making the work of the Human Rights Section more difficult.

I responded by noting that the U.S. government could not control the media. I underlined the fact that participants in the psychiatric visit had recognized and appreciated Soviet openness and had spoken out on that subject. At the same time, I said, individuals connected with this worst form of human rights abuse were still in leading positions in Soviet psychiatry and that was a matter of concern to the West. When asked to name these psychiatrists, I did. I made particular reference to psychiatrists who had invented the supposed illness of "sluggish schizophrenia" and to the role played by the staff of the Serbsky Institute in diagnosing this invented illness, a role that violated the ethical standards of the medical profession.

I could not help going on to point out that if one were to compare the characteristics of sluggish schizophrenia with the personality traits of Vladimir Lenin, one would have to conclude that he suffered from that illness. My comment about Lenin was not objected to. On the contrary, one of the Soviet participants in the meeting observed that psychiatric analysis was often directly related to the state of society. He went on to say that job application forms contained questions designed to reveal the applicant's mental health. One of the questions was: "Do you feel a keen desire to right injustice?" An affirmative answer, I was told, used to indicate mental imbalance. Now the opposite was the case.

My interlocutor continued with the observation that the Western view that younger psychiatrists would be more reform-minded was mistaken. He explained that the Central Committee had found it difficult to arrange the visit of the U.S. psychiatrists. The visit had been strongly opposed by Soviet members of the profession as "humiliating." They argued that "the foreign ministry had dragged them into something of benefit only to the U.S. State Department." However, when the visit was over, some of them agreed that it had "done more good than harm."

One other matter that came up for discussion with the Central Committee staff was the forthcoming CSCE human rights meeting in Paris. Once again, reflecting the new spirit of our relationship, I was asked for particular U.S. concerns and advice. I responded by suggesting that the Soviet Union would be sending a very positive signal if the mechanism for reviewing disputed political prisoner cases was resolved soon. I added that the Ministry of Foreign Affairs had told me that the interagency process of reviewing the matter was 99 percent complete. I was then asked whether the Procurator General had agreed to the proposed mechanism. When I said that he had not as yet consented, I was told that there was no consensus on this issue among the "jurists" and that it was the view of the Human Rights Section that progress on the issue was considerably less than 99 percent complete. I then raised the specific issue of Article 83, which made it a crime for a resident of the Soviet Union to cross the border of the Soviet Union without governmental authorization. I was told that that law was under review and would be revised.

Secretary Baker reports in his memoirs that he had a good meeting with Foreign Minister Shevardnadze at this May ministerial, strengthening the friendly relationship that they had established in Vienna. Talking to Mrs. Shevardnadze, an ardent Georgian nationalist, Baker says he came to a better understanding of the nationalities problem that the Soviet Union faced.[11]

In the human rights dialogue, it was clear that we had come a long way toward a truly cooperative relationship. At the conclusion of the ministerial meeting, I made the following assessment in a formal message:

---

11. Baker, *Politics of Diplomacy*, 78.

> The human rights dialogue associated with Secretary Baker's May 10–11 Moscow visit was productive. It is clear that the message from the top is that the dialogue should be pursued in a manner which would be constructive in effecting improvements in Soviet domestic affairs in line with the leadership's intentions and which would also contribute to improved bilateral relations. The United States, in turn, considers Soviet human rights improvements of the utmost importance regarding confidence-building between our countries.[12]

When our intensive human rights dialogue began a little over two years earlier, we had focused on three major issues: the criminalization of unapproved political or religious activities, severe restrictions on emigration, and abuse of psychiatry. By May 1989, the persons serving prison terms under the laws that criminalized political or religious activity had been released and the laws at issue had been repealed, most of the rules that had restricted emigration had been set aside and hundreds of thousands of exit permits were being issued, and abuse of psychiatry had ended. All that was left of our old agenda were cases in which we contended that persons convicted ostensibly for ordinary crimes had, in fact, been punished for their political activities, and the cases of denials of exit permits on the ground that the applicant possessed classified information. On both these issues, the Soviet foreign ministry tried to assist in resolving the cases by getting the Ministry of Justice to review the cases of what we contended were the remaining political prisoners and the Ministry of Defense to review the cases of refuseniks whose once-classified information we contended was obsolete.

While my substantive discussions in the course of my May 1989 visit to Moscow were very positive, I had one exchange with Anatoly that I thought unimportant at the time but that turned out to be of major significance. At the very beginning of our exchange of thoughts, Anatoly wanted to know why the close relationship between our two countries was not continuing. I answered that there was no need to be concerned; that the current administration wanted to be Bush I, not Reagan III. Anatoly responded: "But when will Bush I start?"

Bringing Anatoly Back In

The May meetings brought us back to where we had been in our human rights dialogue at the end of the Reagan administration, ready to move forward toward the goal of a democratic Soviet Union. In the interim between January and May, Anatoly had been shifted to other responsibilities. Although we were making significant progress, I believed that we would move further and faster if Anatoly were to remain fully engaged. I thought

---

12. State Department message, "U.S.-Soviet Human Rights Dialogue," May 17, 1989.

that, although he did not need to attend to matters of detail, the broader policy issues with which we continued to be concerned made it critically important that we deal with all these questions in a manner that maximized our opportunities for constructive work. It was clear to me that Anatoly could play an important role in that context.

In light of these considerations, a message was sent to the Soviet government making the point that the U.S. government was greatly pleased by the progress in our human rights dialogue—and that we were looking for approval of a mechanism on the exchange of information regarding purported ordinary criminal cases that could have a political slant, favorable resolution of the remaining refusenik cases, and an expanded dialogue on the new agenda. The message continued:

> While the Humanitarian Affairs Administration is doing a fine job working on the details of the old agenda and laying the foundation for work on the new agenda, progress on the new agenda will require the active involvement in the MFA [Ministry of Foreign Affairs] of persons at a higher level. We are looking, in particular, for the re-engagement of [redacted, Deputy Foreign Minister Adamishin]. It would be our recommendation that we arrange for a comprehensive consultation with him in Washington.[13]

Note needs to be taken of what was involved here: the U.S. Department of State was requesting that the Soviet foreign ministry assign a specific, named Soviet official to work with the United States and send him to the United States for discussion of outstanding issues. One of the truly amazing aspects of the relationship that had evolved was that the Soviet foreign ministry promptly responded positively to this suggestion: Anatoly was reengaged in our human rights work and visited Washington for a thorough consultation on all outstanding issues. It was a successful visit.

In December, Anatoly and I met in Paris a few days after the Bush-Gorbachev meeting in Malta. We reviewed the broad domestic issues of the Soviet Union, seeking to complete the work on issues of the old agenda and then to focus on our new agenda. Regarding the old agenda, we continued to discuss cases of prisoners who had been convicted of nonpolitical crimes, but where allegations had been made by interested groups that the charges were trumped up—that the intention was to punish the defendant for political activities.

We also discussed a list of forty persons serving prison terms in the United States that Foreign Minister Shevardnadze had turned over to Secretary Baker, cases in which, it was claimed, the imprisonment was politically motivated. It is my impression that neither Shevardnadze nor any of

---

13. Ibid.

the other foreign ministry officials who dealt with the issue really believed that there were prisoners of conscience in the United States, that is, prisoners who had not committed or planned to commit acts of violence in pursuit of their political objectives. Both the foreign ministry and we acted out this charade, as Anatoly had originally suggested, by assembling the relevant documents from the U.S. attorneys' offices and turning them over to the Soviet foreign ministry.[14] That enabled the ministry, in turn, to call upon the Procurator General's office to reciprocate by providing us with the records of cases in which persons had been convicted of nonpolitical offenses for political reasons.

Moving on to the new agenda, I underlined to Anatoly the interest of U.S. Attorney General Richard Thornburgh in a rule-of-law dialogue. I explained that, to avoid duplication and overlapping efforts, we had created a working group in the United States with the task of coordinating Soviet-U.S. cooperative rule of law programs. The working group consisted of representatives of the Departments of State and Justice, the U.S. Information Agency, and the United States Institute of Peace. The working group would also coordinate its efforts with private groups such as the American Bar Association.

I made it clear that, as we saw it, work on the rule of law encompassed the theory and practice of constitutional law, including the separation of powers, civil liberties, the independence of the judiciary, the division of authority between the national government and its subdivisions, and the procedural aspects of criminal law, including juvenile law.

We did not stop our work with this outline of concepts but immediately discussed concrete next steps. Arrangements were made for a rule of law seminar in Moscow, led by U.S. authorities on constitutional law. Further, ten Soviet judges were to come to the United States to observe U.S. court proceedings, and there would be programs for Soviet lawyers to spend time in the United States to study specific topics of interest, such as issues of constitutional law.

I succeeded in enlisting the help of U.S. federal judges to work with their Soviet counterparts. On one occasion, a U.S. judge told me after having returned from an exchange visit to the Soviet Union that he had been told by a Soviet colleague how happy he was to be able to dispense real justice rather than "telephone justice." When the U.S. judge asked what telephone justice meant, he was told: "When the local party secretary calls you to tell you how to decide a pending case."

Independent associations were being formed, and the country moved toward free elections. We discussed with Soviet officials cooperative programs

---

14. They invariably demonstrated that the defendant had been engaged in an act or acts of violence.

in the fields of psychiatry, the physically handicapped, and mine health and safety. The United States did not urge the Soviet Union to undertake these programs; they resulted from suggestions made by the Soviet side, particularly Anatoly.

A few months later, in addressing the UN Human Rights Commission on March 1, 1990, Anatoly stated his country's commitment to the principles of governance that emanated from the Enlightenment:

> The fact that we belong to one civilization implies that all member countries of the international community conduct their internal affairs in conformity, at least in general terms, with some common ideals. Humanity has formulated certain standards for economy, political life, culture, and as a fusion of all of the above, for human rights and freedoms.[15]

New Problems for Perestroika

A new problem was, however, now coming to the fore: the Soviet Union's nationalities problem, about which Shevardnadze had expressed deep concerns to Baker. Secession was most vigorously advocated in the Baltic states. In view of the fact that the United States had never recognized the absorption of the Baltic states into the Soviet Union, we urged the Soviet Union to negotiate a peaceful change with the leadership of the Baltic states and not use force. During this period, I received a visit from the Georgian leader, Zviad Gamsakhurdia, who urged U.S. support for Georgian independence. I told him, to his great disappointment, that while the United States supported Baltic independence, it would not advocate Georgian independence. We would support the right of the people of Georgia to participate in free elections and to have their language and their culture recognized, but we would not support the dissolution of the Soviet Union. Yet, even without U.S. support, nationalism in the non-Russian republics, particularly Ukraine and Georgia, came increasingly to the fore and ultimately caused the Soviet Union to disintegrate without U.S. engagement.[16]

Rising nationalism in the non-Russian republics gave rise to increased nationalism within Russia, reflecting a concern that Gorbachev's leniency would cause the Russian-dominated Soviet Union to disintegrate. Gorbachev's liberalization program weakened his standing in other respects as well. Free elections to the People's Congress produced a legislature that rejected some of Gorbachev's proposals. While the economy continued to

---

15. A copy of the complete text is in my possession.

16. Gamsakhurdia became Georgia's first president. He subsequently sent me this brief message: "I am not a fascist."

function along socialist principles, the end of centralized control, combined with a relaxed attitude toward those administrators and workers who did not perform well, resulted in a failure to meet targets of economic growth. Strikes called by the newly free labor unions occurred, further hampering efforts to increase production. While Gorbachev continued to be highly regarded by those who appreciated the end of the police state, large numbers of Soviet citizens, concerned about their standard of living and the general feeling of insecurity, became increasingly skeptical of their government's policies.

When I summed up developments in the Soviet Union during the year 1989 in congressional testimony in early 1990, I said that "Soviet reformers have committed themselves publicly to establishing in the Soviet Union a state based on the rule of law, adhering to democratic principles, and respecting human rights." But I also called attention to the fact that we were not home free, that the Soviet reformers faced formidable obstacles. I noted that "opponents of reform, consisting of Russian nationalist extremists, party hacks fearful of losing their positions of authority and privilege, and demobilized army officers who find themselves in a similar situation, may form a significant political bloc" that could stand in the way of progress.[17]

The combination of ultranationalists and Communist apparatchiks came to be referred to as Gorbachev's right-wing opposition. But by the early 1990s, a left-wing opposition had formed itself as well. Its standard bearer was a long-term Communist Party official whom Gorbachev had elevated to the position of first secretary of the Moscow Communist Party Central Committee and member of the Politburo, Boris Yeltsin. He had resigned from these positions in October 1987, after having taken the floor at a Central Committee plenum to attack Gorbachev for concentrating too much power in his hands.

Yeltsin reentered the political arena after Gorbachev had taken another significant step forward in the democratization of the Soviet Union. Under an amendment to the Soviet constitution, a new legislative body had been created, the Congress of People's Deputies. In March 1989, when elections were held for this congress, the Communist Party was still the only party functioning in the Soviet Union, but multiple candidacies were allowed in each constituency, and quite a number of candidates who had not had any official endorsement were elected. One of them was Yeltsin, who soon was

---

17. Anatoly had warned me not to expect the democratic trend to continue without interruption. We should expect zigzags, he had said. I also heard a far more pessimistic assessment from a Russian professor who visited Washington in 1989 and gave a lecture on the Soviet Union's future that was truly disconcerting. During the question period, I made the point that Spain, after living for forty years under Franco, had evolved into a genuine, vibrant democracy. The professor's response was: "You don't understand the difference between authoritarianism and totalitarianism. The Bolsheviks have destroyed the country's social fabric."

able to gain the support of colleagues and form his own group within the congress.

The group argued that reforms had moved too slowly; more fundamental changes needed to take place, and rapidly. The policy positions of this group attracted the support of members of the intelligentsia who had not been part of the party apparatus, particularly former dissidents. Beyond that, Yeltsin attracted support because he exhibited what we in the United States call political charisma, something that Gorbachev lacked. Yeltsin's personality attracted many citizens, particularly in Moscow, where he had served on the local Central Committee and where his populist appeal resonated. In due course, a left-wing movement, with Yeltsin as its leader, was in place.

One of the most significant elements of the political program of that left-wing movement was that, even though it was largely a movement of Russians, it favored local sovereignty. When I met in January 1990 with two of my one-time dissident friends who were now supporting Yeltsin, they started to talk about Russian sovereignty. I called their attention to the fact that if Russia wanted sovereignty, every other republic would want sovereignty and the Soviet Union would break up. In response they shrugged their shoulders. It was then that it dawned on me that by supporting Russian sovereignty, Yeltsin's supporters sought to get rid of Gorbachev and replace him with Yeltsin. The dissolution of the Soviet Union was a price they were prepared to pay to elevate their man to the top leadership post.

Thus, even though nominally the Communist Party was still the Soviet Union's only political party, there were now three distinct political movements, each with its own program. The right wing was eager to return to the country's totalitarian past and was opposed to any form of regional autonomy. It most certainly opposed secession by any of the Soviet republics. It had no single principal leader, but it had a strong cadre of hard-core apparatchiks combined with the military-industrial complex. At the other end was a less well-organized democratic movement that had split into two parts. As far as I could tell, the basic objectives of the two parts were the same: They wanted to establish a free, democratic state. They differed in their articulation of their goals regarding the economy and, above all, in the choice of the leaders that they were prepared to follow. The left wing, led by Yeltsin, called for the prompt movement to a market economy. The centrists, led by Gorbachev, agreed that the socialist economic model had failed, but favored a more gradual approach to fundamental economic change.

Pressing Ahead with the New Agenda

The pattern of U.S.-Soviet relations that had been established by the end of 1989 as a result of the Bush-Gorbachev meeting in Malta—namely, a continuation of the policies of the final years of the Reagan-Shultz leadership—continued in 1990. In the human rights area, our principal focus was now on our new agenda, cooperative working relations between experts in specially selected fields, and major emphasis on the rule of law. In early 1990, we added another item to that agenda: We agreed to discuss and establish U.S.-Soviet cooperation in international human rights fora, namely, the CSCE process, the United Nations, and the International Red Cross. We further agreed to establish a working group consisting of representatives of the Soviet Ministry of Foreign Affairs and the U.S. embassy in Moscow. The working group was to meet regularly to handle the administrative details of projects arising out of our human rights dialogue.

Anatoly, who had overseen the human rights dialogue in addition to other responsibilities, was now most definitely phasing out of it. In May 1990, he moved to Rome to serve as Soviet ambassador to Italy. His successor was Deputy Foreign Minister Vladimir Petrovskiy. When I met Petrovskiy, he stated his readiness to work with the United States and me along the same lines as Anatoly had done. He paid tribute to Anatoly's work, which had resulted "in a changed pattern of attitudes" toward cooperation with the United States on human rights matters. The focus of our meeting was once again the rule of law. As Petrovskiy put it, the Soviet Union did not want to "reinvent the bicycle," and therefore found discussions of U.S. legal procedure very interesting.

We also discussed a problem that had arisen regarding the proposed visit to the United States of Soviet psychiatrists. A delegation had been formed and was ready to travel to the United States when psychiatrists at the National Institute of Mental Health discovered that some members of the delegation had theretofore been engaged in abuse of psychiatry. Because the United States was to bear the cost of the trip, the U.S. government would have been embarrassed if it funded visits to the United States by persons who had violated the principles of their profession. Petrovskiy contended that the cancellation of the trip had made an unfavorable impression in "academic and medical circles." Turning to the forthcoming CSCE human rights conference in Copenhagen, Petrovskiy assured me of Soviet support for a U.S.-U.K. proposal on free elections. The Soviet Union did, in fact, cooperate fully in the conference's work, which concluded with a strong declaration on human rights and democracy.[18]

Indicative of the drastic change in the focus of our human rights dialogue, I met with the Soviet minister of justice, Veniamin Yakovlev, during my May 1990 trip to Moscow. At the outset of our discussion, he mentioned that when

---

18. State Department message, "A/S Schifter's May 16 Meeting with Deputy Foreign Minster Vladimir Petrovskiy," May 29, 1990.

he had first met me in 1988, he had no idea that our "relations would grow so quickly into a full-scale affair." He characterized a recent visit to the United States by a group of Soviet judges as "professionally enriching for the participants and very important to the democratization of the Soviet judicial system." We then made plans for a more intensive program of judicial exchanges.

In the course of a broader discussion of current affairs, Yakovlev made a number of telling points. First, broad masses of people were not yet experienced in democracy, making for problems in the process of democratization. Second, if the rule of law could be established, democratization could certainly take place. Third, the country needed a leadership group of experts, economists, and lawyers, not people who knew nothing other than "ordering people around." Fourth, a new law had given local governmental units authority to decide how to use available funds; they would have to learn to use that authority wisely.[19]

Other exchange programs discussed during the May 1990 visit were the visits to the United States of delegations concerned with the handicapped and the elderly. Both groups had found their visits useful. Arrangements had been made for the production of wheelchairs and prosthetics. The delegation dealing with the elderly was interested in the design of homes for senior citizens.

Highlights of my other visits to the Soviet Union in the course of 1990—and indicative of the entirely new direction of our human rights dialogue—were meetings with Alexander Maximovich Yakovlev of the Institute of State and Law and Minister of the Interior Vadim Bakatin.

Alexander Maximovich Yakovlev, a member of the Supreme Soviet—not to be confused with Aleksandr Nikolayevich Yakovlev, Gorbachev's closest confidant—was another official who showed great interest in bringing the rule of law to the Soviet Union. When I met with him in June 1990, he noted several changes. First, jury trials were authorized by law, but the law had to be implemented at the local level. Second, it was understood that defendants were entitled to truly independent counsel, but the problem was who would pay for the services of such counsel; thus, "implementation in Kirgizia was one thing, in Lithuania another, and in Russia still a third." Third, citizens would be allowed to sue government officials, but crash courses for judges in administrative law were necessary to handle this new caseload. He expressed the concern that I had heard from others that much of the Soviet population had a "peasant family mentality," seeking a strong father figure to rule, and was, therefore, not committed to supporting democratic reforms.

---

19. State Department message, "A/S Schifter's May 18 Meeting with Veniamin Yakovlev, Minister of Justice of the USSR," March 31, 1990.

Regarding the broader issue of governance, Yakovlev expressed concern about the formation of what he called rightist forces. He placed the Communist Party at their center, supported by the military-industrial complex and the most secret sections of the KGB.

One of the brightest stars in the Soviet government of that period was Vadim Bakatin, the minister of the interior, with whom I had an extensive discussion in October 1990. He readily accepted the suggestion that his ministry, which supervised the country's police, participate in the exchange programs with the United States in the field of the rule of law. We then discussed how the division of responsibility between federal, state, and local police in the United States could be studied by Soviet officials as the Soviet Union decentralized its police force. Bakatin agreed and said that he had been greatly concerned that law enforcement was disintegrating, as no clear lines were drawn regarding the responsibilities of different entities of government. "Crime doesn't sleep," he said, as he explained that he had finally been able to negotiate an agreement between the Soviet Union and the individual republics that temporarily delineated a division of responsibility, with a permanent solution to be found in a future all-union treaty.

Turning to the recent Communist Party congress, Bakatin said that it had made "progressive but imprecise" decisions. Reading between the lines, he concluded that the party favored allowing private property, but the final pronouncements had to account for the views of conservative members and, therefore, reflected "the command-administrative method of the past." Gorbachev, he added, was pushing for greater democracy and a free market, but had run into strong resistance from the old guard. An added problem was that the "broad masses, especially in the provinces," feared any sort of instability. Bakatin blamed Prime Minister Nikolai Ryzhkov for his failure to work on an economic plan on which Gorbachev and Yeltsin had agreed.[20]

In short, the Soviet Union's chief law enforcement officer told me that law enforcement was disintegrating and the "broad masses" feared instability. This was a troublesome assessment of the results of the political opening that Gorbachev had initiated. As 1990 came to an end, there were rumors that Gorbachev was increasingly accommodating the concerns of the military leadership in an effort to keep that leadership on his side. Then, on December 20, many supporters of democracy, both within the Soviet Union and outside it, were shocked by Foreign Minister Shevardnadze's speech to the Congress of People's Deputies in which he announced his resignation and warned that the country was moving toward a military coup or dictatorship.

---

20. State Department message, "HA A/S Schifter's Tour d'Horizon with Soviet Interior Minister Bakatin," October 29, 1990.

In reviewing developments in 1990, I said in a media briefing in February 1991 that further progress toward an open society had been made in the Soviet Union but repeated my warning:

> In the Soviet Union in 1990, vast numbers of citizens continued to exercise newly won political rights, including freedoms of expression, assembly, and religion. Hundreds of thousands were permitted to emigrate. However, reforms were unevenly implemented in the country as a whole, and many are not yet secured by law or buttressed by an independent judiciary. Toward the end of the year and in early 1991, the Central Government's moves to reassert authority over the republics, particularly the use of military force in Latvia and Lithuania, raised concern over the future of the recent reforms, with dangerous implications for the entire country. . . .
>
> As . . . we look for further progress in 1991, one of the key questions will be . . . Will the combination of entrenched conservative forces, economic turmoil, and social upheaval bring the reform era to an end? Or alternatively, will the disparate democratic forces and proponents of the free market overcome the counterattack of the hardliners and solidify and institutionalize the human rights progress so far achieved? If they do, their success will be felt not only in the Soviet Union but elsewhere in the world as well.[21]

The following month, I was in Moscow again to continue my dialogue with Petrovskiy. It should be noted that at this point I was no longer traveling to the Soviet Union in the context of a parallel ministerial meeting. There were no ministerial meetings any more; much of Secretary Baker's attention focused on the Middle East.

In my meeting with Petrovskiy, our discussions were far less productive than they had been before, and I wondered whether that was due to Shevardnadze's departure from the foreign ministry.[22]

We began, as usual, with a discussion of the remaining cases of persons who, the United States contended, had been incarcerated on political grounds. As noted earlier, all those who had been convicted under the articles that criminalized anti-Soviet agitation and propaganda or defamation of the Soviet system had been released by the end of 1988. Since then, we had been struggling over cases of persons who had been convicted on other grounds, but with indications that they were being punished for the expression of dissenting political views. We were now down to four cases, and I expressed the hope that these would be quickly resolved.

---

21. State Department message, "Transmittal of HA A/S Schifter's 2/1/91 Press Statement/Introduction to 1990 Human Rights Report," February 9, 1991.

22. My impression was confirmed a few years later, when I met Petrovskiy in Geneva, where he held a position in the UN Secretariat. Without any prompting from me, he expressed his regrets regarding this 1991 meeting. He appeared to have been under instructions to be uncooperative.

Petrovskiy said that some cases were still under consideration but then could not help but add, with reference to the allegedly political U.S. cases that the Soviet Union had called to our attention, that "not many people" had been released from prison on the U.S. side. I responded quite emphatically that the information that we had supplied to the Soviet government demonstrated that each of the persons on the Soviet list had committed an act of violence. I pointed out further that when the Soviet Union had provided information to us that a person on our list had been sentenced for a crime of violence, we had stricken that case from the list, even if the act was politically motivated.

Petrovskiy went on to say that Soviet NGOs had come into existence that would raise cases of U.S. political prisoners at the forthcoming CSCE human rights meeting; that NGOs were mushrooming; and that the Soviet government had to account for public opinion, demonstrating that it did not accept a double standard in this field. I pointed out that the United States had a two-hundred-year tradition of protecting the rights of citizens. We had agreed to review the U.S. cases that had been raised with us merely to assist the foreign ministry in its dealing with the Soviet Ministry of Justice and elicit that ministry's cooperation as well as the cooperation of the procurator general. As for the reference to the alleged concerns of alleged Soviet NGOs, I told Petrovskiy bluntly that I hoped the Ministry of Foreign Affairs would stop playing that game.

Regarding emigration issues, Petrovskiy also offered a number of excuses. When I pointed out that the number of refusenik cases had been significantly reduced and that the remaining cases could be easily resolved by looking at the facts in individual cases, he contended that there would have to be a legal basis for changing administrative decisions, which would have to await the enactment of the proposed emigration law. A proposed draft of an emigration law had been pending for almost three years. He added that some European countries had expressed concern about the emigration law because it would lead to large-scale Soviet emigration to these European countries. I told him that we had heard this contention before and had checked with France and Germany, both of which had assured us that they had not objected to the proposed new Soviet emigration law.

The conversation then turned to the issue of the media. I said that television news programs had returned to the slanted approach of the past, which, I said, "must be as frightening to people in the Soviet Union as it is to those outside." Petrovskiy responded that it was the government's intention to "strengthen the reform process and maintain stability" and that it was necessary to respond to "immoral representations." I, in turn, stressed that old fears were being aroused, which raised the question of whether there were some people working offstage who sought to reestablish the old order.

When we got to the rule of law projects that we had been working on with the Ministry of Justice, I called attention to the fact that the new Soviet proposals appeared to deemphasize some of the issues that we had discussed before and asked whether we were witnessing retrogression—whether human rights considerations were being pushed aside. I was assured that was not the case.

I was back in Moscow two months later. I had the usual meeting at the foreign ministry, where we discussed the remaining items on the old agenda. In the spirit of the post-Shevardnadze era at the ministry, my interlocutor, Yuri Reshetov, brought up a highly publicized case of police brutality in Los Angeles, the case of Rodney King. I conceded that the United States, like the Soviet Union and other countries, had problems in the area of police brutality but pointed out that the police officers involved in the matter had been indicted and would be tried in a court of law. Reshetov continued at length about a Department of Justice study of police brutality in the United States. I responded again that it was a problem that we shared with the Soviet Union and that we both needed to tackle.

In our discussion of the long-pending proposed emigration law, I was told that the proposal would soon become law, but was then told that it would take some time for the new law to be implemented because of the financial burden that it would impose on the Soviet government. For the law to have meaning, I was told, the Soviet Union would have to develop the capability to enable all persons who received exit permits to actually leave the country. It was important, Reshetov said, that the new right to travel was not a mere paper exercise; funds had to be allocated for Aeroflot to purchase five hundred aircraft, for the railway administration to purchase one thousand passenger cars, for the Ministry of the Interior to increase its staff to process the additional applications for exit permits and passports, and for the Ministry of Finance to be able to meet the increased demand for foreign currency for those travelers who would merely make temporary visits to foreign countries.

When I responded that the issue was one of recognizing the principle of freedom to leave the country, not to provide planes and railroad cars, I got another dose of old thinking from Reshetov. He told me that there would be a great many unhappy people if they were granted the right to travel but not provided the means to do so.[23]

---

23. State Department message, "HA A/S Schifter's Meetings with MFA Human Rights Officials April 22 and 25," May 3, 1991.

A Growing Sense of Foreboding

The U.S.-Soviet human rights dialogue continued nevertheless. While we were still making incremental progress in reducing the remaining cases on our old agenda, my April 1991 meeting at the foreign ministry showed that there was reason to be concerned that the warning that Shevardnadze had delivered when he resigned in December 1990 should be taken very seriously. I therefore used the opportunity of my visit to meet with Shevardnadze, as well as with Ivan Laptiev, the chairman of the Supreme Soviet (a position similar to that of speaker of the U.S. House of Representatives), Gavriil Popov, Moscow's mayor, and Vyacheslav Lebyedev, the chairman of the Supreme Court of the Russian Soviet Republic.

My discussion with Chairman Laptiev, so clearly a new thinker, contrasted sharply with the old thinking that had returned to the foreign ministry, as reflected in Reshetov's utterly absurd observations about the need for planes and railroad cars. Laptiev noted that in the preceding year, more than 450,000 people had left the Soviet Union. He assured me that the new approach to emigration would soon be anchored into law by adoption of a law on entry and exit. He added his personal observation that many people who might strive to leave the country "are psychologically not ready for such changes in their fate."[24]

In the preceding months, I had become increasingly concerned that the sharp division in the Soviet Union's democratic camp—between the followers of Gorbachev and those of Yeltsin—would seriously endanger the progress made under perestroika. When I met with Shevardnadze, my first question to him was, therefore, what he thought of the idea of convening a roundtable of the differing democratic political groupings to reach an understanding on a program that they could all support. Shevardnadze thought that was premature. It was his view that only two persons, Gorbachev and Yeltsin, needed to get together to resolve their personal differences. They needed to stop insulting each other. If President Reagan, who had spoken of the Evil Empire, and Gorbachev, who had spoken of the imperialists, could get together, he said, so could these two Soviet political leaders. Once that had happened, a roundtable could succeed.

When I asked about his views of the future of the Soviet Union, Shevardnadze emphasized the need to move to a federal system. He spoke of "the devolution of significant authority from the center to the republics." In his view, the leadership should have begun its work on devolution three years earlier "when it still had strong support," and when it could have held all

---

24. State Department message, "'Izvestiya' Carries Official Report on A/S Schifter's Meeting with Chairman of the USSR Supreme Soviet Council of the Union Ivan Laptev," April 26, 1991.

fifteen republics together. At this point, he thought, it would still be possible to hold nine of them together. I assumed that he thought that, in addition to the Baltic states, Armenia, Georgia, and Moldova would secede from the Soviet Union. He added that the republics' differences in their ethnic backgrounds made the shift from a unitary state to a federal system that much more complicated. In the United States, he said, citizens identified themselves as Americans. In the Soviet Union they defined themselves first on the basis of their ethnicity.

I used this opportunity to ask Shevardnadze whether he had noticed the name of the U.S. general with responsibility for northern Iraq, General Shalikashvili. Shevardnadze laughed and said that he certainly had. He added: "In your country he is an American. Here he would be a Georgian. That's what is so great about your country."

Looking back at the years since the beginning of perestroika, Shevardnadze said that the leadership had made serious mistakes in underestimating the country's social and interethnic problems. There was a tendency either to work at a slow pace or to make hasty decisions. The leadership, he said, should have looked ahead for a longer period, ten to twelve years, recognized the problems the country faced, and moved step by step to effect the transition to a democratic system.

Under the previous system, Shevardnadze noted, the almighty Politburo would make a decision today that would be implemented tomorrow. Without mentioning Gorbachev's name, he suggested that Gorbachev had made a serious mistake in giving decision-making authority to legislative bodies without retaining authority in the executive agencies. He said that from the very beginning, he and others had urged adoption of the presidential system, following the U.S. model, but the idea did not receive sufficient support. Now, he added, presidential decrees were issued, but they were not complied with.

Expressing great concern regarding the present state of affairs, Shevardnadze said that Gorbachev had initially disagreed with him when he spoke of a threat of dictatorship. A month later, however, Gorbachev had said the Soviet Union was facing chaos from which a dictatorship could emerge. He had also spoken "of the threats coming from both right and left."[25]

At the conclusion of this meeting with Shevardnadze, I was certainly more troubled about the Soviet Union's future than I had been when I had arrived.

My next meeting was with Gavriil Popov. The specific reason for my meeting with the mayor of Moscow was to discuss U.S.-Soviet cooperation in

---

25. State Department message, "Former Foreign Minister Shevardnadze's Comments on Current Conditions," April 27, 1991.

the area of humanitarian assistance to Moscow's elderly and handicapped. I proposed a training program for Soviet social workers in Moscow and in the United States who would then be qualified to staff senior citizens' and crisis centers. The mayor said that creating such centers was "an excellent idea." He noted that Moscow was home to approximately two million pensioners, one-fifth of the city's population. He also mentioned that the pensioners were unwilling to support economic reform because that implied price increases, which would reduce the standard of living for persons on fixed incomes.

Regarding the training of social workers, Popov was all for training in Moscow, but did not consider it advisable to provide training in the United States. He said: "There will be one hundred who wish to go for every spot that will be available, and upon their return, few will use their training for our benefit." He mentioned that others who have been trained in the United States "disappear altogether or work in the ministries." Only 5 percent "work for the benefit of the people when they return."

When our conversation shifted to human rights, Popov cautioned against becoming too complacent in the face of gains in the area of human rights in the Soviet Union. He said: "If we speak of specific cases, we see that the numbers have decreased. At the same time, this should not be the origin for illusions about the entire situation. The protection of human rights must ultimately depend on the basis upon which our society lives and develops." He continued with a remark that was truly prophetic: "The problem of human rights is a direct consequence of the mood of our leaders. The moment they change their mood, it can all be reversed. We don't have guarantees. Our laws are still weak and our entire law enforcement system depends upon state structures." I assumed that what he meant by that remark was that the Soviet Union lacked an independent judiciary. He added that "in the West you are visited by highly educated, cultured [Soviet] champions of human rights. In the Soviet Union these same jurists keep silent in the face of unlawfulness."[26]

As in my other meetings on this trip, my discussion with the chief judge of the Supreme Court of the Russian Soviet Republic, Vyacheslav Lebyedev, had a specific administrative purpose, but then broadened into a tour d'horizon regarding the state of human rights in the Soviet Union.

To start with, I apprised Lebyedev of plans for cooperative U.S.-Soviet efforts in the field of judicial reform, to invite the Russian Supreme Court to participate in the effort, and to establish long-term relationships between Soviet and U.S. judges to take the place of the sporadic meetings that had characterized the legal dialogue to date. Lebyedev made it clear that he was interested in having Russian judges participate in the program and stressed

---

26. State Department message, "A/S Schifter Meets with Mayor Popov on Human Rights, Humanitarian Cooperation and Moscow CSCE Meeting," April 29, 1991.

that he, too, had been thinking about the benefits to be derived from long-term contacts.

Regarding the broad issue of human rights, Lebyedev continued, there was a need to provide constitutional guarantees of such rights. He said: "Judges dealing with cases involving human rights find themselves in a difficult position because the decision of the court can be only as just as the law which the judge applies. Therefore, if the laws are not just, the decision of judges dealing with these questions can be according to the law but unjust."

In addition to the need for constitutional guarantees, Lebyedev emphasized the importance of creating a judiciary that was completely independent from the executive branch. He cited numerous examples of cases influenced by extrajudicial considerations. In the past, he said, "the militia, KGB, and prosecutors' offices were used to mete out justice. The court was utilized least of all. That is why problems have accumulated."[27]

I was not aware that, during my stay in Moscow, the Central Committee of the Communist Party had held a plenary session at which a motion had been offered to call for the resignation of General Secretary Gorbachev. In his introductory remarks, Gorbachev had said:

> We have gathered at an exceptionally difficult time. The atmosphere in the country is heating up to boiling point. The atmosphere within the Party is also becoming charged. What is most important now is not to yield to the temptation of emotional decision-making. Obviously the current time is not one for quiet academic analysis. Attempts are being made to deflect the country from the course of reforms, either by driving it into another ultra-revolutionary venture which would jeopardize our statehood or by reverting to a thinly disguised totalitarian regime. I am referring to the plans of the rightist and leftist radicals.
>
> Both these trends are pernicious. And the greatest danger at the moment lies in their convergence notwithstanding their ostensibly irreconcilable animosity.[28]

In the end, the rightists and leftists did not converge to defeat Gorbachev. The people whom Gorbachev called leftist radicals—the Yeltsin supporters—did not vote against him.

A Failed Coup, a Crumbling Union

In an article that I had written in the summer of 1988, I had offered the following thoughts:

---

27. State Department message, "A/S Schifter Meets with RSFSR Supreme Court Chairman Lebedev on Rule of Law and Humanitarian Cooperation," April 29, 1991.
28. Gorbachev, *Memoirs*, 599.

> There are now reformers in the Soviet establishment who have concluded that the doctrines of the past must be put aside and that other standards defining the relationship between the governing and the governed must take their place. Increasingly, they look to the standards which are the products of the Enlightenment of the eighteenth century, the standards to which the Western democracies subscribe.
>
> But lying in wait for Mikhail, as he makes his way through the forest, is the wolf, the opposition to reform. There are those who simply prefer stability and order and consider democratic trends destabilizing. And then there are those who under Gorbachev's reforms would lose jobs, status, and privileges. The Soviet Union, we must keep in mind, is one of the most class-ridden societies now in existence, with its higher aristocracy, its lower aristocracy, and all the hangers-on associated with those who exercise power. Are they willing to accept the new egalitarianism and the meritocracy which the reformers advocate? How hard will they fight to hang on to their positions? What, above all, will be the attitude of the military in the face of sharp budget cuts?[29]

On August 18, 1991, about two months following the first rumor of a possible coup, the wolf struck. Radio Moscow announced that Vice President Gennady Yanayev had taken over as president of the Soviet Union due to Gorbachev's inability to perform his duties for health reasons. A state of emergency had been declared, and a state emergency committee had been formed consisting of Yanayev, Prime Minister Valentin Pavlov, Defense Minister Dmitry Yazov, Interior Minister Boris Pugo, KGB Chairman Vladimir Kryuchkov, and three others. What was not generally known at that time was that Gorbachev, who was vacationing in the Crimea, had received a visit from a group of conspirators who demanded that he bless the coup.

What appeared initially quite troublesome was that the emergency committee contained the leaders of all the forces in the Soviet Union that carried arms: Yazov, who led the army; Pugo, who led the police; and Kryuchkov, who led the KGB. But what happened then was, perhaps, perestroika's finest hour: These three arms-carrying forces did not follow their leader. To paraphrase the hope for the future of the protagonist in Erich Maria Remarque's *All Quiet on the Western Front*, they called a coup and nobody came. Instead, the people of Moscow rose up, roused by Boris Yeltsin's appeal to defend the newly established democratic order.

What I found particularly striking was the report of the behavior of the Alpha Group, a KGB special strike force trained for rapid action against hostage takers. When ordered to move on the Russian government's White House to arrest Boris Yeltsin, the Alpha Group took a vote on whether to carry out the order and decided unanimously to disobey it. By August 23, the coup had ended and the coup leaders had been arrested.

---

29. Schifter, "Glasnost, the Dawn of Freedom," *World Affairs* (Summer 1988): 23.

What the coup had accomplished, however, was to put the Soviet Union back on the radar screen of top U.S. policymakers. It was clear to everyone concerned that with the reactionary forces defeated, the political struggle in the Soviet Union was between the ascending Yeltsin and a seriously weakened Gorbachev, between those who wanted to maintain the Soviet Union in some form and those who wanted to see it dissolved.

That was the setting in which I visited Moscow in October 1991 for what was to be my last visit to the Soviet Union. Once again I met with Ivan Laptiev, the chairman of the Supreme Soviet Council. At the outset of our meeting I reminded Laptiev of a conversation several years earlier in which he had predicted to me that any coup attempt would fail because the people would resist the coup and the soldiers would side with them. In response, Laptiev told me that during the coup attempt, he and other members of the Supreme Soviet had been able to enter the Kremlin unimpeded, although they had to pass through rings of tanks and armored personnel carriers to do so.

The coup, he went on to say, did not fail because the plotters were incompetent or lacked resolve. The coup failed because the plotters were wrong about three matters. First, the people had changed and were no longer willing to let a group of men in the Kremlin decide their fate. Second, Yeltsin—both personally and as the central figure of a specific group of people—was stronger than the plotters thought. Third, the coup plotters failed to size up Gorbachev accurately. They thought Gorbachev was weak and would yield to pressure. "I know Gorbachev well," Laptiev said, "and he is in reality a very tough, even cruel person. The coup plotters went to the Crimea not to ask for forgiveness, as has been reported, but to ask Gorbachev to bless the coup. That shows they did not understand him."

Laptiev went on to discuss the changes that were expected to be made in the Soviet Union's governmental structure in the near future. Although no final decisions had as yet been taken, he made it clear that there would be significant devolution of power from the center to the republics. He said that "if we take the structure of the U.S. Congress and make it more complicated, we will have the new Supreme Soviet."

The lower chamber, to be called the Council of the Union, he explained, would have the power to decide economic issues, human rights, and many other issues. However, its decisions would have to be approved by the upper chamber, the Council of the Republics. That council would operate by consensus, thus allowing each republic's delegation to exercise veto power over the entire legislative process. Beyond that, each republic's Supreme Soviet would have the power to declare the central Supreme Soviet decisions null and void on their respective territories. As Laptiev saw the role of the new central Supreme Soviet, it would serve as a symbol of the continued existence of the Soviet Union, preserving the Soviet Union for purposes of international law, but that would be all.

Turning to the subject of human rights, Laptiev said that "it is difficult to speak of fully guaranteeing human rights in a nation without food and where a great deal of violence is occurring." But he believed that a legal basis had been created for the protection of human rights. The human rights problem, he said, had now shifted to the republics, where presidents, often with the backing of legislators, believed they could fence themselves off from the Soviet government's human rights efforts. He urged me to see to it that the West put pressure on the republics to conform to human rights standards. He added that while the republics might ignore pressure from the Soviet government, they were sensitive to world public opinion.

The State Department's cable reporting on this meeting with Chairman Laptiev contains the following concluding paragraph:

> In closing, Laptiev thanked A/S Schifter for his many efforts to bring human rights to the Soviet Union. Laptiev recalled that, especially during the early years of Perestroika, there had been many tense meetings with A/S Schifter. "In the beginning we resisted," Laptiev said, "but now we have come to realize that you were right to push us so hard. I just want to thank you for all the help you have given us over the years on human rights."[30]

Four and a half years had passed since Anatoly and I had first met and the effort to have the Soviet Union live up to its international human rights obligations had begun. It was good to know that the success of this effort was recognized and appreciated at a high level in the Soviet Union's governmental hierarchy.

On the following day, I had the unique experience of visiting KGB headquarters to meet with the new chairman of the KGB, Vadim Bakatin, whom I had found a most impressive person when I had met him during his service as minister of the interior.

I started our meeting by emphasizing the strong feelings of friendship on the part of the people and government of the United States for the people of the Soviet Union in the wake of the failed coup. I stressed our eagerness to cooperate in finding democratic solutions to the problems the Soviet Union faced. In this context, I noted the programs that were initiated during Bakatin's tenure at the interior ministry, under which ministry officials visited the United States to study the interaction among U.S. law enforcement agencies at the federal, state, and local levels. I referred to the fact that the programs were discontinued after Bakatin was replaced by Boris Pugo as minister of

---

30. State Department message, "Council of the Union Chairman Laptiev Discusses Coup, Outlines Structure of the USSR Supreme Soviet in Meeting with A/S Schifter," October 24, 1991.

the interior. (Pugo was one of the main plotters in the attempted August coup and committed suicide after it failed.)

Bakatin responded with a review of the state of affairs as he saw it. He said that after the tragic days of August, it had been possible to achieve a real breakthrough in "our six-year revolution"—suggesting that the revolution started as soon as Gorbachev was elected general secretary. He did not think that Gorbachev's program of perestroika deserved heavy criticism because "we did what we could." The failure of the coup had made the goals of reform clear, especially in the economic sphere, by which he meant the need to move to a market economy. What troubled him was that, even though the failure of the coup meant that the basic decisions had been made, everyone seemed to be going in circles. There was no forward movement. That, he thought, was dangerous.

Bakatin stressed the point that every aspect of political life in the country had changed. The domination of the country by a power structure reaching from the Politburo down to the district party committees had been wiped away. What was troublesome was that nothing had appeared to take the place of this power structure. As he put it: "The democrats are not clear in their goals and things are just dragging on." He was worried that democratic concepts were sometimes being lost in the shuffle. He thought that outlawing the Communist Party was dangerous, because that could force the Communists underground. He said: "We are talking about building a society based on the rule of law and we cannot go back. But in practice we sometimes do undemocratic things."

On the issue of whether to preserve the union or break it up, he was strongly in favor of the former, thus siding with Gorbachev over Yeltsin. He expressed concern that the central authority had been eliminated. "There is no central government," he said. He pointed out that the restructured Supreme Soviet had not yet been able to meet because some republics—primarily Ukraine—had not designated their representatives. Gorbachev, he said, had been unable to exercise his authority completely because he had to rely so heavily on the presidents of the constituent republics.

Bakatin went on to discuss the possibility of the republics becoming fully independent. In that case, he said, a decision would have to be made as to the powers that the people would want to delegate to the governments of the separate republics. Defense and security should be among them. On the other hand, setting up customs barriers and separate currencies would not be helpful. Finally, he said, thought should be given to the weight of the Soviet Union's role in international affairs and what would happen to its international role if the country broke up into smaller entities.

Gorbachev, in Bakatin's view, was doing his best to speed up the resuscitation of government functions, but much time was being wasted. What was now necessary was to make decisions as to the nature of the future governmental structure: whether it should be federal, confederate, or something else. In his view, a central structure needed to be maintained before the republics could become truly sovereign. He focused in particular on Ukraine, which he believed was looking for an arrangement of the Soviet republics similar to that of the members of the European Community. But making such an arrangement would take time and depend on the views of other members of the union. Immediate independence for Ukraine, he said, would be "a tragedy." Without mentioning Yeltsin's name, Bakatin also had harsh words for Russian leaders who were "toying" with the idea of an independent Russia. They failed, he said, to grasp the historical, unifying role that Russia had played. The coup was over, he said, but the problems had become greater.

I commented that I knew that Bakatin had access to information that was not available to me and that such information might be the source of his pessimistic outlook. On the other hand, I suggested, one could not lose sight of the miraculous nature of what had transpired in August. People with only limited experience in democracy had acted as free people and opposed an attempt to reinstate the dictatorship. I noted also that so little blood had been shed in overcoming the coup. To be sure, Bakatin was right in pointing out that the Soviet Union faced great problems. In dealing with them, I suggested, it would be appropriate to set priorities. Technical assistance from the West could play a valuable role. Bakatin agreed and said that improving agricultural production, increasing the quality of education, and creating a favorable environment for the development of small businesses were his favored priorities.

Turning to a human rights issue, I pointed out the importance of adhering to proper standards in the forthcoming trials of the coup plotters. The whole world would be watching, I said. The trials should be open with a strong defense team for the accused. Given the experience I had in my many discussions with Soviet officials of Paragraph 64 cases—in which the defendant had been charged with treason—I urged a fresh look at the Soviet criminal code to transform it from one of a dictatorship into one of a democracy.

Bakatin agreed. It was important, he said, to avoid something that would resemble the show trials of the 1930s. It was essential to have the trials be open and to start with the presumption of innocence. But he warned that the Soviet legal system was still very weak. Defense lawyers lacked experience in defending the rights of their clients.

Regarding Bakatin's comments concerning the possible outlawing of the Communist Party, I pointed out that under the Helsinki Final Act, individuals had the right to peaceful assembly and association. Bakatin responded that the new union constitution would be based on the Helsinki Final Act and the Universal Declaration of Human Rights.

We ended our conversation with an exchange of thoughts about the future of the KGB. Bakatin noted that the decision had been made to split off the external functions of the KGB from the domestic ones. With his plans still based on the continued existence of the Soviet Union, he discussed the need for a "rational system of state security" that would have to be worked out with the republics and expressed concern that some of their leaders would not understand this. He said that he had succeeded in working out such an arrangement with the Ukrainian National Security Service. As we concluded our meeting, Bakatin told me that if the KGB continued to exist on a federal basis, he would welcome continued cooperation with the United States.[31]

We in the State Department had certainly shared the views of many others that the failure of the August coup attempt had been good news for the democratic cause throughout the world. For me, it was a pleasure to watch, on television, Gorbachev's return from the Crimea. His life had been spared and he had not been deposed from his position as president of the Soviet Union.[32]

But my October visit to Moscow made clear that Gorbachev's standing had been seriously damaged. Following his return from the Crimea and the arrest of the coup plotters, who had held key positions in the Gorbachev administration, the governmental process under which the Soviet Union functioned had been severely disrupted. The continued existence of the Soviet Union was in doubt. Gorbachev personally had lost respect. He could no longer hold the Soviet Union together. The rising star was that of Yeltsin. He was the hero of the opponents of the August coup attempt and was respected by many Russians who admired a person who showed leadership qualities.

Of course, Yeltsin could assume full power only if the Soviet Union were to come to an end. I thought of a conversation, a year and half earlier, with my friends Gleb Yakunin and Sergey Kovalev, who had merely shrugged when I said that the Russian demand for sovereignty would mean the dissolution of the Soviet Union. What they seemed to have anticipated was about to come true: The Soviet Union would disappear, and with it, the position that Gorbachev had held. Russia would be a sovereign state led by Yeltsin. That is what they had hoped for.

---

31. State Department message, "KGB Chairman Bakatin Expresses Worry over Future of the Union in Meeting with HA A/Schifter," October 16, 1991.

32. I recall an impromptu discussion that Gorbachev had with reporters in Moscow as he came off the plane. Speaking of the coup plotters who had tried to extract his resignation, he said: "They were so rude. I was trained not to be rude to people." I thought that statement said a lot about the personality of that leader of the Soviet state.

In November 1991, I used the opportunity of an address to the CSCE human rights meeting in Oslo to pay tribute to Mikhail Gorbachev:

> I attended, in the spring of 1985, the first CSCE meeting devoted purely to the issue of human rights, the Ottawa meeting. It was a meeting at which discussion of human rights did not differ from previous discussions of that issue in the CSCE framework. By that I mean that we divided sharply along ideological lines: John Locke's idea of the role of the state versus that of Vladimir Lenin.
>
> But I also recall what the head of the Hungarian delegation told us at Ottawa. There is a new spirit hovering over us all, he claimed. It is the spirit of the new Soviet leader, Mikhail Gorbachev, who will change everything. Our delegation watched and listened and did not notice any change. We, therefore, did not give a great deal of credence to the observations of our Hungarian colleague. . . .
>
> Now we know, of course, that our Hungarian colleague was right. Profound change did not occur immediately, but it came in due time. As we meet today, at a gathering specifically dedicated to the issue of democracy, all of us define that term in the same manner. We all share a common understanding of the concept that a government in order to be legitimate must obtain its mandate from the people in a free and fair election, that it must respect the fundamental rights of all persons under its jurisdiction.
>
> Regrettably this is, however, not a time for expressions of self-satisfaction. Just as years passed before Western Europe recovered from the devastation of World War II, so years are likely to pass before Eastern Europe will recover from the distortions of the economy created by the command system, the social devastation wrought by totalitarianism. And just as there was concern about the survival of democracy in some parts of Western Europe forty-five years ago, so are there concerns about the survival of democracy in parts of Eastern Europe today. . . .
>
> We should . . . take note of the difficulties which the twelve republics which constituted the USSR will encounter on the road to democracy. The world was truly amazed by the fortitude demonstrated by the people of Russia when confronted by a coup led by the heads of the country's security forces. But as we all know, overcoming the coup was only a first step. The adverse effect of a legacy of more than seven decades of totalitarianism will be felt for years to come, more so in some republics, in some regions, than in others. And just as in Yugoslavia, there is concern about inter-ethnic violence, again more so in some Republics than in others.
>
> We must view it as a responsibility of all of us to help those who must confront these problems directly. We must help them find solutions to these problems in a democratic order, respectful of human rights. What the signatures of our leaders on the Helsinki Final Act should remind us of is that we are indeed our brothers' keepers.[33]

---

33. State Department message, "CSCE Seminar Msg No. 1: U.S. Opening Speech," November 5, 1991.

Anatoly Adamishin

Economic Repercussions of Perestroika

Perestroika brought freedom to the Soviet Union, but it was certainly not a linear process. Growing resistance to reforms, combined with our leaders' miscalculations, made for a twisting path. One of the biggest mistakes committed by Gorbachev and his closest colleagues was the mishandling of the economy, which undermined the political progress that had been made. Many people understood even at the time that profound economic changes were desperately needed. On January 1, 1989, at the beginning of perestroika's fifth year, I wrote in my diary:

> The New Year night passed on in hot debates. Abel Aganbegian, a knowledgeable economist, asserts that our economy is drifting. The General Secretary [Gorbachev] doesn't focus on the issue, entrusting the job entirely to government officials that are not very competent in the financial field. They, in turn, don't heed any of the independent experts. The situation is close to a crisis: the gap between salaries paid to the workers and the availability of goods that could be bought for this money is widening. Unsatisfied demand is near to 80 billion rubles. The federal budget deficit exceeds 100 billion rubles. What is even worse: 50 billion dollars of foreign debt has already accumulated. Sometimes they even lack the special sort of paper needed to print rubles.

Because merchandise was extremely scarce, the quality of everyday life in the Soviet Union deteriorated. First meat and butter disappeared, then milk and other food. Soon the shelves in the stores were empty. The obvious result was widespread discontent.

Why were supplies dwindling?

I heard answers to that question directly from Prime Minister Nikolai Ivanovich Ryzhkov when I accompanied him to Luxembourg, where he met British Prime Minister Margaret Thatcher.[1] She held Gorbachev and perestroika in great respect, though she warned of the difficulties of balancing different kinds of reforms: "You are trying to make people work in a new way, overcoming apathy, being more dependent on themselves and less on

---

1. Kicking off her conversation with Ryzhkov and pouring a scotch for herself, the Iron Lady asked him if he wanted a drink: "I put that question because I don't understand you Russians any more." In the Soviet Union, the anti-alcohol campaign was in full swing, another blunder that deprived the government of the money that the state's monopoly on selling spirits had provided. Ryzhkov courageously said no. I said yes; I couldn't let her drink alone in the presence of two Russians.

the government. At the same time you permit them to speak freely. You may be sure that they would prefer to yell than to work."[2]

Ryzhkov agreed that political reforms had been placed ahead of economic ones. He observed that the economy had been so neglected that modernization might take decades. But the general feeling was that the government's indecisiveness was at the root of the existing economic problems. The government failed to move forward with reforms that would introduce a market economy while the command methods had mainly stopped working.

A big problem was that militarization oozed from all the pores of the economy. The government had initiated the conversion of four hundred plants that worked for defense to producing consumer goods, but the needed changes in technologies and equipment would take at least two years. Yet the people were eager for immediate results. The country's leadership had put off price reform for several years, fearing social unrest, with the result that consumer prices were two to two-and-a-half times less than the cost of production. The economy could no longer sustain huge state subsidies. Ryzhkov believed that the greatest need was to restructure peoples' conception of the economy; only a few were prepared to avail themselves of the new rights that had been promised from above.

The old incentives for working, such as fear of punishment and socialist competition, were gone, but personal interest in earning money to improve one's standard of living was not widespread. The market was beginning to have some effect, however, permitting the rise of small- and medium-size cooperatives. More generally, though, the managers of big industrial plants, the so-called red directors, didn't want to share their power with workers. They were one of the biggest obstacles to economic reform.

Ryzhkov focused on two other themes in his talks with Thatcher. First, he expressed gratitude for the help provided by the United Kingdom and other Western countries in repairing the damage done by the December 1988 earthquake in Armenia.[3] Never before had the Soviet Union received such a wave of global sympathy. (While listening to him I was thinking: Aside from all the other problems, how unlucky have we been during perestroika—first the atomic catastrophe at Chernobyl, then other technological calamities, and now Armenia!)

Ryzhkov's second theme was the hiatus in the development of Soviet-U.S. relations. The U.S. administration that came to power in January 1989 declared

---

2. In Moscow a story about Zhuchka, a small dog who was extremely happy with perestroika, circulated. When asked why, it replied: "It's true, my doghouse is small as before, I have to eat the same bad bones, but at least now I may bark."

3. On December 10, 1988, I was in Brussels for a solemn celebration of Human Rights Day. The king of Belgium crossed an enormous hall to express to the Soviet representatives the solidarity of his country with the Soviet Union over Armenia.

that it was taking a pause to reconsider Washington's policy toward the Soviet Union. "Everything has come to a halt," Ryzhkov lamented. "The Americans should finally make up their minds." Thatcher tried to console Ryzhkov, pledging that she would urge President Bush not to postpone decisions.

Political Ramifications

In Moscow, something had seemed wrong even before Bush took office; at the Politburo meeting in late December 1988, Gorbachev, who had just returned from delivering his famous speech to the UN General Assembly in New York, pointed out that the new administration "wasn't ready for a serious turn in Soviet-American relations that would be adequate when compared to the steps proposed or announced in a unilateral way by the USSR." Shevardnadze agreed, predicting that the new administration would be more cautious and circumspect.

In April 1988, there had still been hope that the cooperation established with President Reagan and Secretary Shultz would continue. In Gorbachev's mind, Reagan understood perestroika and showed himself willing to correct his earlier prejudices.[4] The reality under Bush turned out to be disappointing. The long time-out in Soviet-U.S. relations taken by the new American administration lasted until December 1989 and halted almost all constructive efforts during the entire year. Moscow viewed it as an attempt to undercut the Soviet diplomatic offensive, especially after Gorbachev's UN speech, which had presented many new ideas with potentially long-term implications. They touched the humanitarian field as well. Shevardnadze, Aleksandr Yakovlev, and KGB chairman Vladimir Kryuchkov forwarded a special note to the Central Committee (I wrote the initial draft) in which a number of measures were suggested, approved by the Politburo, and then implemented, allowing Gorbachev to make a statement from the UN podium that in the Soviet Union, not a single person was imprisoned for political views.

The new U.S. indifference toward perestroika placed an additional burden on Gorbachev at the moment when control of the internal situation in the Soviet Union began to slip from his grasp. Was it because he had opened the door to the new freedoms too wide? Or should he have opened it even wider? At any rate, against the backdrop of glasnost—the transparency regarding governmental and public activities—Gorbachev provided new opportunities for political life that we had not witnessed before.

An example is the 1989 election of the first Congress of People's Deputies. The election was not fully democratic; as a result, the Communist Party of the Soviet Union gained 87 percent of the seats. Nevertheless, it was the

---
4. Gorbachev Foundation, V Politburo CK KPSS, 373.

first real election in recent history. Many party functionaries were defeated while some prominent democrats, such as Andrei Sakharov, who had been called back by Gorbachev from exile in Gorky only three years before, were elected.

Following the election, the general public paid a great deal of attention to the proceedings of the congress. Who would have imagined that millions of Soviet citizens would sit in front of their TV sets for hours following the sessions of this new parliament? For the first time in several generations, political passions could be expressed candidly and fearlessly.

On May, 25 1989, I wrote in my diary:

> Even if the apparatus won the first round, we are witnessing the dawn of a real political struggle. The Party authorities are certainly not inclined to cede their absolute power, but now it is more difficult for them, particularly as the Tsar (Gorbachev) is in a radical mood. He did what no Soviet leader dared to do: he permitted his opponents to pursue the political struggle against himself.

In the long run, the leaders of perestroika, unaccustomed to political competition, did not benefit from the same freedoms they gave to their opponents. In its adamant and sophisticated resistance to reformers, the bureaucracy exploited the new freedoms to undermine the leadership, using populist and demagogical slogans to oppose the government of which they were a part.[5] The bureaucratic opposition also began criticizing foreign policy, and not always with constructive results.

As I wrote during that turbulent time:

> The country had been driven into the corner by those who for decades didn't care about it while thinking only how to keep their hold on power. The source of all our troubles is the political system. It is practically the sole key element that causes us to differ from the countries which are ahead of us. We've got all the other features that those other countries have—territory, resources, an educated population. It shouldn't be that there is only one party. Whatever efforts, like glasnost and perestroika, that you might make, you just cannot eliminate the minuses that a one-party system brings to a country. One of them is that the party's closed nomenklatura cuts off a big portion of the country's intellectual potential. We've been told for years: look, in the USA there are two parties but they are just the same, both defending the capitalists' interests. Why then shouldn't we too have two parties? Let them be in principle the same, but vitally interested to criticize each other, to denounce mistakes made by their rival, to compete with it. The population must have the possibility to choose. A new leader when he comes to power, should have the authority to replace people, pour in fresh blood, get rid of incompetent officeholders. Otherwise stagnation is inevitable. Gorbachev's bid to cut

---

5. Yeltsin's position offers a good example: After he was elected chairman of the Russian Federation Supreme Soviet, he could act as a leader of Russia while opposing the authorities of the Soviet Union of which Russia was still a part.

off the apparatus's roots slowly is better than Chinese unlawfulness, Mao's order to "fire at headquarters," but it brings anguish to the process of perestroika. Economic, social, and nationality crises will not wait for long.

I was not the only one tormented by such thoughts. Usually a guarded man, Shevardnadze opened up in a conversation with me in August 1989:

> I feel really bad now: Nanuli [his wife] is in the hospital for an operation, there is turmoil in Tbilisi, and the kids are still there; but worst of all, I am constantly worried about what is happening in our country. By no means can we admit that some people would leave. [There were already indications that the Baltic republics and some other republics might withdraw from the Union.] The Russian people will not forgive us. The situation increasingly gets out of our control. But we shall never use force to cling to the power. If that becomes necessary, we'll quit.

I was thinking about how hard it was to watch this great country breaking down, how the unlucky people were suffering, people who couldn't be blamed for the monstrous experiments being conducted over their heads. Was it possible that democracy could not save what was kept alive by tyranny?

Humanitarian Progress Continues

On the brighter side, the Soviet stance on humanitarian issues continued to be solid. For example, at the forty-fifth session of the UN Commission on Human Rights in March 1989, the issues of the Romanian authorities' behavior toward the Hungarian minority came up. The Romanians should have been condemned, but because Romania was a member of the Warsaw Pact, we were reluctant to denounce them publicly. I suggested to the Romanians that they agree to receive a delegation from the UN Commission to observe events firsthand, as it would close the issue, and the Romanian delegation promised to invite such a mission. However, I feared that Nicolae Ceausescu, the Romanian dictator, would not approve such close observation, so I informed Moscow that the Romanians might reverse their position and got its go-ahead to suggest what we should do if that happened. The very next day, the Romanians retracted their pledge. When a UN resolution to condemn them was put to the vote, we did not oppose it. This marked the first time in the history of the Warsaw Pact that a Soviet delegation had not opposed a resolution condemning a socialist country.

But if the humanitarian aspect of our policy was in good shape, an entire set of new and troublesome issues had arisen. Eastern Europe was of particular concern. Traveling with Shevardnadze to the Warsaw Pact countries, I saw with bitterness the disintegration of the alliance. The situation in the German Democratic Republic became more worrisome every day. Shevardnadze called me back to the European desk and assigned me to the working group tasked with watching evolving German affairs and preparing policy options for the Soviet leadership. Subsequently, I represented my country in the so-called Two Plus Four discussions—the two German states plus the Soviet Union, United States, Great Britain, and France—which dealt with external aspects of the German reunification.

Although officially I did not take off my humanitarian hat, my direct involvement diminished. Still, in July 1989, I traveled to Washington, D.C., where I met with Thomas Foley, speaker of the House of Representatives, as well as the chairs of various congressional committees. I assured them that the Soviet Union would comply with its obligations resulting from the Vienna meeting, in particular to review all the applications for exit—whether temporary or permanent—from the Soviet Union.

It was a fruitful visit. In addition to meeting with five assistant secretaries of state, I spent time with leaders of several important American Jewish organizations. By meeting with Thomas Krens, director of the Guggenheim Museum, I helped to establish contact between the museum and Soviet cultural institutions that led to permanent cooperation. (When I heard that the 2005 exhibition "Russia!" in the Guggenheim enjoyed great success, I thought back to that first encounter.)

Promoting a New Agenda

I usually met Dick on the eve of high-level visits, preparing the foundation for the ensuing discussions. One such meeting was held five days before Secretary of State James Baker arrived in Moscow in February 1990. On that occasion, I had to split my concerns between my human rights agenda and my new European duties, which focused on Germany. I recall this session in our cozy osobnyak in Alexey Tolstoy Street for another reason: Dick was accompanied by Alexander Vershbow, the same Sandy who was to become the American ambassador to Moscow in 2001.

Although the old human rights agenda—namely, emigration, psychiatry, and political prisoners—was much shorter than it had been, Dick emphasized that some issues were still unresolved. I replied that progress in the area of human rights had been greater than in the economic arena. When, I asked, would the Jackson-Vanik amendment be repealed? Dick answered that if the new emigration law is passed the Soviet Union would be found to be in compliance with the J-V standards.

The remaining refusenik cases concerned applicants who had been engaged in classified work, as well as so-called poor relative cases, in which the person who wanted to emigrate needed to prove that those whom he or she left behind would be able to support themselves. Claims by relations against would-be emigrants were decided by the courts. Thus, I responded to Dick that I was not sure how the Ministry of Foreign Affairs could be helpful. Dick skillfully turned around my reply, saying that from his perspective, courts could respond to the ministry's concern and decide the cases in the spirit of the new law, which was in draft form and about to be approved. We both noted the growing numbers of persons who had received permission to emigrate: 235,000 in 1989.

We devoted much more time to the new agenda than to the old one. High on the new agenda were issues such as exchanging experience and information on how to build a society based on the rule of law and very practical topics such as obtaining U.S. help in manufacturing prostheses for Soviet victims of the Afghan War.

Frankly, humanitarian themes of all kinds were overshadowed in the Baker-Shevardnadze discussions by sizzling events on the international stage. Jokingly, Dick and I ascribed the relative lack of discussion of humanitarian issues to our preparatory work.

Closing Out the Old Agenda

Dick and I communicated in writing as well as orally.[6] The U.S. embassy delivered at least three messages from him to my Moscow desk. One message, dated December 1989, indicates the variety of issues on which we were working: dubious criminal cases that the other side considered political; remaining cases of persons who had been refused permission to leave the Soviet Union on the grounds that they possessed secret data; information that a special intergovernmental group had been created to coordinate the cooperative program on the rule of law; cooperation in drug enforcement and combating organized crime; a forthcoming seminar in Moscow that would include the participation of American experts, such as law school professors, judges, and officials from the U.S. Department of Justice; a program for ten Soviet judges to attend a conference in Reno, Nevada; visits to the United States by various Soviet experts; programs for the physically handicapped; and health and safety in mining operations. Dick also referred to federal-state relations and decentralization. Clearly, there was a sense of cooperation and goodwill on both sides.

In April 1990, two weeks before I left Smolenskaya-Sennaya Square, the location of the Soviet foreign ministry, for the embassy in Rome, I received the following letter from Dick:

---

6. Due to the current rules, I was unable to access the confidential archives of my ministry, so I have to rely on my recollections or documents I received later. Dick is in a much better position in that regard.

Dear Anatoly,

In a few days we shall be able to mark the third anniversary of our first dialogue, which ended with your comment that "we shall continue to play this game." In retrospect we can, I am sure, agree that the game was played well.

In November 1987 you presented us with what we can call "Adamishin initiative," which helped create our new agenda. Last month we had, as a result, an extraordinarily successful visit to the Soviet Union by a group of American lawyers led by the deputy attorney general. Within the next six weeks we shall have visits to the United States by delegations to initiate a dialogue on the physically handicapped and on the elderly; thus, as you move on to new tasks, in a warmer climate, in a country for which you have so much affection, you will be able to look back at very significant accomplishments in the human rights dialogue.

But before you do so, I hope, you will also take a look at what remains of our old agenda and help close it out.

You will recall that as long ago as December 1988 we agreed on a procedure for the discussion of questionable criminal cases. In May 1989 I submitted a list of 56 names to the Procurator General's office. At this point we still have no information at all on 17 cases and incomplete information on 8 additional cases. Please, see to it that the Procurator General's office gets the information together for us without further delay.

The Soviet side, in turn, has submitted 40 cases; we have given you information on all of these.

Of this group of 40, 33 are now in prison, 2 have been released, and 5 are free on bail, while the case is being considered in the United States Supreme Court.

To come back to the data requested from the Procurator General's office: it is my sincere hope that it will be possible to get this material to us well before the next ministerial meeting, if at all possible before the end of this month.

Another item still outstanding on our old agenda is that of the long-term refuseniks who are denied permission to leave the country on security grounds. We have given you a list of 50 long-term cases. Most of the persons on the list have not done any security-sensitive work for more than 10 years. In today's world such knowledge as they may have had becomes increasingly irrelevant to security concerns. I sincerely hope that foreign minister Shevardnadze will be able to see to it that these cases are reviewed once more and are reviewed by persons who have a realistic understanding of present-day conditions.

Sincerely,

Dick

A Review of the Situation

On March, 31, 1990, Gorbachev signed a decree that appointed me as Soviet ambassador to Italy. The Italian government issued its agreement three days later; that spring I left for Rome and a completely new set of duties.

Before leaving, I summed up my perception of what was happening in my country:

> The economic situation is deteriorating, although relatively slowly. The defects are always the same: a huge unsatisfied demand, rising inflation, decreasing of the gold and foreign currency reserve due to growing grain purchases abroad. The foreign debt is already twice as huge as it was at perestroika's bright dawn. Nobody wants to work hard for "wooden" rubles which cannot buy anything. A new frightening aspect: the bonds between plants located in different regions of the country are breaking because of nationalist-ethnic tensions. What is really unpleasant is that the government's measures regarding the economy are characterized even by some Party officials, let alone independent experts, like Nikolai Shmelev, as halfway and indecisive. The argument which is commonly used to justify this tactic of "one step forward, two steps back" is that we need to gain time. But what for?
>
> As to politics, there are no breaks in the fierce arguments inside the CC [Central Committee of the Communist Party] and, what is worse, inside the Politburo, in the Supreme Soviet, and in the local authorities. In this way desperately needed decisions are blocked. A terrible amount of effort is wasted in order to explain to the CC, the organ famous for its conservatism, that perestroika's policy is a good one. Is it really necessary to get the CC's consent? Gorbachev thinks that he has to pull behind him the entire awkward caravan and nobody in the leadership seems to dispute him. Quite a few members of Moscow's intelligentsia see the way out in establishing a regime of strong presidential power. When I talked recently with Shevardnadze, he confessed that he considers that as a last chance.
>
> Enmity between various nationalities is assuming awesome dimensions. Just look what is occurring in Azerbaijan! Most probably the regional boyars' goal is to let Gorbachev down and, in the final account, to come back to Brezhnev's times when the periphery and the center lived according to the motto: "Don't touch us, we'll not touch you." We call our country the USSR. In reality we never had a Union, but a strongly centralized state.
>
> The country is being ruled by people who have known each other for decades. "Aliens" are not welcomed. Just like a popular German saying put it, "We know that we are fools, but we are in the majority." I hate to say it, but there are few first-rate people at the steering wheel. Gorbachev's weakness as he seeks to form a good team is showing up more and more. An example: animosity against Shevardnadze is sharply rising. Even Pravda, the main party organ, is involved in these attacks. It cannot be doing so without its editor-in-chief taking part. And who is the guy, Ivan Frolov, just appointed by Gorbachev? Where is a solid team spirit?

The trouble is that Gorbachev tries to pull the country out from the mess without offending those who drove it into troubles. Such a tactic provokes permanent delays. A reasonable solution, which if implemented on the spot would work, cannot be realized today because of conservative resistance; two months later, that solution has no chance of working. You are then forced to move forward in significantly worse conditions. Lithuania is an example. The Kremlin, due to internal disputes, didn't seek an agreement with the Lithuanian moderates. Then the extremists removed the moderates from power and a dangerous tug-of-war is now in progress.

Actually, we, I mean those who work hard to push perestroika forward, have to pay for failures and blunders which have piled up over decades. Perestroika should have been launched at least twenty years ago. The Czechoslovak events of 1968 were a serious wake-up call, but the Soviet leaders of the time did not dare to accept the challenge. They took cover behind petro-dollars, stagnation, and isolating our society from the rest of the world.[7]

And we have to pay not only for the last decades. History has left us with a heavy legacy. What is really tragic is that this legacy is full of bloody crimes. The leaders' impunity allowed them to treat the country, the people, as they wished. The old rulers got away with it. We don't. Gorbachev and his team resist the introduction of market forces, yet have to deal with a sick society, accustomed to equal distribution, to a government that should provide support for everyone. The conservatives do their best to exploit such moods: to their minds, democracy, let alone the "capitalist market," is not for Russia.

Power is finally slipping from the Party's hands, but it hasn't as yet reached the elected organs, the Soviets. This vacuum is particularly menacing when social tension is so high. As one of my colleagues said: "Kerosene has already reached our knees."

The Spiral Downward

When I arrived in Rome, it quickly became clear that the Italians were very excited by the developments of perestroika. I enjoyed my job in Rome, but was troubled by the news from the Soviet Union. I was even more worried when I returned to Moscow for short periods.

In May, Shevardnadze set off for Washington to prepare for a summit, this time without me. It was no longer my business, but I jealously noted that the minister's talking points included not only arms race problems, but also humanitarian issues. The topics for discussion reflected both ours and U.S. needs: the Americans wanted to discuss the freedom of the media in

---

7. I would add nowadays: Who knows if there had not been the Czechoslovakia of 1968, whether there would have been the Afghanistan of 1979? Perhaps we would not have retained control over Eastern Europe, but having started perestroika much earlier, we could have preserved a renewed Soviet Union.

the Soviet Union, whereas we wanted to discuss the conditions under which Soviet diplomatic and consular representatives worked in the United States. Shevardnadze also had directives to invite the United States to join some international human rights agreements and to review the official U.S. attitude toward immigrants from the Soviet Union, who were still considered political refugees.

In July 1990, I was summoned to Moscow because of Gorbachev's meeting with Italian Prime Minister Giulio Andreotti. As always, our leader showed keen interest in international problems, but this time we hoped mostly to borrow some money from Italy. From conversations with my colleagues, I knew that the treasury was almost empty. How would we pay our debts?[8] Any money we had was used to solve immediate problems—including to purchase food—not to help restructure the economy. In addition, according to Stepan Sitarian, responsible for state finance, the treasury wasn't receiving money from taxes collected by the union republics, which were diverting the flows of funds.

I went back to Moscow in September when the Italian minister of foreign affairs, Gianni De Michelis, while visiting the Soviet Union, promised more than two billion dollars in credit. Gorbachev was happy. When I heard him remark that foreign assistance was vital, I considered my stay in Italy justified. I understood him even better when I saw the Moscow stores: The shelves were empty. Even bread was sometimes difficult to obtain. Desperation and anger were palpable. The newly elected democratic officials of Moscow were doing their best, but even city districts, following the examples of the union republics, regions, and towns, were declaring their sovereignty. Paralysis was rapidly seizing the central government.

As I reflected on the problems confronting us, I jotted down my concerns:

1. The country is rapidly breaking down. The old economic system barely works, but there is a reckless resistance to the formation of a new system, which would make many people obsolete along with their positions and privileges. The almighty Gosplan, superministry for economic planning, desperately defends its right to distribute investments in a centralized way. The other old government and party structures are still there.

2. The political leadership is in big trouble. Gorbachev is attacked both from the right (Ligachev, Polozkov, and other old party nomenklatura) and from the left (Yeltsin). The right has the support of the party apparatus, but Yeltsin is especially dangerous. His quest for power is inexhaustible and he has behind him the Supreme Soviet of the Russian Federation. Some weeks ago it seemed that there was an agreement between the two leaders to set up a joint

---

8. The conditions under which we got the credits were strict: We had to repay the money in three years and the interest rate was high.

program of reforms. Instead, Yeltsin made the Russian parliament approve a separate Shatalin-Yavlinsky Program. What role is there for the Union's parliament? For Yeltsin, Russian sovereignty is not the ultimate goal; it is merely a means to grab power for himself.[9] To benefit from the people's indignation, his team plays to aggravate the situation, which is bad as it is, but everything is good that weakens the Center. Because his appearance is much more resolute than Gorbachev's, many people shift to him, including intellectuals. Gorbachev is permanently on the defensive. The rumor is that in the outlying areas Gorbachev's portraits are being taken down. The Russian Federation government has asked me to help them get Italian credits directly, i.e., skirting the Center. Other republics of the Union follow Russia's example and go even further in their separatist trend.

Gorbachev has to devote considerable effort to the task of defending his power, leaving little energy for constructive work. Still, he is hesitant to break with the Party, as many people advise him to do.

3. The two other leaders of perestroika are following Gorbachev too uncritically. Aleksandr Yakovlev once said to me that he sacrificed himself to "this natural talent," Gorbachev. Shevardnadze also doesn't argue with M.S. In general, we have returned to old practice of nodding to the leader, or, as we say in Russian, to look in his mouth.

When we talk eye-to-eye, Shevardnadze is frank: "The present-day apparatus is rotten and corrupt. There are few competent and honest officials. New governmental structures are needed, but Gorbachev is not in the mood to deal with this problem. We, the leadership, would not resort to dictatorship; it will come after us. The first opposition to perestroika consists of the district and regional Party's committees. Probably the principal blunder was made in October 1917."

This last observation struck me as particularly poignant.

The Beginning of the End

Shevardnadze resigned on December 20, 1990. He presented his resignation as a protest against the onset of a coming dictatorship. Afterward, friends in the Ministry of Foreign Affairs told me that Shevardnadze had been disillusioned with Gorbachev, who was moving to the right and didn't defend

---

9. Several weeks later, I talked in Rome with Viktor Yarochenko, the Russian minister for external economic relations. He didn't hide that the plan was to destroy the union. Otherwise, he said, it was impossible to get rid of the union's commanding structures filled with bureaucratic nomenklatura. Afterward, he asserted, "we would create a new, voluntary union around Russia. All the union republics except the Baltics would come back." Some authors of this project used the expression "Republics, including Ukraine, will crawl back. They couldn't live without Russia." These hopes very soon turned out to be absolutely unrealistic. For some, they were a cover for a thrust for power at any price.

his foreign minister when attacked by conservatives. Shevardnadze feared that Gorbachev was ready to sacrifice him as he had sacrificed Interior Minister Vadim Bakatin.

I immediately realized that Shevardnadze's departure would be a big blow to Gorbachev's perestroika. He was a champion of reform and had managed to establish good contacts with the West.

I sent a cable to the minister urging him to reconsider. I received a reply signed by his secretariat chief, Igor Ivanov, future foreign minister of Russia. Ivanov told me that Shevardnadze had been touched by my message, understood my concerns, and counted me among the few persons in the Ministry of Foreign Affairs who had made perestroika possible, but Shevardnadze's decision was firm.

To be candid, I still don't see clearly why Shevardnadze resigned; another's soul is twilight, as a Russian proverb says. I do know that his resignation caused further deterioration in the national situation.

The last year of the Soviet Union's existence was characterized by the aggravation of the trends first evidenced in 1990. With growing concern, I watched from Rome. The economy was headed for collapse. Gorbachev and Yeltsin were engaged in a fierce political struggle. The union republics continued to break away from the center. Gorbachev tried desperately to maintain a transformed Soviet Union while swinging to the right. One nationality problem seemed to follow another without respite.

In Lithuania, having let slip the chance of reaching an understanding with the moderates in Vilnius, Moscow now had to deal with the hard-nosed Landsberghis, whose tactic was to reject constitutional methods and create a fait accompli for the Kremlin. The situation was explosive; blood was spilled in January 1991. Gorbachev denied that he was to blame. Yeltsin, whose people—according to rumors that reached me from Moscow—had encouraged the Lithuanian leaders to stay firm against Gorbachev, rushed to the Baltic, where he promised Lithuania, Latvia, and Estonia the unconditional support of the Russian Federation. He also appealed directly to soldiers not to obey the central government's orders. Thousands of people took to the streets of Moscow and other Soviet cities in support of the Baltic states' independence. The Baltic states seceded from the Soviet Union immediately after the failure of the coup d'état against Gorbachev in August 1991.

As Yeltsin's prestige grew, Gorbachev's power declined. The latter phenomenon was starkly underlined in another part of the Soviet Union, South Ossetia. In Stalin's time, Ossetia had been artificially split into North Ossetia, part of the Russian Federation, and South Ossetia, an autonomous district in Georgia. Many decades later, this ticking time bomb exploded. In 1991, the new Georgian president, Zviad Gamsakhurdia, sent troops to suppress South Ossetians who wanted to unite with their ethnic brethren in the north. Gorbachev, as the Soviet president, ordered that the skirmish stop, but he did not have the means to carry out his decree. That inaction further eroded his authority. (The time bomb exploded once again in 2008, when South Ossetian and Russian forces battled Georgian troops for five days.)

Surprisingly, given the state of affairs in so many other areas, the field of human rights was doing relatively well. This practically unknown feature of our system had begun to take root. Gorbachev, for example, reproached Lithuanian rebels for violating the human rights of Russian-speaking people. And when the all-union referendum was held in March 1991, the question was worded as follows: "Do you want to maintain the Union as a renewed federation of equal sovereign republics in which human rights and freedoms of all nationalities will be fully guaranteed?" The majority's answer was yes—but it couldn't save the Soviet Union.

Conspiracy

The most striking example of how perestroika changed the country occurred in August 1991 with the attempted coup d'état. The plotters' goal was to put an end to the democratic transformation of the Soviet Union, returning the country to its authoritarian past. The attempt was concocted by the highest leaders of the Soviet Union: Vice President Yanayev, Prime Minister Pavlov, Speaker of the Parliament Lukianov, Minister of the Interior Pugo, and Minister of Defense Yazov; the chief of the KGB, Kryuchkov, played the role of organizer. Gorbachev was betrayed by those whom he trusted completely, several of whom he had only recently appointed to their posts. The upheaval failed due to mass resistance in Moscow, Leningrad, and other cities. Hundreds of thousands people responded to Yeltsin's appeal—Gorbachev was under arrest in Crimea—by taking to the streets to defend the White House, the official residence of the government of the Russian Federation.

It is true that the coup was badly organized and the conspirators showed weakness and indecisiveness. But the fact that the conspirators did not arrest those who were bound to resist, including Yeltsin, and that they abstained from storming the White House and avoided bloodshed means that they wanted to make their action look legitimate. Repression would have come later under the appearance of legitimacy. The plotters had to consider the new realities of the country regarding the respect for the rights of individuals, even as they underestimated them.

This assessment is not the product of hindsight. On the second day of the coup, I wrote in my diary: "They will fail."

As an ambassador, I was very interested in my ministry's conduct. It was of some relief to me that Aleksandr Bessmertnykh, who had been appointed minister after Shevardnadze's resignation, was not among the conspirators. Still, Bessmertnykh's first deputy, Yuli Kvitsinsky, sent instructions that our embassy in Rome, like all other Soviet missions, should deliver to the host government a message from Yanayev as acting president of the Soviet Union. (Following an experienced practice of lessening the damage, my embassy managed to avoid full implementation of these instructions.) Kvitsinsky acted in compliance with the ministerial collegium chaired by Bessmertnykh. That's why when Gorbachev returned from Crimea, he fired both Bessmertnykh and Kvitsinsky.

The End

After the failed coup, the centrifugal tendencies became irresistible. In the following weeks, all the union republics declared independence. The only way for party bosses in Kiev or Minsk to avoid Moscow's wrath was to break with Gorbachev; his authority had plummeted compared to Yeltsin, who was then considered the savior of the democracy. Desperate efforts were made to save the union, but it was too late. A federal or confederal arrangement that might have been possible in 1989 was unthinkable in the autumn of 1991. On December 1, 90 percent of Ukrainian voters, including Russians in Ukraine, opted for independence. Four days later, the Ukrainian parliament, the Rada, annulled the republic's entry into the Soviet Union according to the agreement of 1922 that had created the union in the first place.

I made the following entries in my diary:

> September 1991: Alexander Rutskoy, Russian vice president, paid a visit to Italy. [A couple of years later, he and Yeltsin would man opposite sides of the barricades—one on the defensive inside the White House, the seat of the Supreme Soviet, the other ordering army tanks to fire at the building. In 1991, they were singing the same tune.] Running like a common thread though all Rutskoy's official talks—to which I, in my ambassadorial capacity, accompanied him—was this: "You Italians should discontinue your affairs with the Center; your business will not gain anything from you talking to Gorbachev. The RSFSR [Russian Federation] has all power in its hands, as it has all the property. We won't leave the Center even a nail."

> December 8: Upon seeing TV news from Moscow covering the meeting of Yeltsin, Kravchuk [the Ukrainian president], and Shushkevich [the Belarusian leader], at which they declared that the USSR had ceased to exist and signed the agreement creating the Commonwealth of the Independents States: Ukraine, Byelorussia, and Russia—my god, Russia—drove the last nail in the coffin of the Union.

> December 9: This is how the Italian politicians react to the Belovezhskaya Puscha deal, both publicly and in conversations with me: the USSR's disintegration has become inevitable. Of course, the USSR provided the best guarantees regarding ownership of nuclear weapons and a uniform conduct of international affairs. But if the confederation cannot be achieved, a commonwealth is definitely preferable to the loss of time and the threat of complete disintegration.

As I saw it, an agreement had been reached by the parties with the least desire to preserve a semblance of a relationship with the center. The governing elites in the constituent republics were frightened by perestroika. For them, power was more important than democracy; they tried to save their power by proclaiming independence, causing the collapse of the Soviet Union. The main question was whether the commonwealth would prove viable. Yugoslavia's example showed that we must avoid a civil war at any cost. My Italian friends consoled me: The best result would be a commonwealth agreement, even if it bore traces of haste and bad workmanship, rather than the ad infinitum continuation of negotiations. The Italians were rightly displeased with Gorbachev's removal and hoped he would be able to take a position such as commander of strategic forces, an option discussed at the puscha.

During those surreal days, questions buzzed though my mind. Was it possible to save the Soviet Union? Why had perestroika, which had generated so much hope, enthusiasm, and élan, come to such a lamentable end? Could it be mended? I refused to believe that perestroika was dead.

At first, it seemed that not quite everything was lost: the Belovezhskaya Puscha Accords made it possible to keep Ukraine within the union—and without Ukraine, any union was a nonentity. Quickly, however, reality dawned. The ink was not yet dry on the agreement to create the commonwealth when the army was divided. There was never a question of joint command.

Leonid Kravchuk outwitted Yeltsin, taking advantage of his yen for power. Or were both playing the same game? One grabbed Russia while the other grabbed a chance to slip from Moscow's orbit, where Ukraine had been for the past 350 years or so. "It is evident from everything," I wrote in my diary, "that the Commonwealth is not so much for preserving the Union as for dividing it, not so much for keeping Ukraine as for assuring its 'soft departure.'"

During these days, Aleksandr Yakovlev, one of perestroika's ideologists, visited Villa Abamelek, the embassy residence in Rome, where we spoke at length about the situation. Yakovlev offered this postmortem and prediction:

> The Union as it had formerly existed should have been destroyed, but a united state could have been preserved. The coup intervened. The most

important thing now is to do no harm, to bring about no aggravation. We've been outwitted, and there is no one to blame for that but our own selves; I am not going to withdraw into opposition.[10] The problem is that the winners are plunged in internal power struggles; in all likelihood, Khasbulatov's and Rutskoy's parliament will soon be dispersed. It is glasnost that we must defend as much as we can, because it is the last obstacle remaining on the way to Bonapartism. Things will not go as far as a civil war, but even a small amount of bloodshed must not be allowed. The transition to a new state of society has become wild and uncontrolled; a step-by-step evolution failed. While an institutional order is in place, rascals are contained; when it breaks down, the scum have full play. Changes cannot but be illegitimate and unconstitutional under these circumstances, and the transitional period as a whole is traumatic and painful. Gorbachev's biggest mistake was his failure to accept Yavlinsky's economic plan—not because it was good but because his refusal meant an orientation to the rightist forces.[11] Mikhail Sergeyevich was afraid that the democrats wouldn't let him accomplish what he was doing, that the bunglers would ruin everything, including the Union. In consequence, he fell hostage to flatterers and humbugs like Boldin (his secretariat chief and one of the conspirators). For all that, Gorbachev is a great and tragic figure. There are few politicians who wouldn't cling to power.

---

10. These words had a direct impact on me when I was deciding what to do in the new circumstances: I accepted the offer to remain in Rome as the Russian—no longer the Soviet—ambassador.

11. Gorbachev explained his temporary switch to the right in this way: "The country goes to the right so I am going in this direction too." His main objective was to save the Union. The forces in the party, army, and military-industrial complex supported this goal, while Gorbachev couldn't be so sure about democrats. In May 1991, Gorbachev began to understand his mistake; the August putsch must have ended all doubts.

7

Concluding Thoughts

Richard Schifter

This chapter offers reflections on both the work that Anatoly and I accomplished together and the broader issues of the fate of perestroika and the end of the Cold War. In my portion of the chapter, I begin by examining the remarkable role played by Mikhail Gorbachev in bringing an end to the Cold War started by Joseph Stalin forty-three years earlier—a role, however, he could not have performed if President Reagan and Secretary Shultz had not correctly analyzed his intentions and responded accordingly. I then examine the reasons for Anatoly's and my productive relationship and several lessons that might be of interest to other negotiators, whatever their sphere of interest.

Under Gorbachev, a great deal of progress was made in introducing the basic concept of human rights and in democratizing the Soviet Union. It was the failings of his successor, Boris Yeltsin, that gave democracy in Russia a bad name, causing a return to autocracy. This gives rise to the question of whether the United States could have handled matters differently, so as to help the Soviet Union or Russia remain on a democratic course. I suggest that while there were internal problems in the Soviet Union that we could not easily address, there was at least a chance of our doing better if we had remained as fully and effectively engaged in support of the democratic movement in the Soviet Union after January 1989 as we had been when George Shultz was secretary of state.

In his portion of the chapter, Anatoly describes the historical background against which events in the Soviet Union unfolded as Gorbachev lost control, the presence and absence of democratic traditions in Russia, and the errors committed by Gorbachev. He also offers comments on what he regards as the failure of the United States to provide adequate support for democracy in the Soviet Union.

The Unique Role of Mikhail Gorbachev

The totalitarian system of government that Stalin had established in the Soviet Union was one in which ultimate control of all aspects of life in the country was vested in one person, the general secretary of the Central Committee of the Communist Party of the Soviet Union. It was through the party structure and the ever-present and truly feared secret police that not only all aspects of government, including control of the socialist economy, were placed under the general secretary's dictatorial control; what George Orwell called thought control was exercised as well.

After Stalin's death in 1953, his system of governance was modified: collective rule succeeded one-man rule. The power that had once been exercised solely by Stalin was exercised by a group, the Politburo. While the country's system of totalitarian control by the very top of the Communist Party pyramid was maintained, governmental action no longer depended on the whims of a single person. It was the leadership group that was now in charge. It relaxed thought control, but the power that it exercised over all governmental affairs remained unlimited.

Collective rule did not mean that all Politburo members had equal standing. The general secretary was the recognized leader. However, he depended on continuing support from a majority of his colleagues. One general secretary, Nikita Khrushchev, was deposed when he lost such support. A major challenge that faced each general secretary was to maintain a Politburo consensus on key issues.

On March 11, 1985, Gorbachev became the sixth person to occupy the position that Stalin once held. He had climbed up the ranks of the Communist Party and had become a member of the Politburo five years earlier. After his election as general secretary, it took a while for him to assert himself fully. When he did, he brought a majority of the Politburo along to join him in dismantling the Soviet Union's totalitarian system—a system the foundation of which had been laid by Lenin more than eighty years earlier, made significantly more oppressive by Stalin, and slightly relaxed by Stalin's successors. The system had governed the Soviet state for more than two generations.

Mikhail Gorbachev occupies a truly unique role in world history. Can anyone name another leader in whom absolute authority was vested, yet who surrendered that authority voluntarily, without being threatened by force from either domestic or foreign actors?

Margaret Thatcher was the first prominent Western leader to make the point that Gorbachev "was a man that one can do business with." At the outset there was skepticism on that subject in U.S. government circles. Change came about as a result of the development of a close personal relationship between Secretary Shultz and Foreign Minister Shevardnadze. As Shultz describes his first meeting with Shevardnadze in August 1985: "Overall, the substance of the Soviet position was unchanged. But I was struck by Shevardnadze's tone: it was far less polemical. This might just be a different style, but it might also indicate that the Soviets were taking a new look at themselves."[1]

It did not take long for the personal relationship between Shevardnadze and Shultz to become increasingly friendly. To Shultz it became clear that the Soviets were indeed "taking a new look at themselves" and that the person who was responsible for the changes that were taking place was Gorbachev. In November 1985, Gorbachev had his first meeting with Ronald Reagan. It took place in Geneva. As Shultz describes the concluding press conference of the two leaders: "The personal chemistry was apparent. The easy and relaxed attitude toward each other, the smiles, the sense of purpose, all showed through."[2] These vastly improved relations between the heads of government (de facto in the case of Gorbachev) and the foreign minister and secretary of state began to offer hope that, at long last, there was a chance to end the Cold War. But turning the two ships of state around so they could sail a common course still took time.

As noted earlier, Gorbachev divided his close to seven years in office into three periods: the time of "quests, trials, and errors" (1985–88); followed by the period of democratization (spring of 1988 to early 1990); and the struggle among the social, national, and political forces that reform set free (1991). That is evidently how developments, broadly speaking, looked from the top of the Soviet governmental pyramid. Looking at the Gorbachev era as a U.S. official watching the details of Soviet developments during that era, I saw, broadly speaking, the same three periods, but would time and describe them somewhat differently.

In December 1986, when Gorbachev involved himself personally in the return of Andrei Sakharov from banishment to Gorky (Nizhniy-Novgorod) to Moscow, and in January 1987, when he allowed many political prisoners to be released from the gulags, he may very well have thought he was doing no more than returning the Soviet Union to the Khrushchev era. In retrospect, however, it seems that the democratic genie was let out of the bottle in December 1986. In the years that immediately followed, the Soviet Union brought itself, step by step, into compliance with the standards of the Universal Declaration of Human Rights, a set of principles laid down in a 1948 UN General Assembly resolution from which the Soviet bloc—joined by Saudi Arabia and apartheid South Africa—had abstained.

---

1. Shultz, *Turmoil and Triumph*, 574.
2. Ibid., 606.

Many U.S. analysts of the so-called realist school offered an interpretation of the changes brought about by Gorbachev that assumed that he never deviated from his commitment to Marxism-Leninism. As they saw it, Gorbachev recognized that there were serious deficiencies in the operations of the Soviet state and that some repairs were necessary, but, the realists believed, the repairs that Gorbachev was prepared to undertake were not designed to make basic changes in the system. They thought that the traditional Communist system would remain in place domestically and that the Soviet Union would continue to be an adversary of the United States on the international scene.

The political figure with whom the realists sympathized from 1987 onward was Boris Yeltsin. He had criticized Gorbachev for not moving fast enough, for failing to dissolve the Communist Party, and for failing to privatize the economy. Over time they also came to think that Yeltsin was likely to dissolve the Soviet Union, which they viewed as a highly significant beneficial step on the geopolitical scene.

Those who were members of the so-called idealist school—to which I confess to belong—believed, and believe today, that Gorbachev and his closest associates not only recognized that the economy was not working well, but that the entire oppressive totalitarian system, in which much power was concentrated in the secret police, needed to be brought to an end.[3] As George Shultz described his thinking in November 1987: "I felt that a profound, historic shift was under way: the Soviet Union was, willingly or unwillingly, consciously or not, turning a corner; they were not just resting for round two of the cold war."[4]

Gorbachev and his close associates moved too slowly for some and too rapidly for others, but they succeeded in ending totalitarian control of the lives of Soviet citizens. As for the realists' expectation that the Soviet Union might dissolve, the idealists considered it far more important, in terms of U.S. geopolitical concerns, that the Soviet Union under Gorbachev was prepared to cross over to the democratic camp.[5]

With Reagan as president and Shultz as secretary of state, the formulation of U.S. foreign policy was in the hands of two persons who, without having identified themselves formally with any particular school of foreign policy analysis, did subscribe to the idealist approach. They saw in Gorbachev and Shevardnadze statesmen who had concluded that it was in the interest of

---

3. As described in chapter 4, note 16, when Gorbachev was six years old, he had the traumatic experience of the secret police arresting his grandfather without justification and keeping him in prison for two years. That experience may very well have been the cause of the origins of his distaste for totalitarianism.

4. Shultz, *Turmoil and Triumph*, 1003.

5. As early as 1989, Anatoly and I began to discuss the appropriateness of the Soviet Union joining the Group of Seven and making it a Group of Eight.

their country to work cooperatively with the United States on the international scene and to make the domestic changes that would bring the Soviet Union into compliance with international human rights standards.

The initial effort to reach an understanding on arms reduction was not easy. A summit meeting in Iceland in October 1986 suggested an opportunity for further progress even if it did not produce all the desired results. Still, in describing an important positive outcome of Reykjavik, Shultz noted: "The Soviet agreement that human rights belonged on the regular agenda of U.S.-Soviet relations was astonishing."[6]

It was George Shultz who thereafter played a critically important role in linking U.S.-Soviet cooperation on the international scene with domestic change in the Soviet Union. While Gorbachev and Reagan would meet and see each other at the occasional summit meetings, Shultz had not only established good personal relations with Shevardnadze, his counterpart, but with Gorbachev as well. Shultz would meet regularly with Gorbachev on his frequent visits to Moscow.[7] From April 1987 to January 1989, Shultz saw to it that our bilateral contacts on arms control and human rights moved on parallel tracks. As he often put it, he gave the human rights cause pride of place. The point that the U.S. side emphasized was that the U.S. Senate would have more confidence in the good intentions of the Soviet Union and would thus be more likely to ratify an arms control agreement if it were evident that the Soviet Union had become an open society and was adhering to democratic norms.

The linkage between arms control and human rights also served Gorbachev's domestic political purposes. The Soviet Union's military leadership had become increasingly concerned that it did not have the resources to help it keep up with the U.S. arms program. That caused it to support the arms control effort. If the price that had to be paid for arms control was a more open civilian Soviet society, the military leadership could live with that.

In his impact on international events, Gorbachev is one of the most significant personalities on the world scene of the twentieth century. He was undoubtedly the prime mover in ending the Cold War that Stalin had started. Yet recognition needs to be given to the three other persons who responded appropriately to the initiatives of the Soviet Union's leader. On the Soviet side there was Shevardnadze, who as foreign minister not only

---

6. Shultz, *Turmoil and Triumph*, 780.

7. It is important to note the fact that the development of the Gorbachev-Shultz relationship was not based on occasional meetings and on wishful thinking about Mikhail Gorbachev. It was a relationship that developed over an extended period of time, during which the two protagonists met frequently, exchanged thoughts, worked on specific problems, and helped solve them. The conclusions that Shultz reached about Gorbachev's reliability as a partner was based on his practical experience of having worked with him and having joined him in removing obstacles to improved international relations.

shared the general secretary's political outlook, but whose straightforward personality convinced Shultz, his U.S. counterpart, that the United States could have confidence in the commitment of the Soviet leadership to the goal of ending the Cold War and creating an open society in the Soviet Union.

However, these results would not have been attained if President Reagan had not joined Secretary Shultz in correctly assessing the outlook of the new Soviet leadership and responding accordingly. Both of them understood how their Soviet counterparts' views had changed from those held by their predecessors, both on the international geopolitical scene and with regard to respect for human rights domestically.[8] While strongly underlining the U.S. positions regarding the issues on the bilateral agenda, Reagan and Shultz handled these matters and their direct personal contacts with the two Soviet personalities in a way that made it possible to reach agreement and effect fundamental changes both in our bilateral relations and in Soviet compliance with its international obligations in the field of human rights. It took some time for the relationships among the four principals to develop, but when they did, they provided a solid foundation for the U.S.-Soviet relationship generally, as Gorbachev explains:

> On April 14, 1987, I welcomed George Shultz in Moscow. Today I view that meeting as a milestone. The American Secretary of State focused the conversation on intermediate-range nuclear forces and the continuation of strategic arms negotiations. But the issues we discussed went far beyond our prepared briefs. It was the first time that we touched on the philosophical aspects of the new policy, on the roles and responsibilities of our two countries.
>
> It seemed that the Americans' main objective had been to learn more about our views and intentions—an entirely justified purpose. But what was to follow? Another round of propaganda campaigns and battling for public support? Or were these soundings a prelude to real politics?
>
> Incidentally, my own aim had been to find out what lay behind the Reagan administration's rhetoric. I wanted to see whether there was any chance of improving relations with Washington. During the talks, I therefore applied a strategy which encouraged our American partner to be frank, to show us his "fall-back positions" and the extent of Mr. Shultz's powers.
>
> I think that both sides pursued basically the same objective. Rhetorical exchanges of "compliments"—including the traditional accusations of excessive spying—were one thing. But the talks had shown that underlying considerations and intentions were far more important. As we could see from his subsequent actions, the Secretary of State genuinely wanted to sustain the dialogue. His position seemed to

---

8. Shultz, *Turmoil and Triumph*.

> influence the American administration in general, President Reagan in particular.
>
> I realized, maybe for the first time, that I was dealing with a serious man of sound political judgment. Subsequently, he developed his potential even more—as a statesman, an intellectual, a creative and at the same time a far-seeing person.[9]

The Working Level

Given the commitment of the four men in top leadership positions to reaching comprehensive agreements, it was necessary to go beyond friendly exchanges of greetings and get down to specifics. That meant that it was necessary to move from the summit and ministerial levels to discussions at what is often referred to as the working level.

The saying that the devil is in the details is highly relevant in this context. The presidents and the ministers dealt with the broad outlines of human rights problems that seriously clouded the relationship between the Soviet Union and the United States. Anatoly's and my task was not only to operate within these broad outlines, but also to identify in detail the concrete problems that confronted us within these outlines and find solutions for them.

Anatoly and I started our dialogue with the historic background of earlier bilateral and multilateral discussions of Soviet human rights issues well in mind. As we discussed earlier in this memoir, the issue of Soviet compliance with international human rights standards entered into the diplomatic dialogue during the détente period, beginning in the late 1960s. The Nixon administration—more specifically, Henry Kissinger—was by no means eager to place human rights on the agenda of the bilateral discussions. Kissinger focused primarily on geopolitical concerns. It was Congress that initially established the linkage between improved bilateral relations and performance in the field of human rights. As arms reduction treaties would require Senate ratification, the Nixon administration was compelled to accept that linkage, even if it was highly skeptical as to its wisdom.

It was as a result of this congressional intercession that the Soviet Union agreed to modify its long-standing policy of putting severe restrictions on the emigration of any of its citizens. In the 1970s, tens of thousands of emigration permits were granted, primarily to Jews, but also to Armenians and ethnic Germans native to the Soviet Union. (In the Gorbachev era, Pentecostal Christians were added to that list.) Granting exit permits should not have been viewed as a great challenge. It did not bring about change in the

---
9. Gorbachev, *Memoirs*, 440.

structure of the Soviet Union's governmental system. In fact, it could have been welcomed as a way to get rid of potential troublemakers. But that is not the way the Soviet authorities saw it. They viewed an application for an exit permit as a rejection of life in the Soviet Union, an action that suggested enmity of the Soviet system.

With the Soviet invasion of Afghanistan in 1979, the détente policy came to an abrupt end, as did the rather limited U.S.-Soviet human rights discussions and the practice of granting substantial numbers of exit permits. In the years that followed, with the Soviet Union under the rule of the gerontocracy, no effort was undertaken to improve superpower relations.

But in 1987, after a pause of eight years, we were once again tackling human rights issues. Anatoly's and my experience demonstrates that, while broad final policy decisions are made at the highest level of government, the ability of the governmental leaders to make these final decisions ultimately depends on the adequacy of the preparatory work. Anatoly's and my job was to do that preparatory work. While each of us was acting in accordance with the goals and objectives of our respective bosses, it was up to us to determine how their respective goals and objectives could most effectively be reached.

The term used in diplomatic contacts to describe the role of the state asking for action by another state is demandeur. Thus, with the United States as demandeur, it came to be my task to spell out concretely what the president and the secretary of state had in mind when they called for Soviet progress in the field of human rights.

My view was that little could be achieved if the United States were to ask that the Soviet Union turn itself overnight into, say, a Swiss-style democracy. Rather than declaiming in general terms the virtue of democracy and asking that the Soviet Union proclaim its rejection of Communism, I sought to identify specific problems that the Soviet government, under Gorbachev's leadership, might be prepared to resolve—problems that upon resolution, first, would be viewed as appropriate and meaningful by Congress and the general American public, and second, could in the long run lead to a change in the system. The immediate goals we set were designed to help large groups of individuals who had been victimized by the system, through incarceration, commitment to mental hospitals, and denial of exit permits, rather than calling for prompt fundamental structural change.

One of the problems that could be corrected quickly was the problem of exit permits. It was a problem Congress underlined when it enacted the Jackson-Vanik amendment to the Trade Act of 1974. Both before and after the enactment of the amendment, the Soviet Union had allowed large-scale emigration. That emigration had clearly not done any damage to the Soviet

Union, or, for that matter, to the structure of the Communist state. It seemed easily possible to return in the late 1980s to the policies of the 1970s.

Next, there was the issue of abuse of psychiatry—the commitment to mental institutions of perfectly sane persons because they were alleged to have committed a political offense. The practice had been roundly condemned internationally and gave the Soviet Union and its psychiatric profession a particularly bad name among intellectuals.

The third issue that we raised got us closer to the matter of challenging the system. We were, in effect, calling for an end to restrictions on freedom of expression, because we urged the release from imprisonment of persons who had been convicted and were serving prison sentences or banishment under what the Soviet criminal code identified as either anti-Soviet agitation and propaganda or defamation of the Soviet Union. Yet on that issue, with the large-scale release of prisoners from the Gulag in January 1987, Gorbachev had shown that he was ready to effect change, returning at least to the Khrushchev years.

Finally, we were looking for an end to the practice under which only a limited number of religious denominations were authorized to engage in religious practices while engagement in religious practices by members of unauthorized denominations was a criminal offense. I assumed that this limitation had nothing to do with the cause of religion as such. It was most likely connected to the police state's unwillingness to tolerate the existence of private groups that would hold meetings without KGB surveillance. A limited number of properly licensed religious groups could be appropriately spied on, particularly if the clergy provided help to the KGB. If that number increased substantially, however, the KGB's task of supervision would be increasingly difficult.

In one instance, there was another reason to refuse recognition to a religious denomination and punish the unauthorized practice of religion: the Eastern-rite Catholic Church was suspected of being imbued with Ukrainian nationalism and supportive of the independence of Ukraine.

In my discussions with Anatoly, I presented specific cases formally and expressed concern regarding the underlying policies informally. I placed emphasis—again in an unpublicized, nonthreatening fashion—on the fact that Soviet practices were in conflict with the International Covenant on Civil and Political Rights, a covenant negotiated by the Soviet foreign ministry. I pointed out that this fact gave the foreign ministry a basis for raising the issue of violations of the covenant with Soviet governmental agencies that were responsible for these violations.

As noted earlier in this volume, Anatoly had himself been concerned over some of the violations of international standards that I pointed out to him. As to some of the others, he was really unaware of how serious the violations were. Having heard the areas of U.S. concern spelled out by me, Anatoly recognized them as issues that the new leadership was indeed prepared to resolve and then went about the task of finding constructive solutions, using his contacts in his own ministry and in other Soviet governmental agencies as well as on the staff of the Central Committee of the Communist Party.

What made it possible for Anatoly and me to succeed was our relationship to our respective bosses, Eduard Shevardnadze and George Shultz. Both of them wanted to cooperate with each other in identifying problems and finding solutions to them. While they were not focused on the fine details, they had confidence in Anatoly and me, who reported directly to them and who, in turn, had a thorough understanding of what Shevardnadze and Shultz were seeking to achieve. What was also important is that Anatoly and I viewed the issues with which we had to deal the way our respective bosses viewed them.

As we write this memoir, more than twenty years have elapsed since our first meeting. As the years have passed, Anatoly and I have become close personal friends. We have thus come a long way since our first encounter in April 1987 in the foreign ministry in Moscow. At that time we were still in a period known in history as the period of the Cold War. We most certainly did not expect that our efforts would make a modest contribution to ending it.

There are those who contend that the Cold War ended in December 1991 with the disintegration of the Soviet Union. Both of us believe that that is a mistaken reading of the history of that period. We believe that the Cold War ended on January 17, 1989, when the Vienna CSCE meeting adopted its concluding document, the first document to come out of the CSCE process to reflect the new relationship of friendship between the Soviet Union and the United States. And we do not believe that it is a reflection of an exaggerated feeling of self-importance if we say that we played an important role in attaining that result. Yes, the fundamental decisions were made at the highest levels of government, that of Gorbachev and Reagan, Shultz and Shevardnadze. It was Reagan and Shultz who insisted that there must be progress in the human rights field before the negotiations on the treaty regarding conventional forces in Europe could begin. But as the account of the sixty days prior to the adoption of the concluding document shows, there were those who wanted to derail any agreement and it was the two of us who thwarted their efforts.

Accidents of bureaucratic history had placed us in positions from which we were able to negotiate and resolve issues that would otherwise have prevented agreement at the Vienna meeting. We had agreed not to deal with each other, as Anatoly put it, as if we were in a bazaar. We worked on a formula that would enable Secretary Shultz to obtain President Reagan's agreement to the Vienna document and would, at the same time, reflect the new thinking advocated by President Gorbachev. Anatoly was among those who saw to it that that new thinking was well reflected in the speech that Gorbachev delivered at the United Nations in December 1988, a speech that caused me to run up to Secretary Shultz and tell him excitedly: "He has repudiated Leninism."[10]

What were the factors that made it possible for us to play the roles that we did? First of all, and most important, we had the confidence of our immediate superiors, the foreign minister and the secretary of state. They knew that we understood their respective policy objectives and were confident that we would do our best to reach them. Further, we had become personal friends and had come to trust each other. Each of us knew that we both were trying to attain the same result.

The Vienna concluding document would not have been adopted if we had been required to spend weeks exchanging diplomatic notes, which, in turn, would have had to go through a multilevel clearance process. On each of the issues that we resolved, we did so by talking to each other and then letting our bosses know what conclusions we had reached.

Thus, the lesson can be drawn from our experience that, in future negotiations like ours, it is essential that, first, the basic policymakers are in close touch with the officials responsible for working on details; second, the officials working on the details fully understand the goals of the policymakers and are committed to attaining them; and third, the policymakers have sufficient confidence in the working-level officials to allow them to operate without the customary bureaucratic constraints.

The Soviet Union's New Three-Party System

During my frequent visits to Moscow in the Soviet Union's last three years, from 1989 to 1991, the years in which it functioned as a democracy, I saw a drama unfold. The bureaucracy, the military, and the Communist Party

---

10. There was another occasion—truly accidental and not really within the scope of our mandate—where the two of us helped along the process toward ending superpower tension. In March 1988, Shevardnadze was in Washington to negotiate an understanding on Soviet withdrawal from Afghanistan. At issue was an agreement between the United States and the Soviet Union to end the supply of arms to the contending Afghan forces. Anatoly, who had come along to negotiate with me, was told to postpone the human rights negotiations and, instead, to participate in the discussion of Afghanistan. At this meeting Shultz and Shevardnadze could not find agreement and Shevardnadze left Washington abruptly.

The next morning we met to start discussions on human rights. At the outset, Anatoly told me how deeply upset Shevardnadze had been over the failure of the Afghanistan discussions. I passed that message on to one of my colleagues and was told that Shultz had been equally upset. The word that came back from the secretary's office was a request that Anatoly convey the message to Shevardnadze that the United States was interested in continuing the Afghanistan discussions. That led to further meetings and ultimately an agreement acceptable to both sides.

apparatus had for decades marched to the beat of a single drummer, the party's general secretary. In these last years, its members were on their own. There were those who had for years hoped for change and highly welcomed the Gorbachev reforms. But there were also those who liked to hold on to their special status and privileges and deeply resented the changes brought about by perestroika. They were also deeply resentful of what they viewed as the humiliation of the Soviet Union on the international scene and the role the United States played in its negotiations with the Soviet Union—negotiations that helped bring about the reunification of Germany and Soviet withdrawal from its sphere of influence in Eastern and Central Europe.[11]

The major international events of 1989 involved the replacement of the Communist governments that had ruled the countries that were the junior members of the Warsaw Pact. One Communist government after another was replaced, either as a result of a negotiated change or, as in the case of Czechoslovakia, through what came to be called the Velvet Revolution. Only in Romania was there bloodshed, including the death of the dictator and his wife. The Soviet Union took no action to prevent these states from leaving the Communist orbit. In Bulgaria, Shevardnadze assisted with the ouster of the Communist dictator, Todor Zhivkov.

The most spectacular event by far was the fall of the Berlin Wall in November 1989. That event was followed by difficult negotiations, in 1990, between the Soviet Union, the United States, Germany, the United Kingdom, and France with regard to the future of East Germany. The end result was the unification of Germany, with the unified German state being part of NATO. It was very difficult for Gorbachev to assent to this outcome and his decision to do so was highly unpopular among Russian nationalists.[12]

To add to Gorbachev's domestic political problems, the nationalities issue—the claims for independence from Russia of Soviet republics populated by non-Russians—began to raise its head and came most strongly to the fore in 1991. One of the major consequences of the introduction of fundamental freedoms into the Soviet Union was that national minorities began to assert themselves, with quite a number of their spokesmen calling for total independence from Russian control and thus for secession from the Soviet Union. That call for total independence was particularly pronounced in the Baltic states. As the United States had never recognized the incorporation of the Baltic states into the Soviet Union, the United States supported the Baltic

---

11. Resentment that has not been forgotten to this day and was most clearly expressed by Prime Minister Vladimir Putin in 2008, close to twenty years later.

12. Another international issue that took a prominent place on the bilateral agenda in 1990 and 1991 was the Gulf War, Saddam Hussein having once been a client of the Soviet Union. That issue, on which the Soviet Union also accommodated the concerns of the United States, was of lesser interest to Soviet public opinion.

call for independence, which was added to the bilateral U.S.-Soviet agenda, causing Gorbachev an additional problem with his right-wing opposition: Understandably, conservatives in the bureaucracy and the party apparatus found this development most troubling and began to view Gorbachev and his supporters as engaging in traitorous activities. The nationalities issue thus added significantly to the deep division between the Gorbachev reformers and the right wing. As it was, that division had been in evidence prior to 1989, when Gorbachev had to deal with the opposition to his reform efforts within the Politburo, led by Yegor Ligachev. Gorbachev and his supporters had no problem overcoming their opponents within the Politburo. It was an exercise they were able to handle well.

Yet while Gorbachev and his friends knew how to outmaneuver opponents in the Politburo, they found it far more difficult to deal with the challenge posed by the right-wing opposition that had established itself after 1988 in the governmental and party apparatus. In years past the leadership had laid down the line and the underlings had carried out their instructions. But in the new, democratic Soviet Union, underlings were allowed to make their own decisions. That meant that if Gorbachev wanted to continue to have their support, he needed to persuade them to render it. That, in turn, required the creation of an organized effort to reach out to regional and local leaders and make the case for reform. Regrettably, Gorbachev and the supporters of reform lacked the know-how needed to perform this task of persuasion.

The right-wing opposition was not the only force that Gorbachev and his supporters had to reckon with. Aside from the politically engaged establishment, which then divided between reformers and hard-line conservatives, there was a third group: the pre-Gorbachev-era dissidents and their sympathizers. These dissidents were gradually coming together to form a force on the Soviet political scene. Their visceral opposition to the Soviet Union's establishment caused them to distrust Gorbachev and the reformers that were part of it. The person whose public pronouncements they found increasingly attractive was Boris Yeltsin.

And so the so-called left-wing opposition to Gorbachev came into being. Its leader was a man who had been a member of the party establishment, too, but the emphatic tone with which he denounced the Communist Party impressed the long-term opponents of Communism. They were also impressed by Yeltsin's sharp criticism of Gorbachev and the reformers for having moved too slowly.

Thus, three political groupings were on the scene in the new, democratic Soviet Union. Two of them emanated from the establishment and the third from the dissidents and their sympathizers. Most of them were reasonably well educated. But where was the bulk of the people? The general population did have points of view regarding developments on the political scene, but they had not been used to engaging actively in public affairs. Most Soviet citizens were preoccupied with the economic decline that the Soviet Union was experiencing, as well as the deterioration of conditions regarding law and order. What we were thus witnessing were three groupings of deeply committed actors playing the political game while the general public watched them with interest but without participating in that game.

On my visits to Moscow there were no occasions that brought me together with the right-wingers, but I did have frequent meetings with both the Gorbachev reformers and Yeltsin's left-wing opposition. I used these opportunities to ask them, first, about the issues on which each of these groups differed from the others. I could not detect any such differences other than opinions as to the speed with which conditions should be changed. Both groups were committed to an open society respectful of human rights and favored movement toward privatizing the economy. Regarding the latter, in particular, the left wing urged much faster movement than did the Gorbachev supporters.

Still, given the similarity in the outlooks of Gorbachev's and Yeltsin's forces, I used whatever opportunity I had in speaking to my contacts in Moscow to urge them to unite. Given the threat posed by the right-wing forces, I would quote Benjamin Franklin to them: "If we do not hang together, we'll hang separately."

I have made reference earlier to the rise of the nationality issue. To the consternation of the right-wing opposition, the Gorbachev leadership, as they saw it, was not aggressive enough in keeping the Baltic states within the Soviet Union. Georgian nationalism was then once again in evidence, as was Ukrainian nationalism. These were not merely threats to the existence of the Soviet Union as a Communist state. Going back in history before 1917, it was the state that once constituted the Russian Empire that appeared to be disintegrating.

The right wing was virulently opposed to such a development. The centrist reformers wanted to avoid such an outcome but were hesitant about the use of force in preventing it, particularly in the Baltic states, the Soviet occupation of which, under the Hitler-Stalin Pact, had never been recognized by the United States.

But where was the left wing on this issue? As I have mentioned earlier, in January 1990 I had had a discussion with two of my one-time dissident acquaintances, who had told me that they were in favor of Russian sovereignty. From that conversation I gleaned that they supported the dissolution of the Soviet Union as a way of finally getting rid of a leadership that was viewed as tainted by the past and getting a fresh start for Russia with Yeltsin in the lead.

Oddly enough, the chain of events that led to the end of Gorbachev's leadership—and with it, the dissolution of the Soviet Union—began in August 1991 with a striking demonstration of the progress that had taken place in the Soviet Union under Gorbachev. The attempted right-wing coup, organized by the leaders of the three Soviet forces that bore arms—the army, the secret police, and the ordinary police—failed because the rank and file of these three armed forces, including high-ranking officers, were unwilling to follow the leadership of the top command and had the courage to disobey orders.

The failure of the August coup was thus the result of the new thinking that Gorbachev had brought to the Soviet Union. But it did not help Gorbachev maintain his standing among his countrymen. On the contrary, the hero of the hour was Gorbachev's adversary, Boris Yeltsin, who was viewed as the man who had turned the tide against the coup plotters and had helped bring Gorbachev back from his vacation resort unharmed.

It would have been an ideal time for the two exponents of democracy in the Soviet Union to join in an effort to move forward together. But that was not to be. There were no profound disagreements between them on public issues. What separated them was the profound dislike they had for each other. Gorbachev was an uncharismatic leader who discharged his responsibilities in a thoughtful, systematic fashion, after having done his homework and having thought matters through with great care. He was a sober leader in every respect, including his rejection of alcohol. His administration was free of any taint of corruption.

Yeltsin's personality was the exact opposite. In his appeal to the general public he was charismatic. He would not spend a great deal of time studying and analyzing problems of government. If an idea appealed to him, he would seize it and make it his own. And he had a serious problem with alcoholism, and often drank until he could no longer function. Later, during his years of leadership of the Russian Federation, questions were raised regarding the financial dealings of personalities who had close connections to his administration.

Fate propelled these two prominent personalities into a contest for leadership in the autumn of 1991. Gorbachev's title at that time was president of the Soviet Union. Yeltsin's was that of president of the Russian Federated Soviet Socialist Republic. As the weeks passed, it became increasingly clear that Yeltsin and his supporters believed that the most effective way to defeat Gorbachev was to dissolve the Soviet Union, thereby eliminating his job and leaving Yeltsin in his position in the Russian Federation.

Given Yeltsin's charisma and Gorbachev's lack thereof, the Soviet general public, particularly the public in Moscow, very clearly preferred Yeltsin to Gorbachev. Gorbachev was also blamed for the sharp decline in the economy and the increase in crime.

Still, democracy had not advanced to the point at which the general public was given a clear voice in the decision-making process. What was decisive in this period was that Gorbachev, once the all-powerful chairman of the Politburo, whose orders were punctiliously followed, was no longer able to cause his government to function. His writ no longer ran. Still, Gorbachev, Yeltsin, and other leaders of individual Soviet republics sought to negotiate a transition to a more decentralized Soviet Union. But the people close to Yeltsin were not interested in anything other than the dissolution of the Soviet Union. With the government of Russia—the principal component of the Soviet Union—joining the leaders of many of the other Soviet republics in supporting the dissolution of the Soviet Union, Gorbachev had no other option but to leave the scene.

The Sequel

The dissolution of the Soviet Union did not mean that all of the one-time Soviet republics would immediately return to dictatorial rule. The annual report of Freedom House, which had in 1990 moved the Soviet Union from its "not free" category to its "partly free" category, maintained that classification for the Russian Federation until 2005, when it moved Russia back to being classified "not free." Freedom House's 2007 report classifies Ukraine and the Baltic states as "free" and Armenia, Georgia, and Moldova as "partly free." The other eight successor republics are, alas, in the "not free" category.

Focusing on the Russian Federation, we need to note that Yeltsin maintained the democratic structure that he had inherited from Gorbachev. Regrettably, however, he managed governmental affairs so poorly that he gave democracy a bad name with the Russian public. As promised, the economy was privatized, but under conditions that raised serious ethical questions. The public continued also to be concerned about lawlessness and thus the threat to public safety. Further, there was doubt as to whether the president was in effective control of the government at all times.

Thus, when Vladimir Putin became president of the Russian Federation and began to curtail individual freedom in Russia, the general public did not object. The Russian citizenry welcomed the reestablishment of order, both in internal governmental affairs and on the streets, through guarantees of public safety. As it was, Putin did not return Russia to the state of affairs in the Communist period. He went back further. Governance in today's Russia resembles that in place during the days of Tsar Alexander III: Individuals may speak their minds as long as they are not viewed as a threat to the incumbent government. If they are viewed as such a threat, they are dealt with harshly—very harshly.

Note need also be taken of the fact that the policy of friendly relations with the world's major democracies, which had characterized the final years of the Gorbachev era, was continued under Yeltsin. In 1997, the Russian Federation joined the Group of Seven, the group of major industrialized democracies, to form the Group of Eight. Putin has now distanced Russia from the world's democratic camp.

Many casual observers of the international scene did not believe in 1991 that the end of Gorbachev's leadership of the Soviet Union would be detrimental to the causes of democracy and respect for human rights. As a matter of fact, they thought that Yeltsin would improve on Gorbachev's accomplishments. To this day, there are many such observers who truly believe that it was Yeltsin, not Gorbachev, who brought democracy and respect for human rights to Russia. A careful assessment of developments would necessarily lead to the conclusion reached by Freedom House: the Soviet Union became "partly free" under Gorbachev, Russia continued to be "partly free" under Yeltsin and in the early years of Putin, and has regressed in recent years to being "not free."

Could such regression have been prevented? It is not clear whether the people of Russia, after decades of totalitarianism, were ready to move quickly toward Western-style democracy. As we have shown here, there were members of the intelligentsia, both inside and outside the government, who wanted the country to progress in that direction. Both Anatoly and I agree that the chances of moving toward democracy on a solid footing would have been greater if the leadership of the country had remained in the hands of the solid, clear-thinking Gorbachev, an instinctive democrat, instead of being assumed by the somewhat irrational and confused Yeltsin.

The Bush Administration's Skepticism about Perestroika

In chapter 6, I describe the continuation of U.S. human rights work in the Soviet Union during the last three years of that state's existence. There was a significant difference between the work that I was doing in 1989, 1990, and 1991 and the work I did in the immediately preceding years. In the earlier years, I focused on issues and problems that were central to U.S. Soviet policy, as expressed by both the president and the secretary of state. But by early 1989 the basic human rights concerns of the United States had been satisfactorily resolved under the Soviet Union's perestroika policy. There were a few details still to be cleaned up, of vital importance to the people directly affected, but the broad policy issues had been resolved and we were increasingly focused on what we were calling "the new agenda," programs focusing on the rule of law and on assistance for the handicapped and the elderly.

Both the remaining details on the old agenda and the effort we undertook regarding the issues on our new agenda were not central to U.S. policy under the Bush administration. The secretary of state did not stand in the way of any of my activities. I was able to move forward without hindrance. But it was a struggle to find funding for our new projects at this time, when the doors in Moscow were wide open for humanitarian and rule-of-law activities in cooperation with the United States. Chapter 6 contains a brief discussion of what appeared to be the outlook of the White House and State Department on Soviet policy. That discussion deals with just the tip of the iceberg. If we want to reach conclusions as to what the United States might do most effectively if faced again with a similar situation, we need to dig more deeply.

In September 1991, following the aborted coup, Secretary Baker visited Moscow and then wrote an extraordinarily perceptive message to President Bush:

> The simple fact is we have a tremendous stake in the success of the democrats here. Their success will change the world in a way that reflects both our values and our hopes. What may be at stake is the equivalent of the postwar recovery of Germany and Japan as democratic allies, only this time after a long Cold War rather than a short, hot one. The democrats' failure would produce a world that is far more threatening and dangerous, and I have little doubt that if they are unable to begin to deliver the goods, they will be supplanted by an authoritarian leader of the xenophobic right wing.... Given the long odds, I think we need to be realistic in recognizing that success might amount to simply holding off a counterreaction and giving the democrats the space and time to stay with what will be a long journey. But that in itself would be an historic legacy.[13]

What is deeply regrettable is that this extraordinarily perceptive and far-sighted analysis was produced in September 1991, two years and eight months after the Bush administration had taken office. The long delay in reaching this conclusion may very well be the consequence of a mindset described by George Shultz as he was leaving office: "the 'new team' did not understand or accept that the Cold War was over."[14]

Confirmation of Shultz's assumption can be found in the very first chapter of Baker's memoirs, entitled "The Day the Cold War Ended." As Baker sees it, the Cold War ended in early August 1990, when the United States and the Soviet Union agreed on a joint statement criticizing Iraq's invasion of Kuwait.[15]

---

13. Baker, *Politics of Diplomacy*, 535–536.
14. Shultz, *Turmoil and Triumph*, 1138.
15. Baker, *Politics of Diplomacy*, 16.

There is no doubt that Secretary Baker and Foreign Minister Shevardnadze and their respective staffs had produced a highly important statement, a statement of profound international significance, on the subject of Iraq. But that statement was not the result of a sudden impulse of the leaders of the two countries to find a subject on which they could agree. It was the product of years of extended close contacts between the leadership of the two countries—close contacts which, as we have already noted, reached a high point with Gorbachev's repudiation of Leninism in December 1988, his readiness to cross over into the democratic camp, and the signing of the CSCE Vienna Document on January 17, 1989.

Back then, in January 1989, the incoming administration should have followed the approach recommended by Baker close to three years later. But the assessment by the new U.S. leadership of the Reagan-Shultz policy toward the Soviet Union ranged from skepticism to hostility. Secretary Shultz, as he left office, had been concerned about the outlook of the new administration, in which realists such as Brent Scowcroft, the new national security adviser, would play a significant role. While President Bush and Secretary Baker did not belong to the realist camp, they had sufficient doubts about the Reagan-Shultz policies to allow for a pause in the development of U.S.-Soviet relations that would permit conducting a top-to-bottom policy review. In the meantime, as he came to note, President Gorbachev felt like the bride left at the altar. As he put it in his memoirs:

> The [Bush] administration was apparently in no hurry to develop Soviet-American relations. The first meeting between Eduard Shevardnadze and Secretary of State Baker, which took place in Vienna in mid-March—nearly two months after George Bush assumed office—left us with the impression that the new administration was biding its time, waiting for … what were they waiting for? Some of the signals we were receiving were quite alarming. There were people in our country and in the Soviet leadership who were ready to interpret the drawn-out interval as evidence that Washington was plotting against the Soviet Union, or at least had no intention of improving relations.[16]

Contrary to these initial assumptions, Secretary Baker developed a good relationship with Foreign Minister Shevardnadze after they had met a few times, and President Bush, after his meeting with Gorbachev in Malta, in December 1989, was satisfied that profound changes had occurred in the Soviet Union. But the intimacy in the relationship of the Shultz years was gone, as was the deep U.S. interest in the success of perestroika and glasnost. Furthermore, the national security adviser remained unconvinced, creating a split of opinion on Soviet policy at the highest level of the U.S. government.[17]

---

16. Gorbachev, *Memoirs*, 496–497.
17. Baker, *Politics of Diplomacy,* 157.

There is little doubt that by 1990 both President Bush and Secretary Baker thought well of Gorbachev and wanted him to succeed. But in his memoirs Baker makes it clear that while he had come to the conclusion that Gorbachev's intentions were good, he was, from the very beginning, doubtful that perestroika would succeed. As early as April 1989, then–Secretary of Defense Dick Cheney let the cat out of the bag when he said in a CNN interview that Gorbachev would "ultimately fail." Baker strongly objected to Cheney's statement, but as he put it in his memoirs, he "didn't disagree with his substantive analysis."[18]

The Cheney incident of March 1989 was at risk of repeating itself in October when Robert Gates, then serving as deputy to Scowcroft, sent to the State Department a draft of a speech that he intended to give. Baker describes his reactions after he had read the draft:

> My feeling was that Bob had made a fundamental mistake by failing to distinguish between what the administration thought privately and what we said publicly about those views. His speech was extremely pessimistic about Gorbachev's chances of survival. While that view was shared by most of us, highlighting it in our public comments would have had the effect of pulling the rug out from under the President's statements that we supported perestroika. Analytically, I didn't have any serious disagreement with Gates's assessments. . . . But in terms of the policy approach of our new administration, it would be a disaster.[19]

It would indeed have been a disaster. Secretary Baker was just then in the process of delivering speeches that, as he put it, "outlined the administration's own 'New Thinking' on perestroika and the nature of the new U.S.-Soviet relations." He describes "the logic chain" of his speeches as follows:

> I argued that perestroika was a "true revolution" that transcended economics to encompass globally all of Soviet society and its relations. "It is an ongoing experiment," I told the Senate, "relying on a fair amount of seat of the pants logic." The fate of perestroika's success would be determined by what the Soviets themselves did, I said, but there was room for a new relationship. I said that the President and I wanted perestroika to succeed "not because it is our business to reform Soviet society or to keep a particular Soviet leader in power—we can really do neither—but because perestroika promises Soviet actions more advantageous to our interests."[20]

There are aspects of these statements that deserve close attention. As already noted, Secretary Shultz says in his memoirs that President Reagan and he "were handing over real momentum." That is most certainly what they

---

18. Ibid., 70.
19. Ibid., 156–157.
20. Ibid., 155–156.

had done, having worked with Gorbachev and Shevardnadze for close to four years and having established excellent relations with the Soviet Union. One might have expected the new administration to seek to build on what they had accomplished rather than laying out new thinking.

Equally of concern, in retrospect, is the view that it was not "our business to reform Soviet society," that we wanted perestroika to succeed "because perestroika promises Soviet actions more advantageous to our interests." The approach taken by President Reagan and Secretary Shultz was that reform of Soviet society was a worthy goal that transcended narrow U.S. geopolitical interests. Causing the Soviet Union to respect human rights, adhere to the rule of law, and establish a democratic system of government would bring it into compliance with its international obligations and would make it a better partner in maintaining world peace.

A few months earlier, Baker had had another meeting with Shevardnadze, his third. In that meeting, Baker writes, a brief statement by Shevardnadze "fundamentally changed our relationship."[21] What Shevardnadze had said was this:

> The trends developing in the Soviet Union have been difficult. Democratization, perestroika, and renewal are affecting every part of our society … and every person, and every family, too. We are now in the most crucial stage in what we call our revolution. . . . Our country's social and economic problems are enormous. The financial situation is in very grave condition. There are big imbalances in our markets and money supply, and goods are also vastly out of balance.

As Baker saw it, Shevardnadze "had not only conveyed just a political position in which the Gorbachev government found itself, but also the emotional struggle in which he was engaged." But Shevardnadze had also gone on to speak of "cooperation":

> We know that only we can solve our own problems. We agree with what both President Bush and you have said about the Soviet people being responsible for themselves and for making perestroika work. Of course, cooperation helps, and we seek it from the United States, Europe, and Asia. We also know that the capability of our partners is limited especially with regard to our needs—and we are not about to require you to take 100 million Soviet people under your wing.[22]

Baker's response was cautious:

> I want to repeat that we are strongly committed to the success of perestroika, recognizing that this very much depends on what you do and how you respond to the challenges you face. The vast majority of

---

21. Ibid., 138
22. Ibid., 139.

> Americans support your efforts. But how effective we can be in trying to assist you depends on our public opinion continuing in this favorable direction.[23]

The question of cooperation came up again in a meeting in May 1990 between Gorbachev and Baker. Baker reports:

> Gorbachev said the Soviet Union was facing a significant funding gap over the next few years, and would need $20 billion in loans and credits. He said he needed the symbol of our involvement in the loan effort—in large part, I suspected, so he could demonstrate how his policies were succeeding in getting the United States to contribute to Soviet needs. Gorbachev said the next few years would be critical, because Moscow was going to move to a market-based economy. To cushion the impact and expedite the transition, he needed resources to buy consumer goods to invest in the conversion of defense plants to civilian output.[24]

The U.S. response was to encourage the International Monetary Fund to grant the Soviet Union substantial loans. That, however, was not enough to turn the Soviet economy around.

In chapter 6, Anatoly vividly describes the serious economic downturn that accompanied the coming of freedom to the Soviet Union. To be sure, the United States did not have an obligation to straighten out the economic mess created in the Soviet Union by its command economy and the disintegration of that economy in the perestroika years. But, as Secretary Baker correctly pointed out in September 1991, it was in the best interest of democrats everywhere, and most certainly of democrats in the United States, for the Soviet Union's democrats to succeed. He implied that if the Soviet Union's democrats decided to move forward on economic reform, the West should do its part to be of help. That conclusion was, alas, reached too late.

Could the United States Have Helped Perestroika Succeed?

What is clear, in retrospect, is that without effective help from the West, perestroika was doomed to fail. There is no certainty that the converse was true as well—that with Western help perestroika would have succeeded. What is worth considering, however, is whether the approach outlined in Secretary Baker's September 1991 memorandum, if it had been written in January 1989 and promptly implemented, would have changed the course of history.

---

23. Ibid.
24. Ibid., 249.

When the Bush administration took office, experts on the Soviet Union presented it with two contrasting assessments of the state of affairs in that country. One side argued that the Cold War was over, that democrats were leading the Soviet Union and that they respected human rights, but that they had economic difficulties and needed and deserved economic assistance. The other side argued that there had been no substantive change in the Soviet Union and that the Gorbachev leadership wanted to solve some internal problems, but continued to be committed to Leninism and would resume the Cold War as soon as the internal problems had been resolved.

Secretary Baker and President Bush ultimately rejected both assessments. They gave Gorbachev and his team credit for trying to effect change, but held to the view that they would ultimately fail. Under these circumstances, an effort was made by the United States to continue friendly relations with the Soviet Union, but not to get one's hopes too high, and certainly not have us go out of our way to provide help for what would surely be a lost cause.

As Baker got to know Shevardnadze and ultimately Bush got to know Gorbachev, their views that both men were trying to effect significant reforms were significantly strengthened. But, as noted, it took until September 1991, in the wake of the unsuccessful August coup, for Secretary Baker to come to the conclusion that there really was a chance that the Soviet Union's democrats might succeed and that our help to them could make a difference.

It was too late to help Gorbachev at that point. The intramural struggle in the Soviet Union's democratic camp was won by Yeltsin and led to the dissolution of the Soviet Union in December 1991. The following month, the United States organized a coordinating conference to provide humanitarian and economic assistance to the newly independent states of the former Soviet Union.[25]

There were those in the U.S. government who viewed that outcome as the best of all possible results: the dissolution of the Soviet Union and what they viewed as a genuine democrat in charge of the Russian Republic. There were others who saw the situation differently. They considered Yeltsin's personality to be unstable and doubted whether he would be an effective leader of the new Russian democracy.

These memoirs do not analyze developments in the post–Soviet Union period. What can be stated briefly, though, is that Yeltsin's leadership of Russia turned out to be as erratic as at least some in the U.S. government had expected. What had not been expected, but what did indeed happen, is that the Yeltsin administration was thoroughly corrupt and utterly inept in handling the economy, thus discrediting the democratic cause among the Russian people. After anointing Vladimir Putin as his successor, Yeltsin

---

25. Ibid., 617–619.

resigned in December 1999. Putin, in turn, reestablished authoritarian rule in Russia.

Was that outcome inevitable? Is democracy simply not suitable for Russia? That very question was asked in 1945 with regard to Germany and Japan. It could, of course, be argued that Germany had experience as a democracy prior to 1933. But Japan had never had such an experience. Yet, ever since Freedom House started its country ratings in 1973, Japan has been rated "free." Before 1945, Russia certainly had been exposed to democratic thought and the spirit of the Enlightenment far more than had Japan. Experience has shown that that thought and that spirit can surmount geographic and cultural barriers.[26]

Would a different end result have been reached if the Reagan-Shultz policies had been continued? We obviously cannot be certain but we need to consider the following: President Reagan and Secretary Shultz were fully committed to the task of protecting the national interests of the United States. But they measured U.S. national interest not only in terms of relative military strength, but also in terms of the spreading of the idea of freedom. One can say that they had an ideological, emotional attachment to the international human rights cause.

In February 1983 it was Ronald Reagan who took time out in a conversation with Soviet ambassador Dobrynin to discuss the issue of the Siberian Seven, Pentecostal Christians who had taken refuge at the U.S. embassy in Moscow five years earlier and were still living there, fearful of arrest by Soviet authorities if they left. As Reagan put it: "If you can do something about the Pentecostals or another human rights issue, we will simply be delighted and will not embarrass you by undue publicity, by claims of credit for ourselves, or by 'crowing.'"[27]

And in April 1985, it was George Shultz who donned a yarmulke and attended a seder with refuseniks at the U.S. embassy. He used that opportunity to express his emotions to the refuseniks: "You are on our minds; you are in our hearts. We never give up, we never stop trying, and in the end some good things do happen. But never give up, never give up. And please note that there are people all over the world, not just in the United States, who think about you and wish you well and are on your side."[28]

---

26. Following the abolition of totalitarian control in Mongolia in 1990, I had a visit, as U.S. assistant secretary of state for human rights, from leaders of the Democratic Party of Mongolia. My first question to them was: "How did the idea of democracy reach you?" Their answer was that the best students at their secondary schools were sent abroad to study at foreign universities, but they had to be in the Soviet bloc. So they went to Warsaw, Prague, and Budapest. As my interlocutors put it: "And they came back with ideas about freedom."

27. Shultz, *Turmoil and Triumph*, 165.

28. Ibid., 887.

Both Reagan and Shultz knew what Communism was all about and had reached the conclusion that by 1988 the Soviet Union was no longer led by Communists, but by people who shared our commitment to democracy and respect for human rights. What would their reaction have been if they had still been in office when the serious economic problems developed in the Soviet Union that Anatoly has described? There is every reason to believe that they would have adhered to the message that Shultz had given the refuseniks: "We never give up, we never stop trying, and in the end some good things do happen."

Would Reagan and Shultz have succeeded in helping Gorbachev stabilize democracy in the Soviet Union? There is obviously no way of telling for sure. But given Shultz's expertise in the field of economics[29] and Gorbachev's high regard for Shultz,[30] the Soviet leader might well have listened to advice, especially if it was accompanied by a comprehensive program of economic assistance. A comprehensive economic assistance program like the Marshall Plan could very well have made a signifancant difference.

In Conclusion

What lessons can be learned from our experience? The most important lesson is that the placement of the human rights issue on the U.S.-Soviet diplomatic agenda led to a beneficial result, the end of Soviet totalitarianism. That end might well have come later, but it came sooner because the United States sent a clear message and the leader of the Soviet Union understood it and ultimately agreed with it.

What was, of course, unique about the dialogue about which we have written was that it was a dialogue between two superpowers that had for more than forty years been engaged in a cold war. The United States had theretofore found it easier to inject human rights into diplomatic dialogues with smaller states, particularly those that had a special interest in good relations with the United States. It was a unique set of circumstances—most important, the accession of Gorbachev to the position of general secretary—that ended totalitarianism in the Soviet Union.

---

29. Before serving as secretary of state, he had also served as secretary of labor, director of the Bureau of the Budget, and secretary of the treasury.

30. As quoted above, Gorbachev considered Shultz "a statesman, and intellectual, a creative, and, at the same time, a far-seeing person."

Anatoly Adamishin

What roles did glasnost, democratization, and perestroika play in the destiny of my country? Did they make a positive impact on our history, or did they lead to the breakdown of the Soviet Union, which many still consider to be a national tragedy? Was it possible, as Gorbachev wanted, to marry socialism and democracy? Nancy Ries, an American who lived in the USSR during perestroika, believes that "a moment of opportunity, a rational combination of socialist and market systems could have occurred."[1]

After the disastrous 1905 Russian Revolution, future Menshevik Georgi Plekhanov coined the phrase "one shouldn't have taken up arms." Should Gorbachev have similarly refrained? This question encompasses another one: Was our unprecedentedly broad, open, and honest cooperation with the Americans, including in the human rights field, productive for the Soviet Union, or did it contribute to our troubles? I have heard the reproaches: By conceding to the Americans in the human rights domain, we softened and then destroyed our regime. But if we follow this logic we have to come to the conclusion that the worse people's conditions become, the stronger grows the regime. Was the inoculation of democracy a lethal injection, or was the dose insufficient to overcome resistance from conservative antibodies?

These questions are argued, sometimes fiercely, in today's Russia and beyond. Some authors, like British historian Mark Almond, assert that stagnation served the Soviet Union's interests better than perestroika did because stagnation posed no threat to the people who maintained the country's cohesion and stability.[2] My colleague Yuli Kvitsinsky, former first deputy foreign minister of the Soviet Union, recently expressed a similar idea: "If it were not for Gorbachev we could have lived another two decades without woe." Gorbachev is still being cursed in Russia.

In this chapter, I try to answer the above questions, first, by revisiting the history of democratic tendencies in Russia.

An Inevitable Authoritarian Regime?

Russia is typically characterized not only as having a history of authoritarian rule, but also as being unsuitable for any other system of governance. I give

---

1. Nancy Ries, *Russian Talk* (Ithaca, NY: Cornell University Press, 1997), 16.

2. See Mark Almond, "1989 without Gorbachev: What If Communism Had Not Collapsed?" in *Virtual History: Alternatives and Counterfactuals*, ed. Niall Ferguson (New York: Basic Books, 2000), 392–415.

the floor to Catherine the Great: "The sovereign must be autocratic, for no other form of government but that which concentrates all power in his person is compatible with the dimensions of a state as great as ours.... Any other form of government would not only be harmful, but utterly ruinous for Russia."[3] Three hundred years later, many Russians still side with the empress.

The proponents of the autocratic interpretation of Russia's history believe that, despite the profound outward changes in the nature of Russian regimes—from tsarist autocracy to Soviet ideological authoritarianism—the substance remained the same: The state was everything, an individual was nothing. For centuries, Muscovite Russia had been run like a private estate, its inhabitants treated as the property of the tsar. The theme of disrespect toward the small man, the famous hero of Nikolai Gogol's novel, winds through all great Russian literature. Louis XIV declared that *"l'etat c'est moi,"* but Stalin was even more explicit when he, toasting the simple men and women, the people at the grassroots who won victory in the Great Patriotic War, referred to them as the "screws" or cogs—innumerable, anonymous parts of the huge state machine. Many in the current ruling elite in Russia view this tradition as inescapable, even if they do not say so openly.

They forget that Russia—unlike, say, China—wasn't always autocratic.

For several centuries, until the Tartar-Mongolian hordes invaded medieval Russia, it absorbed the social mores of its western neighbors, even though it was on the periphery of Europe. Daughters of Russian princes regularly married European kings. Landlocked, Russia had to conduct much of its trade with or through Western partners, compelling Russian merchants to follow the rules of the West. A mercantile economy was only one of the characteristics that the old Russian cities shared with their Western counterparts. The free cities also had high levels of literacy and fashioned their social structures on Western European, specifically northern Italian, models.[4]

Novgorod was the capital of the huge territory that embraced all land north of the Great Russian plains. Its four hundred years of democratic evolution corresponded with that of cities in Europe. As in Western Europe, democracy began with a rebellion against a local prince to limit his powers. But Novgorodians went further, establishing what could be defined as popular rule. The most important issues were discussed and settled at an all-town meeting, the famous veche. For centuries, Novgorod maintained close relations with its western neighbors, including on matters that would now be considered to lie within the humanitarian field.

---

3. I found this quotation in a survey dedicated to Russia in the *Economist*, May 22, 2004, 4.

4. See S. Pushkarev, *A Survey of Russian History* [in Russian] (New York: Chekov Publishing House, 1953), 79 and following.

Novgorod's laws encouraged commerce, the acquisition of property, and compliance with contracts. Hired labor was widespread. The practice of consensual taxation differed from the coercion that was characteristic of tax collection in the territories under Tartar rule, which Russian feudal princes copied. Like their Western counterparts, Novgorod and Pskov didn't maintain regular armies—every able-bodied man would become a combatant if needed.

The Imposition of the Asian Matrix

The Tartar-Mongolian invasion was the major interruption in the democratic path that Russia seemed to be on. The Tartars imposed a so-called Asian matrix—backward politically and socially but strong militarily—on a European country. When I touched on this topic, speaking to Gorbachev, he pointed out that many features of our social and political structures have their origins in Tartar dominance.

But the Tartars were not the only obstacle on the path to a democratic Russia. Religion played a role, too. The Rus' took Christianity from the Byzantines before the East-West schism. The Christians flowing in from the south after the fall of Constantinople brought a radical Orthodox version of the religion. That ideology accelerated the sometimes antagonistic division from Catholic Europe. Russia was cut off from Western Europe, particularly after the Reformation, and from Europe's democratic traditions and economic and social reforms.

That, and not the fact that a huge part of the Russian territory lies in Asia, explains Russia's ambivalent self-identity. The country is European in its main conceptions and philosophy, but employs Asian methods of structuring life. Like Europeans, Russians have believed in the need for change, reform, and democracy; like Asians, they have waited for change to be brought from above.

The territories not affected by the invaders from the East developed in a more European way. Again, the best example is Novgorod. When Ivan III, "collecting the Russian lands together," conquered Novgorod, initially in a peaceful way, one of his first ukases (edicts) was to close a German trading station. Ivan the Terrible finished the job by looting the city completely: He realized that merchants were a threat to autocratic rule. Throughout Russia, what had not been sacked or destroyed by the Tartars was decimated by the tsars.

Attempts at Reform

In the 1800s, attempts were made to reform the system from above. Alexander II abolished serfdom, thus preventing the situation from degenerating into a civil war—a result that the United States, when tackling similar problems, failed to achieve. This "last brave tsar" introduced, in 1864, a system of *zemstvo*, or limited local self-government.

Reformist movements were always marked by a human rights emphasis. The university strike in 1899—considered by some historians to be the start of the Russian Revolution of 1905— proclaimed an urgent demand to promote "the most sacred rights of the development of human individuality." Another demand was to eliminate bezglasnost, the opposite of glasnost.[5] In the early twentieth century, a liberal appeared—Prince Sviatopolk Mirski. As minister of internal affairs, he tried to prevent revolution through concessions and reforms. He partly succeeded when Nicholas II issued a law on the improvement of political order, which provided for the introduction of some civil rights. Unfortunately, the tsar and his entourage didn't dare go further. Their priority was to save the autocracy. Yet, for a brief period after the election of the first state Duma, Russia seemed to be squarely on the road to democracy, providing freedom of expression, assembly, and association.

In the Soviet era, Khrushchev's thaw was promising from a democratic perspective. And some degree of democracy existed in the exhilarating initial years of the independent Russia, after the breakdown of the Soviet Union. Although the Russian regime during that time had been correctly called a "surrogate of democracy," some democratic components were present— free elections, an open media, free public opinion—that served to check the government.

Gorbachev Arrives

For us, a small group of so-called children of the Twentieth Congress, belief in a democratic future for Russia confirmed by historical reminiscence was unbreakable. It inspired us to use all the available tools—frankly, there weren't many, though cooperation with the West was among them—to make this future arrive earlier. That's why we were so enthusiastic about Gorbachev. He tried to accomplish nothing less than to eliminate the authoritarian matrix and to pull Russia off the Asiatic track; moreover, he tried to do so by convincing people of the benefits of a democratic society, not by forcing them into it. For hundreds of years, Russian public life had followed no evolutionary course; instead, it had experienced occasional and abrupt convulsions. For years and years, people would silently tolerate all kinds of injustices and difficulties, and then suddenly they would explode and revolt. Gorbachev believed in a more pacific political evolution.

---

5. See Richard Pipes, *The Russian Revolution* (New York: Alfred A. Knopf, 1990), 7.

His achievements were truly remarkable. He managed to get the Communist Party Congress to approve a program entitled "Toward a Human, Democratic Socialism," which proclaimed that "our main objective is the spiritual and political liberation of the society" and that "human rights are the main criteria of democracy."[6] Who had heard such words from this party before? He publicly raised the issue of whether the people had authorized the party to rule. He believed that if the Communists could win democratic elections, they would legitimately retain power.[7] Gorbachev did more than talk—he did his best to make freedoms concrete, including the freedom to decide one's own destiny.[8]

Was it reasonable to wait until the entire country would accept this new way of thinking? Much later Gorbachev confessed that he had made a mistake in not splitting the mammoth Communist Party and creating a real reformist wing, a social democratic one. Yakovlev, Shevardnadze, and others had urged him to do so when they saw that the party was dragging its feet in implementing democracy because its nomenclatura did not want to yield power. Gorbachev believed that his project was so obviously good for the country that he could convince everybody simply by explaining it.

The Western Contribution to the Fall of Perestroika

It is our own fault that perestroika failed. Even so, many liberals believe that the United States could and should have done more to support this courageous attempt to transform Russia. Others contend that U.S. cooperation could not have saved Gorbachev anyway. For myself, I am sure that Gorbachev's chances of survival would have increased if the United States had led the West in pledging political and material support for perestroika, as Thatcher urged Bush Sr. to do.[9] A similar, earlier appeal to help Gorbachev made by the West German chancellor Helmut Kohl had also met with a negative response. The most the Americans pledged was that the International Monetary Fund would thoroughly study the situation in our country, a task that could take many months.[10] I cannot help adding that the United

---

6. *Pravda*, July 14, 1990. Incidentally, this was the last congress of the Communist Party of the Soviet Union.

7. Gorbachev Foundation, V Politburo CK KPSS, 359, 379.

8. In contrast to Stalin, Gorbachev urged his colleagues: "Switch on the people! They must decide who should rule the country and who should not. The people are not 'screws' any more.... The Party must serve the society and not vice versa." See Gorbachev Foundation, V Politburo CK KPSS, 140.

9. See also Matlock, *Autopsy on an Empire*, 336–339.

10. Philip D. Zelikow and Condoleezza Rice, *Germany Unified and Europe Transformed* (Cambridge, MA: Harvard University Press, 1995), 259, 333.

States bet not only on the most likely winner—Yeltsin—but also on a man who wanted to destroy socialism whereas Gorbachev kept speaking about its renovation.

In my view, many in the United States failed to understand that Gorbachev's democratic socialism offered a better chance than Yeltsin's program did for lasting reconciliation between Russia and the West. The West neglected the opportunity to turn Russia toward Europe and away from the Asian matrix; had it taken that opportunity, relations between Russia and the West would not today be so problematic.[11]

Gorbachev began to lose U.S. support, if it ever existed, long before the coup. The Bush administration was miles away from supporting the economic and political transformation that Gorbachev projected. As we saw it then, one of the reasons for the U.S. attitude was the abiding influence of the American military-industrial complex.[12] Another reason was that, beginning in 1989, the Bush administration was busy pushing the accelerator of two parallel processes: German reunification and the ousting of the Soviet Union from Eastern Europe. This policy encouraged Gorbachev's opponents inside the country. Even when the United States needed—and received—Soviet assistance in the Gulf War, the U.S. administration offered Gorbachev little more than verbal expressions of support and pledges. For all intents and purposes, the Cold War was still on.

Despite the role the United States played or did not play, it must again be emphasized that the main cause of perestroika's failure was in ourselves. As Shevardnadze later confessed to a foreign guest, "At the beginning of perestroika, we were naïve." I would add: "Not only at the beginning."

What Is Russia?

The Soviet leaders rarely understood the country they governed. Who did? We suspected that we lived in the "Kingdom of Distorting Mirrors," to borrow the title of a fairy tale, but almost no one could fathom the whole dis-

---

11. In the early 1990s, most young Russians were pro-American. They regarded the United States as a model for their country and were hopeful that the fall of Communism would usher in an era of cooperation between the United States and Russia. The Clinton administration threw cold water over these hopes when it launched a policy of expanding NATO to include former Warsaw Pact countries. President Clinton also lost much credibility with Russia by pushing NATO to bomb Yugoslavia because of events in Kosovo in 1999. The administration of George W. Bush added insult to injury by sponsoring NATO membership for portions of the former Soviet Union itself—the Baltic states. So, to my mind, one could talk about lost opportunities only by stretching the imagination: The American side simply had not taken them into account.

12. Ambassador Matlock is explicit regarding this. "Washington still seemed more concerned with getting Congressional approval for new weapons systems than finding ways to reduce the dangerous overstock in both nations." See *Autopsy on an Empire,* 274.

ordered picture.[13] Even Yuri Andropov, a man who passed through all the phases of a party and state career, including serving as the KGB chief, once exclaimed in a fit of temper: "We should yet look into what society we have been building." Curiosity, however, was an alien idea. Restrictions and prohibitions were many and strong, and secrecy was an obsession.[14]

Everybody knows about the Iron Curtain, but there was another curtain inside the Soviet Union, and it obscured what was happening in the country. It either concealed the full truth or revealed straightforward lies. All kinds of secrets were kept from the public. Who knew that Russia was facing a demographic crisis—that by 1982 the death rate was higher than the birth rate and that ethnic Russians were a minority in the Soviet Union? Who realized that none of the five-year plans had actually been fulfilled and that the budget had always been in deficit? Who knew about the incredible levels of alcoholism? Information about per capita consumption of alcohol—which in 1984 was 8.3 liters annually in pure alcohol equivalent, twice that of prerevolutionary Russia and four times more than in 1950—was classified as top secret.[15]

The Soviet rulers of that time knew some of those figures, but they hid in their safes the desperate appeals they received from experts. Foreign minister Gromyko kept one such report for several months without acting on it and eventually threw it into the archives. Gorbachev's campaign against alcoholism may have been a failure—in part because the economy lost 34 billion rubles from decreased sales of vodka in 1985–87[16]—but at least he made the information about alcoholism public and tried to do something about the problem.

When the country's leadership was confronted with the Chernobyl tragedy, it turned out that they had been poorly informed about the situation in the atomic energy sphere because it was closely connected with military matters. Few people, I believe, fully understood that although the military and space sectors were relatively advanced, most industrial sectors were underdeveloped. Some machinery had been in operation since before the revolution. Infrastructure, ignored for decades, finally collapsed—but when this happened, Gorbachev was already in power and he was blamed for it.

---

13. The absurdity of the Russian and subsequently Soviet life was depicted by such great writers as Nikolai Gogol and Mikhail Bulgakov. The latter in his novel, *The Master and Margarita*, calls the Devil himself to help bring some justice.

14. We had been raised on prohibitions. Once an employee of the U.S. embassy in Moscow told me a funny story: He hired a Russian nanny for his baby, and the first word the little one uttered in Russian was "nelzia!" (you mustn't!).

15. I quote here the notes in my diary (May 25, 1985, i.e., perestroika time) evidently taken from an official document. I marked also that the expenses per capita for alcohol amounted to 190 rubles per year, more than what was spent for bread, meat, and milk combined.

16. Gorbachev Foundation, V Politburo CK KPSS, 445.

The country lagged in the development of science and technology. Gorbachev himself admitted once that "our science is equipped only about 25 percent according to world standards." There were nearly five thousand research and development institutes in the Soviet Union, but their productivity was often extremely low.[17]

Even before perestroika, people in the Soviet Union had money at home and in savings accounts, but they could buy hardly anything with rubles. At the same time, the most popular word was "deficit."[18] Shops had plenty of merchandise that nobody wanted because of its poor quality. Soon, however, there was a deficit in bread and we imported grain for billions of dollars. Brezhnev implored Nixon to sell us wheat and maize.[19] Money was periodically invested in agriculture, but it never resulted in enough food for the people or enough forage for cattle.[20]

The policy of leveling wages irrespective of the value and quality of work deprived people of incentives to work and learn. Gorbachev commented on the Soviet habit of viewing people as a cheap commodity. People felt alienated from the enterprises where they worked.[21]

The Main Adversary

Bureaucracy has always been the plague of Russia and the Communist Party bureaucracy became a peculiar breed. In the minds of Soviet ideologues, at least, party bosses were meant to act much like priests; instead, they became wedded to power, and if they resembled clerics, it was the mullahs of post-revolutionary Iran. At the top of this bureaucratic hierarchy stood a small group of old men who were not unintelligent but who saw life in a distorted light. The gerontocracy tormented the country, clinging to power and barring the way for younger, more adventurous generations.

---

17. Ibid., 24 and 154.

18. My university friend Boris Vladimirov, who reached a high position in the Central Committee, told me about letters received from the periphery, filled "not with anger, but with grief: in recent years we have seen neither meat nor milk, and now other food has disappeared, we eat potatoes and cabbages. . . . Help us at least for the anniversary of the October Revolution."

19. Dobrynin, *In Confidence*, 262.

20. A story circulated in those years through Moscow, which I transcribed on February 1, 1982, in my diary: "The Party Secretary in charge of agriculture, Kulakov, had long been preparing proposals on how to improve our countryside productivity and living standards, to facilitate individual farmers and so on. Finally he presented them to the Politburo. The 'Grey Cardinal,' M. Suslov, immediately argued against 'restoration of capitalism, creating a class of kulaks.'" He was supported by Brezhnev. Kulakov is said to have asked, "What do we need, grain and meat, or word labels?" He was rebuffed even more harshly.

21. Gorbachev Foundation, V Politburo CK KPSS, 76. Gorbachev even used the word "colonizers" once when speaking about the authorities' way of treating the so-called small ethnicities.

But no regime can eliminate political rivalry. In the Soviet Union, such fights took place behind the scenes, leaving most Russians none the wiser and prompting a cohort of Kremlinologists in the West to try to decipher the few signs of discord that did slip into public view. In the days immediately preceding the March 1985 death of Secretary General Chernenko, Gromyko was nervous and out of sorts. A knowledgeable friend explained that Gromyko, bored with decades of standing behind another man, was considering throwing his hat into the ring. After he made up his mind not to risk a struggle with Gorbachev, and, moreover, to be the first to support him, Gromyko's proverbial imperturbability returned. When Chernenko died, no one except a few at the top knew it. That evening, Gromyko met French foreign minister Roland Dumas at the Moscow airport—Dumas' visit had been planned some time before—and discussed the following day's schedule. Gromyko mentioned that the schedule might be revised. I had drafted and redrafted the itinerary dozens of times, and thus when Gromyko made this comment, I was a little worried. Not until the next morning did we understand that Gromyko was referring to the cancellation of a scheduled meeting with Chernenko.

Will They Fill Their Cars with Water?

The country was kept alive almost exclusively by the export of energy. This export brought in revenue and sustained the might of the gerontocracy, but it also promoted material and intellectual stagnation: With a steady source of income, no one needed to worry too much about modernizing the economy. Some people, including Alexei Kosygin, tried to introduce moderate reforms, but their efforts were aborted because those at the top did not want to dilute their own power. Two decades in which we could have modernized the country were essentially lost. Control of the economy by administrative methods, first developed under Stalin and then solidified during the war of 1941–45, was strengthened even further during the Cold War. The confrontation with the United States and the military threat helped preserve such methods. There was no room for a Soviet Deng Xiaoping, with his famous saying that "it doesn't matter what color a cat is; it's more important whether it catches mice."

Our economic planners believed in the prevailing theory that oil prices would continue to rise because "people can't fill their cars with water." Innovations in the West and energy-saving technologies were entirely ignored. When oil prices fell drastically, the Soviet Union faced catastrophe. In the autumn of 1985, as Prime Minister Ryzhkov reported to the Politburo on July 11, 1986, the price of oil had been 172 rubles per ton; at the time of his report, it had fallen to 52 rubles and was soon expected to drop to 40. That resulted in losses of 9 billion rubles. Among other measures, this necessitated a significant reduction in imports, which intensified the empty-shelves effect in stores. Overall losses from decreased prices for Soviet exports (fuel) made up 13 billion so-called hard-currency rubles in 1985 and another 15 billion in 1986.[22]

To many in the Soviet Union, the collapse was not accidental; it was the result of combined actions by the United States and Saudi Arabia. The latter out of the blue increased oil output from two to nine million barrels a day. The former declared it was reducing oil imports. The price of a barrel of oil in November 1985 was US $30; by April 1986, it had fallen to $12.[23] Later it was Gorbachev who had to find a way out of this crisis.

The Biggest in the World—Militarily

Sometimes, the picture seemed to be surreal. We supplied the West with our mineral resources and received the food—35 million tons of grain in 1987—without which we couldn't survive. Still, the general mood in the country was that the Soviet Union was completely surrounded by enemies, most significantly the United States, and thus needed a strong defense tous azimuts. Like Tsar Dadon from Pushkin's poetry, we maintained a numerous host. The military was probably the biggest in the world and nobody knew how much we spent on it. Often expenses were hidden in the budget. We don't spend a single ruble more than necessary for defense, Brezhnev used to say from the podium during party congresses. But was he, the top man in the Soviet hierarchy, even aware of the real expenditures?

Militarization pervaded the entire social organism; the interests of the military were given priority over the health of the country. Entire regions were contaminated with uranium residue. One could see beautiful lakes and forests on the map, but realize on arriving that they were uninhabitable. This seemingly absurd policy of giving an enormous portion of the national pie to the military-industrial complex was partly tied to the collective memory of the terrible war in 1941–1945, as well as to fear of new calamities. The people's willingness to overlook all kinds of errors and expenses to prevent another war was exploited.

---

22. Gorbachev Foundation, V Politburo CK KPSS, 66, 102, 169.

23. Cited in an article (in Russian) by Nadia Kampaner that appeared in Russia in *Global Affairs* 5, no. 6 (November–December 2007): 93–94.

The International Burden

Another drain on the country's resources came in the shape of its socialist friends. The party leadership had an irresistible desire to pull some countries from the opposite camp to our side to demonstrate that socialism was winning its historic ideological battle. Any movement that declared itself Communist, or close to it, could rely on our support.

A fortune was spent on this ambition. The Afghan war cost six billion rubles each year. I never found the exact figures of the costs of our support to Cuba—and not only to the island in itself, but to its troops in Angola, Ethiopia, and elsewhere. Once, when in Cuba, I talked to many people to try to determine the level of the aid. I came to the conclusion that the entire nation could live without lifting a finger for two months of every year on the aid sent from Moscow. Cuba was not alone on our assistance list; aid to Vietnam amounted to a dozen billion dollars, while Syria received six billion. The export of capital from Russia began much earlier than the arrival of the modern oligarchs.[24]

What Is Democracy?

When Gorbachev became secretary general, he had to contend with the nearly absolute absence of democracy, not only in the country but also within the party. Who among my generation doesn't remember party meetings that nobody was willing to attend except those trying to make their way up the ladder? As for joining the Communist Party, we were obliged to do so if we wanted to build a career. In the most important departments, such as the Ministry of Foreign Affairs, what we called a party layer filled the length and breadth of the organization.

The selection of human resources for the party was often carried out on the basis of perverted criteria, with ambition, not ability, the most important quality. Mediocrity generated mediocrity. One might presume that at least there was room for free discussion behind the closed doors of government agencies. Alas, this rarely occurred. I worked closely with Gromyko for years, but he would think nothing of reproaching me with a phrase like, "Who gave you the right to express your opinion?"[25]

---

24. In this sphere, too, Gorbachev tried to change things abruptly; he saw that some of our friends in the third world were willing to "squeeze all they could" from us and then to drag us into adventurous military conflicts. "Everybody wants us to work for their benefit. And now they want us to fight wars for them as well—we cannot make concessions to that" (Gorbachev Foundation, V Politburo CK KPSS, 46–47, 58, 94, 209).

25. This vividly reminded me of the character of our great poet Aleksandr Griboyedov's immortal comedy who had trained himself "to dare not to have a judgment of one's own."

Like some other countries, the Soviet Union was only an imitation of democracy. Many of democracy's characteristics—elections, public organizations, mass media—were present, but they lacked substance. Elections presented no choices. The gap between everyday life and its official portrayal gave birth to a huge deception. People were unaccustomed to the truth; they were used to thinking that authority and truth were incompatible. This explains the very low level of political trust among ordinary people. Gorbachev encountered this directly.

Soviet society was deprived of the possibility of expressing its opinion, let alone influencing events. The last genuine political demonstration in Moscow was on November 7, 1927, when those who supported Lenin's ideas marched against Stalin. It was brutally dispersed, and those who participated were eliminated one by one. Before perestroika, the only really free discussions were the "kitchen talks" involving one's closest relatives and friends (a lot of ideas realized in Gorbachev's time were born during these passionate debates).

One of our most talented cinema directors, Elem Klimov, made a film, "Agony," about the last days of Tsar Nicholas II in which he tried to warn people about where we were headed. "Agony" was shelved for seven years under the pretext that Klimov lied about Russia—not the tsars, not the regime, but Russia.

The poet Bulat Okudzhava sang that "life was beautiful when judged by the reports"— party reports, naturally. A huge number of propagandists were paid to convince us that everything was going well. In every workplace there was a so-called first department or a special director who worked exclusively studying the loyalty of employees. Many people suffered because they talked too freely. Later, during the last years of Gorbachev, it became known that even Politburo members had bugs in their offices and that different departments inside the KGB were in competition with each other in this respect. Some of our American friends can vouch for the quality of Soviet surveillance technology.[26]

Who Ran the Country?

Aleksandr Yakovlev, a great intellect and dedicated supporter of perestroika, was a guest at our dacha just a few months before his death. I mentioned

---

26. When the U.S. embassy in Moscow was told, in the spirit of perestroika, by the Soviet authorities that its newly built edifice was full of bugs, it was debated whether it would be worthwhile to pull the entire structure down. When Ambassador Jack Matlock touched on this issue in conversation with me, I suggested, "If you decide to demolish the building, try to do it in this way: one floor yes and another floor no." Incidentally, we haven't had reciprocity for that very unusual gesture.

that I was writing a book looking back on the Soviet era, and he volunteered the following observation:

> It is wrong to think that the Communist Party ruled the country. There were two powers, the KGB and the party. In many instances, the KGB was more important than the Central Committee or the Politburo. I don't remember a single case during my years in the Politburo and the Secretariat when objections from the KGB on one or another question were ignored. Everybody felt that the KGB had to be heeded. It was an absolute priority because we thought they by definition have something that we cannot know. The KGB knew everything that was happening in the Central Committee, but the Central Committee didn't know what was happening in the KGB. Maybe the general secretary knew it, but to my mind it is unlikely. The KGB was a closed corporate organization. For all serious projects, even those dealing with economic development, the greatest policy expertise was in the KGB Institute.
>
> When I was a Politburo member, I had fifteen bodyguards, all from the KGB; three cooks, all from the KGB; and the woman who cleaned my house was a KGB officer with a military rank. The man who worked in the garden was from the KGB, too, and everybody wrote a daily report on what I was doing.

The extent of the problem prompted Gorbachev to remark: "Let's not mix up the functions of the CC and the KGB. Ideological work is the domain of the CC. And the KGB should be preoccupied with state security. We do not need an ideological gendarmerie. If we mix up one with the other, we will get nonsense, like it has been before."[27]

Storming the Heavens

By the time Gorbachev came to power in 1985, the Soviet Union, thanks to all the previous leaders from Stalin to Chernenko, was doomed. Anatoly Chernyaev, an aide to Gorbachev, wrote, "When the chief looked in the eyes of truth, the country was already near the abyss."[28]

In Russia, as in any other country, there are always many people who are unhappy with their situation. But in the Soviet Union, this unhappiness wasn't matched by a capacity to act, to struggle for improvement. Gorbachev belonged to a rare (for Russia) category of people in that he was ready to realize practical change without using force. He began to prepare the project of perestroika long before he came to power.

---

27. Gorbachev Foundation, V Politburo CK KPSS, 172.

28. Anatoly Chernyaev, *Six Years with Gorbachev* (Moscow: Progress Publishers, 1993), 40 (in Russian). Contrast this with V. Falin, a notable party functionary and no supporter of Gorbachev, who wrote, "The USSR's agony started yet in the second half of the seventies" (Kommersant-Vlast, April 16, 2005).

In his memoirs, Gorbachev affirms that he had begun planning for perestroika in 1982. He felt compelled, seeing the nation in a dramatic crisis and holding a high government position, to try to fix the situation.

In those days, a trip to Moscow to attend Central Committee sessions was a holiday for district party chiefs, involving little work other than listening to reports and the opportunity to shop, drink, and in general enjoy life. A party secretary told me that Gorbachev never joined in such festivities. He was more inclined to have serious talks about the country's situation with a few like-minded comrades. Speaking with me recently, Shevardnadze confirmed this impression.

I honor Gorbachev for his concern for the destinies of the Soviet people.[29] A harvester operator from Stavropol province acted like a genuine member of the intelligentsia of old Russia—he felt personal responsibility for the fate of the country and put its interests above his own. He was not afraid, in Karl Marx's expression, to storm the heavens.

The Crisis of Nationalities

This is not to say that Gorbachev's judgment was infallible. A clear example of how badly Gorbachev and his team misunderstood the country they governed was their conception of the ethnic problem. On November 2, 1988—three years after perestroika began—he described it thus:

> Comrades, we're entitled to say that we have settled the nationalities question. The revolution paved the way for equality of rights among the national groups, not only on the legal level but also on the social and economic level, and made a notable contribution to equalizing the economic, social and cultural levels of development of all the republics and regions and of all the peoples. The friendship among the Soviet peoples is one of the greatest triumphs of the October Revolution. In itself this is a unique phenomenon in world history, and for us one of the fundamental pillars of the power and solidity of the Soviet state.[30]

Three years later, the Soviet state fell apart along the lines of nationality. The disintegration wasn't sudden. The national republics had long lived according to their own laws, obeying the center only nominally. Brezhnev, particularly during the last years of his rule, created the illusion that he was

---

29. Jack Matlock is absolutely right when he asserts that "if he [Gorbachev] had not subsequently set out to change the system, he might have remained in power longer than Brezhnev." *Autopsy on an Empire*, 53.

30. See Helene Carrere d'Encausse, *The End of the Soviet Empire: The Triumph of the Nations*, trans. Franklin Philip (New York: Basic Books, 1992), 1. There is clearly a tribute to the customary rhetoric here. But Gorbachev remained convinced for a long time that even the Baltic republics "won't go anywhere . . . they will eventually steady down." For decades, ethnic relations were beyond politics, were excluded from critical analysis.

ruling and the republics created the illusion that they were obeying. Below this quiet surface, nationalistic and even anti-Russian passions were boiling, but they were ignored, dismissed, or hidden.

We Won the Battle, But Not the War

Hundreds of books and articles have sought to pinpoint the reasons why Gorbachev's noble project failed. Having watched events unfold from inside, it seems to me that the biggest factor was the sheer scale of the opposition to perestroika. The bureaucracy—the professional party and state apparatuses, especially the military and KGB, local administrations, and the feudal lords of the republics and provinces[31]—were stronger than a handful of reformers. The party had nineteen million members, most apathetic, the rest driven by personal ambition and afraid of losing their privileges and power. They could not but betray a reformist like Gorbachev. Even in the Politburo, few people stood firmly for perestroika.[32]

When the ideological nomenklatura—the mourners of socialism—began to fail, the economic nomenklaturs became the second echelon of defense. They had something to fight for—theoretically, the people's property, but in practice very much their own assets. All-union ministries were a formidable power. According to Nikolay Ryzhkov, as of November 1988 the republics were controlling no more than 10 to 15 percent of their economies.[33] Clearly, the main shareholders—the all-union ministries—were desperately resisting change. As a result of this standoff, administrative levers in the economy grew weaker, whereas the economic tools of control never began to function. A similar discrepancy between dismantling the old mechanisms and introducing new ones also took place in the political and ideological spheres. At first the struggle was restricted to the Kremlin's corridors, but soon it became impossible to hide.

Faced with formidable resistance, Gorbachev did not adopt Mao's strategy and "fire at headquarters," although many urged him to do so. He spoke directly to the people. But society was not prepared for radical changes and inevitable losses, especially because the economic situation quickly deteriorated and store shelves were soon empty. As Richard Pipes notes, "the public, kept silent for seventy years, availed themselves of glasnost not to reinforce

---

31. Gorbachev Foundation, V Politburo CK KPSS, 226.

32. This must have been a reason why Gorbachev reshuffled his cadres so much at the final stages. Out of the 1985 Politburo members, he was the only one to remain there by the end of the perestroika period.

33. Gorbachev Foundation, V Politburo CK KPSS, 416.

the regime but to tear loose from it."³⁴ This was manifested in the ideological sphere by intensified debunking of the ideals, in the social sphere by mass strikes, and in the sphere of nationalities by ethnic conflicts. Unaccustomed to freedom, people did not know how to handle this sudden gift or the bitter truth about the society in which they lived. The final winners—using Dick's term—were the Bolsheviks, even if later they wore the garb of democracy.³⁵

Like Khrushchev in the 1960s, Gorbachev did not have sufficient strength around him to carry out the giant reconstruction called for. His reforms were engulfed in a swamp of unprofessionalism and undermined by sabotage. In any revolution, including a peaceful one, the main issues are power and authority. At the early stages of perestroika, democratic instruments—glasnost, pluralism, human rights—improved respect for authority and therefore strengthened its power. The peak of this stage was 1988, when Gorbachev felt that the Communist monolith could be melted by democratization. But the reformers neglected to maintain their power, nor did they learn to make proper use of the new tools of political struggle, such as free elections and freedom of speech. In the end, those tools were better employed by the forces that were hostile to perestroika.

What Has Been Won?

Yet one should have taken up arms. Perestroika produced substantial results. Gorbachev undermined several features of the Stalinist regime: the one-party system, control by a single ideology, belligerent atheism, highly centralized administration, the economic monopoly of the state, judicial arbitrariness, and the inordinate influence of the military and the KGB. Most important, Gorbachev's initiatives eased the tension regarding unresolved fundamental problems that had been accumulating over decades. Gorbachev may very well have averted the kind of explosion that has characterized Russia's political evolution for centuries.

When Gorbachev's international accomplishments are added to the tally, perestroika's record of accomplishment becomes yet more impressive. Perestroika made Soviet-U.S. cooperation possible, which in turn lessened the burden of the arms race, brought an end to the Cold War and to ideological confrontation, and enhanced respect for human rights and thus the quality

---

34. Pipes, *The Russian Revolution*, 215.

35. Stephen Kohen, an expert on Russian affairs, speaking at a Kennan Institute symposium on October 13, 2006, has no doubts: "If you ask me who destroyed Russia, I will tell you that the blame rests with Yeltsin," adding terms like "Stalin-style destruction." I would add, with reference to already mentioned Nancy Ries, the stupidity, egoism, and sadism of the ruling elites on all levels as opposed to the intrinsic wisdom, generosity, and kindness of the grassroots people.

of life for people throughout the world. The reforms in the Soviet Union showed clearly that we won a battle—indeed, a series of battles. In the end, though, given the melancholy fall of Gorbachev, we lost the war.

Personally, perestroika, especially in its first three years, was when my hopes coincided with my actions. My only sadness is that this period was so short. In the words of the poet and diplomat Fiodor Tiutchev, "Blessed are those who visited this world in one of its fateful moments." Perestroika was, without a doubt, a fateful moment.

Index

Academy of Sciences, Soviet, 115
ACLU (American Civil Liberties Union), 30
ADA (Americans for Democratic Action), 29
Adamishin, Anatoly
   address to UN Human Rights Commission, 89, 194
   Afghanistan invasion and, 42–43, 94
   awareness of Soviet human rights violations, 133, 242
   on Bush administration, 191
   diplomatic career, 2
      effect of Schifter on, 105
      under Gromyko, 19–20
      in Italy, 16, 18–19, 160, 183, 197, 223–24, 231n10
      promotion, 22
      reengagement in human rights, 191–94
      under Shevardnadze, 84, 84n10, 93–94
      in United Kingdom, 16n16, 90
   education, 1, 9–12, 16
   on emigration, 89
   on end of perestroika, 215–231
   falsely labeled as Jewish, 22
   first meeting with Schifter, 3, 23, 94, 129–30, 132–35
   on human rights agenda, 111–25
   "kitchen talk," 20–21
   meetings with American Jewish organizations, 220
   military service, 16
   OVIR meeting, 139–40
   parents of, 8–9
   on perestroika, 224, 275
   personal history, 1, 5, 7–22
   on political prisoners, 117, 144, 146
   preparatory work done by, 240
   proposed humanitarian cooperation program, 124
   on Reagan, 81n3
   role of, 242–43
   at Ryzhkov-Thatcher meeting, 215, 215n1
   Schifter's relationship with, 2–3, 111, 132, 242–43
   Shevardnadze's relationship with, 242
   similarities between Schifter and, 1, 5, 23–24
   on Soviet breakdown, 223, 225–26
   on Soviet-U.S. relations after perestroika, 79–94
   before perestroika, 35–47
   support for reform, 142, 146n17
   Vienna Conference and, 151–60, 176–78
   written communication with Schifter, 221–22
Adamishin, Viktor, 13
Adamovich, Alesia, 123
Aeroflot, 202
Aeroflot hijacking, 124
Afghanistan
   Soviet invasion of, 39–40, 76, 224n7, 240
   Adamishin and, 42–43, 94
   cost of, 269
   Soviet withdrawal from, 41, 42, 243n10
Africa, 94, 269
Aganbegian, Abel, 215
agriculture, 266, 266n20
Aksyonov, Vassily, 21
Alber, Solomon, 90n19
alcoholism, 215n1, 265, 265n15
Aleksandrov, Andrei, 153
Alexander II, 261–62
Alexeyev, Volodia, 10
Alexeyeva, Ludmilla, 44
All Quiet on the Western Front (Remarque), 207
Almond, Mark, 259
Alpha Group, 207
al Qaeda, 43
Amalgamated Clothing Workers, 26
Amalrik, Andrei, 63, 71
American Association for the Advancement of Science, 133
American Civil Liberties Union (ACLU), 30
American Psychiatric Association, 163
Americans for Democratic Action (ADA), 29
American Veterans Committee (AVC), 28–29
Amin, Hafizullah, 40, 41
Amnesty International, 125
Andreevich, Andrei, 155
Andreotti, Giulio, 225
Andropov, Yuri, 96, 155, 265
   decision to invade Afghanistan, 40–42, 40n7
   Shultz meeting, 99
Angola, 94
anti-alcohol campaign, 215n1, 265, 265n15
anti-Semitism, 58–60
Arbatov, Georgi, 153
Armenia
   earthquake, 216, 216n3
   emigration, 131, 137–38, 143, 162, 239

277

Freedom House ranking, 248
Armenian Helsinki Group, 73
arms control
  as factor in Soviet democratization, 145
  during Gorbachev years, 4, 38, 81, 81n4, 127–28, 137–38
  link to human rights, 2, 6, 129, 145, 180, 237, 239
  Reykjavik summit, 81, 105, 237
  at Vienna Conference, 158–59, 162, 180
  Washington summit, 142–45
arms race, 17, 36–37
Article 70, 116
Article 83, 190
Article 188, 171
Article 190-1, 116, 147
Article 227, 171
artists, 15, 15n15, 120–21
Asian matrix, 261
August coup attempt, 206–13, 227–29, 247, 255
Austria, Soviet treaty with, 17
automotive plants, 22, 45, 152
AVC (American Veterans Committee), 28–29

Bakatin, Vadim, 198, 199, 209–12, 227
Baker, Jim, 165
  on end of Cold War, 250–51
  Gorbachev meeting, 254
  Moscow visit, 220–21
  on perestroika, 250, 252, 255
  on Shevardnadze, 186, 186n8
  Shevardnadze meetings, 186, 190–91, 221, 251, 253–54
  Soviet relations policy, 184–86
Baltic states. *See also specific state*
  Freedom House ranking, 248
  NATO membership, 264n11
  secession of, 194, 227, 244–46
Baturin, Yuri, 119
Bea, Agostino, 18
Belgrade Conference, 75–76, 98, 151, 156
Belovezhskaya Puscha Accords, 230
Beria, Lavrenty, 11, 11n6, 56–57, 112, 115, 147, 147n18
Berlin, Isaiah, 20
Berlin Wall, fall of, 244
Beschloss, Michael, 47
Bessmertnykh, Aleksandr, 229
bezglasnost, 262
bill of rights, international, preparation of, 53–54
Bill of Rights (U.S.), 97
bin Laden, Osama, 43
Blatov, Anatoly, 40n7, 153, 155
Bobkov, Fillip, 157
Boldin, 231

Bolshevik movement, 24, 49
  end of, 180
  media control by, 119
  naval revolt against, 32
Bonner, Yelena, 72
Bonnie, Richard J., 114, 115, 187
border disputes, 67–70
Bovin, Aleksandr, 153
Bowles, Chester, 51
brain drain, prevention of, 62, 88
Brandt, Willy, 152
Brasinzkas, 124
Brezhnev, Leonid, 11–12
  Adamishin's career under, 19–20
  arms race, 37
  artists persecuted by, 15n15
  assault on intellectuals, 19–20
  on CSCE conference, 153–54
  decision to invade Afghanistan, 40n7, 41
  emigration during rule of, 21
  on Fenwick, 74
  on Helsinki Final Act, 69
  on human rights, 45
  Nixon summit meeting, 66–67
  political repression under, 96, 116
  U.S. relations with, 57, 95
Brezhnev Doctrine, 80
Brodsky, Iosif, 20
Bronfman, Edgar, 47
Bukovski, Vladimir, 14, 114n4
Bulgakov, Mikhail, 122n18, 265n13
Bulgaria, 98, 244
Bund, 27–28
bureaucracy, as obstacle, 266–67
Bureau of European Affairs (U.S. State Department), 103–06, 150, 167, 168n2
Bureau of Human Rights (U.S. State Department), 103–09, 186–87
Bush, George H. W.
  Adamishin's view of, 191
  at Chernenko's funeral, 4, 89, 101
  compared to Reagan, 185, 217, 251
  failure to support perestroika, 254–57, 263–64
  on Gorbachev, 101–02
  Gorbachev meeting, 82, 89–90, 186, 196–97, 251
  Gorbachev's view of, 217, 251
  human rights policy, 186–87
  as realist, 165, 185, 251
  skepticism about perestroika, 249–54
  Soviet relations policy, 183–86, 196–202, 216–17, 249–54
Byelorussia, 229

Index

Cannonites, 24
capitalist ideology, versus socialism, 80–81, 104
Carter, Jimmy
  human rights policy, 44, 70, 76, 82, 95, 154
  response to Afghanistan invasion, 41
  Soviet view of, 46, 46n20
  trade policy, 46
Catherine the Great, 260
Catholic Church
  as Helsinki Final Act author, 154
  relations between Communists and, 18
  Ukrainian, 134, 241
Ceausescu, Nicolae, 219
Central Committee (CPSU)
  on emigration policy, 88
  Human Rights Section, 188–90
  Ideology Department, 189
  motion calling for Gorbachev's resignation, 206
  on Paris Conference, 190
  on psychiatric incarceration, 114
Central Intelligence Agency (CIA), 185
Chasov, Evgeny, 115, 157, 163
Chebrikov, Viktor, 15n14, 116
Cheney, Dick, 252
Chernenko, Konstantin, 4, 89, 101, 267
Chernobyl disaster, 216, 265
Chernyaev, Anatoly, 88, 271
Chetverikov, Sergey, 168
CIA (Central Intelligence Agency), 185
civil rights
  versus social/economic rights, 96–98
  in Soviet totalitarian system, 115, 129–30
Clifford, Clark, 54–55
Clinton administration, 264n11
Coalition for a Democratic Majority, 33
Cold War, 1, 33–34, 54–57
  end of, 151, 237, 242
    different interpretations of, 250–51
    Gorbachev's role in, 233
    Soviet-American relations at, 149–50
collective farm system (Soviet), 98
College of City of New York, 24–28
Commission on Human Rights. *See* United Nations Human Rights Commission
Commission on Rehabilitation of Political Repression's Victims, 8n1
Commission on Security and Cooperation in Europe (Helsinki Commission), 95, 95n1
Committee on Human Rights, 70
Committee on the Present Danger, 33
Communism
  Schifter's ideological opposition to, 24–30, 34
  Soviet assistance for international, 269, 269n24

Communist(s)
  in American Veterans Committee, 28–29
  in Hollywood, 27, 30–31, 95
  relations between Catholics and, 18
  Schifter falsely labeled as, 28n6
  U.S. legislation against, 30–31
  at Yale Law School, 29–30
Communist apparatchiks, opposition to Gorbachev, 195–96
Communist Party of France, 76
Communist Party of the Soviet Union (CPSU)
  Central Committee (*See* Central Committee)
  democratization and, 120, 195–96, 211–12, 217, 269
  interference in legal system, 93
  role of, 271
  Schifter's visit to, 163
  three political movements within, 196
  totalitarian system under, 234
  "Toward a Human, Democratic Socialism" program, 263
Communist Party of the United States, 25–32, 95
Communist propaganda, 270
Communist youth movements
  American, 25
  Soviet, 1, 9
Conference on Security and Cooperation in Europe (CSCE), 67–70
  as bridge to détente, 151
  Human Rights Experts Meeting, 102
  military aspects of, 158–59
  Soviet view on, 169
  topics ("baskets"), 156, 157
  U.S. Congressional Commission, 171
  U.S. participation in, 152–53, 197
Congress (U.S.). *See also specific member of Congress*
CSCE Commission, 171
  Helsinki Commission, 95, 95n1
  Helsinki Final Act monitoring, 74–75
  role in foreign policy, 45–46, 57–58
  Soviet Jewry issue and, 58–67
Congress of Industrial Organization, 75n39
Congress of People's Deputies, 42, 195, 217–18
Congress of Winners (Seventeenth Party Congress), 11n7
Constitutional Review Commission, 188
consumer prices, 216
conventional forces in Europe (CFE), treaty for reduction of, 166
Copenhagen Conference, 159
Council of Europe, 160
Council of the Republics, 208
Council of the Union, 208

coup, failed, 206–13, 227–29, 247, 255
CPSU. *See* Communist Party of the Soviet Union
criminal code (Soviet)
  political and religious activities, 73–74, 130–31
  reform of (*See* legal reform)
CSCE. *See* Conference on Security and Cooperation in Europe
Cuba, Soviet assistance to, 269
Cuban Missile Crisis, 16–17, 33, 56, 140
cultural rights, versus political/civil rights, 96–98
culture, democratization and, 120–21
Czechoslovakia
  anti-Semitism in, 59
  Charter 77 movement, 76
  Soviet intervention in, 41
  Velvet Revolution, 244
Czechoslovak Spring (1968), 19, 80, 152, 224, 224n7

Daniel, Yuly, 19
Daniloff, Nicholas, 105
death penalty
  in Soviet Union, 93, 116
  in the United States, 124
Declaration for the Rights of Those Who Work and Are Being Exploited, 82
defamation, Soviet criminal code on, 73–74, 140, 147, 241
demandeur, the United States as, 240
De Michelis, Gianni, 225
democratization
  arms control as factor in, 145
  characteristics of, 269–70
  economic reform and, 216
  under Gorbachev, 120, 144, 184, 193–94, 195–96, 199, 233, 235, 249, 262–63, 269–70, 274
  history of, 259–61
  opposition to, 195–96, 195n17
  role of, 259
  rule of law and, 195, 198, 210–11
  Schifter's view on, 200, 207
  Shevardnadze's view of, 203–04
  Soviet power structure and, 210, 274
  U.S. support for, 233, 254
Deng Xiaoping, 267
Deriabin, Yuri, 159
détente
  first steps toward, 17–19, 17n17, 36–37, 57
  Nixon's goal of, 61
  Vienna Follow-Up Meeting and, 151
DeWitt Clinton High School (New York), 24

dissidents (Soviet), 44, 70–77, 117–18. *See also specific person*
  incarceration of (*See* political prisoners; psychiatric incarceration)
Djilas, M., 114n4
Dobrynin, Anatoly
  on Carter, 46n20
  goals for Soviet-U.S. relations, 36n2
  Reagan meeting, 99
  on Soviet Jewry issue, 58, 61, 66
  on trade-emigration link, 45–47
doctors' plot (1953), 60
Doctor Zhivago (Pasternak), 15
Dubinsky, David, 26
Dumas, Roland, 267

Economic and Social Council (UN), 53
economic assistance, foreign, 225, 225n8, 254, 263
economic planning, 267–68
economic repercussions, of perestroika, 215–16, 225, 227, 273
economic rights, versus political/civil rights, 96–98
Ehrenburg, Ilia, 14n13
Eidelman, Natan, 20
Eisenhower, Dwight, 17
elderly services, exchange programs on, 150, 198, 205
elections, free, 193, 197, 217–18
emigration
  by Armenians, 131, 137–38, 143, 162, 239
  congressional intercession on, 239–40
  currency exchange and, 88
  decree on, 88–90, 176, 220
  effect of perestroika on, 79, 85–87
  by ethnic Russians, 85, 131, 135, 143
  to European countries, 201
  historical prohibition on, 85
  on human rights agenda, 111, 191, 201
  ideological battle over, 87–88
  importance in U.S. agenda, 142–43
  as issue at Vienna Conference, 133–34, 158, 162, 170–73, 176
  Jewish (*See* Jewish emigration)
  by Pentecostal Christians, 137–38, 162, 239
  potential groups for, 137–38, 143, 162
  quota policy, 143
  refusal of (*See* refuseniks; *specific person*)
  right of
    under Helsinki Final Act, 73, 86, 154
    progress in gaining, 135–41, 162, 239–40
    restrictions on, 131–32
  statistics on, 86n12, 123–24, 203, 221
  to the United States, 90–91, 138, 163–64

Index

by Volga Germans, 90, 131, 137–38, 143, 162, 239
voluntary, 21, 26–27
energy exports, reliance on, 267–68
Enlightenment, 49, 96, 194, 207, 256
Entin, Vladimir, 119
equal opportunity
  Soviet belief in, during postwar years, 9–10
  Soviet Jewry and, 59–60, 131
Estonia, 227
ethnic Russians, emigration by, 85, 131, 135, 138, 143
EUR. *See* Bureau of European Affairs
European countries. *See also specific country*
  emigration to, 201
European security conference. *See* Conference on Security and Cooperation in Europe
exchange programs
  judiciary, 193, 198, 205–06
  social services, 150, 198, 205
Export-Import Bank, 64, 149–50
extrajudicial practice, 116–17, 206

Falin, V., 271n28
Fanfani, Amintore, 18
fear, culture of, 13
Fedotov, Mikhail, 119
Fenwick, Millicent, 74–75
Fiat, 22, 45, 152
Final Act. *See* Helsinki Final Act
first-degree relative requirement (*vyzov*), 138, 140, 143, 145–46
Fischer, Louis, 31–32
Foley, Thomas, 220
food supply, 215, 225, 266, 266n18, 268
Ford, 45
Ford, Gerald, 46, 64, 75
foreign assistance
  economic, 225, 225n8, 254, 263
  from Soviet Union, 269, 269n24
foreign policy
  formulation of, 57–58
  importance of Soviet-American relations in, 35–36, 95, 104
Franklin, Benjamin, 246
Freedom House report, 248, 256
freedom of expression, 111, 118–20, 130–31, 241
freedom of religion, 117–18, 134, 241
  legal restrictions on, 73–74, 130–31, 140
  as Vienna Conference issue, 169, 171, 176
Freeh, Louis, 28n6
French Communist Party, 76
Frolov, Ivan, 223
frontiers, inviolability of, 68, 154

Gagarin, Yuri, 16
Gaidar, Timur, 39
Gamsakhurdia, Zviad, 194, 194n16, 227
Gates, Robert, 185, 185n4, 186, 252
Geneva Accords, 42
Geneva meeting, Reagan-Gorbachev, 81, 94, 102–03, 235
Genscher, Hans-Dietrich, 83n7
Georgia
  Freedom House ranking, 248
  independence, 194, 227–28, 246
Georgian Helsinki Group, 73
German Democratic Republic, 219
Germany
  border dispute, 67, 69
  democracy in, 256
  Nazi, 50–51
  Ostpolitik (Eastern policy), 152
  reunification of, 220, 244, 264
  Schifter's military career in, 28–29, 50, 54n3
gerontocracy, 21, 266
glasnost (openness), 217
  discrimination against Jews and, 131n7
  freedom of expression and, 119
  intellectual life and, 121–22
  role of, 259, 274
  Schifter on, 106–07
Glorious October Revolution, 3, 180
Glukhov, Alexei, 84n10, 143, 145, 147–48, 163
  Schifter meeting, 168, 171–72
Gogol, Nikolai, 260, 265n13
Goldberg, Arthur, 70
  background, 75n39
  at Belgrade conference, 75–76, 98
  on Soviet Jewry issue, 58
Gorbachev, Mikhail, 79–109
  Andreotti meeting, 225
  anti-alcohol campaign, 265
  arms control efforts, 4, 38, 81, 81n4, 127–28, 137–38
  attacks on U.S. human rights violations, 102, 103
  Bakatin's view of, 210–11
  Baker meeting, 254
  on Bush administration, 217, 251
  Bush meeting, 82, 89–90, 186, 196–97, 251
  Central Committee's call for resignation of, 206
  on Communist Party, 271
  compared with Yeltsin, 247
  coup attempt against, 206–13, 227–29, 247, 255
  decision to quit Afghanistan, 41, 42
  decline in power of, 227–28
  democratization by, 120, 144, 184, 193–94, 195–96, 199, 233, 235, 249, 262–63, 269–70, 274

divisional periods, 235
early personal experience with totalitarianism, 144n16, 236n3
election as general secretary, 101, 234
emigration policy, 88–90, 90n18
on foreign aid, 269n24
foreign policy revolutionized by, 80–82, 82
freedom of expression under, 118–20
gerontocracy pushed out by, 12
human rights policy, 4, 5, 45, 81, 83, 102, 142, 160, 233
idealist support for, 236
Jackson-Vanik amendment and, 47
on KGB, 271
legal reform under, 91–93, 117
military leadership and, 199
Ministry of Foreign Affairs and, 84
mistakes made by, 215, 231, 231n11, 272
Moscow summit meeting, 149–50
on one-party system, 84n11, 119
opposition to, 195–96, 203, 206, 212, 225, 227, 245–46
perestroika (*See* perestroika)
political prisoners released by, 116–17, 127, 134, 235, 241
public opinion of, 247, 249, 259
on Reagan, 239
Reagan meetings, 81, 94, 102–03, 235
Reagan's view of, 27
on religious freedom, 118
repudiation of Leninism by, 174
respect for Soviet people, 263n8, 266
role of, 1, 233–39, 257, 262–63, 271–72, 274
on rule of law, 174
Sakharov's release by, 108, 116, 235
Schifter's tribute to, 213
Shevardnadze's view of, 204, 226–27
on Shultz, 257n30
Shultz meeting, 4, 128, 134–37, 142
Shultz's relationship with, 237n7, 238
Shultz's view of, 4, 128
Shvernik Commission, 15n14
on Soviet-U.S. relations, 238–39
at Stalin's funeral, 10
Thatcher's view of, 4, 234
on travel permits, 87, 120–21
UN General Assembly speech, 173–74, 177, 178, 217, 243, 251
"universal human values" defined by, 156n5
U.S. support for, reduction in, 183–86, 264
U.S. view of, 101–03, 234–36
Vienna Conference and, 156–57, 162, 181
Washington summit meeting, 142–45
Grachev, Andrei, 81
grain embargo, 46n18
Great Patriotic War. *See* World War II

Griboyedov, Aleksandr, 269n25
Grigorenko, Pyotr, 112
Gromyko, Andrei
Adamishin's career under, 19–20
on Afghanistan invasion, 39–42
alcoholism report ignored by, 265
on arms race, 37, 38
on Cuban Missile Crisis, 17
on human rights, 154
on internal diplomacy, 153
on Jewish emigration, 64
leadership style, 84n10, 269
at Madrid Conference, 155, 155n3
political ambition of, 267
proposal of CSCE conference, 152
Shultz meeting, 99, 100
on UNESCO, 122
Gronchi, Giovanni, 18n18
Grossman, Vassily, 121–22
Group of Seven/Eight, 236n5, 249
Gubenko, Nikolai, 122
Guggenheim Museum, 220
The Gulag Archipelago (Solzhenitsyn), 71
gulags, 9, 13, 13n10, 15, 115–16, 132, 133. *See also* political prisoners
Gulf War, 244n11, 264

HA. *See* Human Rights Bureau
handicapped services, exchange programs on, 150, 198, 205
Helsinki Commission, 95, 95n1
Helsinki Final Act, 67–70, 68–70
authors of, 154
emigration rights under, 73, 86, 154
monitoring of
by Soviet dissidents, 71–72, 99, 127
by U.S., 74–75
as nonbinding, 144n15, 154
Second Follow-Up Meeting, 96
signing of, 151
Soviet compliance with, 144, 172, 173, 220
Soviet democratization and, 212
violations of, 76
Helsinki Group, 72–75, 74
Helsinki Process. *See* Conference on Security and Cooperation in Europe
Herzen, Alexander, 118
Hill, Charlie, 140
Hillman, Sidney, 26
Hiss, Alger, 30
Hitler-Stalin Pact, 32, 246
Hollywood (California), Communist movement in, 27, 30–31, 95
Holocaust, 50–51, 58
Hoover Institution, 122n18
Housing Act of 1937 (U.S.), 52

Index 283

human rights
  arms control linked to, 2, 6, 129, 145, 180, 237, 239
  differing definitions of, 96–98
  effect on U.S.-Soviet relations, in pre-Gorbachev period, 5–6
  goal-oriented dialogue on, 127–32
  Helsinki Final Act concerning (*See* Helsinki Final Act)
  in international relations field, 49–51, 65, 76–77, 95–98, 197
  post–World War II evolution of, 5–6
  Soviet Jewry and, 61–67 (*See also* Jewish emigration)
  Soviet progress in, 137–41, 162–64
    at end of perestroika, 219–20
    measurement of, 135–37
  Soviet view of, before perestroika, 43–44, 49
  trade linked to, 45–47, 62–67
  U.S. view of
    after perestroika, 95–96, 98–101
    before perestroika, 54–55, 65, 76–77
  U.S. violations of, Gorbachev's attacks on, 102, 103
human rights advocates (Soviet), 70–77
human rights agendas, 111–50
  issues on, 111, 130–32, 191, 241–42
  new versus old, 188, 191, 196–202, 220–22, 249
  preparatory work for, 240–41
  widening of, 123–25
Human Rights Bureau (U.S. State Department), 103–09, 186–87
Human Rights Commission. *See* United Nations Human Rights Commission
human rights documents. *See also specific document*
  binding versus nonbinding, 144n15, 155–56
  failure to comply with, 155–56
  U.S. failure to sign, 156
Humphrey, Hubert, 29
Hungarian CSCE delegation, 102
Hungarian minority, in Romania, 219
Hungarian revolt (1956), 16, 16n16, 32, 80
Hussein, Saddam, 244n11

Ibarrury, Dolores, 12
ideological battles
  between capitalism and socialism, 80–81, 104
  over emigration, 87–88
  between realist and idealist camps, 165–66, 185, 236, 251, 256
Indian tribes (American), legal representation of, 52
intelligentsia
  Soviet
    Brezhnev's assault on, 19–20

    democratization and, 249
    perestroika and, 120–22, 184
  U.S., impact of Communists on, 30
Intermediate-Range Nuclear Forces Treaty, 142
international cooperation, Soviet view of, 111
International Covenant on Civil and Political Rights, 53–54, 69
  as binding, 144n15, 156
  emigration rights under, 86
  prisoners of conscience and, 141–42
  Soviet compliance with, 144, 241–42
International Covenant on Economic, Social, and Cultural Rights, 53–54
International Ladies Garment Workers Union, 26
International Monetary Fund, 254, 263
International Red Cross, 197
international relations, human rights as issue in, 49–51, 65, 76–77, 95–98, 197
Ioseliani, Otar, 121
Iraq, invasion of Kuwait, 250
Iron Curtain, 265
Isaacson, Walter, 62, 66
Israel
  emigration to, 46, 90n18, 138, 163–64
  Schifter's visit to, 164
  Six-Day War, 60, 85
Italy
  Adamishin's diplomatic service in, 16, 18–19, 160, 183, 197, 223–24, 231n10
  relations with Russia, 152, 229–30
  Soviet request for loan from, 225, 225n8
  as waystation for Jewish emigration, 163–64
Ivan III (Tsar), 261
Ivanov, Igor, 227
Ivan the Terrible, 261
Izvestia, 69

Jackson, Henry M., 46, 62, 62n13. *See also* Jackson-Vanik amendment
Jackson Hole (Wyoming), Baker-Shevardnadze meeting in, 186, 186n8
Jackson-Vanik amendment, 45–46, 62–67, 240–41
  ethnic Russian migrants and, 135
  precedent set by, 65–66
  repeal of, Soviet hopes for, 220
  text of, 63
Japan, 256
Jaruzelski, Wojciech, 40n7
Jewish emigration, 137–38
  exit tax on, 62, 63
  historical perspective on, 85
  to Israel, 46, 90n18, 138, 163–64
  as issue at Vienna CSCE conference, 133–34, 162

restrictions on, 131–32
statistics on, 61, 65, 65n19, 86n12, 96, 123, 143, 239
trade linked to, 45–47
U.S. emphasis on, 138–39
vyzov requirement, 138, 140, 143, 145–46
Washington rally on behalf of, 142
Jewish population (Soviet), 10n3
discrimination against, 58–60, 131
Johnson, Lyndon, 45
John XXIII (Pope), 18
judicial reform. *See* legal reform
judiciary exchange programs, 193, 198, 205–06
jury system, 188, 198

Kahane, Meir, 45
Kampelman, Max, 75n39, 96, 100, 149
Kapitsa, Mikhail, 21n24
Kashlev, Yuri, 105, 106, 157, 158, 159
Kennedy, John F., 17, 18, 58
KGB, 148
  Alpha Group, 207
  democratization and, 212
  on emigration policy, 88
  Helsinki Group and, 72, 74
  psychiatric incarceration and, 114, 130
  religious groups and, 241
  role of, 271
Khasbulatov, 231
Khrushchev, Nikita
  Adamishin meeting, 18n18
  antimilitary measures, 16
  arms race, 37
  communist ideology, 80
  Cuban Missile Crisis, 16–17, 56
  inconsistent policies of, 14–15
  political death of, 18–19
  political repression under, 116
  thaw, 13–14, 57, 262
  totalitarian system under, 234
  Twentieth Party Congress speech, 11–13
    effect on American Communism, 27, 31–32
    international aspects of, 15–17, 57
  Western relations with, 17–19, 57
Khrushchev, Sergei, 18n19
Khrushcheva, Julia, 19n20, 21
Kiev, 7–8, 13
King, Rodney, 202
Kirkpatrick, Jeane, 33–34
Kishinev pogrom (1903), 59
Kissinger, Henry
  on CSCE conference, 153
  on Helsinki Final Act, 69, 74–75
  on Jackson-Vanik amendment, 63–66
  as realist, 165

on Soviet Jewry issue, 58, 61–62, 66–67
Soviet-U.S. relations under, 57, 239
"kitchen talk," 20–21, 270
Klimov, Elem, 20, 270
Kohan, John, 88n15
Kohen, Stephen, 274n35
Kohl, Helmut, 263
Kolokol (magazine), 118
Kolosov, Sergei, 20
Komplektov, Viktor, 43n13
Komsomol, 1, 9
Kornienko, Georgy, 38
Korotich, Vitaly, 121, 121n16
Koryagin, Anatoly, 109, 109n22
Kosovo, 264n11
Kostin, Andrei, 117n13
Kosygin, Alexei, 19, 22, 267
Kovalev, Anatoly, 84, 123, 153, 158, 168–72
Kovalev, Sergey, 44n16, 212
Kozyrev, Semen, 14n13, 18
Kravchuk, Leonid, 229, 230
Krens, Thomas, 220
Kronstadt rebellion, 31–32
Kryuchkov, Sergey, 148
Kryuchkov, Vladimir, 148, 207, 217, 228
Kulakov, 266n20
Kuvalda, Peter, 91
Kuwait, Iraqi invasion of, 250
Kvitsinsky, Yuli, 229, 259

labor code (Soviet), reform of, 92–93
labor movement (U.S.), 26–27, 32
Landsberghis, 227
La Pira, Giorgio, 18
Laptiev, Ivan, 203, 208–09
Latvia, 227
law enforcement, reform of, 199
Lebyedev, Vyacheslav, 203, 205–06
Leffler, Melvyn, 37n4, 83n6
left-wing opposition, to Gorbachev, 195–96, 206, 245–46
legal reform (Soviet), 91–93, 188–91. *See also* rule of law
  after Vienna Conference, 159, 169
  Gorbachev's UN speech on, 174
  on mental health issues, 115
  political prisoners and, 117, 132, 140, 241
  prisoners of conscience and, 142
  Soviet-U.S. cooperation on, 193, 197–99, 202, 205–06
legislation
  against Communists, in the United States, 30–31
  Helsinki Final Act monitoring, 74–75
lend-lease debt, 45–46
Lenin, Vladimir, 49, 93, 189

Leninism
  collapse of, 98
  repudiation of, 174, 243, 251
Levitsky, Mel, 166
l'Humanite (newspaper), 76
Lichachev, Dmitri, 123
Life and Destiny (Grossman), 122
Ligachev, Yegor, 119, 121, 121n16, 245
"line 5 problem," 60
Linnas, Karl, 124
literature under glasnost, 121–22
Lithuania, 224, 227
Lithuanian Helsinki Group, 73
loans
  Export-Import Bank, 64, 149–50
  International Monetary Fund, 254, 263
  from Italy, 225, 225n8
Longo, Gigi, 12n8
Louis XIV, 260
loyalty-security program (U.S.), 30–31
Lublin (Poland), 50
Lukianov, Anatoly, 119
Lukin, Vladimir, 90
Lyubimov, Yuri, 21, 122

Madrid Conference, 96, 151, 155, 156
Major, Frederic, 123
Malenkov, Georgy, 17, 17n17, 19n20
Malta meeting, Bush-Gorbachev, 82, 186, 196–97, 251
Manege (Moscow), 15
Mao Zedong, 62
Marcantonio, Vito, 26n2
Marxism-Leninism, in postwar Soviet Union, 9
mass media
  freedom of, 118–20 (*See also* freedom of expression)
  U.S., coverage of Soviet issues, 189–90
Materials Policy Commission, 52
Matlock, Jack, 168
  on emigration, 89n17, 157n6
  on Gorbachev, 168n3, 272n29
  Komplektov meeting, 43n13
  on military-industrial complex, 264n12
  on Soviet surveillance technology, 270n26
  Vienna Conference and, 175, 176
M'Bow, Amadou-Mahtar, 123
McCarthy, Joseph, 30–31
McGovern, George, 33
medium-range missiles (SS-20s), 37–38
Meir, Golda, 13
Melekhin, Gennadiy, 125
mental illness, institutionalization for. *See* psychiatric incarceration
Mercuriev, Stanislav, 123

Metropolitan Uvenaly, 123
militarization (Soviet)
  economic effects of, 37, 216, 268
  emphasis on, 265, 268
military aspects, of Soviet-American relations, 33, 55. *See also* arms control
military coup, failed, 206–13, 227–29, 247, 255
military-industrial complex (U.S.), influence of, 264, 264n12
military service
  by Adamishin, 16
  by Schifter, 28–29, 50
Ministry of Foreign Affairs (Soviet)
  collegium meeting on Afghanistan, 39
  coup attempt and, 229
  disputes with other Soviet agencies, 94, 145–48
  Humanitarian Department, 83–85, 117, 168, 192
  ideological objection to emigration, 87–88
  implementation of Vienna Conference by, 159
  party layer in, 269
  on psychiatric incarceration, 113–15
  working group on human rights, 93–94
Ministry of Health (Soviet), 114–15
Ministry of the Interior (Soviet), 146
Mirski, Prince Sviatopolk, 262
missiles, 37–38, 129. *See also* Cuban Missile Crisis
Moldova, 248
Molotov, Vyacheslav, 13, 59, 67
Mongolia, 256n26, 261
Moscovskie Novosti (magazine), 121
Moscow
  Adamishin's early career in, 19–20
  Adamishin's early life in, 8–9
  Baker's visit to, 220–21
  human rights conference in, 2, 125, 125n19, 159–60
  proposal for, 135–36, 157, 161–62
  Manege exhibitions, 15
  Reagan-Gorbachev summit meeting, 149–50
  rule of law seminar in, 193
  Schifter's May 1989 visit to, 188–91
  U.S. embassy in, Siberian Seven at, 77, 99–100, 138, 256
Moscow University, 9–12, 16, 60
most-favored-nation status, human rights linked to, 46, 62–67

Nagy, Ferenc, 32
Na Taganke (theater), 21, 122
National Institute of Mental Health (U.S.), 197
nationalities problem. *See also specific group*

Baker-Shevardnadze discussion about, 190
  Gorbachev's misreading of, 272
  perestroika and, 194–96
  during Soviet breakdown, 223, 227–28, 244–46, 272–73
National Security Council, U.S., 105–06, 161
NATO
  arms race, 37–38, 166
  European security conference (*See* Conference on Security and Cooperation in Europe)
  former Warsaw Pact countries joining, 264n11
Nazi extradition, 124
Nazi Germany, 50–51
needle trades unions, 26
neoconservatives, 33
Netherlands, 38, 91, 138
"the new agenda," 3
New Class (Djilas), 114n4
New Deal, 24–26, 97
New Deal–Fair Deal program, 29
New Delhi (India), 51–52
New Left, 33
New York Times, 51, 72, 74, 148
Nicholas I (Tsar), 85
Nicholas II (Tsar), 270
Nikitin, Sergei, 21
Nikitin, Tatiana, 21
Nitze, Paul, 33
Nixon, Richard
  arms control treaty, 153
  Brezhnev meeting, 66–67
  on CSCE conference, 153
  Khrushchev meeting, 17
  Mao meeting, 62
  Soviet-U.S. relations under, 57, 61–62, 239
  trade policy, 45–46
NKVD, 112, 112n, 147
Nobel Prize, 15, 20, 70
Novgorod, 260–61
Novoe Vremia (magazine), 114n4
nuclear arms race, 17, 37–38, 37n4
Nudel, Ida, 141

Office of Visas and Registration (OVIR), 139–40
Ogonek (magazine), 121
oil prices, 267–68
Okudzhava, Bulat, 14, 270
One Day in the Life of Ivan Denisovich (Solzhenitsyn), 15
Orlov, Yuri, 70, 71–72, 74, 76
Oslo Conference, 213
Osten-Saken, Baron, 21n23
OVIR (Office of Visas and Registration), 139–40

Paragraph 64 cases, 211
Paris, Adamishin-Schifter meeting in, 192
Paris Conference, 159, 190
Pasternak, Boris, 15
Paul I (Emperor), 21n23
Pavlov, Valentin, 207, 228
Pella, Giuseppe, 18n18
penal code
  Russian Federation, 112
  Soviet, reform of (*See* legal reform)
Pentecostal Christians
  emigration by, 137–38, 162, 239
  Soviet treatment of, 77, 99–100, 256
perestroika, 82–83
  Adamishin's view of, 224, 275
  attempted coup and, 228–29, 247, 255
  Bush administration's skepticism about, 249–54
  democratization under, 120
  economic repercussions of, 215, 225, 227, 273
  effect on Soviet-American relations, 79, 111
  emigration policy and, 85–87
  end of, 183–31
  failure of, Western contribution to, 254–57, 263–64
  freedom of expression under, 118–20
  Gorbachev's preparation for, 271–72
  intelligentsia and, 120–22
  legal reform and, 91–93, 115, 117, 130–32
  nationalities problem and, 194–96
  opposition to, 226, 273
  political amnesty during, 116–17, 127
  religious freedom under, 118
  results of, 274–75
  role of, 259
  travel permits, 121
  Universal Declaration of Human Rights and, 155n5
  Vienna Conference and, 162
Perm 36, 133
Pershing-2 missiles, 37–38
Petrovich, Yuri, 122
Petrovskiy, Vladimir, 197, 200–02, 200n22
Pimen, Patriarch, 118
Pipes, Richard, 44n16, 80n2, 273
Pisarev, Sergei, 112
Plekhanov, Georgi, 259
poets, role of Russian, 122
Poland
  border dispute, 67, 69
  labor movement in, 27–28
  Schifter's parents in, 50
  street demonstrations in, 16
police brutality (U.S.), 202
police force (Soviet), decentralization of, 199

Politburo
  freedom of conscience law, 118
  media law, 119–20
  totalitarian system under, 234
  on UNESCO, 122
political prisoners, 111, 115–16. *See also* gulags; prisoners of conscience; psychiatric incarceration
  Adamishin on, 117, 144
  on human rights agenda, 191–93, 201, 222, 241
  as issue at Vienna CSCE conference, 133–34, 158
  legal reform and, 73–74, 117, 132
  release of, 116–17, 127, 140, 235, 241
    reciprocity for, 146–47
  statistics on, 115–16, 116n11
  trumped-up charges, 171–72
  in the United States, 117, 146–47, 192–93, 201
political rights, versus social/economic rights, 96–98
political science experts, in humanitarian working group, 125
Ponomarev, Boris, 41
poor-relative cases, 220–21
Popov, Gavriil, 203, 204–05
Potsdam agreement, 54, 54n3, 153
Powell, Colin, 185
power structure, Soviet democratization and, 210, 274
Poznan (Poland), 16
presidential system, 204
pretrial incarceration, 93
price reform, 216
prisoners of conscience, 111, 117–18, 130–32. *See also* political prisoners
  decline in, 162
  release of, 132, 176
  Schifter's work on behalf of, 141–42, 171, 193, 200–01
propaganda, Communist, 270
prosecutor's office, role of, 188
psychiatric incarceration, 109, 109n22, 112–13
  American visit investigating, 114–15, 162–63, 170, 187, 189–90, 197
  under Andropov, 96
  as CSCE conference issue, 157, 169
  end of, 132, 140, 144, 162
  on human rights agenda, 111, 130, 132, 191, 241
  statistics on, 112–13
Public Group of Assistance to Implementation of the Helsinki Agreements in the USSR, 72–75
public opinion (Soviet)
  of Gorbachev, 247, 249, 259
  of Soviet breakdown, 244–46
  of the United States, 264n11
  of Yeltsin, 247
public opinion (U.S.)
  of emigration issue, 142–43
  role in foreign policy formulation, 58
  of Soviet Union, 4, 55–56, 95, 103
public organizations, compulsory registration of, 120
publishing houses, 120–21
Puerto Rican nationalists, as political prisoners, 146–47
Pugo, Boris, 207, 209–10, 228
Pushkin, Aleksandr, 11
Putin, Vladimir, 12, 244n11, 248–49, 255–56

radio broadcasts, Soviet jamming of, 76, 158, 174
Radio Moscow, 207
Ratford, David, 125
Reagan, Ronald
  Adamishin's view of, 81n3
  capitalist ideology, 80
  compared with Bush (George H.W.), 185, 217, 251
  Dobrynin meeting, 99
  early experience with Communism, 27, 95
  Gorbachev meetings, 81, 94, 102–03, 235
  Gorbachev's view of, 239
  human rights policy, 79, 99–100
  as idealist, 236–37
  internal administrative disputes, 185
  Jewish emigration and, 138
  Moscow summit meeting, 149–50
  on nuclear war, 37n4
  presidential campaign, 95
  role of, 238
  Schifter's vote for, 33
  on Soviet Jewry issue, 58
  Soviet-U.S. relations under, 1, 236–38, 253, 256–57
  Soviet view of, 4
  Washington summit meeting, 142–45
realist camp, versus idealist camp, 165–66, 185, 236, 251, 256
red directors, opposition to economic reform, 216
Refugee Act of 1980 (U.S.), 164
refuseniks, 90n19, 91. *See also specific person*
  on human rights agenda, 191, 192, 201, 220–22
  release of, 140–41, 174
  for security concerns, 88, 134, 147–48
  Shultz meeting with, 132, 134–35, 256–57
  Shultz-Shevardnadze discussion about, 138
  statistics on, 123, 159, 162, 170

as Vienna Conference issue, 133–34, 157, 157n7, 162, 170–73
religion. *See also specific religion*
  freedom of (*See* freedom of religion)
  as obstacle to democracy, 261
  Soviet persecution of, 77
Religious Affairs Commission (Soviet), 134
Remarque, Erich Maria, 207
Reshetov, Yuri, 140–41, 144, 202
Reuters, 72–73
Reykjavik summit, 81, 105, 237
Ridgway, Roz, 103, 168n2
Ries, Nancy, 259, 274n35
right-wing opposition, to Gorbachev, 195–96, 245–46
Rogers, William, 66
Romania, 219, 244
Romanov dynasty, 49
Roosevelt, Eleanor, 29, 53, 97
Roosevelt, Franklin Delano, 24–25
Roosevelt, Theodore, 59
Rosenberg, Julius, 30
Rostow, Eugene, 33
Rostropovich, Mstislav, 21
Rostropovich, Vishnevskaia, 21
Roth, Loren, 163, 187
Rubenstein, Eli, 164
rule of law, 188–91. *See also* legal reform (Soviet)
  democratization and, 195, 198, 210–11
  Gorbachev's UN speech on, 174
  Soviet-U.S. cooperation on, 193, 197–99, 202, 205–06
Run (Bulgakov), 122n18
Rusk, Secretary, 140
Russia
  demographic crisis in, 265
  history of democracy in, 49, 259–61
  independence, 211, 229
  mental health law, 115
  nationalism within, 194–96, 246
  overview of, 264–66
Russian-American Treaty of Commerce and Navigation, 59
Russian Empire
  democratic movement in, 49, 259–61
  emigration control during, 85
Russian ethnics, emigration of, 85, 131, 135, 138, 143
Russian Federation
  emigration law, 90
  Freedom House ranking, 248
  Penal Code, 112
  Putin as leader of, 248–49, 255–56
  religious freedom under, 118
  Yeltsin as leader of, 247, 249, 255–56, 274n35

Russian Orthodox Church, 118
Russian Revolution (1905), 259, 262
Russian Supreme Court, 205
Rutskoy, Alexander, 229, 231
Ryzhkov, Nikolai, 199, 215–17, 267, 273

Sakharov, Andrei
  Adamishin's view of, 44
  on death penalty, 93
  dissident activities of, 70–71
  election to Congress of People's Deputies, 218
  exile of, 21
  Helsinki Group and, 72
  on Jackson-Vanik amendment, 47
  message to Belgrade conference, 75
  return from exile, 108–09, 116, 127, 218, 235
  warnings sent to, 63
Salachov, Tair, 123
San Francisco Conference, 50–52
Schifter, Richard
  Adamishin's relationship with, 2–3, 111, 132, 242–43
  arrival in United States, 24
  Bakatin meeting, 209–12
  on democratization, 200, 207
  diplomatic career, 2, 23
    beginning of, 34, 51, 95–96
    foundations of, 50
    Human Rights Bureau, 103–09, 186–87
  education, 1–2, 24–30, 51
  on end of perestroika, 183–213
  on EUR-HA dispute, 106
  falsely labeled as Communist, 28n6
  first meeting with Adamishin, 3, 23, 94, 129–30, 132–35
  first visit to Soviet Union, 23
  on glasnost, 106–07
  Glukhov meeting, 168, 171–72
  on Gorbachev's UN speech, 174, 243
  on human rights agenda, 127–50
  Kovalev meeting, 168–72
  Laptiev meeting, 208–09
  last visit to Soviet Union, 208
  Lebyedev meeting, 205–06
  legal career, 2, 31, 52
  memo on Soviet human rights progress, 136–37
  military service, 28–29, 50, 54n3
  OVIR meeting, 139–40
  parents, 1–2, 23–25, 50
  personal history, 1, 5, 23–34
  Petrovskiy meeting, 200–02, 200n22
  Popov meeting, 204–05
  preparatory work done by, 240
  on psychiatric incarceration, 130

on release of political prisoners, 127
role of, 242–43
on Sakharov, 108–09
Shevardnadze meeting, 141–42, 144, 203
Shultz's relationship with, 242
similarities between Adamishin and, 1, 5, 23–24
on Soviet breakdown, 218–19
Soviet human rights checklist, 107–08
on Soviet political turmoil, 142
on Soviet-U.S. relations
    after perestroika, 95–109
    before perestroika, 49–77
suggested U.S. approaches, 136–37
tribute to Gorbachev, 213
on UN Human Rights Commission, 34, 52, 95–96, 100–01
on Vienna Conference, 161–81
view on Communism, formation of, 24–30, 34
volunteer activities, 52
written communication with Adamishin, 221–22
Yakovlev meeting, 197–99
scientists, in humanitarian working group, 125
Scowcroft, Brent, 165, 185, 186, 251
Screen Actors Guild, 27, 95
secrecy, media freedom and, 119
security concerns, emigration prohibition based on, 88, 134, 147–48
September 11, 2001, attacks, 43
Serbsky Institute, 189
serfdom, abolition of, 261–62
Sergeyevich, Nikita, 13, 14, 18n18
Service, Robert, 44
Seventeenth Party Congress (Congress of Winners), 11n7
Shachnazarov, Georgi, 153
Shachtmanites, 24
Shalikashvili, General, 204
Shamir, Yitzhak, 90n18, 164
Sharansky, Natan, 46n20, 73, 74, 76, 105
Shatrov, M., 121n16
Shcharansky, Anatoly. *See* Sharansky, Natan
Shcharansky, Avital, 99
Sheindlin, Alexander, 123
Shestack, Jerome, 76
Shevardnadze, Eduard
    Adamishin's relationship with, 242
    on Afghanistan invasion, 40, 42, 243n10
    arms control negotiations, 137, 139
    Baker meetings, 186, 190–91, 221, 251, 253–54
    Baker's view of, 186, 186n8
    on Brezhnev era, 21
    on Bush administration, 217
    on democratization, 203–04
    on emigration policy, 86–87, 89
    on Gorbachev, 204, 226–27
    on human rights issues, 83, 93–94
    leadership style, 84, 84n10
    on Lyubimov, 122
    on perestroika, 264
    on prisoners of conscience, 117, 141–42, 193
    proposal for Moscow human rights conference, 157
    on psychiatric incarceration, 114
    on release of political prisoners, 144n15
    resignation of, 199–200, 203, 226–27
    respect for science, 125
    role of, 1, 237–38
    Schifter meeting, 141–42, 144, 203
    Shultz letter to, 173
    Shultz meetings, 3, 128–29, 138–39, 243n10
    Shultz relationship with, 234–35, 237, 238
    Shultz view of, 128
    on Soviet breakdown, 219, 226
    on UNESCO, 123
    on U.S. psychiatrists' visit, 162–63
    Vienna Conference and, 158, 175–76, 178–79
    at Washington summit meeting, 224–25
Shmelev, Nikolai, 223
Shultz, George
    on Afghanistan invasion, 42
    Andropov meeting, 99
    arms control negotiations, 127–28, 139
    on Bush administration, 250, 252–53
    at Chernenko's funeral, 4, 101
    EUR-HA dispute and, 106
    on Gorbachev, 4, 101, 104
    Gorbachev meeting, 128, 134–37, 142
    Gorbachev's relationship with, 237n7, 238
    Gorbachev's view of, 257n30
    Gromyko meeting, 99, 100
    human rights policy, 79, 98–191
    on human rights working group, 132–33
    as idealist, 236–37
    on internal disputes, 165–67, 185
    Jewish emigration and, 138
    on Moscow human rights conference, 161
    Moscow visits, 81, 128–29, 149–50
    refusenik meeting, 132, 134–35, 256–57
    on release of political prisoners, 127
    role of, 1, 237
    Schifter's relationship with, 242
    Shevardnadze letter, 173
    Shevardnadze meetings, 3, 128–29, 138–39, 243n10
    Shevardnadze's relationship with, 234–35, 237, 238
    Siberian Seven case, 99–100
    on Soviet Jewry issue, 58

support for Soviet democratization, 233, 236
    Vienna Conference and, 158–59, 165, 166–67, 169, 172–73, 175, 178–80
    on Washington, 168
Shvernik, Nikolay, 113
Shvernik Commission, 15, 113, 117
Siberian Seven, 77, 99–100, 138, 256
Siniavski, Andrei, 19
Sitarian, Stepan, 225
Six-Day War (Israeli-Arab), 60, 85
Slansky, Rudolf, 59
Slipyi, Cardinal, 18
"sluggish schizophrenia," 113, 189–90
small- and-medium-size cooperatives, 216
Smekhov, Venyamin, 21
Smith, M., 16n16
socialist ideology, versus capitalism, 80–81, 104
Socialist Party (U.S.), 25, 26
social rights, versus political/civil rights, 96–98
social workers, exchange programs for, 150, 198, 205
Sokolov, Sergei, 17
Solzhenitsyn, Aleksandr, 15, 21, 63, 71
South Africa, 53–54, 54n2
South Ossetia, 227–28
Soviet-American relations
    during Bush administration, 183–86, 196–202, 216–17, 249–54
    Cold War (*See* Cold War)
    effect of perestroika on, 79, 111
    at end of World War II, 82n6
    failure of perestroika and, 254–57, 263–64
    human rights agendas (*See* human rights agendas)
    importance in foreign policy, 35–36, 95, 104
    as international issue, 33–34
    military aspects of, 33, 55 (*See also* arms control)
    as model, 125
    during Nixon administration, 57, 61–62, 239
    before perestroika, 35–77
    during Reagan administration, 236–38, 253, 256–57
    Vienna Conference and, 161–62, 180–81
    working-level discussions, 239–43
Soviet dissidents, 44, 70–77, 117–18. *See also specific person*
    incarceration of (*See* political prisoners; psychiatric incarceration)
Soviet Jewry Movement, 61–63, 66, 138
Soviet-Nazi Pact, 32, 246
Soviet satellite states. *See also specific state*
    anti-Semitism in, 59
    devolution of power to, 208–09
    flow of funds diverted by, 225
    Helsinki Groups in, 73
    human rights protections in, 209
    nationalism in, 194, 204, 245–46
    NATO membership, 264n11
    revolutionary shift in, 80
    secession of, 204, 210, 219–20, 227–28, 229–31, 244
Soviet Union
    accession to international human rights covenants, 53
    border dispute, 67, 69
    dissolution of, 229–31, 242, 244, 247
    aftermath of, 248–49
    prediction of, 212
    Yeltsin's role in, 196
    German invasion of, 25–26
    last year of, 227
    three-party system, 243–48
    U.S. view of, 4, 55–56, 95, 103
Spiridonova, Maria, 112
spying, 105
SS-20s (medium-range missiles), 37–38
Stalin, Joseph
    crimes committed by, awareness of, 12–15, 27–29, 56–57, 83n6
    cult of personality, 10–11, 11n5, 14n12
    death of, 10–11, 234
    on death penalty, 93
    denunciation of, 11–13, 57
    diktat on America as enemy, 36
    disrespect for Soviet people, 260, 263n8
    dissent against, 70
    legal reforms, 93
    mass purges, 116, 116n10, 145n16
    during postwar years, 9
    totalitarian system under, 234
    treatment of Jews under, 58–60
    U.S. view of, 54–56, 83n6
    during World War II, 8
Stalinists (U.S.), 25
Stars and Stripes, 51
State Department (U.S.)
    Bureau of European Affairs, 103–06, 150, 167, 168n2
    Bureau of Human Rights, 103–09, 186–87
    on Helsinki Final Act monitoring, 74–75
    internal dispute over Vienna Conference, 164–65
    on Jackson-Vanik amendment, 63
state interests, emigration prohibition based on, 88, 134, 147–48
state security system, democratization and, 212
Stevenson, Adlai III, 64, 149
Stockholm, Shultz-Gromyko meeting, 100

Strategic Arms Reduction Treaty, 153
Student Defenders of Democracy, 27–28
Suez crisis, 16
Supreme Soviet
    Committee on International Affairs, 159–60
    decree on emigration, 87–90
    media law, 120
    reorganization of, 208–09
surveillance technology, 270, 270n26
Sushkevich, 229
Suslov, Mikhail, 121–22, 266n20
Syria, 269

Talbott, Strobe, 47
Taliban, 43
Tartar-Mongolian invasion, 261
Tass, 64–65, 72
"telephone justice," 193
telephone law, 93
Terebilov, Vladimir, 92, 157
terror, culture of, 13
Thatcher, Margaret
    on Gorbachev, 4, 234
    Ryzhkov meeting, 215–17, 215n1
    support for perestroika, 263
thaw (Soviet), 13–14, 57, 262
The Thaw (Ehrenburg), 14n13
The Thaw Generation (Alexeyeva and Goldberg), 44
Thornburgh, Richard, 193
Tito, Josip Broz, 17
Tiutchev, Fiodor, 275
Todorov, Professor, 123
Togliatti, Palmiro, 12n8
Tomahawk cruise missiles, 37–38
trade, emigration linked to, 45–47, 62–67
Trade Act of 1974, Jackson-Vanik amendment to. *See* Jackson-Vanik amendment
travel abroad, facilitation of, 87, 120–21, 202
treason, Soviet criminal code on, 73–74, 158
Treaty on Conventional Forces in Europe, 2
Trotsky, Leon, 32
Trotskyists, 24–25
Truman, Harry
    administration of, Schifter's role in, 28n6, 52
    legislation against Communists, 30–31
    Schifter's support for, 29
    Soviet-U.S. relations under, 33, 55, 83n6
trumped-up charges, 171–72
Tukhachevsky, Mikhail, 24, 32
Tvardovski, Aleksandr, 15
Twentieth Party Congress
    Khrushchev's speech to, 11–13
    effect on American Communism, 27, 31–32
    international aspects of, 15–17, 57
    as milestone to democracy, 15
Twenty-Seventh Party Congress, 81
Twilight (Yakovlev), 8
Two Plus Four discussions, 220

Ukraine
    Freedom House ranking, 248
    independence, 211, 229, 230, 246
Ukrainian Catholic Church, 134, 241
Ukrainian Helsinki Group, 73
Ukrainian National Security Service, 212
UNESCO, 122–23, 148
United Kingdom
    Adamishin as ambassador in, 16n16, 90
    assistance for Armenian earthquake, 216
    Soviet relations with, 125
United Nations, as human rights forum, 197
United Nations Charter, adoption of, 49–54
United Nations Economic and Social Council, 53
United Nations Educational, Scientific, and Cultural Organization (UNESCO), 122–23, 148
United Nations General Assembly,
    Gorbachev's speech to, 173–74, 177, 178, 217, 243, 251
United Nations Human Rights Center, 161
United Nations Human Rights Commission
    Adamishin's speech to, 89, 194
    creation of, 97–98
    criticism of Soviets by, 76
    Romanian case, 219
    Schifter's participation in, 34, 52, 95–96, 100–01
    speechmaking ritual, 100–01
United States
    foreign policy formulation in, 57–58
    presidents (*See also specific president*)
    role in foreign policy formulation, 58
    Soviet view of, 36, 36n3, 46, 46n20
    ratification of international human rights covenants, 53n1, 54
    Soviet relations with. (*See* Soviet-American relations)
Universal Declaration of Human Rights, 53, 155, 155n5
    as nonbinding, 144n15
    rights defined by, 97–98
    Soviet democratization and, 212, 235
universal human values, 156n5
university strike (1899), 262
U.S. News & World Report, 105

Ustinov, Dmitri, 14, 40–42, 40n7

Vanik, Charles, 47. *See also* Jackson-Vanik amendment
Varshavskaya, Irinia, 147–48
Vatican. *See* Catholic Church
Vaz, 22
Venice human rights conference, 145
Vershbow, Alexander, 220
Vienna, 24
Vienna Conference, 2, 105–06, 114, 151–81
   arms control and, 158–59, 162, 180
   Concluding Document, 149, 178–81, 242–43
   effect on Soviet-American relations, 161–62, 180–81
   emigration as issue at, 133–34, 158, 162, 170–73, 176
   implementation of, 159–60
   religious freedom as issue at, 169, 171, 176
   Soviet delegation to, 133
   U.S. intramural conflict over, 164–68
Vietnam, 269
Visbor, Jury, 21
Vladimirov, Boris, 12–13, 266n18
Vladimov, Georgy, 21
Vlasikhin, Vassily, 125
Vlasov, Albert, 157
Volga Germans, emigration by, 90, 131, 137–38, 143, 162, 239
voluntary societies, foreign aid to, regulation of, 120
Vorontsov, Ambassador, 84n10
Voroshilov, Klement, 122n18
Voznesenski, Andrei, 14, 123
Vyshinsky, Andrei, 93, 155n4
Vysotsky, Vladimir, 14
vyzov (first-degree relative requirement), 138, 140, 143, 145–46

wages, 266
Wallace, Henry, 29–30
Warsaw Pact, 219, 244
Washington, D.C.
   Adamishin's visit to, 192
   Jewish emigration rally, 142
   Schifter's legal career in, 31, 52
   summit meetings, 142–45, 224–25
Whitehead, John, 123, 124, 141, 142
The White House Years (Kissinger), 67

working level, discussions at, 239–43
World Jewish Congress, 47
World War II (Great Patriotic War), 7–9, 25–26, 260
   end of
      European borders at, 67, 69, 152
      Soviet-U.S. relations at, 82n6
writers, travel by Russian, 120–21,

Yakovlev, Aleksandr, 8, 8n1, 144, 198, 217, 226, 230–31, 270–71
Yakovlev, Alexander Maximovich, 198
Yakovlev, Egor, 121
Yakovlev, Veniamin, 125, 197–99
Yakunin, Gleb, 212
Yale Law School, 29–30
Yalta agreement, 54, 54n3, 152
Yanayev, Gennady, 207, 228
Yarochenko, Viktor, 226n9
Yavlinsky, 231
Yazov, Dmitry, 207, 228
YCL (Young Communist League), 25
Yeltsin, Boris
   Afghanistan policy, 42
   autocracy under, 233, 248, 255–56, 274n35
   charisma of, 196, 247
   compared with Gorbachev, 247
   coup attempt and, 207–08, 227–28, 247, 255
   foreign relations under, 249
   opposition to Gorbachev, 183, 195, 203, 206, 212, 226, 227, 245–46
   political position of, 218n5
   realist support for, 236
   reentry into political arena, 195–96
   role in dissolution of Soviet Union, 12, 196
   support for Baltic independence, 227
   U.S. support for, 255, 264
Yevsukov, Ludmilla, 135
Yevtushenko, Yevgeny, 14
Young Communist League (YCL), 25
Young Pioneers, 1, 9
Yugoslavia, 264n11

zemstvo (limited local self-government), 262
Zhivkov, Todor, 244
Zimmerman, Warren, 149, 169
Zionism, 36n2, 60–61
Zivs, Samuil, 148
Zumwalt, Elmo, 33
Zumwalt, Mouza, 33

About the Authors

Anatoly Adamishin is president of the Euroatlantic Association and a visiting professor at the University of Virginia. During a distinguished career in the Soviet Ministry of Foreign Affairs, he rose to the position of deputy foreign minister of the Soviet Union and held the lead position on the Soviet side in its dialogue with the United States on human rights. In the 1990s, he served as the Russian Federation's ambassador to Italy and the United Kingdom, as first deputy minister of foreign affairs, and as the federation's minister to the Commonwealth of Independent States countries.

Since retiring from government service, he has held fellowships at the Russian Academy of Science's Institute of Europe, the Woodrow Wilson Center for Scholars, Stanford University, and the United States Institute of Peace.

He has published numerous articles in Russian and foreign periodicals dealing with foreign affairs, human rights, and the situation within Russia. He is also the author of two books: *The Fall and Rise of a Great Power* (in Italian, 1995) and *White Sun of Angola* (in Russian, 2002).

He received his Ph.D. in history from the Diplomatic Academy of the USSR and graduated with honors in economics from the University of Moscow.

Richard Schifter was born in Vienna, Austria, in 1923 and arrived in the United States as a refugee in 1938. He graduated in 1943 from the College of the City of New York summa cum laude. From 1943 to 1948 he served in the United States Army in Europe and then in the U.S. Military Government for Germany. Upon returning to the United States, he entered Yale Law School, from which he graduated in 1951.

From 1951 to 1984 he practiced law in Washington, D.C., specializing in the representation of American Indian tribes. He reentered government service in 1981, initially part-time, as U.S. representative in the United Nations Commission on Human Rights, and from 1984 to 2001 held full-time positions, successively, as deputy U.S. representative in the United Nations Security Council with the rank of ambassador, assistant secretary of state for human rights and humanitarian affairs, counselor in the United States National Security Council, and special adviser to the U.S. secretary of state.

He is a former member of the board of directors of the United States Institute of Peace. He now chairs the American Jewish International Relations Institute and serves on the board of trustees of the Institute for Christian and Jewish Studies.

Jennings Randolph Program for International Peace

This book is a fine example of the work produced by Senior Fellows in the Jennings Randolph fellowship program of the United States Institute of Peace. As part of the statute establishing the Institute, Congress envisioned a program that would appoint "scholars and leaders of peace from the United States and abroad to pursue scholarly inquiry and other appropriate forms of communication on international peace and conflict resolution." The program was named after Senator Jennings Randolph of West Virginia, whose efforts over four decades helped to establish the Institute.

Since 1987, the Jennings Randolph Program has played a key role in the Institute's effort to build a national center of research, dialogue, and education on critical problems of conflict and peace. Fellows come from a wide variety of academic and other professional backgrounds. They conduct research at the Institute and participate in the Institute's outreach activities to policymakers, the academic community, and the American public.

Each year approximately twelve senior fellows are in residence at the Institute. Fellowship recipients are selected by the Institute's board of directors in a competitive process. For further information on the program, please contact the program staff at (202) 457-1700, or visit our Web site at www.usip.org.

United States Institute of Peace Press

Since its inception, the United States Institute of Peace Press has published over 150 books on the prevention, management, and peaceful resolution of international conflicts—among them such venerable titles as Raymond Cohen's *Negotiating Across Cultures*; *Herding Cats* and *Leashing the Dogs of War* by Chester A. Crocker, Fen Osler Hampson, and Pamela Aall; and William I. Zartman's *Peacemaking and International Conflict*. All our books arise from research and fieldwork sponsored by the Institute's many programs. In keeping with the best traditions of scholarly publishing, each volume undergoes both thorough internal review and blind peer review by external subject experts to ensure that the research, scholarship, and conclusions are balanced, relevant, and sound. As the Institute prepares to move to its new headquarters on the National Mall in Washington, D.C., the Press is committed to extending the reach of the Institute's work by continuing to publish significant and sustainable works for practitioners, scholars, diplomats, and students.

Valerie Norville
Director

Board of Directors

J. Robinson West (Chair), Chairman, PFC Energy, Washington, D.C.

George E. Moose (Vice Chairman), Adjunct Professor of Practice, The George Washington University

Anne H. Cahn, Former Scholar in Residence, American University, Washington, D.C.

Chester A. Crocker, James R. Schlesinger Professor of Strategic Studies, School of Foreign Service, Georgetown University, Washington, D.C.

Kerry Kennedy, Human Rights Activist

Ikram U. Khan, President, Quality Care Consultants, LLC

Stephen D. Krasner, Graham H. Stuart Professor of International Relations, Stanford University

Kathleen Martinez, Executive Director, World Institute on Disability

Jeremy A. Rabkin, Professor of Law, George Mason University, Fairfax, Va.

Ron Silver, Actor, Producer, Director, Primparous Productions, Inc.

Judy Van Rest, Executive Vice President, International Republican Institute, Washington, D.C.

Nancy Zirkin, Executive Vice President, Leadership Conference on Civil Rights

Members ex officio

Robert M. Gates, Department of Defense

Hillary R. Clinton, Department of State

Richard H. Solomon, President, United States Institute of Peace (nonvoting)

Frances C. Wilson, Lieutenant General, U.S. Marine Corps; President, National Defense University.

Human Rights, Perestroika, and the End of the Cold War

Text: Palatino
Display text: Narrowband, Raleigh, and Optima
Cover Design: The Creative Shop
Interior Design and Page Makeup: Katharine Moore
Developmental Editor: Nigel Quinney
Copy Editor: Brian Slattery
Proofreader: Amy Thompson
Indexer: Mary Coe